Turkish Perspectives on Secularization and Media

Mustafa Derviş Dereli · Metin Eken
Editors

Turkish Perspectives on Secularization and Media

Springer

Editors
Mustafa Derviş Dereli
Sociology of Religion
Necmettin Erbakan University
Konya, Türkiye

Metin Eken
Journalism
Erciyes University
Kayseri, Türkiye

ISBN 978-3-032-16435-3 ISBN 978-3-032-16436-0 (eBook)
https://doi.org/10.1007/978-3-032-16436-0

This Springer imprint is published by the registered company Springer Nature Switzerland AG
The registered company address is: Gewerbestrasse 11, 6330 Cham, Switzerland

Contents

Contributors

Merve Bahadur Antalya, Türkiye

Musa Süheyl Baysal Department of Legal History, Hacettepe University, Ankara, Türkiye

Mehmet Birekul Department of Sociology, Necmettin Erbakan University, Konya, Türkiye

İhsan Çapcıoğlu Department of Sociology of Religion, Ankara University, Ankara, Türkiye

Gülsen Çankal Department of Sociology, Bartın University, Bartın, Türkiye

Hüseyin Çil Department of Sociology, Selçuk University, Konya, Türkiye

Mustafa Çuhadar Ankara, Türkiye

Mustafa Derviş Dereli Department of Sociology of Religion, Necmettin Erbakan University, Konya, Türkiye

Sedat Doğan Department of Sociology, Kırklareli University, Kırklareli, Türkiye

Metin Eken Department of Journalism, Erciyes University, Kayseri, Türkiye

Yunus Ergen Department of Public Relations and Publicity, Hatay Mustafa Kemal University, Hatay, Türkiye

Fatma Eroğlu Genç Konya, Türkiye

Yusuf Ziya Gökçek Department of Radio, Television and Cinema, Marmara University, İstanbul, Türkiye

Faruk Karaarslan Department of Sociology, Necmettin Erbakan University, Konya, Türkiye

İbrahim Nacak Department of Sociology, Selçuk University, Konya, Türkiye

Yasin Yılmaz Department of Philosophy and Sociology of Law, Necmettin Erbakan University, Konya, Türkiye

Chapter 1
Introduction

Mustafa Derviş Dereli and Metin Eken

Secularization has long been a fertile ground for conceptual and theoretical inquiry within the social sciences. Initially, it was formulated as a grand narrative grounded in the assumptions of rationalization, functional differentiation, and disenchantment, positing that religion would undergo a progressive decline—both institutionally and in individual consciousness—culminating in its eventual disappearance. Over time, however, this linear and evolutionary model was subjected to growing critique, giving rise to alternative paradigms that challenged its historical determinism. These were followed by eclectic perspectives that emphasized the coexistence and mutual entanglement of the religious and the secular. At this juncture, secularization is increasingly understood not as the erosion of religion per se, but as a heuristic for analyzing the transformation of religiosity into more individualized, culturally embedded, and contextually adaptive forms.

In this context, the book does not interpret the decline of traditional religious forms merely as evidence of secularization, nor does it assume that the increasingly visible emergence of new modes of religiosity in today's world is unrelated to the dynamics of secularization. Particularly in societies such as Turkey, where the religious and the secular are not perceived as fixed, binary categories, and where the experience of religion and modernization follows a distinct trajectory, articulating a context-specific position on secularization is essential to framing the book's overall perspective.

Accordingly, this study approaches secularization as a mode of consciousness—an orientation of thought that manifests itself in everyday practices shaped by this mindset and reflected in the lived experience of daily life. While the structural influence of culture shapes these practices, they are also conditioned by the possibilities of agency. In this sense, secularization is conceptualized not merely as a modern

M. D. Dereli (✉)
Department of Sociology of Religion, Necmettin Erbakan University, Konya, Türkiye
e-mail: mdervisdereli@erbakan.edu.tr

M. Eken
Department of Journalism, Erciyes University, Kayseri, Türkiye

M. D. Dereli and M. Eken (eds.), *Turkish Perspectives on Secularization and Media*,
https://doi.org/10.1007/978-3-032-16436-0_1

phenomenon but as a historically recurring form of "religious estrangement" that can be observed throughout human history (Eken, 2020, 2021).

In this regard, media—emerging as an increasingly influential social reality in modern societies—is understood not merely as a neutral communication channel, but as a value-laden medium shaped by both its cultural embeddedness and technical affordances. Accordingly, the secularizing effect of mediatized processes is approached not as a deterministic or coercive force, but as a potential—one that gains significance depending on how the symbolic resources of the media field intersect with belief, spirituality, religion, and transcendence through the exercise of human agency (Dereli, 2019, 2022; Eken, 2021).

The volume titled *Turkish Perspectives on Secularization and Media* comprises thirteen complementary chapters, in addition to the Introduction. In the second chapter of this book, titled "A Glance at the Secularization of Law from the Perspective of Journals: From the Ottoman Empire to the Republic," Yılmaz and Baysal examine legal changes in Turkey through journal articles that influenced public debate during the transition from the Ottoman Empire to the Republic. Focusing on the journals *Sebilürreşad* and *İctihad*, this study compares the views of Islamists and modern thinkers on legal changes and the replacement of Sharia with Western law. Looking back at history, it becomes clear that these journals also shaped the struggles over religion, modernity, and national identity while establishing a secular legal system.

In the third chapter, titled "Secularization Debates in Islamist Journals Post-1990," Ergen examines how Islamist periodicals in Türkiye have perceived and problematized secularization since the 1990s. Using qualitative thematic analysis on writings published *in Altınoluk, Umran*, and *İktibas*, the study reveals that secularization is predominantly viewed as a Western-origin ideology incompatible with Islam and detrimental to religious and moral integrity. These journals interpret secularization as both an existential and social crisis, advocating a return to "fıtrat," revelation-centered consciousness, and the reconstruction of Islamic values. Ergen concludes that Islamist journals operate not merely as vehicles of information but as intellectual arenas that generate counter-discourses to modernity and articulate alternative moral and civilizational visions.

In the fourth chapter, titled "Secularization in Turkish Cinema: Yeşilçam Neighborhood Against the State Ideal," Gökçek investigates the reflections of secularization and modernity in Turkish cinema, particularly the cultural tensions between the state's secular vision and the traditional ethos of Yeşilçam's neighborhood narratives. Based on historical and thematic analysis, the study traces the evolution of cinema from a state-directed medium into a localized cultural arena that articulates its own moral and social order. It argues that Yeşilçam developed a form of "local secularism" rooted in everyday life and emotional realism rather than in ideological opposition, creating a hybrid synthesis of modern and traditional values. In this framework, the neighborhood becomes a symbolic counter-space to state secularism, promoting a moral universe grounded in communal justice and cultural authenticity.

Focusing on the intersection of religion, media, and state ideology, Çuhadar's chapter titled "Restricted Islam: Religious Program Principles in The Turkish

Radio and Television Corporation (TRT) General Broadcasting Plans (1977–2004)" analyzes how Türkiye's public broadcaster mediated secularism through its programming policies. Drawing on official TRT documents and content analysis of broadcasting plans, the study identifies two dominant categories—reductive and exclusionary references—revealing that laicism, national unity, and modernization were central to the framing of religious content. Between 1977 and 2004, TRT's policies promoted a positivist and secular worldview, presenting religion as compatible with modern civilization and scientific rationality while discouraging political, sectarian, or emotional expressions of faith. As Çuhadar concludes, these principles institutionalized a form of "restricted Islam," reflecting the broader effort of the republican state to align religious broadcasting with its secular modernization project.

In their co-authored chapter titled "Is the Family Spell Being Broken? The Secularization of the Family Concept in Turkish TV Series: The Case of Aile Series," Birekul and Eroğlu Genç explore how contemporary Turkish television represents the transformation of family values within a secular cultural framework. Through discourse analysis of the first five episodes of Aile, they examine how the series redefines the family by prioritizing individual autonomy over collective bonds and portraying the family as a source of personal conflict rather than moral refuge. The study situates these representations within Max Weber's concepts of Entzauberung (disenchantment) and rationalization, suggesting that Aile reflects a broader process in which traditional values—such as sacrifice, loyalty, and chastity—are eroded and replaced by self-centered, pleasure-oriented lifestyles. The authors conclude that by normalizing materialism, individualism, and non-traditional relationships, the series exemplifies the secularization of the institution of family.

In Karaarslan's chapter, "Post-Secular Religion and Society in Türkiye: The Case of Kübra Series," the discussion centers on how artificial intelligence reconfigures religious experience and identity within a post-secular framework. Using the Turkish TV series Kübra as a case study, Karaarslan investigates how technology mediates belief, transforming revelation from the divine to the digital. Through a sociological reading of the series, the chapter argues that Kübra exemplifies a new hybrid religiosity—neither wholly traditional nor secular—where algorithmic messages replace sacred texts and digital communities supplant conventional congregations. Interpreting this transformation through Habermas's theory of the post-secular society, Karaarslan demonstrates that Türkiye's modernity embodies a coexistence of secular and religious logics, now extended into the technological realm, revealing a distinctive synthesis of faith, reason, and digital modernity.

Addressing the conceptual foundations of media theory, Doğan's chapter titled "Public Sphere and New Media in Türkiye: A Metatheoretical Observation Related to Literature" offers a critical reflection on the epistemological conditions required to evaluate whether new media weakens or transforms the political public sphere. Rather than answering this empirical question directly, Doğan scrutinizes the theoretical premises that make such inquiry possible, situating his analysis within and beyond Habermasian frameworks. By mapping Turkish scholarship on media and public discourse, the study exposes a lack of metatheoretical reflexivity and overreliance on data-driven or citation-based reasoning. In conclusion, Doğan warns that without deeper theoretical self-awareness, academic discussions risk secularizing their own intellectual substance—reducing complex sociopolitical phenomena to mechanistic interpretations devoid of genuine critical engagement.

In his chapter titled "Secular Language in Generation Z Discourses in Digital Environments: The Case of Twitter/X," Dereli investigates how secular expressions emerge and circulate in social media discussions about Generation Z in Türkiye. Employing qualitative document analysis on 134 tweets collected through purposive sampling and analyzed, the study uncovers that discourses surrounding Generation Z often frame the generation through the lens of secularization, reflecting shifts in values, beliefs, and authority. Dereli shows that these online narratives oscillate between portraying young people as agents of moral decline and as symbols of pluralism and creative transformation. The chapter concludes that digital environments not only mirror but also reshape the sociocultural boundaries of belief, identity, and tradition, underscoring the analytical potential of generational studies for understanding secularization in contemporary Turkish society.

In Eken's chapter, "Online Strategies of Atheistic Movements in Türkiye: The Case of Ateizm Derneği," the focus is on how Türkiye's first official atheist organization utilizes social media to construct visibility, legitimacy, and collective identity. Drawing on the main thematic frameworks of global atheist activism—such as minority discourse, religious mimicry, inversion, and reclaiming patriotism–the study conducts a qualitative analysis of the Ateizm Derneği's online communication strategies. Eken demonstrates that although these strategies parallel Western counterparts in certain respects, they acquire a distinctive form shaped by Türkiye's sociopolitical and cultural context—merging secular advocacy with elements of popular science, humor, and polemical critique. While these strategies cultivate an alternative secular public sphere and articulate dynamics of existence and resistance against Islam as the cultural "other," they also contribute to the normalization and public visibility of nonreligiosity within the Turkish context.

In their collaborative chapter titled "Hybridizing Beliefs in the Age of Secularization and the Search for Meaning on Social Media: The Case of the Dark Retreat," Çapcıoğlu and Bahadur explore how digital platforms facilitate the emergence of hybrid and individualized spiritual practices in contemporary Türkiye. Using qualitative content analysis of YouTube materials, including Çetin Çetintaş's channel and the Dark Retreat: Kaya Yalpa documentary, the study examines how yoga, meditation, and retreat rituals respond to existential crises produced by secular modernity. The authors demonstrate that these practices provide alternative frameworks for meaning-making, serving as digital sanctuaries for self-discovery, psychological relief, and emotional renewal. Their findings reveal that the growing popularity of such rituals reflects not the disappearance of the sacred but its transformation into new, syncretic, and media-mediated forms that reconcile spirituality with modern lifestyles.

In Çil's chapter, "'Loose' Muslim – 'Strict' Opponent: Religion as an Object of Humor in Social Media Stand-Ups," the complex intersection of religion, humor, and sociopolitical polarization in contemporary Türkiye is explored through the analysis of 25 stand-up performances published on YouTube. Using thematic analysis, Çil reveals how the increasing individualization and interpretive openness of religion in the postmodern era have made it more accessible to ironic and ambivalent humor. Comedians neither wholly reject nor fully embrace faith; instead, they embody a "believing without belonging" stance that mirrors broader cultural transformations. By situating religious references within spatial and symbolic codes – such as contrasts between Konya, İzmir, and Kadıköy— the study demonstrates how humor maps Türkiye's secular–religious divide. Ultimately, Çil argues that stand-up comedy serves as both a mirror and a mediator of the shifting role of religion in public life, where political satire and religious commentary are increasingly converging within digital spaces.

Exploring the evolving relationship between technology, memory, and spirituality, Çankal's chapter, "Remembrance and Mourning Rituals in Digital Cemeteries," analyzes how digital platforms reshape traditional mourning and commemoration practices. Through a netnographic examination of Instagram and Facebook profiles belonging to deceased individuals, the study demonstrates that comment-based interactions—ranging from expressions of grief to symbolic acts of remembrance—constitute new forms of digital mourning. Over time, these interactions evolve from immediate emotional responses to routinized memorial behaviors, signaling the secularization of post-death rituals. Çankal concludes that the solace and communal connection once offered by religious traditions are now reproduced through digital communication, transforming virtual memorials into secular spaces that redefine how death, remembrance, and the sacred are experienced in modern society.

In Nacak's chapter titled "Social Reflections of Smart City Applications in Turkey: Konya Metropolitan Municipality Applications (Youth Culture Card)," the impact of digital urban initiatives on the social and cultural lives of young people in metropolitan environments is examined. Based on interviews with 28 university students in Konya, the study examines the Youth Culture Card as an example of a smart city application that increases access to cultural, artistic, and educational opportunities. Nacak found that this card promotes socialization, participation, and a sense of belonging, particularly among students new to the city, by removing financial and social barriers to civic life. However, participants also expressed the need for more career-focused programs, participatory youth platforms, and transparent communication about existing services. This section highlights how Konya's smart city policies not only support urban well-being through digital innovation but also demonstrate how technology can strengthen civic participation and cultural inclusivity among urban youth.

The chapters compiled in Turkish Perspectives on Secularization and Media illuminate the multifaceted relationship between religion, modernity, and secularization in Türkiye's sociocultural landscape. Across diverse thematic and methodological frameworks—from legal and cinematic analyses to studies on digital platforms, humor, and urban policy—these contributions reveal that secularization in Türkiye does not follow a linear trajectory of decline in religiosity but rather unfolds through negotiation, reinterpretation, and hybridization. Media, in this context, emerges as both a mirror and an agent of this transformation, mediating tensions between the sacred and the secular, the individual and the community, and tradition and modernity. Whether through the reformist and oppositional tones of early periodicals, the moral reconfigurations in film and television, or the secularized expressions of belief and identity on social media, each study underscores that Türkiye's secular experience is not characterized by rupture but by dynamic interaction. These chapters offer a nuanced, interdisciplinary understanding of how secularization is continuously redefined within the media and technological networks of contemporary Turkish society.

References

Dereli, M. D. (2019). Dinî kimliklerin siber uzamda akışkanlaşması. *İnsan ve Toplum Dergisi, 9*(1), 85–116. https://doi.org/10.12658/M0301

Dereli, M. D. (2022). *Sanala veda: Sosyal medya ve dönüşen dindarlık.* Sakarya Üniversitesi Yayınları.

Eken, M. (2020). Modern görsel kültürde m nesli'nin online inanç pratikleri. *Bilimname, 43*, 31–71. https://doi.org/10.28949/bilimname.762744

Eken, M. (2021). *Çevrim içi dindarlık: M neslinin inanç pratikleri.* Nobel Akademik Yayıncılık.

Chapter 2
A Glance at the Secularization of Law from the Perspective of Journals: From the Ottoman Empire to the Republic

Yasin Yılmaz and Musa Süheyl Baysal

2.1 Introduction

The transition from the Ottoman Empire to the Republic of Türkiye marks a period of profound transformations in the secularization of law. These transformations were not confined to the political and social spheres but also encompassed significant changes in the legal domain. Particularly with the Second Constitutional Period (1908–1920), the surge in press and publishing activities provided a platform for the formation of public opinion and the discussion of legal reforms. As Birinci notes, the re-proclamation of the Constitution opened the floodgates of publishing activity, sparking intense debates among various segments of society (Birinci, 2012, p. 89). During this period, journals and newspapers emerged as critical platforms where diverse perspectives on the secularization of law were expressed, shaping society's perception of these reforms.

As Tunaya points out, the intellectual currents of the period were divided into three main streams—Westernism, Turkism, and Islamism—with Ottomanism serving as their common ground (Tunaya, 1948, p. 590). These currents also manifested in discussions on the secularization of law: some journals advocated for the continuation of secular legal reforms, while others resisted, defending the influence of Sharia law. The secularization process, which began during the Tanzimat period and culminated in 1926 with the comprehensive adoption of Western law in the Republican era, represented a profound transformation for large segments of society. This study aims to examine the secularization of law through a selected sample of journal publications from the Second Constitutional Period and the Republican era. Ictihad's support for

Y. Yılmaz (✉)
Department of Philosophy and Sociology of Law, Necmettin Erbakan University, Konya, Türkiye
e-mail: yasinyilmaz@erbakan.edu.tr

M. S. Baysal
Department of Legal History, Hacettepe University, Ankara, Türkiye
e-mail: musabaysal@hacettepe.edu.tr

M. D. Dereli and M. Eken (eds.), *Turkish Perspectives on Secularization and Media*,
https://doi.org/10.1007/978-3-032-16436-0_2

secular law and Sebilürreşad's opposition to Western-inspired legal reforms will be analyzed as key axes reflecting the diversity and conflict within the intellectual landscape of the period.

The transition from the Ottoman Empire to the Republic of Türkiye marked a transformative period in the secularization of law, profoundly shaped by intellectual debates reflected in journals. This article examines this process through the lens of two influential publications: Sebilürreşad and Ictihad. Sebilürreşad (1908–1925) staunchly defended Islamic principles, criticizing secular reforms as incompatible with Turkish-Islamic society, while Ictihad (1904–1932) championed Western-inspired legal reforms. By analyzing the contrasting perspectives in these journals, this study aims to illuminate the ideological tensions and intellectual currents that defined the secularization of law during the Second Constitutional Era and the early Republican period, highlighting their roles as platforms for shaping public discourse and societal transformation.

The research was conducted through a selected sample of journals from the Second Constitutional Era and the early Republican period. In particular, Ictihad and Sebîlürreşâd were chosen as the primary focus due to their representation of opposing perspectives in secularization debates. The articles published in these journals, as well as writings discussing legal reforms and editorial policies, were evaluated using qualitative content analysis.

2.2 Seeing Law Through the Lens of Journals: Legal Reforms During the Second Constitutional Era and the Republic Period

In the final century of the Ottoman Empire, law was shaped at the intersection of traditional structures and modernization efforts. The reform process, initiated during the Tanzimat period, brought discussions on secularizing the legal system to the forefront. Journals of the era served as a mirror, reflecting this transformation process and conveying the ideological foundations, societal implications, and intellectual debates surrounding legal reforms to the public.

Before the Tanzimat, Ottoman law in its classical period was a synthesis of Sharia and the sultans' law (örfi/'urfi). Some scholars regarded the dimension of sultans' law (örfi) as representing a secular sphere. According to Ekinci, characterizing the legal and judicial reforms following the Tanzimat solely as the secularization of law is misleading, as secular provisions not contrary to religious principles existed in Ottoman law before the Tanzimat (Ekinci, 2016, p. 541). While sultans' law derived its legitimacy from Sharia law, secular/laic reforms had no such concern. Sultans' law served as a tool to reinforce the state's authority in the legal domain. This authority became particularly evident in the post-Tanzimat period through debates over the compatibility of new laws with Islam (Otacı, 2004, p. 351). The central authority of the state largely neutralized the opposition of the ulema on this matter, allowing reforms to proceed along a pragmatic and modernization-driven trajectory, prioritizing practical considerations over religious sensitivities. This duality exemplifies legal pluralism, where multiple legal systems interact within a single social field, raising questions about the nature of law in stateless or semi-autonomous contexts (Mollaoğlu, 2024).

During the Second Constitutional Era and the early Republican period, the ideological foundation of legal reforms was shaped by Western-originated ideas, including positivism and materialism. According to Korlaelçi, schools offering French-language education, minority schools, students sent abroad, and educators arriving from foreign countries played a significant role in introducing these ideas to the Ottoman Empire. These educational institutions created a conducive environment for Ottoman intellectuals to adopt a neutral, or even supportive, stance toward the secularization of law (Korlaelçi, 1986, p. 377). Western-style education generated an epistemological divide between Islamic knowledge and new "scientific" knowledge (Göçek, 1999, p. 162), which emerged as a key factor in legitimizing legal reforms. The journals of the period contributed to presenting legal reforms as a scientific and modern necessity through articles reflecting this intellectual transformation. At the same time, some journals, emphasizing traditional values, adopted a conservative and critical stance in their publishing policies. This study will explore the diverse perspectives represented in these journals through their influential writings.

2.3 Sebilürreşad's Resistance to the Secularization of Law (1908–1925)

Sebilürreşad, initially launched in 1908 under the name Sırat-ı Müstakîm and renamed in 1912, emerged during the liberal environment ushered in by the Second Constitutional Era in the Ottoman Empire, a period when diverse ideas found expression. Founded by Ebul'ula Zeynelabidin (Mardin) and Eşref Edib (Fergan), both graduates of the Law School, the journal Sebilürreşad quickly became a prominent platform for Islamist thought. However, it was closed under the Takrir-i Sükun Law due to the Eastern uprisings, ceasing publication after its 641st issue on March 5, 1925 (Efe, 2009). Embracing the notion that Islam encompasses not only spiritual but also worldly and legal order, Sebilürreşad published content aligned with this perspective. Compared to other Islamist journals and newspapers, it adopted a relatively moderate editorial stance, consistently and effectively advocating Islamist ideas, thereby reaching a broad readership (Kara, 2014, pp. 28–29).

Throughout the final years of the Ottoman Empire and the early years of the Republic, Sebilürreşad held a significant place in debates on modernization and Westernization (Özkorkut, 2021, p. 6). While generally aligning its editorial line with state policies, the journal criticized the emerging secular state framework, including measures such as the abolition of Sharia courts, the closure of madrasas, and changes in the legal and judicial systems (Özkorkut, 2021, p. 27). In response to the secular legal reforms that began during the Tanzimat period and accelerated in the Republican era, the journal emphasized the necessity of a system rooted in Islam's moral, social, and legal principles, arguing that Western laws were incompatible with the spirit of Turkish-Islamic society. This section examines Sebilürreşad's opposition to secularization and its defense of Sharia's supremacy, drawing on articles by its various contributors.

The Tanzimat period, initiated in the early nineteenth century, is considered the starting point of secular legal reforms in the Ottoman Empire. Eşref Edib argued that the Tanzimat aimed to secularize the state by aligning the Islamic order with Christian systems, ultimately leading to the empire's downfall. He maintained that reforming an entity by altering its identity leads to its destruction. He criticized the judicial procedures and education systems borrowed from Europe as incompatible with the nation's spirit, traditions, and needs, resulting in the loss of time and generations (Eşref Edib, 1921b).

In an article addressing the separation of religion and state, Muhammed Hamdi argued that the laws enacted during this period amounted to little more than propaganda for change. Quoting Gustave Le Bon, he noted that transforming society through laws disrupts social order and contradicts the wisdom of legislation. He criticized Ottoman laws for lacking influence in people's hearts due to their superficial nature (Muhammed Hamdi, 1918). The seeds of legal duality were sown during this period, and by the Second Constitutional Era, the notion of this duality as a problem was deemed laughable, with calls for unity seen as absurd (Muhammed Hamdi, 1918, p. 328).

The Tanzimat's efforts to modernize by imitating the West were harshly criticized by Sebilürreşad's contributors. For instance, in a 1919 article, Ömer Rıza attributed the state's collapse to Western-style reforms, which he argued had already failed and were incompatible with Islam, threatening the essence of Muslim society. The fear that adopting Western civilization wholesale would destroy Islam and social order was a recurring concern during this period (Ömer Rıza, 1919).

The 1876 Constitution (Kanun-ı Esasi), regarded as a continuation of the Tanzimat reforms and a step toward a constitutional order, was criticized for elements deemed contrary to Sharia law. An article titled "The Incompatibility of the Constitution with Sharia," initially published in Âtî and republished in Sebilürreşad, argued that the 1876 Constitution, which was repeatedly amended, was a "makeshift law" not rooted in the nation's spirit. Criticized as a hasty and blind translation, the Constitution was seen as conflicting with Sharia and the Ottoman Empire's spiritual, social, and moral fabric. The critique particularly focused on the caliphate, noting that translations of European laws, combined with Christian notions of sanctity, portrayed the sultan as unaccountable and sacred. In contrast, Sharia and the practices of the Rightly Guided Caliphs emphasized the caliph's accountability ("Kanûn-ı Esâsî'nin Şer'a da Mugayereti", 1918).

Selâhaddîn Âsım, in a comparative analysis of legal systems, noted that during periods when Arabs adhered to Sharia, they achieved material, spiritual, and moral superiority. However, lapses in its application led to significant declines in its effectiveness. He argued that only Sharia could establish societal rules, relationships, happiness, and mutual obligations with depth and refinement, emphasizing that previous religious laws, being corrupted, were incapable of achieving this goal (Selahaddin Asım, 1909a). Addressing objections to Sharia's application due to the presence of non-Muslims in the Ottoman populace, he asserted that their happiness, prosperity, and peace could only be ensured through Islamic Sharia. Selâhaddîn Âsım also extensively criticized the moral and societal decline caused by European laws in various articles, stressing that while Europe's civilization, industry, and education could be utilized, its customs, morals, and behaviors should not be adopted in the homeland (Selahaddin Asım, 1909b).

Said Halim Pasha argued that the best political system for Islamic society is one based on Sharia. Every Muslim is duty-bound to oversee Sharia's implementation, granting the right to hold the government accountable to Islamic principles. Representation, he argued, should come from an elite assembly united around Sharia's common purpose, rather than class conflicts. Legislative authority rests with jurists well-versed in Sharia, with the Assembly of Deputies serving as a supervisory body. Sharia-based laws must align with society's spirit and ensure justice (Said Halim Paşa, 1922). Rejecting claims that Islam caused decline, Kırşehir Deputy Müfîd argued that adherence to Sharia prevents collapse, with ignorance to be addressed through knowledge and science (Kırşehir Mebusu Müfîd, 1922). Similarly, M. Şemseddin stated that irreligion destroys morality, legal concepts, and laws, emphasizing that law rests on sacred moral principles and that justice, a virtue, collapses when morality declines (M. Şemseddin, 1919).

Islamist thought was rooted in the belief that Islam encompasses not only spiritual but also worldly and legal order. In a 1916 article in Sebilürreşad, Aksekili Ahmed Hamdi argued that the caliph is both the religious and worldly leader of Muslims, and the state's separation from Sharia would equate to the destruction of Islam (Aksekili Ahmed Hamdi, 1916, p. 178). Similarly, Babanzade Ahmed Naim maintained that religion and the state are inseparable, with religion encompassing legal rules that extend beyond mere worship and ritual. The state's duty to protect religion was deemed essential for maintaining the nation's moral and social order, lest the people neglect their religious and moral responsibilities (Ahmed Naim, 1918).

The emphasis on Islam as a religion governing worldly affairs implied Sharia's adaptability to modern needs through ijtihad. Throughout the journal's publication, especially before the Republic, ijtihad was a recurring topic, with lengthy debates on whether its gate was closed. These articles addressed claims that Islamic Sharia was outdated or inadequate, providing clear responses to such assertions (Halim Mağribi, 1910; Sabit, 1910).

In one article, Hasan Hikmet discussed the nature of modern laws, critiquing Westernists' claims that Sharia-based legal systems lack contemporary or civilized value. Despite Western characterizations of Islamic law as "medieval, theocratic, and clerical," Hikmet argued that Western legal systems were more primitive, supporting his view with examples from Bolshevik Russia, France, and England. He further contended that democracy, often presented as a secular principle, already existed in the Islamic world (Hasan Hikmet, 1923c).

The suitability of Western legal systems for Turkish society became a topic of debate, particularly after the Lausanne Peace Conference. On May 24, 1923, Ahmet Cevdet, writing in İkdam, criticized the proposal at Lausanne for foreign jurists to draft a civil code, arguing that foreigners unfamiliar with Anatolian society would not be able to create suitable laws. He cited the Swiss Civil Code, which was developed over the years to align with Switzerland's traditions and mentality, as evidence that Turkish society needed a legal system rooted in its own culture (Ahmed Cevdet, 1923).

Another debated issue was the dual court system, with Sharia courts operating alongside nizamiye (secular) courts. An article addressing this duality noted that discussions on judicial unity often led to calls for the abolition of Sharia courts. It referenced Egyptian jurist Helbavi Bey, who proposed unifying the courts by codifying Islamic rulings, thereby integrating nizamiye courts under Sharia-based principles to achieve judicial unity (Hasan Hikmet, 1923b). Eşref Edib noted that even the symbolic presence of Sharia courts, despite their limited authority, was a source of comfort for Muslims, suggesting that a fully Islamic judicial system would reduce objections (Eşref Edib, 1921a). Rumors about abolishing Sharia courts alarmed Sebilürreşad. A July 31, 1923, article criticized reports in some newspapers that the new constitution would eliminate Sharia courts ('Mahkeme-i Şer'iyyeler Kalıyor Mu?', 1923), with Akşam claiming the People's Party viewed their abolition as "reform." The journal argued that these courts were foundational to the nation's religious and moral ties, deeming their removal "irrational and childish" and asserting that secular ideas clashed with the people's values ('Ankara Haberleri', 1923).

The notion that civilization is a whole, with one aspect being the separation of religion and politics in Europe, was rejected by Ahmed Nazîf, who criticized proponents for conflating the Quran and the Bible. He explained the differences between Islamic and Christian legal systems and their historical impacts. He argued that a nation cannot be created but governed, and laws should address deficiencies or establish new ones as needed. If laws fail to meet modern needs, the issue lies with individuals, not Islam, which, unlike Christianity, can address all aspects of life. He suggested that laws could draw from other Islamic schools of thought beyond the Hanafi school when necessary (Ahmed Nazif, 1923).

Akşam's editor-in-chief, Necmeddin Sadak, argued that republican governance and Sharia were incompatible, advocating for modern laws over Sharia courts. In response, Sebilürreşad defined the republic as a system that fully reflects the nation's spiritual, social, and emotional aspects, with the best republican governance representing and implementing the national will. Sadak later distinguished between "spiritual and temporal sultanates," viewing modernization as a means of separating spiritual from temporal authority and advocating for a complete separation of religion from state affairs by embracing a European identity (Hasan Hikmet, 1923c). Sadak's views are parallel to those of Ictihad, which will be discussed in the next section. His claim that "religion and Sharia no longer apply to state affairs or interpersonal relations," despite the Constitution's declaration of Islam as the state religion and the Assembly's duty to enforce Sharia, provoked backlash. His labeling of adherence to Sharia as "reactionary" implied that the entire nation, Assembly, and government were reactionary ('Teceddüd Ahkâm-ı Dîniyyenin Nesih ve İbtâli Demek Midir?', 1923).

In the early years of the Republic, secularism was perceived as a significant threat by Islamist thinkers. On August 30, 1923, Hasan Hikmet argued that secularism was not synonymous with modernity, asserting that Muslim societies were inherently modern, but secularism would undermine the national structure. He viewed secularism as dangerous for Islamic societies. The three laws passed by the Turkish Grand National Assembly on March 3, 1924—abolishing the Ministry of Sharia and Foundations, enacting the Law on Unification of Education, and abolishing the caliphate—were seen as cornerstones of secularism and harshly criticized by Sebilürreşad. The journal argued that abolishing Sharia courts and closing madrasas were incompatible with the people's religious values. A July 31, 1924, article, citing the 1924 Constitution's clauses designating Islam as the state religion, criticized claims of the state's secular nature (Hasan Hikmet, 1923a).

The 1924 Constitution's clause stating "The religion of the Turkish State is Islam" and provisions for enforcing Sharia were strong anchors for secularism's opponents ('Laiklik-Lâ-Dinilik: Hükûmete Laiklik İsnad Olunması Doğru Mudur', 1924). On January 17, 1924, Ahmet Emin Bey's article in Vatan, suggesting religion be limited to worship and belief, was met with resistance from Islamists, who argued it would negate Sharia's role in social order. Sadrettin Celal's claim that the Constitution's "Islam is the state religion" clause was insincerely added also drew criticism. Sebilürreşad argued that secularism claims contradicted the Constitution, which explicitly tasked the Assembly with enforcing Sharia ('Ahmed Emin Bey'den Bir Sual', 1924). Statements by ministers or deputies treating the Constitution as mere paper reflected a disregard for its authority. The journal emphasized that the Constitution defines the government's structure, and claiming a secular state contrary to it was contradictory, noting that ministers could not act against the Constitution and laws.

In 1926, following the comprehensive adoption of Western legal systems, Justice Minister Mahmut Esat Bozkurt stated that the new laws were based on secular state principles, noting that prior family law decrees had restricted polygamy but should be abolished, as it hindered civilized family life. Sebilürreşad rejected Bozkurt's view, denying a link between polygamy and the civility of family life, and harshly criticized his emphasis on secularism and polygamy's abolition as contrary to Islam and the Constitution ('Adliye Vekîlinin Beyânâtı', 1925).

2.4 Ictihad's Paving the Way for Secular Law (1904–1932)

The Second Constitutional Era marked a pivotal phase in the Ottoman Empire, during which discussions on modernization and secularization crystallized into an intellectual movement. Launched in 1904 in Geneva under the leadership of Abdullah Cevdet, the journal Ictihad emerged as a prominent platform laying the ideological and practical foundations for modernist reforms. Published in both Turkish and

French, the journal introduced Ottoman intellectuals to the ideas of Western thinkers such as Gustave Le Bon, Ludwig Büchner, and D'Holbach, fostering a positivist intellectual framework (Akgün, 1988, p. 130; Ayluçtarhan, 2007, p. 185; Hanioğlu, 1981, pp. 134–137; Hanioğlu, 1997). The group known as Westernists, rallying around Ictihad, advocated radical ideas such as a superstition-free "scientific Islam," opposition to monarchy, and a secular legal system, thereby shaping the secularization process from the Ottoman Empire to the Republic, until Ictihad ceased publication following Abdullah Cevdet's death (1932).

Unlike earlier movements that supported partial Westernization in areas such as state administration, law, and finance, Westernists during the Second Constitutional Era advocated for the comprehensive adoption of Western models of governance. Drawing from Enlightenment philosophy and French culture, this movement shaped the intellectual world of the future Republican cadres. Ictihad served as a central platform for these ideas until Abdullah Cevdet died in 1932, disseminating the views of Westernist intellectuals to the public (İnalcık, 2016, p. 309). The journal criticized Tanzimat-era reforms as imitative and superficial, advocating for the prioritization of public education to achieve socio-economic development. It emphasized that the Westernist movement was not a blind imitation, but rather adapted positivism's widespread influence in nineteenth-century Europe to propose a rational and scientific modernization project for the Ottoman context (Tansü, 2002, p. 276; Tunaya, 1948, p. 593; Yılmaz, 2025, pp. 116–120).

Westernists acknowledged the societal role of religion, even selectively using religious references to legitimize secular reforms (Ceyhan, 2019, p. 13). However, they viewed Islam's superstition-laden interpretation as an obstacle to modern civilization. Inalcık notes that Westernists proposed a morality-centered, superstition-free understanding of religion (İnalcık, 2016, p. 347). This perspective was frequently explored in Ictihad's pages, with the journal taking on the mission of combating false dervish practices, religious charlatanism, and superstitions.

Westernists distinguished between the ibâdât (matters of worship, concerning the relationship between individual and God) and muâmelât (interpersonal relations or civil law) aspects of Islamic law, focusing their reform proposals on the latter. Ictihad's jurist Celal Nuri argued that both science and religion aim to enhance human welfare, asserting that religion should not contradict empirical truths or hinder scientific progress. In his concise words, "Religion was created for humanity; humanity was not created for religion." (Celal Nuri, 1913, pp. 63–64). While advocating for the secularization of muâmelât, he viewed European law as an "open treasure," but recommended its localization to align with Islamic jurisprudence (Celal Nuri, 1914, p. 46). This approach facilitated the adoption of Western law under the guise of Islamic jurisprudence, aiming to balance the defense of Islamic law with the support of Western legal principles (Celal Nuri, 1912).

Ictihad infused Young Turk ideas with a radical anti-monarchist stance (Mardin, 2008, p. 252). Abdullah Cevdet's opposition to the sultanate planted the seeds of a modern state concept, positioning the journal as a pioneer of an intellectual movement that recognized the responsibilities of a modern state in the Ottoman context (Tunaya,

1948, p. 627). Additionally, its emphasis on the separation of religion and state paved the way for secular legal reforms (Ardıç, 2012, p. 35; Ceyhan, 2019, p. 78).

In his 1912 article "A Very Awake Sleep," published in Ictihad, Kılıçzade İsmail Hakkı presented radical proposals in areas such as military, politics, education, women's rights, economy, religion, law, and dress, offering a distinct "utopia" compared to other intellectuals of the Second Constitutional Era (Kılıçzade Hakkı, 1913). Kılıçzade argued that religion should address individual consciences and be separated from state affairs and law, with its worldly rulings reduced to advisory moral guidance (Kılıçzade Hakkı, 1915; Zeren, 1999). Combined with Ictihad's call for combating superstitions and promoting a rational understanding of religion, these proposals strengthened the intellectual foundation for secular legal reforms.

The activities of Westernists around Ictihad had a profound influence on the intellectual world of the cadres who founded the Republic. Mustafa Kemal, a product of modern educational institutions, drew inspiration from Westernist ideas and put them into practice. While Westernists could not transform their ideas into a cohesive ideology, during Atatürk's era, these ideas were blended with Turkish nationalist elements to form the official ideology (Creel, 1980, p. 9; İnalcık, 2016, p. 347). By advocating a superstition-free religious understanding, a rational legal system, and a modern state vision, Ictihad built a bridge from the Ottoman Empire to the Republic, paving the way for secular law.

Bilgişin, emphasizing the insufficient study of Turkish legal history in the early Republican years, aimed to contribute to the development of a national legal consciousness by demonstrating the existence of ancient Turkish law. The Ulu Yasa laws of Genghis Khan were presented as a written example of Turkish law, rooted in national spirit, customs, and traditions (Bilgişin, 1922a). This suggested that Ictihad's secular legal proposals could be grounded in the national legal tradition. The task ahead was to liberate Turkish law from the dominance of religious scholars and foster its development as an independent science by drawing on Western legal doctrines (Bilgişin, 1922b).

The adoption of the Swiss Civil Code in 1926 marked a turning point in the Republican era's legal landscape. Ictihad regarded this event as one of Mustafa Kemal's "spiritual victories." However, Abdullah Cevdet cautioned that adopting a nation's civil code does not automatically render it civilized; it merely removes barriers to progress. This view reflects Ictihad's perspective that secular law should be internalized through a societal evolution aligned with customs and traditions to be effective. The journal emphasized that laws must become "natural, customary, and traditional" to have impact, advocating for the internalization of secular law through societal transformation (Abdullah Cevdet, 1926a). Citing Justice Minister and legal revolution pioneer Mahmut Esat Bozkurt, Ictihad praised the Civil Code's innovations—such as abolishing polygamy, strengthening women's legal status, ensuring gender equality in inheritance law, recognizing freedom of religion, and removing religious differences as barriers to marriage—as essential for a modern and civilized society (Abdullah Cevdet, 1926b).

2.5 Conclusion

The transition from the late Ottoman Empire to the early years of the Republic of Türkiye represents a critical juncture in the secularization of law, characterized by intense ideological debates that found expression in the contrasting narratives of Sebilürreşad and Ictihad. Sebilürreşad, as a stronghold of Islamist thought, consistently championed the preservation of Sharia's moral, social, and legal authority, viewing secular reforms as a profound threat to the Turkish-Islamic identity. From the Tanzimat period through the early Republican era, the journal critiqued Western legal frameworks as incompatible with the nation's traditions, values, and spiritual ethos, emphasizing the role of Sharia in ensuring justice, societal cohesion, and moral order. Its extensive legal-themed articles condemned key secular measures, including the abolition of Sharia courts, the closure of madrasas, and the transformative laws of March 3, 1924. These laws, foundational to the principle of secularism in the new Turkish state, were seen by Sebilürreşad as undermining the Constitution's recognition of Islam as the state religion and the nation's moral fabric. The journal's steadfast advocacy for judicial unity under Sharia, the preservation of Islamic family law, and the inseparability of religion and state underscored its vision of an Islamic order as the guarantor of societal well-being.

In contrast, Ictihad served as a vanguard for modernist and positivist ideals, advocating a secular legal framework as indispensable to modernization. By promoting a rational, superstition-free interpretation of religion and drawing on Western intellectual currents, Ictihad laid the ideological groundwork for the Republic's legal reforms. It celebrated milestones, such as the 1926 adoption of the Swiss Civil Code, which it viewed as a triumph of secular progress, introducing innovations like the abolition of polygamy, enhanced legal status for women, and gender equality in inheritance law. While selectively engaging religious references to legitimize reforms, Ictihad emphasized the need for laws to align with societal customs and evolve through rational, scientific principles, thus bridging Ottoman intellectual traditions with the Republic's secular vision.

Collectively, Sebilürreşad and Ictihad encapsulate the polarized intellectual landscape of the era, with Sebîlürreşâd defending Islamic legal traditions and İctihad primarily championing Western-inspired secular modernity. Their contrasting stances reflect the broader tension between preserving Islamic legal heritage and adopting rational, secular legal systems. Within these journals, diverse perspectives emerged: Sebilürreşad featured debates on the scope of ijtihad, with some contributors adhering strictly to the Hanafi school and others advocating for broader ijtihad to adapt Sharia's core principles to contemporary needs, while Ictihad, during the late Ottoman period, included voices that supported modernizing Islamic law to sustain its relevance, though it shifted to exclusively promoting secular legal reforms after the establishment of the Republic. These multifaceted debates underscore the pivotal role of journals as platforms for shaping public discourse and navigating Türkiye's complex legal and cultural transformation.

References

Abdullah Cevdet. (1926a, March 1). Kanun-ı Medenî. *Ictihad, 199*, 3893.

Abdullah Cevdet. (1926b, June 1). Kanun-ı Medenî ve Adliye Vekilimiz. *Ictihad, 205*, 3989–3992.

Adliye Vekîlinin Beyânâtı. (1925, January 22). *Sebîlürreşâd, 25*(635), 175.

Ahmed Cevdet. (1923, May 24). Garplılaşmak isteyenlerin nazar-ı ibretine: Usûl ve kavâninin tesirleri. *Sebîlürreşâd, 21*(530–531), 86–88.

Ahmed Emin Bey'den Bir Sual. (1924, January 17). *Sebîlürreşâd, 23*(584), 192.

Ahmed Naim. (1918, November 28). Bizde din ve devlet. *Sebîlürreşâd, 15*(380), 293–295.

Ahmed Nazif. (1923, December). Teceddüd–tekemmül: Mecelle mes'elesi. *Sebîlürreşâd, 23*(579, 580), 121; 75–77.

Akgün, M. (1988). *Materyalizmin Türkiye'ye girişi ve ilk etkileri*. Kültür ve Turizm Bakanlığı.

Aksekili Ahmed Hamdi. (1916, October 19). Din ve devlet yahud hilâfet ve saltanat (İngiliz Gazetelerine Cevap). *Sebîlürreşâd, 14*(359), 178.

Ankara Haberleri. (1923, October 11). *Sebîlürreşâd, 22*(567–568), 175–176.

Ardıç, N. (2012). *Islam and the politics of secularism: The caliphate and middle eastern modernization in the early 20th century*. Routledge.

Ayluçtarhan, S. (2007). *Dr. Abdullah Cevdet's translations (1908–1910): The making of a Westernist and materialist 'culture repertoire' in a 'resistant' Ottoman context* [Master Thesis]. Boğaziçi University.

Bilgişin, Ş. M. (1922a, January 31). Milli tetebbular: Eski Türk hukuku. *Ictihad, 142*, 2986–2988.

Bilgişin, Ş. M. (1922b, March 15). Milli tetebbular: Yeni Türk hukuku. *Ictihad, 145*, 3031–3033.

Birinci, A. (2012). *Hürriyet ve İtilaf Fırkası -II. Meşrutiyet devrinde İttihat ve Terakki'ye karşı çıkanlar-*. Dergah Yayınları.

Celal Nuri. (1912, January). İslamda vücub-i teceddüd. *Ictihad, 4*(55), 970–973.

Celal Nuri. (1913). *Tarih-i istikbal*. Yeni Osmanlı Matbaası.

Celal Nuri. (1914). *Havaic-i kanuniyemiz*. Matbaa-i Ictihad.

Ceyhan, A. F. (2019). *Accommodating Islam and modernity: The case of Abdullah Cevdet's Ictihad (1904–1926)* [Master's Thesis]. İstanbul Şehir Üniversitesi Sosyal Bilimler Enstitüsü.

Creel, F. W. (1980). Abdullah Cevdet: A father of Kemalism. *Journal of Turkish Studies, 4*, 9–26.

Efe, A. (2009). Sebîlürreşâd. In *TDV İslam Ansiklopedisi* (Vol. 36, pp. 251–253).

Ekinci, E. B. (2016). *Osmanlı hukuku*. Arı Sanat Yayınları.

Eşref Edib. (1921a, May 14). Şer'iyye vekâletinin beyannâmesi Münâsebetiyle. *Sebîlürreşâd, 19*(480), 126–128.

Eşref Edib. (1921b, July 2). Tanzîmâtçılık bu memleket için mahz-ı felâket olmuştur. *Sebîlürreşâd, 19*(486), 193–201.

Göçek, F. M. (1999). *Burjuvazinin yükselişi imparatorluğun çöküşü* (İ. Yıldız, Trans.). Ayraç Yayınları.

Halim Sabit. (1910, February 24). Ictihada Dair. *Sırat-ı Müstakim, 3*(77), 392–394.

Hanioğlu, M. Ş. (1981). *Doktor Abdullah Cevdet ve dönemi*. Üçdal Neşriyat.

Hanioğlu, M. Ş. (1997). Garbcılar: Their attitudes toward religion and their impact on the official ideology of the Turkish Republic. *Studia Islamica, 86*, 133–158. https://doi.org/10.2307/1595808

Hasan Hikmet. (1923a, August 30). İçtimâiyyâtta garpçılık-bozgunculuk: Laiklik-asrilik. *Sebîlürreşâd, 22*(555–556), 73–74.

Hasan Hikmet. (1923b, November 8). İctimâiyâtda garbcılık ve bozgunculuk: Asrî Aile. *Sebîlürreşâd, 23*(574).

Hasan Hikmet. (1923c, November 29). İctimâiyâtta garbcılık ve bozgunculuk: Asrî kanun. *Sebîlürreşâd, 23*(574, 577, 579), 21; 74–77; 104–106.

İnalcık, H. (2016). *Devlet-i Aliyye 4*. Türkiye İş Bankası.

Kanûn-ı Esâsî'nin Şer'a da Mugayereti. (1918, November 7). *Sebîlürreşâd, 15*(377), 252.

Kara, İ. (2014). *Türkiye'de İslamcılık düşüncesi 1*. Dergah Yayınları.

Kılıçzade Hakkı. (1913, February). Pek uyanık bir uyku. *Ictihad, 4*(55), 1226–1228.

Kılıçzade Hakkı. (1915). *İtikadat-ı Batıla'ya ilan-ı harb.*
Kırşehir Mebusu Müfîd. (1922, August 3). İslâmiyet'in vaz' ettiği mebde'ler. *Sebîlürreşâd, 20*(512), 211–213.
Korlaelçi, Murtaza. (1986). *Pozitivizmin Türkiye'ye gelişi.* İnsan Yayınları.
Laiklik-Lâ-Dinilik: Hükûmete laiklik isnad olunması doğru mudur? (1924, July 31). *Sebîlürreşâd, 24*(610), 185–186.
M. Şemseddin. (1919, January 9). Beşerî cem'iyetler için dînin lüzûmu. *Sebîlürreşâd, 15*(386), 388–391.
Mağribi. (1910, February 10). Müctehidler yetiştirelim. *Sırat-ı Müstakim, 3*(75), 364–366.
Mahkeme-i şer'iyyeler kalıyor mu? (1923, October 25). *Sebîlürreşâd, 22*(571–572), 206–207.
Mardin, Ş. (2008). *Jön Türklerin siyasi fikirleri (1895–1908).* İletişim Yayınları.
Mollaoğlu, A. E. (2024). Hukuki çoğulluk bağlamında hukukun neliği sorununa muhtasar bir bakış. *DiHA: Journal of Interdisciplinary Legal Studies, 1*, 64–87. https://doi.org/10.5281/zenodo.13857197
Muhammed Hamdi. (1918, December 12). Dinimiz, devletimiz. *Sebîlürreşâd, 15*(382), 324–329.
Ömer Rıza. (1919, March 27). İslam mefkûresine doğru. *Sebîlürreşâd, 16*(400–401), 107–109.
Otacı, C. (2004). *Hukukun laikleşme serüveni.* Birey Yayınları.
Özkorkut, N. Ü. (2021). Sebilürreşad Dergisi'nin Türkiye Cumhuriyeti'nin kuruluş sürecinde batılılaşma ve laiklik Düşüncesine Yaklaşımı. *Türk Hukuk Tarihi Araştırmaları, 31–32*, 5–40.
Said Halim Paşa. (1922, August 3). İslâm'da teşkîlât-ı siyâsiyye: İslâm usûl-i siyâsiyyesi. *Sebîlürreşâd, 20*(512), 50–52.
Selahaddin Asım. (1909a, March 4). İctimâiyyât ve şerî'at-i İslamiyye. *Sırat-ı Müstakim, 2*(28), 24–26.
Selahaddin Asım. (1909b, April 1). İlm-i ictima'a nazaran İslamiyet. *Sırat-ı Müstakim, 2*(32).
Tansü, Y. E. (2002). *Batıcı düşüncenin etkili bir sözcüsü olarak Ictihad Dergisi* [Master's Thesis]. Ankara University.
Teceddüd Ahkâm-ı dîniyyenin nesih ve ibtâli demek midir? (1923, December 6). *Sebîlürreşâd, 23*(578), 87–90.
Tunaya, T. Z. (1948). Amme hukukumuz bakımından İkinci Meşrutiyetin siyasi tefekküründe garpçılık cereyanı. *İstanbul Üniversitesi Hukuk Fakültesi Mecmuası, 14*(3–4), 585–630.
Yılmaz, Y. (2025). *Son dönem Osmanlı hukuk düşüncesi -Ictihad dergisi üzerinden bir inceleme-* (2nd ed.). Layiha Yayınevi.
Zeren, S. (1999). *İsmail Hakkı Kılıçoğlu'nun eserleri ve fikirleri* [Master's Thesis]. İstanbul Üniversitesi Sosyal Bilimler Enstitüsü.

Chapter 3
Secularization Debates in Islamist Journals Post-1990

Yunus Ergen

3.1 Introduction

In Türkiye, where the modernization experience spans approximately two centuries, religion has consistently maintained its central position in social, cultural, and political life (Kara, 2024). The modernization efforts that became more pronounced during the late Ottoman Empire took on a more comprehensive structure with the proclamation of the Republic, particularly within the framework of national-state identity. The transition from a multiethnic empire to a unitary nation-state endowed Turkish modernization with distinctive characteristics. These unique features become especially evident when compared with Western experiences of modernization (Mardin, 1991). Undoubtedly, religion has emerged as a more intensely scrutinized and debated structure throughout this process. Considering that modernization also entails a process of secularization, the role of religion in the transformation from empire to republic has given rise to secularization debates specific to the Turkish context (Ertit, 2019b; Shlykov, 2019).

The fact that Islam was a founding element in the Ottoman political structure shaped religion-state relations and secularization policies during the Republican period in a multidimensional and negotiated manner. Indeed, in the early years of the Republic of Türkiye, which was introduced into the modernization process with strict laic (as distinct from secularism) policies based on the French experience and a top-down approach, a concentrated effort was made to reduce the influence of the religious sphere not only in political governance but also in social life. That is, while the state was becoming laic, it was also desired that the public secularize within the framework of these laic policies and enacted laws (Kuru, 2009). Although this was a state policy, it was also implemented for many years within the framework of various ideologies, such as Kemalism. In contrast, the religious sphere, intended to

Y. Ergen (✉)
Department of Public Relations and Publicity, Hatay Mustafa Kemal University, Hatay, Türkiye
e-mail: yunusergen@mku.edu.tr

M. D. Dereli and M. Eken (eds.), *Turkish Perspectives on Secularization and Media*,
https://doi.org/10.1007/978-3-032-16436-0_3

be bracketed politically and socially both as a state policy and through the ideological orientations of those who governed the state, was attempted to be preserved in terms of its legitimacy through opposing ideologies, in order to regain functionality in political and social life. Islamism undoubtedly led these ideologies (Sözeri, 2019; Yavuz & Öztürk, 2019). At the root of the ideology of Islamism, whose intellectual origins go back further than Kemalism, lies the idea that Islam, as a political governance model, constitutes an alternative to the models shaped by the secular and imperialist West (Çiğdem, 2004; Kara, 2004, 2014). The ideology of Islamism, roughly shaped on this intellectual basis, has made its presence felt in every period of modern Türkiye's historical adventure as a current of thought and social movement (Bulaç, 2004; Mert, 2004). Thinkers, intellectuals, or men of letters who adopted this ideology have made efforts to express their ideas through various platforms. It can be said that intellectual journals are at the forefront of these platforms. Islamist journals that began publishing in the early twentieth century continue to exist today.

The idea of Islamism and Islamist journals, which constitute the foundational ground of this idea, have been shaped throughout history around various orientations. The course of this thought, which evolved in different directions according to the conjunctural structure of each period, has taken form through continuities and ruptures as a movement and an ideology. Efforts to make a period-based classification of these forms continue to exist in the literature on both Islamism and Islamist journals (Işık, 2020; Sunar, 2019b). Among these, the intensity of discussions focused on the post-1980 and post-1990 periods is remarkable. The post-1990 period is especially significant, as it was a time when both the political structuring of Islam gained strength and the effects of global neoliberal transformations were deeply felt. During this period, Islamist journals became essential platforms where the intellectual and ideological positions of Islamist circles were more intensively produced and gained increased visibility.

A growing and expanding body of literature has developed on the issues addressed in Islamist journals. In fact, national-level surveys reveal that dozens of articles, review essays, and theses have been written on the subject. The topics of these writings vary. While there is a concentration on the historical trajectory of journals, either those that have concluded their publication or those that continue to be published, within a specific thematic framework (Budak, 2020; Çoban, 2018; Çöpoğlu, 2023; Gürpınar, 2017; Karataş, 2024; Kaya, 2023; Selçuk, 2023), some studies examine how a particular event or phenomenon has been discussed in Islamist journals (Altun, 2024; Karaman, 2020; Küçükosman, 2022; Küçüktığlı, 2024; Maviş, 2017; Polat & Uzun, 2024). Among these, a large number of studies focusing on the image of women and the status of women in social life are particularly noteworthy (Ahnas, 2025; Meşe, 2015; Yiğit, 2020; Yıldırım, 2021). The most comprehensive studies on Islamist journals, however, have been published in the form of edited volumes. The first of these is the study titled *1960–1980 arası İslamcı dergiler-toparlanma ve çeşitlenme* (Islamist journals between 1960–1980: Consolidation and diversification) (2016). This study thoroughly examines the formation of Islamist thought and its processes of change and transformation, with a focus on Islamist journals in general and the debates featured in various journals. The other study, consisting of four volumes and edited by sociologist Lütfi Sunar, is titled *"Bir Başka Hayata Karşı:" 1980 sonrası İslamcı dergilerde meseleler, kavramlar ve isimler* ("Against Another Life": Issues, concepts, and names in post-1980 Islamist journals) (2019a). In this study, Islamist thought and the journals in which it emerged are addressed in detail. While the study focuses on how Islamism has developed and what ruptures it has undergone throughout the historical process, it also provides an in-depth analysis of the approaches Islamist journals adopted during political, economic, and cultural transformation processes. Furthermore, it provides a detailed examination of various Islamist journals, the debates surrounding these journals, prominent figures, and key concepts.

It is possible to state that the literature on Islamist journals has developed across various focal points and is progressing toward becoming a comprehensive corpus. However, within the relevant body of literature, there is no comprehensive study on how the phenomenon of secularization has been addressed, nor on how debates on secularization reflect the relationship between Islamist thought and social change and transformation. Only one master's thesis related to the subject was found in the conducted surveys. This thesis, which focuses on debates over laicism in Islamist journals, analyzes the understanding and attitudes of Islamists in Türkiye toward laicism (Özbey, 2023). Although the thesis includes some discussion of secularization, it has been determined that a comprehensive evaluation was not conducted, since the primary focus was laicism. Therefore, the lack of a study that directly focuses on secularization debates in Islamist journals, where Islamist thought takes shape, stands out as a gap. Based on this gap, this study aims to examine writings on secularization published in Islamist journals in post-1990 Türkiye and reveal the intellectual and discursive attitudes of Islamist thought toward secularization. In this respect, this study seeks to answer the question of how secularization is perceived and interpreted by those who adopt an ideology that aims to increase the influence of religion (Islam) in social and political life. It also reveals how secularization theory, which explains the weakening of the power of metaphysical elements to organize individual and social life (Berger, 2020; Casanova, 2014; Ertit, 2019a), and the process of secularization itself are evaluated by Islamists who aim to reverse the claims of the theory.

3.2 Method and Research Design

This study, which aims to examine the writings on secularization published in post-1990 Islamist journals and to reveal the intellectual and discursive attitudes of Islamist thought toward the process of secularization, was conducted within the framework of a basic qualitative research design. In essence, the qualitative research paradigm focuses on how individuals or communities make sense of and interpret their experiences related to an existing phenomenon or event, how they construct these meanings through the interactions they engage in within social life, and what values they attribute to this construction. In the basic qualitative research approach, uncovering these meanings is the primary aim of the study (Güler et al., 2013; Merriam, 2018). In this respect, it was considered that a basic qualitative research design would be appropriate for exploring the reflections on the societal and individual manifestations of the secularization process in writings published in journals issued by those who embrace Islamist thought, and for understanding how the discourse built upon these reflections is constructed.

3.2.1 Data Sources and Sampling

The field of the study consists of writings on the subject of secularization that appear in journals that are either aligned with Islamist thought or identified as Islamist and that continued their publication in the post-1990 period. The reason for focusing on journals from 1990 onward is that this period witnessed significant transformations in the political, social, and intellectual dimensions of Islamist thought in Türkiye. Following the fragmented and disorganized appearance of the 1980s, the 1990s emerged as a period during which Islamist circles both expanded into mass movements and experienced noticeable diversification of ideas. The rise of the Refah Party, the search of Islamist circles for a liberal democratic order, the intertwining of radical tendencies with aspirations for pluralism, the initiatives and investments of Muslim businessmen resulting in the rise of the "green capital," the acceleration of economic development, and especially the sociocultural conditions brought about by the political power shift post-2000 all contributed to a more favorable environment for the formation of Islamist thought during this period (Erkilet, 2004, p. 691; Maviş, 2017, pp. 11–16; Sunar, 2019b, pp. 11–12). Therefore, examining the writings on secularization published in post-1990 Islamist journals will enable a more accurate understanding of the intellectual and discursive attitudes of Islamist thought, which entered a new phase of structuring and transformation in relation to the secularization process.

Islamist journals published in Türkiye were digitized and made available to researchers in 2013 by the İlmi Etütler Derneği-İLEM (Scientific Studies Association) under the title of the İslamcı Dergiler Projesi-İDP (Islamist Journals Project) (*İlmi Etüdler Derneği*, n.d.). Through the digital catalog and database of this project, which has its own website, researchers have been granted the opportunity to research topics of their choice (*İDP*, n.d.). In this study, the digital database of İDP was initially utilized, and a search was conducted for writings containing the keywords "secular," "secularization," "secularism," and "secularisation." However, owing to the inability to access all relevant writings and the subsequent maintenance status of the project's website, the project coordinators were contacted and informed about this research. To access analyzable writings, the project coordinators were requested to provide an inventory of journals that continued to be published in the post-1990 period. The inventory provided access to information on 658 Islamist journals. Among these, the

20 journals with the highest number of issues were listed and sent to the project coordinators. From this list, the top five journals containing the highest number of writings that included the designated keywords were selected using a purposive sampling strategy. The journals identified were *Altınoluk*, *İktibas*, *Mektup*, *Umran*, and *Yedi İklim*. *Yedi İklim* and *Mektup* journals were excluded from the study because they primarily publish literary-themed content, do not engage in intellectual/discursive debates on secularization in writings containing the keywords, and are inaccessible due to the lack of relevant writings. Accordingly, writings on secularization published in the journals *Altınoluk*, *İktibas*, and Umran were selected for analysis.[1]

3.2.2 Data Analysis

The writings comprising the study sample were subjected to thematic analysis. Themes are structures created by the researcher that represent a particular meaning based on recurring patterns in the data set. They provide an in-depth understanding by establishing connections across different data and are generally derived from small units of meaning (codes). Thematic analysis is a flexible data analysis technique used to systematically uncover themes (Braun & Clarke, 2006, 2022; Scharp & Sanders, 2019). Strategies such as the reflexive, code reliability, and codebook approaches are prominent in thematic analysis. In this study, a reflexive thematic analysis strategy was employed because of its flexible structure (Braun & Clarke, 2022; Morgan, 2022). Accordingly, the 53 writings were divided into themes within the framework of various codes based on patterns of meaning, and data analysis was performed.

The analyses were conducted using the qualitative data analysis software MAXQDA. The writing of each journal was transferred to MAXQDA, and the coding process was conducted within the program. An inductive approach was adopted for coding. Rather than focusing on the central issue problematized in each writing, attention was given to how the issue was examined in the context of secularization itself. In this regard, an initial open coding phase was followed by a selective coding phase (Kuckartz, 2014). During the coding process, the texts were read repeatedly several times, and the final themes were determined within the framework of peer feedback. The codes were not mutually exclusive. In other words, more than one code can be assigned to a particular section of the text. Thus, a more comprehensive analysis of the text's semantic patterns was sought.

[1] For information on the journals and their editorial orientations, see: (*Altınoluk Dergisi*, n.d.; *İktibas Dergisi*, n.d.; *Umran Dergisi*, n.d.).

3.2.3 Validity and Reliability

To ensure the validity and reliability of the study, the strategy of peer debriefing was employed. Peer debriefing, which involves an external review of the research process, refers to inviting one or more neutral peers (experts) who are not involved in the research to share their thoughts and feedback on the research process (Creswell, 2013; Merriam, 2018). Qualified peers facilitate the review and evaluation of documents related to the data collected by the researcher, including the provisional and final codes and themes derived from their analysis, as well as the study findings (Ahmed, 2024; Amin et al., 2020; Janesick, 2015; Spall, 1998). In this study, three academics who had previously worked on the subject, were well-versed in the qualitative research process, and had experience in thematic analysis, were included in the process. Each of the three academics was asked to evaluate the research and analysis processes of the study independently. Through interviews conducted via online meetings, simultaneous feedback on the research was obtained from academics. As a result of this feedback, the data analysis process was reassessed, and the codes and themes created for data analysis were finalized. In this way, consistency in the analysis process was methodologically reinforced.

3.3 Results

3.3.1 Quantitative Overview

When examining the general profile of the 53 writings on secularization published in the journals that constitute the sample, the highest number of writings is found in *İktibas* (30), followed by *Umran* (14) and *Altınoluk* (9). The writings were published between 1994 and 2016 (Fig. 3.1). A significant portion of them (84.91%) were published after 2002. The highest number of writings was authored in 2008.

Thirty-nine different authors authored the writings found in the journals that constitute the sample. The types of writing vary. The most frequent type is "opinion pieces," and the journals also include writings in the form of "panel discussions," "essays," "interviews," "book reviews," and "articles." The content of these writings is examined in detail under the relevant themes in the following sections.

3.3.2 Conceptual and Theoretical Discussion

Within this theme, which includes matters related to the conduct of conceptual and theoretical discussions on secularization, the writings found in the journals that constitute the sample were coded into seven categories (Fig. 3.2). Based on the findings, it is observed that the journals demonstrate an effort to construct a theoretical

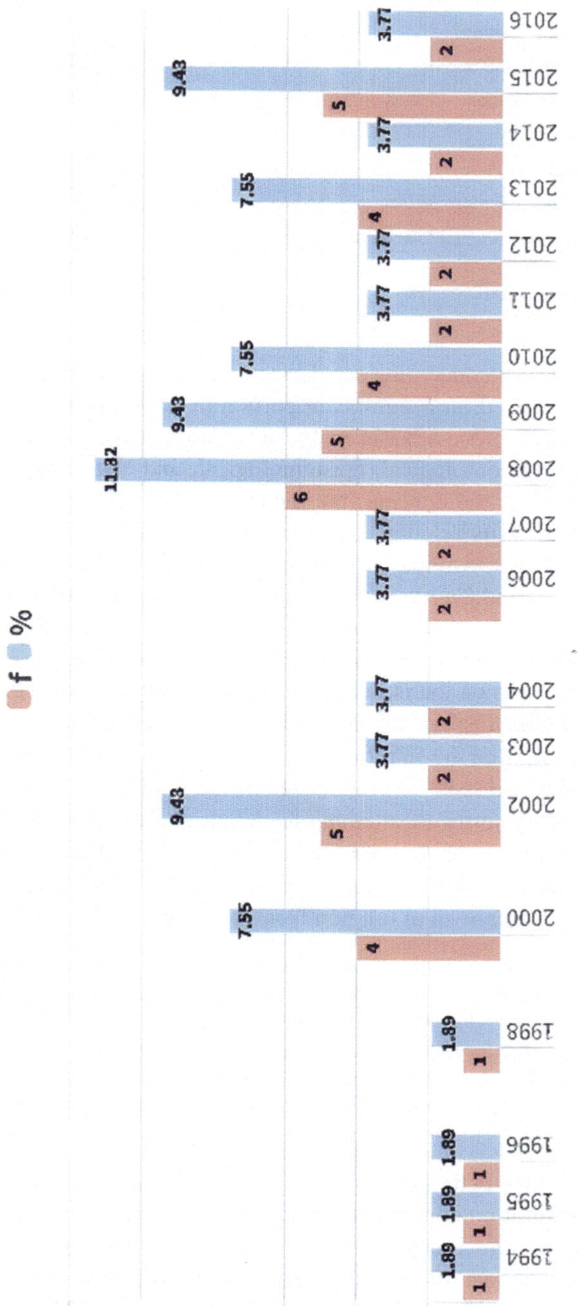

Fig. 3.1 Number of papers

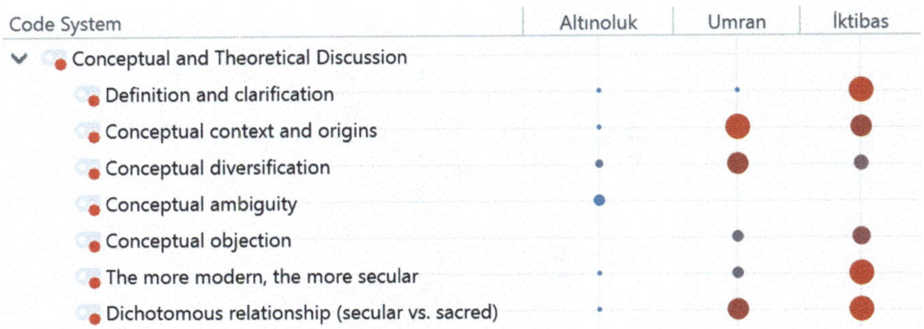

Fig. 3.2 Code matrix of theme 1

and conceptual framework concerning secularization. Indeed, although not present in all the writings examined, in a significant portion of them, secularization is not merely treated as a social process but is analyzed within a multilayered structure of meaning that includes its ontological, epistemological, and historical dimensions. The origin and context of the concept, its boundaries and derivatives, its contradictions and ambiguities, its relation to modernization processes, and its critical analyses are central to the writings on it. When viewed in terms of specific journals, particularly *İktibas* and *Umran*, secularization is positioned both as an essential extension of modernity and as a social process that poses a threat to Islamic thought and way of life. In the writings published in *Altınoluk*, although such positioning is less frequent, the emphasis on the individual and societal impacts of secularization is more prominent. In this respect, the theme also bears traces of an approach that, rather than focusing solely on the empirical outcomes of secularization, questions its conceptual foundations and seeks to produce alternative intellectual grounds for it.

The overwhelming majority of attempts to define and explain the concept of "secular" and its derivatives have developed within a critical framework. This is because secularization, in addition to the meanings inherent in its etymological origin, is also interpreted as the removal of religion from social and individual life.

> Secularism, by severing the connection with the Creator, the transcendent, and with superior natural principles, presents a materialistic perspective; it does not seek any remaining association with the religious, but complete disconnection. (Rahim, 2015, p. 36)
>
> …Secularism, on the other hand, is the corruption in practice, creed, and consciousness; a shift toward worldliness, the exclusion of religious thinking from all areas of life, the nullification of religious symbols, and the positioning of religion solely as a matter of personal conscience. (Yazçiçek, 2015, p. 33)

This critical attitude in the definitions and explanations suggests that secularization is not viewed as a natural outcome of the modernization process; rather, it is seen as a deliberate process aimed at accelerating it. In other words, secularization is viewed as a deliberate project of individual and social transformation. The writings strongly imply that secularization constitutes an ideological and cultural assault. This is most apparent in narratives concerning the context and origin of the concept. These narratives interpret secularization as a Western invention. There is a strong emphasis on the idea that secularization, considered to have emerged as a result of the West's social, cultural, political, and theological tensions, is an "imported" concept or phenomenon for Muslim societies:

> Although the concepts of laicism, laicist ideology, and secularism have occupied our agenda intensely in recent years, they are generally confused with one another and used interchangeably. Undoubtedly, the fact that these are 'imported' foreign concepts plays a role in this confusion. (Arslan, 1994, p. 10)

However, conceptual discussions have also been conducted through the use of analytical definitions. In some texts, secularism is used synonymously with laicism, while in others, efforts have been made to define it by distinguishing it from similar concepts such as laicism. Furthermore, the family of secular concepts has been explained alongside philosophical currents, such as "atheism," and ideologies, including "nationalism," "socialism," and "liberalism," thereby increasing semantic diversity. This diversity, on the one hand, points to the broadness of the concept's semantic boundaries, while on the other hand, it also leads to ambiguity. Although not overwhelmingly emphasized, there is a noticeable indication that some of the theoretical and conceptual discussions in the writings contain confusing interpretations. In particular, the writings in *Altınoluk* focus on the semantic ambiguities between the concepts of "secular" and "laic." It is also understood that this ambiguity is interpreted as an obstacle to theoretical consensus:

> Today, the word 'laic' and its derivatives have become outdated and worn out. Due to the unconscious use of these concepts, people in the country have come to the point of grinding their teeth at one another, making them unappealing in the eyes of the masses—except for the militants themselves. Moreover, officials and even those who debate and write on these issues often confuse them with one another; as a result, everyone ends up listening only to themselves, and thus complete ambiguity prevails. (Yazıcıoğlu, 1995, p. 50)

In some texts, the emphasis on the ambiguity of the concept extends to a critical rejection of the concept itself. In these narratives, which present a shared perspective, it is emphasized that the concept of "secular" and its derivatives do not align with the cultural and historical experience of the Muslim-Turkish society and that they possess a coercive and exclusionary character. The epistemological rejection of the concept emerges not as a matter of terminological preference but as a form of resistance against the distortion of truth. Accordingly, not only the family of secular concepts of family but also its origin and function are questioned.

The discourse that modernization gives rise to secularization is frequently found in secularization literature (Berger, 2020; Casanova, 2014; Coleman, 2015). A definition of secularism and a narrative of secularization that parallels this discourse are also present in Islamist journals. Indeed, in the writings analyzed, an organic connection is established between modernity and secularity, often framed within a critical causality. In this framework, secularity is not seen merely as an extension of modernity but is evaluated as an inherent outcome of it. Moreover, the ideals of modernity and the processes of modernization are not portrayed as neutral elements with no effect on secularization, but rather as a conscious project deliberately pursued to promote the spread of secularization processes:

> To speak of modernity is to speak of secularism. Regardless of the topic, the cause, the ideology, the struggle, or the policy—when it refers itself to modernity, it suddenly becomes legitimized, or can be legitimized. (Müftüoğlu, 2014, p. 14)

> Secularity is one of the most fundamental parameters of modernization. (Yazçiçek, 2015, p. 35)

In the conceptual and theoretical discussion of secularization, the most prominent emphasis is placed on the sharp distinction made between the secular and the sacred. The concepts of the secular and the sacred, addressed through a relationship of opposition, are interpreted within a framework of conflict and irreconcilability. The fact that secularity is of Western origin is evaluated as an "imported" concept and phenomenon, is considered alien to the fabric of Muslim societies, and is often viewed as an ideological project aimed at transforming or eliminating the religious structures of these societies—namely Islam—is reflected throughout the narratives. This dichotomous relationship, which stands out in the writings, is grounded at various levels, primarily historical, cultural, and political. While secular thought and the process of secularization are subjected to criticism for absolutizing the worldly through a rationalist orientation and thus excluding the sacred, religion itself—as the most valuable sacred—and the fundamental elements of the tradition formed by its teachings are highlighted as the essential foundation of individual and social salvation:

> There is no sword sharper than that of the holy books for distinguishing between right and wrong. Whatever has retained its truth in all of humanity's accumulation of knowledge and wisdom has been borrowed from holy books. The light of secular culture fades; the light of sacred culture does not fade. (Gürdoğan, 2009, p. 8)

> Today, while Islam is advancing powerfully, secularism (laicism) is rapidly collapsing. Islam attracts those who seek justice, whereas the main pillars of secularism are disintegrating, and secularism is losing even its ability to defend itself—except through violence. (El-Gannuşi, 2002, p. 96)

> Secularism is in no way compatible with Muslim life. (Rahim, 2015, p. 47)

As can be seen, the secular vs. sacred dichotomy is examined at the conceptual and theoretical levels as phenomena that are irreducible to one another. In this analysis, a value hierarchy is constructed through the distinction built on the axis of the temporary and artificial versus the permanent and authentic. Moreover, this hierarchy does not merely involve opposition; it also gives rise to new forms of questioning and synthesis from political, social, and moral perspectives. Thus, the discussion evolves beyond a mere reflex to protect religious values, encompassing an active confrontation and resistance against the normative values or systems represented by the secular, the other, and the opposing. This mode of interpretation also manifests as a form of individual and social identity. In more precise terms, secularization itself is subjected to criticism as an empirical process and positioned as the opposite. At the same time, the identities of those "on the other side" are defined by incorporating them into the family of secular concepts. As a result, the emergence of new opposing identities, such as Muslims vs. secularists or Islamists vs. secularists, on the discursive level is facilitated.

The secular vs. sacred dichotomy is constructed not only as a theoretical and conceptual distinction but also as a vision of civilization and a process of identity construction. This construction, formulated based on the concept of *ummah* consciousness, resonates in various contexts specific to Türkiye. Although a significant portion of the writings in the journals that constitute the sample critically engage with the phenomenon of secularization through issues concerning Türkiye, it is difficult to claim that an adequate level of in-depth analysis and examination has been conducted. It is observed that the evaluations specific to Türkiye are primarily addressed in connection with the modernization process.

3.3.3 The Trajectory of Türkiye's Secularization

In this theme, which encompasses critical evaluations published in Islamist journals regarding the secularization process intertwined with Türkiye's modernization trajectory, the relevant writings were categorized into three groups (Fig. 3.3). In the journals that constitute the sample, Türkiye's unique experience of secularization is addressed as the outcome of a problematic and externally dependent modernization from a historical perspective, with an emphasis on the insufficiency of the process in terms of its intellectual and institutional infrastructure. Moreover, albeit rarely, more flexible and pluralistic approaches can be found, indicating that the secular and sacred may coexist not through absolute opposition but in transitional and hybrid forms. This approach is particularly prominent in *İktibas*. The emphasis on the inadequacy of modernization is more pronounced in *Altınoluk*. While the narrative of distorted modernization and secularization appears in all three journals, the most intensive discussions occur in *İktibas*. On a broader scale, this theme provides an opportunity to understand both the distinctive course of secularization in Türkiye and the reflections of criticisms of Turkish modernization within Islamist thought.

In the Islamist journals, particular emphasis is placed on the problematic or distorted aspects of Türkiye's experience with modernization and, consequently, secularization. Rather than being evaluated independently of one another, both experiences were examined within the context of a cause-and-effect relationship. This relationship is often regarded as problematic. Turkish modernization and secularization are portrayed as a top-down transformation project that contradicts the cultural

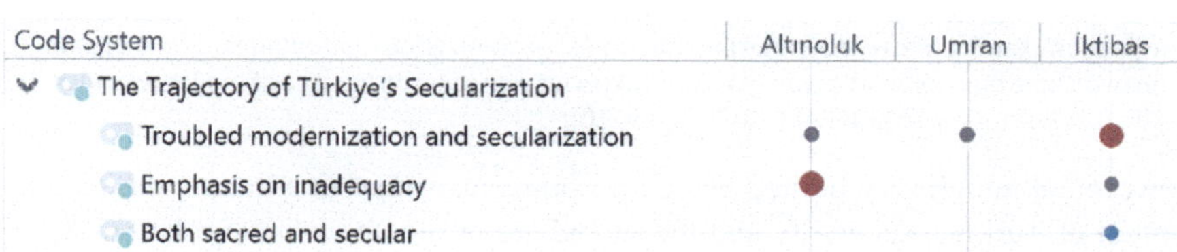

Fig. 3.3 Code matrix of theme 2

structure and fails to meet local/national needs. This approach, frequently encountered in conceptual and theoretical discussions, is also evident in narratives regarding Türkiye's secularization experience. Secularism is positioned as an ideological apparatus aimed at altering and transforming the essential identity of Turkish society. Moreover, there is a consensus around the view that this apparatus was implemented through political imposition rather than societal consensus:

> Undoubtedly, there must be different methods for secularizing an Islamic society. The crudest and most aggressive—therefore the most unacceptable and most repulsive—of these methods are top-down (Jacobin) laicism programs. The most acceptable one is the moderate understanding of laicism. In Türkiye, it is this second type (authoritarian) laicism policy that has been consistently implemented. (Aras, 2009, p. 36)

> In general, the projects of modernization, renewal, contemporization, and Westernization implemented in non-Western societies—and specifically in the Islamic world—were not projects developed or invented by these societies based on their own experiences and their own cultural and intellectual dynamics. They were either imported or, in certain situations, exported. In fact, what was attempted on a global scale was the secularization of the world—and especially of the Islamic world. (Kaplan, 2002, p. 27)

The cultural tension created by processes based on the narrative of distorted modernization and secularization is presented as a justification for the emergence of sociopolitical crises and identity conflicts. Remarkably, the narrative that secularization was constructed as a disconnected phenomenon from cultural continuity and through paradigms belonging to the West leads to questioning the legitimacy of the process. Moreover, the perception that modernization and secularization are not merely political or structural transformations but also impositions of identity and lifestyle is clearly felt. In such a situation, the views emphasizing the lack and inadequacy of resistance on the part of those subjected to these processes draw attention. In other words, the failure of those exposed to modernity and secularism in a top-down manner to produce an adequate intellectual response due to their intellectual weakness is put forward as a justification for the functionality of a distorted, incomplete, or flawed process:

> Unfortunately, in Türkiye, the most talented minds have for years spent their valuable efforts—and undoubtedly, if they had focused on our real problems, very productive outcomes could have been achieved—and their precious time discussing and writing about this concept, some of them without even properly knowing its meaning. (Yazıcıoğlu, 1995, p. 50)

> Today, if we are being dragged in the direction desired by modern-secular history, it is due to the inadequacy of our intellect/thought/contemplation, our sincerity, and our efforts. …Because we have failed to produce comprehensive, in-depth, and encompassing analyses/critiques/examinations concerning the rise and fall of civilizations and cultures, we are unable to overcome the profound weakness we are experiencing today in the face of modern-secular-liberal civilization. (Müftüoğlu, 2013, pp. 9–10)

However, although very limited, there are comments suggesting that, in the specific context of Türkiye, secularity and the sacred are not in an absolute relationship of opposition, but rather are shaped within an intertwined, "hybrid," and often tension-filled coexistence. Indeed, both secular and sacred narratives are articulated by sociologist Göle in an interview featured in *İktibas*. Known for her studies focusing on Türkiye's sociological structure, Göle extensively examines this narrative in her works that analyze the processes of Turkish modernization and secularization (2017a, 2017b). According to her, these processes in Türkiye have a distinctive structure:

> The case of Türkiye is, on the one hand, an experience that exists within the secular while also trying to maintain its connection to the sacred. …If the sacred exists, the secular cannot exist; or if it is secular, it must reject the sacred. The Turkish experience challenges the 'either/or' interpretations—either secularization or Islamization theses. (Göle, 2012, p. 71)

As Göle points out, the experience of Türkiye presents not an "Islamic resistance" positioned directly against secular modernity, but rather an intermediate form that seeks to coexist with secular structures while retaining the sacred. This condition allows for a questioning of the classical dichotomous framework regarding the process of secularization, such as the "either secular or sacred" approach. However, such a line of questioning does not appear in other writings found in the Islamist journals that constitute the sample. However, this hybrid or mixed structure that has formed at the societal level opens the door to a discursive space in which the sacred is not entirely excluded, and secular norms are not radically rejected. It can be clearly stated that a narrative that allows space for such a discursive ground and a comprehensive debate on secularization within that narrative is not conducted in the writings analyzed. Instead, there exists a strong discourse that secularization itself is of Western origin, that it is therefore incompatible with the sociocultural fabric of Muslim-Turkish society, and that, consequently, the problems arising from secularization undermine the values of Muslim societies and damage their way of life.

3.3.4 The Influences of Secularization

In this theme, which analyzes the effects of secularization on individual and social life, the relevant sections of the writings were coded into eight categories and six subcategories (Fig. 3.4). Secularization is believed to exert a wide-ranging influence on the public sphere and social life, extending from media to politics, economy to education, and cultural structure to the language and discourse used. Indeed, the most intense discussions of secularization have been conducted within the framework of its effects on individual and social life. It is particularly observed that greater emphasis is placed on the moral and religious transformation of individual and social lives. It is argued that in this process of transformation, the individual becomes distanced from core values, exhibits an increased tendency toward materialism, experiences a metaphysical void that leads to individualization, and consequently suffers from a weakening of their religious affiliation.

All three journals exhibited a hostile stance toward secular effects. However, differences in approach among journals are noticeable. *Altınoluk*, for example, addresses the transformation in individual and social life resulting from the effects of secularization with a sensitivity that prioritizes traditional or conservative references.

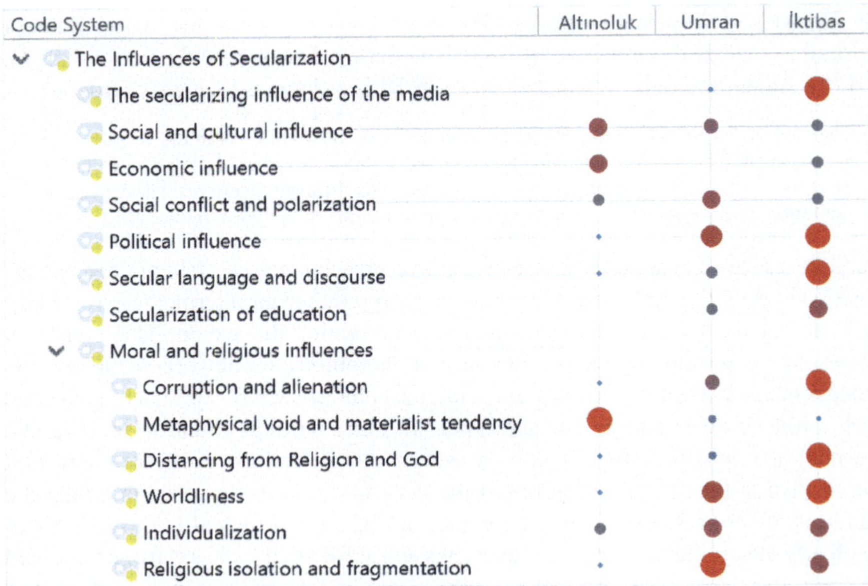

Fig. 3.4 Code matrix of theme 3

Umran approaches the relationship between secularization and structural transformations from a more theoretical perspective. *İktibas*, which provides the most extensive coverage of these effects, focuses more intensively on the political and ideological dimensions of the issue, particularly emphasizing the secularizing influence of the media and the secularization of language. Thus, while the journals agree on a hostile stance toward the effects of secularization, they express this stance from different perspectives. Based on the relevant sections included in this theme, it can also be stated that secularization is perceived as a crisis by journals that adopt Islamist thought. However, the dimensions of this crisis vary.

Among the elements influencing the secularization of individual and social life, the media is presented as a primary factor. It is understood that the writings published in *İktibas* focus more heavily on the media's secularizing effects. In these writings, the media is depicted as a hegemonic apparatus that functions ideologically in spreading the secular worldview and lifestyle. The media is examined as a structure that weakens the public visibility and legitimacy of religion. Within this framework, the media is evaluated as a tool that hinders the preservation of religious values through popular culture, the entertainment industry, and manipulative propagandist content:

> The influence of secularism on social and cultural life can be observed through information and communication technologies such as the media and the Internet, which occupy a central place in contemporary life. These have negative effects—primarily on Muslims, but also on other believing communities—because these tools are in the hands of individuals who lack religious sensitivity and who give rise to alternative values that are completely contrary to religious teachings. (Rahim, 2015, p. 40)

The idea that the most general effect of secularization manifests in social and cultural life is reflected in various ways across all three Islamist journals. It is argued that social and cultural practices have secularized, resulting in the widespread adoption of secular culture. This culture, through its hegemonic superiority, transforms religious values and distances religion from being a common reference point in society, or causes it to be distanced. In particular, the weakening of the public visibility of religious rituals and acts of worship, the psychological pressure faced by religious individuals within modern-secular society for their actions and behaviors, and the domination of new secular cultural codes/values are presented as evidence supporting the argument that secularization has not only an ideological dimension but also a behavioral and emotional impact:

> ...In a secular society, religion has ceased to be a common reference point; in its place, other shared references, other sanctities, and other common values have taken hold. Now, it is their institutions and sanctions that are in effect—not those of religion.... (Kademoğlu, 1996, p. 40)

Alongside the social and cultural effects of secularization, references to its economic impacts, although limited, have also drawn attention. The economic effects, mentioned briefly only in *Altınoluk* and *İktibas*, appear as a critique of the secular economic order. In particular, this order is criticized through the discourse that money has become an end in itself, rather than a means to an end. Within this framework, it is emphasized that capitalist competition and market dynamics have been absolutized, that the individual serves money, and that an economic mentality centered on individual interest, power, and consumption—rather than sacred values—has been constructed. Secular culture is presented as the primary agent responsible for this condition.

Some argue that secularization leads to social conflict and polarization. A narrative is presented suggesting that societal reflections of the dichotomous relationship (secular vs. sacred), discussed under the theme of theoretical and conceptual debate, materialize through conflict and tension. It is emphasized that, based on the belief that there is no reconciliation between secular values and sacred values, a confrontational culture—distant from dialog—has emerged within the binary of "us" and "the other."

One of the areas in which the effects of secularization are most intensely discussed is in politics. Writings that focus on the political effects of secularization are primarily found in *Umran* and *İktibas*. The analyzed texts emphasize that secularism transfers political legitimacy from divine references to human and worldly foundations, thereby generating a profound transformation in the realm of politics. Moreover, this process of transformation is argued to extend beyond the mere exclusion of religion from the public sphere, significantly restricting the political discourse and representational possibilities of religion-based demands. In evaluations centered on Türkiye, it is asserted that secular regimes throughout history have been closely intertwined with Kemalist ideology and military-bureaucratic tutelage mechanisms, that political pluralism has been limited, and that the participation of religious political actors in the political arena has been systematically obstructed. In broader-scale analyses, it is emphasized that democratic (laic) governance models are incompatible with the Islamic world, that these models serve the strategic interests of Western powers, and that they contradict the unique political demands of Muslim societies. Furthermore, secular regimes are claimed to be linked to imperialist interventions, and the discourse of democracy is argued to be instrumentalized to suppress the will of societies and conceal legitimacy crises. The discussions conducted within this framework demonstrate that the influence of secularity on politics should not be understood solely as a structural transformation but must also be evaluated as an intervention with epistemological and normative dimensions:

> ...Perhaps the greatest dilemma of secular power is that it claims the source of legitimacy lies in human beings. In doing so, power and the desire for power are placed within individuals. In this sense, power ceases to be vertical and becomes horizontal— spreading and expanding. However, in vertically structured power, there is no relationship between power and society; it is not intertwined with society, and therefore, such power does not concern itself with monitoring individuals' social lives. This is why society can rise to the point we call the meaning of spontaneity in life. ("Toplumun Otopsiye İhtiyacı Var -Açıkoturum-," 2002, p. 49)

> Secular regimes both mortgaged the will of the peoples in the Middle East and created artificial tensions between the state and the people; and they also allowed the resources of the region to be exploited not by its own populations, but by the Western colonial powers to whom they were dependent in every respect. (Kaplan, 2004, p. 49)

In Islamist journals, as well as in everyday conversations and discourses, the prevailing narrative is that language itself has undergone a process of secularization and transformation. This transformation is emphasized not only as a change in the semantic structure of language but also as an indicator of a broader cultural shift. It is not merely associated with the selection of different word variations but also highlights a paradigmatic rupture that reshapes modes of thinking and value hierarchies. The purification of language from religious references is argued to undermine the Islamic mindset and way of life at the individual and societal levels. Moreover, it is emphasized that secular language has come to dominate everyday life and that resistance to this domination has remained weak. Therefore, it is asserted that the secularization of language inevitably leads to secularization in thought and action:

> Regretfully, we must say that our language has become profane; it has been conditioned to serve secular reason and laicism. Speaking of the sacred, of what is holy, has been confined to homes or to certain associations and foundation activities. (Atav, 2011, p. 39)

> Expressions that referenced God and conveyed information about Him have now been replaced by phrases like 'Wishing you healthy days,' 'Wishing you happiness,' 'Have a good trip,' 'Take care,' 'Damn it,' 'Goodbye,' and 'Oleyy'—forms of secular language that bear no divine reference, that disregard God. (Vatandaş, 2007, p. 39)

The writings analyzed strongly emphasize that secularization also affects education, giving rise to a secular model of education. The modern-secular education system is criticized for reducing human beings to a "homo economicus" model—transforming individuals from creative and sacred subjects into functional objects within the cycle of production and consumption. It is particularly emphasized that the secular education system has lost its capacity to generate values, adopted a worldview devoid of otherworldly purposes, and operates with an approach that prioritizes purely worldly objectives. Within the framework of the madrasa–mektep (traditional–modern school) dichotomy, a deep conflict is said to exist between the classical Islamic understanding of knowledge and the secular epistemic regime. The removal of religious references from educational institutions is seen as a kind of departure from divinely endowed nature (*fıtrat*).

When examined by the journal, *İktibas* presented more theoretical and systematic critiques, arguing that the secular understanding of education weakens public morality and diminishes individuals' awareness of God. *Umran*, on the other hand, focuses more on the lack of spiritual and moral dimensions in modern educational practices. Overall, education is presented as the most institutionalized and impactful domain in which secularization manifests itself; as such, the need for a profound transformation at both theoretical and practical levels is strongly emphasized.

The most extensive discussions concerning the effects of secularization revolve around its moral and religious impact on individual and social lives. The harshest criticisms are directed toward the notion that both individuals and society are undergoing a process of corruption and alienation. Secular culture is depicted as a mindset that detaches individuals from their values, spiritual world, and social affiliations. Within this framework, the individual is portrayed as devoid of identity, confronted with spiritual emptiness, and drawn into a state of existential disorientation. The modern-secular lifestyle is said to replace trust, sharing, and meaning in human relationships with selfishness, hedonism, and loneliness. Examples such as the commodification of women, the detachment of youth from moral references, and the trivialization of worship rituals illustrate how secularism manifests in everyday life. Moreover, the weakening of an individual's bond with faith is a significant factor in deepening alienation. The marginalization or belittlement of Islamic values is also presented as evidence that this corruption constitutes a moral as well as a cultural crisis. Thus, strong critiques suggesting that Islamic societies are drifting under the influence of secular ideologies and practices—and are experiencing intellectual and moral colonization—form the most prominent common denominator in the writings reviewed:

> …The modern-secular mindset, which shows extreme tolerance toward all kinds of immorality, vice, evil, theft, degeneracy, corrupting habits that ruin an entire youth, drugs, alcoholism, the sex industry, human trafficking, etc., can exhibit an incredible lack of understanding and hostility toward the noble manifestations of noble Islam (Müftüoğlu, 2008, p. 50)

> The pure minds corrupted by secularism recognize no right to life for anything other than itself, turning hostile; even the common denominator of being human is denied. This is not a situation exclusive to the Western world but poses a threat to humanity as a vulnerability of other cultures and identities as well (Yazçiçek, 2015, p. 36)

Critiques suggesting that individuals' metaphysical inclinations are increasing daily, yet they are simultaneously falling into a void within their world of meaning and values, and growing distant from the metaphysical, are also noteworthy. These critiques reflect the profound spiritual crises that modern-secular societies have fallen into. The prevailing view in the analyzed writings is that secularization severs individuals from transcendent values and metaphysical orientations, which, in turn, leads to loneliness, a loss of inner wholeness, and descent into meaninglessness. This deprivation is being suppressed through integration into a culture of consumption. However, such suppression efforts are believed to weaken further an individual's inner relationship with truth, the metaphysical, and the spiritual. Another point highlighted in this regard is that the aforementioned metaphysical void and materialistic inclination are not confined to the individual level but also give rise to broader societal deterioration. Indeed, expressions frequently encountered in the texts—such as "loss of meaning," "spiritual void," or "hunger of the soul"—are used to describe the conditions of both individuals and society. These expressions are also employed to characterize modern-secular individuals:

> The excessive development and growing support for materialist thought and secular understanding have created a spiritual void in people's lives. In a sense, physical satisfaction has given rise to metaphysical voids and hungers (Yılmaz, 2002, p. 15)

Islamist journals frequently emphasize that the metaphysical void produced by secularization fosters a tendency to distance oneself from religion and God. According to the shared narratives, religion, under the influence of secularization, has not only withdrawn from the public sphere but has also ceased to function as a common point of reference in people's lives. God, in this framework, has been virtually "expelled" from daily life or "shelved." The absolutization of human reason, the elevation of intuition, experience, and pragmatism as alternatives to religious knowledge, and the relativization of "good" and "evil" are all seen as contributing to the erosion of a shared moral foundation. This, in turn, is associated with outcomes such as the erasure of the concept of sin and the replacement of the sacred with false and transient values.

This situation is also viewed as a contributing factor to the worldliness of individuals and society. Indeed, one of the prominent categories concerning the effects of secularization in the examined journals is worldliness. The writings define worldliness as a form of internal deformation. It is stated that tendencies such as ambition for rank, wealth, and status lead to the fading of the awareness of the hereafter and to the reduction of religion to merely a matter of conscience. Throughout this process, frequent references are made to the negative connotation associated with the concept of "worldly life" in the Qur'an. In the texts, where critiques of modernity are also prevalent, the decline of interest in the inner world of the individual, the materialistic lifestyle focused on external success, pleasure-seeking driven by consumption, and the instrumentalization of moral values within market relations are presented as common manifestations of worldliness. Particularly, the emphasis on the notion that happiness in secular modernity is equated solely with success, prosperity, and prestige is the primary focus of this category.

It is also stated that individuals, influenced by secular culture, have withdrawn from social life and adopted a more self-centered attitude. It is argued that individualization, encouraged by the secular mindset, has reduced even acts of worship to the level of "personal and private preferences," thereby gradually diminishing the role of religion in social life. Religion is detached from its social context and transformed into merely an inner feeling or intellectual engagement, while worship loses its visibility and becomes a silent, private, and individual practice. Accordingly, it is believed that the public influence of religious life has been weakened. Furthermore, the self-centered lifestyle of modern individuals is considered one of the fundamental dynamics behind the disintegration of social relations. This individualism promoted by secularization is regarded as a process that erodes traditional and Islamic virtues such as altruism, empathy, and sharing. In this context, secular individuality is evaluated not only as a lifestyle but also as an indicator of moral and cultural disintegration. On the other hand, the transformation of the concept of privacy in accordance with secular norms and the changes experienced by the family in this process clearly reflect the tension between individualization and religious values. It is claimed that with the rise of individual autonomy, communal relations have dissolved, that the transition from "a religious individual belonging to a community" to "an individual who is religious" has accelerated, and that, as a result, the social character of religion has been significantly weakened:

> The secular mindset has turned life into a prison of egoism. Everyone has come to live alone in plain sight of each other. Those who could not visit the neighbor upstairs considered going to the moon an accomplishment. (Temel, 2009, p. 12)

> In secular processes, we observe that people who were once religious individuals belonging to a community have transformed into religious individuals in the singular sense. (Arslan, 1994, p. 17)

The final reflection of the moral and religious effects of secularization manifests in the form of religious isolation and fragmentation. In this significant category, where the writings show a clear consensus, it is asserted that the social visibility and role of religion have weakened. Religion is no longer seen as an essential unifying element of society, and its capacity to construct a shared world of meaning is thought to have diminished. Consequently, the influence of religion in public life is claimed to be limited to a symbolic and ceremonial level. This situation is said to pave the way for social fragmentation, identity rupture, and cultural alienation. The authors also emphasize that secularization involves not only cultural transformation but also epistemological rupture. In this process, accelerated by Enlightenment thinking, the meaning and place of the sacred were redefined, and a secular worldview—where "the heavens no longer intervene in the affairs of the earth"—began to dominate. In this context, the realm of religion was reduced to theology, while the social and political spheres were reshaped by rationality and pragmatism. Additionally, the top-down importation of secularization into the Islamic world is presented as a model that is incompatible with authentic religious structures and conflicts with local traditions. As a result, religion became fragmented and isolated from social life:

> Modern-secular culture has caused major fragmentations and disconnections in all areas of life. (Müftüoğlu, 2008, p. 49)

> Since secularism centers physical reality (=this world), it separates the otherworldly from the worldly, represses the otherworldly / 'religious,' and views life as confined solely to this world. (Kaplan, 2004, p. 49)

As is evident, the primary focus of writings on secularization is its effects. In particular, criticisms that focus on the moral and religious implications of secularization are examined through themes such as estrangement from religion and God, the isolation and fragmentation of religious institutions, and the process of individualization. This suggests that secularization is viewed as a phenomenon or project that aims to dismantle both individual and collective spirituality and religious structures. Evaluations of the consequences of this phenomenon emerged as another central theme emphasized by the authors.

3.3.5 The Consequences of Secularization

The consequences of secularization are sometimes addressed directly, while at other times they are evaluated through the lens of various phenomena or concepts. This approach was similar across all three journals (Fig. 3.5). Moreover, the outcomes of secularization's impact on individual and social life are notably framed within a shared narrative of the crisis. This crisis, embedded in a multidimensional and layered structure, is interpreted as a crisis of religion and morality. As highlighted in previous sections, under the influence of secularization, religion has begun to lose its functionality both in theory and practice, and moral erosion has occurred in individual and social life. The process of secularization, which has led to profound erosion and structural dissolution in the individual's world of meaning and value, as well as in society's cultural memory, has accompanied the absolutization of modern values such as individualism, freedom, and rationality. Consequently, this has led to a decline in the status of sacred, transcendent, and conservative values as well as traditional morality. As a result, concepts such as "identity crisis," "spiritual void," "sense of meaninglessness," "alienation," and "anomie" have been emphasized, with evaluations, recommendations, and proposals offered concerning the condition of modern-secular individuals and society.

Evaluations of the consequences of secularization emphasize that modern individuals and society are being driven into an existential impasse. The marginalization of religious values from social life is argued to lead to an individual's isolation in the search for meaning and a weakening of their connection to truth. In the long run, this is claimed to produce destructive consequences not only at the individual level but also in terms of collective consciousness and the moral structure. It is suggested that the

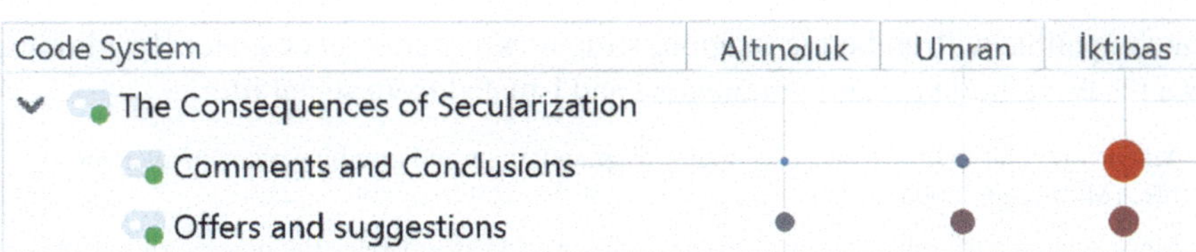

Fig. 3.5 Code matrix of theme 4

intervention of laic governments in the social fabric deepens societal polarization and that policies denying religious legitimacy and truth accelerate the disintegration of cultural structures. Moreover, the modern manifestations of religion are seen as inherently at odds with their essence, posing a significant risk. These risks are considered more likely to result in adverse outcomes.

Another noteworthy point in the general assessments of the secularization process is that it is not perceived as a "conclusion," but rather as an ongoing and potentially worsening drift and disintegration. Importantly, this is seen not only as a threat to Muslims but also as a structural danger to individuals and societies of other faiths, undermining their shared value systems. A strong critical stance is also evident regarding the replacement of core social values—such as trust, solidarity, wisdom, and justice—with selfishness, individualism, and the loss of truth. Therefore, evaluations and conclusions regarding secularization indicate that its impact extends beyond religious life, posing a broader threat to individual consciousness and the collective world of meaning.

In response to this grim picture, various suggestions and proposals have been put forward. Primarily focused on the question of "what is to be done?", these proposals propose strategies for addressing the ruptures caused by secularization. While the recommendations shed light on different perspectives, the central emphasis is placed on the reconstruction of Islamic thought, values, and institutions:

> …We cannot be the props, operators, or slaves of systems that do not belong to us. Therefore, we must construct our own society and present our values to the public by distinguishing them from falsehoods. In the life we live, we must be visible with a clear identity, without concealing the truth. (Ertürk, 2015, p. 22)

> Let us reunite in the vast universe of truth and justice with our pure souls and vibrant minds; let us rediscover ourselves and our innate beauty so that we may free ourselves from postmodern captivity! Let us initiate change within ourselves! (Cepe, 2006, p. 81)

In a world shaped by the secular paradigm, the idea that Muslims should not remain passive is strongly expressed. Critical thinking, moral resistance, a return to divinely endowed nature (*fitrat*), and consciousness based on revelation are proposed as the primary paths. Islam is emphasized not only as a nostalgic heritage but also as a dynamic system capable of producing solutions to contemporary crises. The transformative power of Islam's principled stance is highlighted in response to issues such as moral corruption, economic injustice, and spiritual collapse. In particular, these discourses calling for "a return to the self" and "authenticity" criticize the insufficiency of solutions offered by modern-secular culture and underline the need to develop an alternative civilization perspective. In this context, the proposals are also considered systematic approaches that encompass practical and principled solutions, rather than ideological reactions.

3.4 Conclusion

Journals, which stand out as a traditional mass communication tool as well as a periodical publication format, constitute a unique medium that combines both current and theoretical content, positioned between the daily nature of newspapers and the longevity of books. This format, which emerged as a carrier of information during modernization, has also evolved into an intellectual platform for counter-modern stances over time (Aydeniz, 2016, p. 19). The emergence and development of Islamism, which represents the most significant counter-modern stance in Türkiye, have been mainly shaped by intellectual discourse. This trajectory, extending from *Sırat-ı Müstakim* to *Sebilürreşad*, from *Büyük Doğu* to *Hareket*, and to many journals today, demonstrates that Islamism possesses a publishing culture that produces ideas and sustains them by situating them within a historical context (Karaman, 2020, p. 1). Within this culture, discussions have been and continue to be conducted on a wide range of topics. A substantial body of literature has emerged, comprising numerous studies that analyze the perspectives from which these discussions are approached. This study, aiming to contribute to the existing literature, focuses on debates on secularization in Islamist journals published post-1990. Within this scope, writings on secularization in *Altınoluk*, *Umran*, and *İktibas*, which embrace Islamist thought, were analyzed thematically.

The results of the analyses indicate that the concepts of secularism and its derivatives are generally addressed within a framework that portrays them as imported from the West and incompatible with the essence of Islamic societies. The emphasis on the concept being "imported" is extreme, as reflected in the explanations and definitions presented in the writings. Moreover, the term is frequently used synonymously with laicism. The prevalence of interpretations framing the concept as imported positions it within an anti-Islamic context. Most authors contributing to these journals examine secular and derivative concepts through a dichotomous lens. The emphasis on the concept, having emerged from the Western Christian experience, is often employed to argue its incompatibility with Islam. Within this framework, numerous objections to secularization have been articulated on both theoretical and conceptual grounds.

However, most of the writings examined either address the meaning of secularization as a process only superficially or neglect it altogether, rather than providing a comprehensive and in-depth intellectual framework for understanding it. It remains debatable to what extent the formats offered by these journals are conducive to sustained discussion. Intellectual production, often shaped by the pressures of public visibility, may at times be reduced to superficial content that is quickly consumed and easily digestible, rather than fostering rigorous analysis and critical thinking. This convenience, offered by periodicals such as journals and newspapers, carries the risk of weakening the substance of intellectual debate and limiting its depth (Aydeniz, 2016, p. 20). In addition, the brevity of many of the writings analyzed constitutes another obstacle to deepening intellectual engagement. For this reason, the lack of comprehensive and sustained analysis of secularization in Islamist journals can be attributed to the ontological structure of the media in which these writings appear.

The secularization processes experienced by Muslim societies are often explained in terms of the concepts of secularism and its derivatives, which have been developed in modern Western societies. This results in the uncritical and unexamined transmission of these concepts, portraying them as the primary cause of the transformations occurring within these societies. The modern lifestyle that emerges from secularization is, in this context, almost designated as a scapegoat, treated as if it were solely responsible for the moral crises and social underdevelopment faced by Muslim societies. Consequently, a relationship of opposition is established between Western modern values and Islamic values through the conceptual and theoretical debates surrounding secularization. In other words, a dichotomous approach is adopted along the axis of "us" (Muslims) versus "the other" (modern-secular-West). As a natural outcome of this approach, the legitimization of Islamist ideology through these opposing identities is facilitated.

In this regard, the evaluations specific to Türkiye in the writings featured in the journals remain relatively limited. Assessments of secularization are generally framed around the imagination of the *ummah*, and the discussions are analyzed within the dichotomy of the Western world and the Islamic world. In contrast, Türkiye's experience of secularization is more closely tied to its modernization. The secularization experience, regarded as a natural outcome of the distorted and problematic aspects of Turkish modernization, is considered a phenomenon arising directly from modernization itself. The trajectory of Turkish secularism, constructed in the formula of "the more modern, the more secular," and the lack of resistance to it, are associated with the social and cultural conditions produced by the prevailing laic-political regime. It is also observed that an emphasis on inadequacy at times underscores this critical linkage.

The primary focus of the writings featured in the journals appears to be the effects of secularization. While the processes of secularization and their consequences in macro-level domains such as culture, economy, politics, education, language, and media are addressed, the moral and religious impacts of secularization on individual and social life are also examined in detail. The vast majority of evaluations concerning these effects are negative. Criticisms related to individualization, worldliness, alienation, and spiritual emptiness—consequences of secularization—are frequently articulated in these writings. Secularization is depicted not merely as the exclusion of religion but as a profound and destabilizing process that results in a comprehensive existential crisis. Within this process, it is repeatedly emphasized that both individual and social life have become distanced from religion and God, that worldly tendencies have intensified while the otherworldly has been set aside, and, as a result, Muslim societies have become corrupted and alienated from their core values. Writings that analyze this multidimensional crisis present the spread of the secular lifestyle as the primary driving force behind it.

The multilayered crisis caused by secularization at both the individual and social levels is addressed in the examined writings within a shared framework of concern, and this crisis is generally interpreted as a dissolution centered on religion and morality. The individual's isolation in the search for meaning, the erosion of collective consciousness, and the replacement of social values with individualism and self-interest are identified as the main consequences of this process. The proposals developed in response to this negative picture emphasize the reconstruction of Islamic values and thought, efforts to develop an alternative civilizational perspective in the face of the destructive effects of the secular paradigm are characterized by calls for a return to *fitrat*, moral revival, and revelation-based awareness. In this context, secularization is depicted as both an existential and a social threat, and systematic, authentic solutions grounded in the principled stance of Islam are advanced in response.

Ultimately, this study reveals that journals embracing Islamist thought in Türkiye perceive secularization as both a historical process and a contemporary challenge that shapes today's world of meaning, influences religious identity, and generates multidimensional crises. Although the proposed solutions to this crisis at times rely on traditional values and at other times adopt a critical and intellectual stance, their common ground lies in a profound questioning of modernity and an effort to construct an alternative intellectual framework. While the lifestyle brought about by secularization is criticized in Islamist writings, it is also regarded as the foundation for a call to transformation and a search for a new social, moral, and intellectual structure. At this point, the function of journals as mass communication tools becomes significant. These publications serve as reflections of a particular ideology and simultaneously act as platforms for public discourse, cultivating a collective consciousness and generating a counter-narrative against secularization. In this context, beyond being mere content producers, journals emerge as actors shaping the meanings of both individual and social life, making visible the transformations, ruptures, and reconstruction tendencies within Islamist thought.

One of the most significant limitations of this study is its exclusive reliance on journal articles as primary sources. Although books, polemical texts, and memoirs written by the exact intellectual figures could shed additional light on the debates discussed here, incorporating such materials lies beyond the scope of the present analysis. For the same reason, the study does not systematically situate these journals within the broader political and social context of the period. While doing so would undoubtedly add historical depth, it would also substantially expand the aims and length of this study. Future studies may, through in-depth analyses of journals with different editorial lines, examine how these discourses intersect with media and communication practices, how these journals interact with their readers, and whether they generate alternative public spheres in response to secularization. Moreover, by incorporating books, polemical texts, and memoirs produced by the exact intellectual figures, future research could provide further insights into how themes only briefly addressed in journal articles were elaborated in other genres of writing.

Acknowledgements I would like to express my profound gratitude to the *İslamcı Dergiler Projesi (Islamist Journals Project)* team for granting me access to the data, as well as to the administrators of the *İlmi Etütler Derneği (İLEM)* for their valuable support and assistance.

References

Ahmed, S. K. (2024). The pillars of trustworthiness in qualitative research. *Journal of Medicine, Surgery, and Public Health, 2*, Article 100051. https://doi.org/10.1016/j.glmedi.2024.100051

Ahnas, M. O. (2025). İslamcı dergilerde cinsiyet kimliği ve modernleşme: Kadın kimliği dergisi örneği. *Çukurova Üniversitesi Sosyal Bilimler Enstitüsü Dergisi, 34*(1), 634–650. https://doi.org/10.35379/cusosbil.1586512

Altınoluk Dergisi. (n.d.). Retrieved July 1, 2025, from https://www.altinoluk.com.tr

Altun, F. Y. (2024). *Türkiye'de İslamcı dergilerde hilafet söylemleri* [Doctoral Dissertation]. Mimar Sinan Güzel Sanatlar Üniversitesi Sosyal Bilimler Enstitüsü.

Amin, M. E. K., Nørgaard, L. S., Cavaco, A. M., Witry, M. J., Hillman, L., Cernasev, A., & Desselle, S. P. (2020). Establishing trustworthiness and authenticity in qualitative pharmacy research. *Research in Social and Administrative Pharmacy, 16*(10), 1472–1482. https://doi.org/10.1016/j.sapharm.2020.02.005

Aras, A. (2009). Türkçe sekülerleştirme olimpiyatları. *İktibas, 367*, 34–37.

Arslan, A. (1994). Sekülerizm kendi içinde helak taşıyan bir süreçtir. *Umran*, 10–17.

Atav, M. (2011). Konuştuklarımızın gösterdiği adres. *İktibas, 390*, 37–39.

Aydeniz, H. (2016). Dergi: Bir imkân ve zaaf olarak entelektüel arayış zemini. *Dergiler Dergisi (TÜRDEB), 2*, 19–21.

Berger, P. L. (2020). Dinin krizinden sekülerizmin krizine. In A. Köse (Ed.), *Kutsalın dönüşü: 21. yüzyılda dinin geleceği* (2nd ed., pp. 100–115). Timaş Yayınları.

Braun, V., & Clarke, V. (2006). Using thematic analysis in psychology. *Qualitative Research in Psychology, 3*(2), 77–101. https://doi.org/10.1191/1478088706qp063oa

Braun, V., & Clarke, V. (2022). *Thematic analysis: A practical guide.* Sage.

Budak, H. (2020). İslamcı dergicilik: Vahdetin içinde bir ses "İslam'ın İlk Emri Oku" dergisi. *Gümüşhane Üniversitesi Sosyal Bilimler Dergisi, 11*(1), 117–135. https://doi.org/10.36362/gumus.621995

Bulaç, A. (2004). İslam'ın üç siyaset tarzı veya İslamcıların üç nesli. In Y. Aktay (Ed.), *Modern Türkiye'de siyasi düşünce: İslamcılık* (Vol. 6, pp. 48–67). İletişim Yayınları.

Casanova, J. (2014). *Modern dünyada kamusal dinler* (M. M. Şahin, Trans.). Sakarya Üniversitesi Kültür Yayınları.

Cepe, N. (2006). Postmodern tutsaklıktan kurtulmak. *Umran*, 81–82.

Çiğdem, A. (2004). İslamcılık ve Türkiye üzerine bazı notlar. In Y. Aktay (Ed.), *Modern Türkiye'de Siyasi Düşünce: İslamcılık* (Vol. 6, pp. 26–33). İletişim Yayınları.

Çoban, B. Z. (2018). Sebilürreşad dergisinde Hıristiyanlık ve papalık. *Tarih ve Gelecek Dergisi, 4*(2), 8–26. https://doi.org/10.21551/jhf.431932

Coleman, J. A. (2015). Seküler: Sosyolojik bir bakış (Ö. F. Darende, Trans.). In M. A. Kirman & İ. Çapcıoğlu (Eds.), *Sekülerleşme: Klasik ve çağdaş yaklaşımlar* (pp. 45–55). Otto Yayınları.

Çöpoğlu, M. (2023). *Türkiye'de İslamcı dergilerin dönemin din anlayışına etkileri: Hilal Dergisi örneği (1958–1993)* [Master's Thesis]. Ondokuz Mayıs Üniversitesi Sosyal Bilimler Enstitüsü.

Creswell, J. W. (2013). *Nitel araştırma yöntemleri: Beş yaklaşıma göre nitel araştırma ve araştırma deseni.* Siyasal Kitabevi.

El-Gannuşi, R. (2002). İslami hareketler: Özeleştiri ve yeniden-düşünme (T. Kışlakçı, Trans.). *Umran*, 96–100.

Erkilet, A. (2004). 1990'larda Türkiye'de radikal İslamcılık. In Y. Aktay (Ed.), *Modern Türkiye'de Siyasi Düşünce: İslamcılık* (Vol. 6, pp. 681–697). İletişim Yayınları.

Ertit, V. (2019a). *Sekülerleşme teorisi.* Liberte Yayınları.

Ertit, V. (2019b). Türkiye'nin sekülerleşme pratiği. In M. A. Kirman & V. Ertit (Eds.), *Sekülerleşme Tartışmaları* (pp. 267–329). Kadim Yayınları.

Ertürk, H. (2015). Ödünç kimlikler. *İktibas, 35*(438), 19–22.

Göle, N. (2012). Müslümanlar artık mazlum değil aktör. *İktibas, 407*, 70–73.

Göle, N. (2017a). *Melez desenler: İslam ve modernlik üzerine* (5th ed.). Metis Yayınları.

Göle, N. (2017b). *Seküler ve dinsel: Aşınan sınırlar* (3rd ed.). Metis Yayınları.

Güler, A., Halıcıoğlu, M. B., & Taşğın, S. (2013). *Sosyal bilimlerde nitel araştırma yöntemleri.* Seçkin Yayıncılık.
Gürdoğan, N. (2009). Paradan para kazananların beklenen krizi. *Altınoluk, 275*, 8–9.
Gürpınar, B. (2017). Hilâl dergisi ve dünya siyasetine bakışı. *Bilecik Şeyh Edebali Üniversitesi Sosyal Bilimler Dergisi, 2*(2), 436–452.
İDP. (n.d.). Retrieved July 1, 2025, from https://idp.org.tr/
İktibas Dergisi. (n.d.). Retrieved July 1, 2025, from https://iktibasdergisi.com/
İlmi Etüdler Derneği. (n.d.). İLEM-İlmi Etüdler Derneği. Retrieved July 1, 2025, from https://www.ilem.org.tr/
Işık, V. (2020). Türkiye'de İslamcılığı yeniden düşünmek: Muhafazakâr yahut modernist reddiyecilik arasında. In L. Sunar (Ed.), *Müslüman Dünyada Çağdaş Düşünce: Türk Düşüncesi* (Vol. 1, pp. 183–217). Yurtdışı Türkler ve Akraba Topluluklar Başkanlığı Yayınları.
Janesick, V. J. (2015). Peer debriefing. In *The Blackwell encyclopedia of sociology*. John Wiley & Sons. https://doi.org/10.1002/9781405165518.wbeosp014.pub2
Kademoğlu, M. R. (1996). İbadetler için yaptırımın anlamı. *Altınoluk, 128*, 37–40.
Kaplan, Y. (2002). İslam'ın özne olarak yeniden tarih sahnesine çıkışı ve İslâm'ı protestanlaştırma projesi. *Umran*, 26–31.
Kaplan, Y. (2004). Sekülarizmin ve seküler ideolojilerin çöküşü. *İktibas, 312*, 48–49.
Kara, İ. (2004). İslamcı söylemin kaynakları ve gerçeklik değeri. In *Modern Türkiye'de Siyasi Düşünce: İslamcılık* (Vol. 6, pp. 34–47). İletişim Yayınları.
Kara, İ. (2014). *Türkiye'de İslamcılık düşüncesi: Metinler/kişiler 1* (2nd ed.). Dergah Yayınları.
Kara, İ. (2024). *Resimli cumhuriyet din kitabı* (Vols. 1–3). Dergah Yayınları.
Karaman, Y. V. (2020). *1990'lı yıllarda İslamcı dergilerde kapitalizm tartışmaları* [Master's Thesis]. Marmara Üniversitesi.
Karataş, M. V. (2024). Tezkire dergisi: İslamcılık düşüncesine yönelik bir çözümleme. *Muhafazakar Düşünce Dergisi, 20*, 194–218.
Kaya, T. (2023). *Türkiye'de İslamcı dergilerin dönemin din anlayışına etkileri: Mektup Dergisi örneği (1985–2010)* [Master's Thesis]. Ondokuz Mayıs Üniversitesi Sosyal Bilimler Enstitüsü.
Kolektif. (2016). *1960–1980 arası İslamcı dergiler-toparlanma ve çeşitlenme.* İlem.
Kuckartz, U. (2014). Qualitative text analysis: A guide to methods, practice & using software. *SAGE Publications Ltd.* https://doi.org/10.4135/9781446288719
Küçükosman, H. (2022). İslamcı dergilerde hadis tartışmaları meseleler, dönemler ve isimler. *Kalemname, 7*(14), 587–594.
Küçüktığlı, M. S. (2024). Islamophobia agenda in Islamist magazines in Türkiye: A content analysis. *Journal of Media and Religion Studies, Special Issue 1*, 147–185. https://doi.org/10.47951/mediad.1524288
Kuru, A. T. (2009). Secularism and state policies toward religion: The United States, France, and Turkey. *Cambridge University Press.* https://doi.org/10.1017/CBO9780511815096
Mardin, Ş. (1991). *Türk modernleşmesi: Makaleler 4.* İletişim Yayınları.
Maviş, N. (2017). *Türkiye'de İslamcılığın değişen siyasal dili: 1990'lı yıllarda İslamcı dergiler* [Doctoral Dissertation]. Hacettepe Üniversitesi Sosyal Bilimler Enstitüsü.
Merriam, S. B. (2018). *Nitel araştırma: Desen ve uygulama için bir rehber* (S. Turan, Trans.). Nobel Akademik Yayıncılık.
Mert, N. (2004). Türkiye İslamcılığına tarihsel bir bakış. In Y. Aktay (Ed.), *Modern Türkiye'de Siyasi Düşünce: İslamcılık* (Vol. 6, pp. 411–419). İletişim Yayınları.
Meşe, İ. (2015). İslami bir moda dergisi örneğinde moda ve tesettür: Ne türden bir birliktelik. *Fe Dergi, 7*(1), 145–158. https://doi.org/10.1501/Fe0001_0000000138
Morgan, H. (2022). Understanding thematic analysis and the debates involving its use. *The Qualitative Report, 27*(10), 2079–2091. https://doi.org/10.46743/2160-3715/2022.5912
Müftüoğlu, A. (2008). Algısal soysuzlaşmalar. *Umran*, 49–50.
Müftüoğlu, A. (2013). Ağır hasarlı algılar, ağır hasarlı zihinler. *İktibas, 418*, 9–10.
Müftüoğlu, A. (2014). Sekülerizmin saltanatı. *İktibas, 431*, 14–15.

Özbey, M. A. (2023). *1990–2000 arası İslamcı dergilerde laiklik tartışmaları* [Master's Thesis]. Dokuz Eylül Üniversitesi Sosyal Bilimler Enstitüsü.
Polat, A., & Uzun, M. B. (2024). Türkiye'de dini grupların Diyanet İşleri Başkanlığına bakışı: Altınoluk, Köprü ve İktibas dergilerinde Diyanet tartışmaları. *Medya ve Din Araştırmaları Dergisi, 7*(2), 63–81. https://doi.org/10.47951/mediad.1570300
Rahim, A. B. A. (2015). Sekülerizmin dini inanç ve hayat üzerine etkisi (İ. Türe, Trans.). *İktibas, 443*, 36–48.
Scharp, K. M., & Sanders, M. L. (2019). What is a theme? Teaching thematic analysis in qualitative communication research methods. *Communication Teacher, 33*(2), 117–121. https://doi.org/10.1080/17404622.2018.1536794
Selçuk, E. K. (2023). Türkiye İslamcılığında özgün bir odak: Ercüment Özkan ve İktibas dergisi. *International Journal of Communication and Media Research, 3*(2), 83–101.
Shlykov, P. (2019). The secularization and desecularization nexus in the Turkish context: What is behind? *Politics and Religion Journal, 13*(2), Article 2. https://doi.org/10.54561/prj1302199s
Sözeri, C. (2019). The transformation of Turkey's Islamic media and its marriage with neoliberalism. *Southeast European and Black Sea Studies, 19*(1), 155–174. https://doi.org/10.1080/14683857.2019.1579413
Spall, S. (1998). Peer debriefing in qualitative research: Emerging operational models. *Qualitative Inquiry, 4*(2), 280–292. https://doi.org/10.1177/107780049800400208
Sunar, L. (Ed.). (2019a). *Bir başka hayata karşı: 1980 sonrası İslamcı dergilerde meseleler, kavramlar ve isimler* (Vols. 1–4). Konya Büyükşehir Belediyesi Kültür Yayınları.
Sunar, L. (2019b). İslamcılığı konumlandırmak: Genel bir giriş. In L. Sunar (Ed.), *"Bir Başka Hayata Karşı": 1980 Sonrası İslamcı Dergilerde Meseleler, Kavramlar ve İsimler* (Vol. 1, pp. 1–14). Konya Büyükşehir Belediyesi Kültür Yayınları.
Temel, A. R. (2009). Aç gözlülük krizi. *Altınoluk, 277*, 11–13.
"Toplumun Otopsiye İhtiyacı Var" -açıkoturum-. (2002). *Umran*, 37–50.
Umran Dergisi. (n.d.). Retrieved July 1, 2025, from http://www.umrandergisi.com.tr/index.html
Vatandaş, C. (2007). Nasıl ve neye göre bir hayat tarzı. *Umran*, 37–42.
Yavuz, M. H., & Öztürk, A. E. (2019). Turkish secularism and Islam under the reign of Erdoğan. *Southeast European and Black Sea Studies, 19*(1), 1–9. https://doi.org/10.1080/14683857.2019.1580828
Yazçiçek, R. (2015). *İslâm, laiklik ve sekülarizm ekseninde devlet. İktibas, 444*, 28–37.
Yazıcıoğlu, H. (1995). Yeni bir kavram kargaşasına doğru laiklik-secularizm. *Altınoluk, 109*, 50–51.
Yiğit, E. (2020). *1980 sonrası İslamcı dergilerde kadının dini politik dönüşümü* [Doctoral Dissertation]. Hitit Üniversitesi Sosyal Bilimler Enstitüsü.
Yıldırım, F. (2021). *1980 sonrası İslamcı dergilerde kadın ve kadının çalışma hayatı: Kadın Kimliği dergisi örneği* [Master's Thesis]. Necmettin Erbakan Üniversitesi Sosyal Bilimler Enstitüsü.
Yılmaz, K. H. (2002). Neden tasavvuf? *Altınoluk, 191*, 15–17.

Chapter 4
Secularization in Turkish Cinema: Yeşilçam Neighborhood Against the State Ideal

Yusuf Ziya Gökçek

4.1 Introduction

When we evaluate secularism in Turkey in terms of its removal from the "sacred" aspects of tradition and religion, we see that specific legal regulations and practices in the early Republican period progressed in line with this evaluation, that it was a state project under the control of the bureaucratic elite, and that the radical implementation of modernity was characterized by Westernization/Modernization. The term "modernization" was first associated with the principle of progress and a concept related to "time." The spirit of time, meanwhile, points to a techno-cultural interval where progress and development are embodied, located in the West. Abandoning the sacred and abolishing tradition, among other burdens of the past on the path to modernization, are lightened through secularization. When modernization is seen as "the narrowing and neutralization of the sacred sphere in economic, technological, political, educational, sexual, and intellectual life" (Berkes, 2006, p. 23) as a state policy, secularization and modernization practices become equivalent. At the same time, secularization is comprehensive enough to encompass a debate that is more frequently discussed in Turkey, such as secularism. The centralization of rationalization, along with the deterministic nature of technology, has diminished the power of religion in the public sphere in favor of science (Weber, 2011) and the loss of dominance of religious institutions and symbols over social and cultural institutions (Berger, 2025) has made secularization the most effective ideology of the cinematic century as a language and process of modernity. The end of the nineteenth century and the following centuries were a period marked by a cinematic vision that brought explanation and meaning to facts and events through an imaginative narrative presence. There are two dimensions to the concept of secularization in Turkey. The first is

Y. Z. Gökçek (✉)
Department of Radio, Television and Cinema, Marmara University, İstanbul, Türkiye
e-mail: yusuf.gokcek@marmara.edu.tr

M. D. Dereli and M. Eken (eds.), *Turkish Perspectives on Secularization and Media*,
https://doi.org/10.1007/978-3-032-16436-0_4

the transformation of daily life through the top-down implementation of secularization by the state, utilizing legal, educational, cultural, social, and other instruments; the second is the participation of Turkish society in the secularization process (Tekin, 2012, p. 191).

Secularization, which determined the economic, political, and social policies of the state during the early Republican period; the abolition of the Caliphate, the Sheikh al-Islam, and the Ministry of Religious Endowments in 1924, the establishment of the Presidency of Religious Affairs, the abolition of Sharia courts, the enactment of the Law on Unification of Education, the adoption of the Gregorian calendar in 1925, the enactment of the Hat Law, the closure of tekkes, zawiyas, and tombs, the banning of Sufi orders, the adoption of the Swiss Civil Code and the Code of Obligations in 1926, and the constitutional amendment in 1928 removal of the phrase "The religion of the state is Islam" and the phrase "application of Sharia law" from the powers of the Grand National Assembly, removal of religious references from the oath of the Grand National Assembly, adoption of the Latin alphabet, removal of religious classes from primary and secondary education in 1930 (starting with schools in cities), the translation of the call to prayer into Turkish in 1932, the change of the weekly holiday to Sunday in 1935, and the introduction of the principle of secularism into the constitution in 1937. All secularization practices based on secularism in Turkey are focused mainly not on the separation of religion and state affairs, but on strengthening the state's control mechanisms. The reforms carried out during the Atatürk period "focused on creating a new collective identity within an order that rejected the role of religion in reform politics" and "aimed to expand the independence of the individual within society." However, asymmetric secularization, implemented by the bureaucratic elite, while limited to state control and institutions, did not seem sufficient to permeate spatial and social areas, such as the "neighborhood" and "community," in state programs resistant to secularization. Conflictual secularization aims to eliminate neighborhood-level collectivity in order for the individual to emerge: "...the neighborhood is more than an administrative unit; it is a dense Gemeinschaft with boundaries protected by tough guys and loyal dogs, and it is an environment that shapes most of the normal life of an ordinary Ottoman citizen (Mardin, 1991)." The emergence of films with a "neighborhood" theme in Turkish cinema, especially following the transition to a multi-party system, suggests that it is not the modern individual but a nostalgic trio of person, neighborhood, and sociality that is emphasized.

Cultural policies implemented during the Ottoman period were primarily limited to the bureaucracy due to the intelligentsia it had created. However, with the newly established country, this policy aimed not only at a bureaucratic scope but also at a cumulative design for the entire population, seeking to bind everyone and everything to the defined "new." The book "Civil Knowledge for Citizens," prepared by Afet İnan and used as a textbook in middle schools and high schools throughout the 1930s, a significant portion of which was written by Atatürk, states that the Islamic religion loosened the national bonds of the Turks and numbed their national feelings due to its ummah politics. Furthermore, the "fear of God," the fundamental basis of religious morality, was criticized, and it was stated that this restricted freedom of conscience ()… (However, in the 1940s) Within the framework of Hasan Âli Yücel's educational initiative, the 1940s also witnessed the dissolution of the ruling bloc. With the help of now mature conservatives, the aim was to restore the relationship between religion and morality, based on observations of spiritual decline and moral collapse. (Çelikoğlu, 2013, pp. 282–286). The 1940s were not only a period when secularization ceased to be an authoritarian, regulatory, and confrontational tool of early Republican policy, but also a time when new methods of secularization based on the principles of pluralism and adaptation emerged in Turkish cinema.

Cinema activities in Turkey began before the establishment of the Republic of Turkey. With the proclamation of the Republic in Turkey (1923), cinema did not immediately become a state ideological tool. Since cinema was not considered a priority art form by the state in Turkey, and it did not fall within the scope of high art inherited from the Ottoman Empire, it was positioned as a tool with a high propaganda effect in the early years of the new regime. Although references to cinema by Republican ideologues remained limited, entrepreneurs were keenly aware of cinema's power. Republican intellectuals prioritized the performing arts, viewing cinema as a means of reaching broad segments of the public. In Yakup Kadri Karaosmanoğlu's articles (2024) in Kadro magazine and in his novel Ankara, cinema was assigned a Soviet-style role in showcasing the achievements of the Republic and making the revolution the property of the Turkish nation. Kadri's understanding of cinema is evident in his comparison between Istanbul, which he viewed as a place of debauchery, and Ankara, which he saw as a center of national consciousness. "Istanbul" is portrayed as a place of tasteless and degenerate entertainment, likened to Sodom and Gomorrah. Cinema finds its place by distinguishing its dual nature as both a cure and a poison in Turkey, specifically in relation to these two cities (Gökçek, 2022, p. 170).

4.2 Cinema as the Threshold of the New Regime

In the early years of the Republic, cinema was the most essential pillar of the relationship established with the Soviets. The presence of Muhsin Ertuğrul, one of the most influential film directors of the Republican era, who was accused by some film writers of establishing a "cinema dictatorship" (Özön, 2013, p. 109), and his filming of Tamilla (1925) and Spartacus (1926) in the Soviet Union were also outcomes of young Turkey's cinema policies. At the same time, while the film "Ankara: Heart of Turkey" (Lüleci, 2014, p. 50), prepared by Sergey Yutkevich and Lev Arnshtam in 1933, was being shot in Turkey, Soviet directors were assisted by Reşat Nuri (Güntekin) and Fikret Adil (Vandov, 2014, p. 274). This film showcases the achievements of the Republic and the changes that accompanied the establishment of the new regime. The film constructs a discourse of progress based on modernity and does not include any representation of religion. The promise of the "new man," emphasized in early Soviet films, is reflected in the discourse of the new regimes of that period.

The producers of the period emphasized that Turkish cinema was not shaped solely by entertainment and the public's expectations for amusement, but also by education and social responsibility. In the report prepared by Şakir Seden for the Ministry of Education in 1925, Şakir Bey first listed the necessary steps for using cinema as an educational tool in three main points. Accordingly, he first addressed the establishment of cinema halls in schools and the organization of screenings for students by utilizing city and town cinemas in areas without schools. Secondly, he stated that cinema screenings should be organized through mobile cinemas for those in cities, towns, and villages without cinemas, provided that the roads were suitable. Thirdly, it is stated that cinema should be used as a propaganda tool to highlight Turkishness and Turkish culture (Yıldız, 2021, p. 50). Furthermore, the proposal for "Ibret Yerleri" (Places of Instruction) by Commander of the Eastern Front Kazım Karabekir Pasha, which remained an unrealized project, was included in a memorandum sent to the Presidency of the Grand National Assembly of Turkey approximately five months before the proclamation of the Republic. According to Pasha's proposal, there would be cinema and theater performances at the Places of Instruction, and young people would be trained as filmmakers. These venues would serve, in his own words, "solely for the nation's advancement." Designed as a multi-dimensional venue, the "Place of Instruction" would, however, primarily be used for cinema-related activities. In his proposal that cinema should be seen as an educational tool, Kazım Karabekir grouped "films that corrupt society's morals" under the heading of "nudity films," while viewing "scientific, technical, and industrial films" that "broaden the public's horizons and understanding" as "educational films for the public" (Öztürk, 2004, p. 80). However, although Kazım Karabekir's proposal did not come to fruition, the pasha's sensitivity regarding films did not align with the social paradigm of the early Republic.

During the early Republican period, cinema was a predominantly urban art form. A platform for discussing rural tastes in cinema had not yet emerged. Erotic imagery in films from the late Ottoman period and the early Republican era hindered cinema's expansion of its reach. For example, works such as Sedat Simavi's Pençe (1917) are labeled with concepts like "exploitation" (Öngören, 1982) and "erotic" (Evren, 1995; Özgüç, 2006) in studies describing the early period of Turkish cinema. Noting the audience's reception of the scenes featuring girls in swimsuits in Muhsin Ertuğrul's 1933 film "Karım Beni Aldatırsa" (If My Wife Cheats on Me), writers of the time stated that "cinema audiences bowed their heads, found the scene too explicit, and left the cinema" (Öngören, 1982, p. 67). Although such scenes increased audience numbers, they also generated a "problematic" judgment about cinema films among many people.

Alongside this trend in popular cinema, the state was also establishing its own cinema agenda. Although there was no common consensus on how to establish the relationship between national education and cinema within the traditional framework, the practices of the People's Houses established in the 1930s were designed to open up space for secularism, in sharp contrast to projects that prioritized adaptation, such as the "House of Instruction," which intertwined cinema with tradition. The contrast between the "ignorance" of rural areas and the "enlightenment" of modern city life in the Republic's People's Houses films, documentaries, and representative dramas reflects the secular-modern imagination in cinema.[1] "In the provinces, especially in towns or small cities, the role of the Turkish Ocakları (Turkish Hearths), which functioned almost like a state-affiliated civil society organization rather than a private enterprise, was significant in the establishment of the first permanent cinemas." (Özyılmaz & Çeliktemel-Thomen, 2022, p. 21). Following the closure of the Turkish Associations in 1931, the People's Houses (Halkevleri) were established in 1932.[2] They were founded "to strengthen and make effective the political ideology through clubs, publications, and events, adhering to government policy, similar to the Turkish Associations during the Second Constitutional Era (1908–1920)" (Arıkan, 1999, pp. 262–263).

Considering the cinema activities of the People's Houses, it is worth noting that this art form was predominantly viewed as an ideological tool and utilized for propaganda purposes. Turkey's political and military successes were highlighted in these films. An important feature of the films shown in the People's Houses and People's Clubs in villages during the war years was that images of political cadres' tours, important events, and speeches were integral to the films (Öztürk, 2022, p. 182). During the single-party political era, the primary purpose of cinema was to foster social solidarity, create a new social ethos, promote positivism in processes of explanation and interpretation, and break the spell of the religious sphere with the spell of the new regime. In "civil" films, such as Muhsin Ertuğrul's "Bir Millet Uyanıyor" (A Nation Awakens, 1932), Ottoman representations are positioned as antagonists, while religious representations are constructed as those who collaborated with the enemy during the War of Independence or undermined the struggle for independence. Secularization in Turkey was not only coded in the political persuasion efforts of the People's Houses and the "indecent" images in popular films; through screenings organized either by the state or through political associations, the "harem-selamlik" audience began to cease to be a category. Cemil Filmer, one of the first filmmakers of the Republic, recounts in his memoir how male and female audiences watched films together: "Muzaffer said, 'Go downstairs and bring the women outside inside.' And Yaver went, and after a while, the cinema was packed with women. It was there, in Ankara Cinema in Izmir, that women, men, and Atatürk watched films together for the first time in Turkey." (Filmer, 1984, p. 126)

[1] In 1912, during the final period of the Ottoman Empire, the Turkish Associations were established in Istanbul to research Turkish culture and develop the idea of nationalism. In 1932, the newly established Republic sought to bring all nationalist and cultural activities under state control, so it closed the institution and transferred its assets to the People's Houses, which were established that same year.

[2] The People's Houses, established in 1932, the year the Turkish Clubs were closed, were founded by the state for the purpose of public education and cultural development. During the Democratic Party's rule, they were closed in 1952, accused of being "the CHP's propaganda center."

4.3 Transition to a Multi-Party System, Pluralization of Film Language

With the advent of World War II, Turkey imported many films for screening from neighboring countries such as Egypt. For Turkey, which had previously imported a large number of films from Europe and America, this situation would disrupt the positivist-oriented development of the early Republic and potentially create a new "medieval" climate in terms of image. Secularization was inherent in the Westernization paradigm, and from the late Ottoman period onward, Turkey was seen as a center operating a modelable modernity program for many countries in the Middle East. However, Egypt was considered a country with a "reactionary" and "escapist" cinema map that one wanted to break away from. It was clear that Egypt's characterization as "undeveloped," "traditional," and "backward" was an incomplete assessment made by the regime's intellectuals, as there was a more radical implementation of modernity in Egypt than in the late Ottoman period (Küçük, 2010). Turkey's opening its doors to Egyptian films was not a historical necessity but rather the result of a significant audience's interest. The Egyptian film "Tears of Love" (Damu' al-Hubb) (1936), directed by Muhammad Karim and released in 1938, garnered significant interest from audiences, a fact confirmed by witnesses of the period (Özemre, 2023). The film's success triggered other producers to start importing films from Egypt (Cantek, 2000, pp. 32–33; Özön, 2013, p. 127). It is estimated that approximately 130 Egyptian films were screened in Turkey between 1938 and 1948. Only 53 Turkish films were produced during these ten years, with 20 of them shot between 1947 and 1948. During this period, when American films were only popular in large cities, Egyptian films, which were much loved by Turkish audiences, were shown for weeks even in small towns (Gürata, 2004; Yılmaz, 2024). This situation also ensured that Egyptian films, which had a significant impact on Turkish cinema history, reached the Turkish public (Evren, 2014). With the changes that occurred in the post-war conditions, there was also an increase in domestic film production. While one fiction film was shot in 1945 and another in 1946, the number of domestic films increased significantly after the establishment of the Association of Domestic Film Producers. In 1947, the number rose to 12, followed by 18 in 1948, 19 in 1949, and 22 in 1950 (Özgüç, 1988, pp. 15–18).

The growing influence of Egyptian films was mainly cultural. This would also influence the melodramatic language of Turkish cinema. The influence of Egyptian films drew the attention of the political establishment of the time, leading to efforts to prevent these films. Reports also reflected the emphasis on Westernization in films in an attempt to counter the influence of Egyptian films. The Republican People's Party, in its letter dated February 10, 1942, numbered 8/44280, stated to the Ministry of the Interior that Arabic films in Mersin and Adana were reducing the public's interest in Turkish, and that The Republican People's Party, in its letter dated February 10, 1942 (No. 8/44280), stated to the Ministry of the Interior that Arabic films in Mersin and Adana were reducing the public's interest in Turkish, and wrote an official letter summarizable as follows: "In cities under the influence of Arab culture, the public's interest in Turkish has decreased due to the influence of Arabic films; therefore, the screening of Arabic films should be banned (Cantek, 2000, p. 35)." The melodramatic effect in Egyptian films that were shown reinforced class solidarity through coincidences and feelings. Songs and singers were the carriers of culture, the unifiers of the nation, and examples and references showing how love could be experienced. In this respect, Egyptian films operated outside the idea of progress that the Republic controlled through its own institutions.

The report prepared by Nizamettin Nazif Tepedelenlioğlu on January 1, 1947, was submitted to the CHP General Secretariat. According to Tepedelenlioğlu, it was considered possible to make films with the available means, to "promote" specific ideas by making these films appealing to the public, and to win over the public. According to the report, which sought to answer the question "Why should we make films?", the reasons were: "to prevent the love of the old days, which Egyptian cinema spreads imperceptibly," "to save on foreign exchange going to Egypt," "to reduce the popularity of some European and even American films, and to reserve imported films for the highest works of art…" (Duman, 2018, p. 404). We can interpret Egyptian cinema before Yeşilçam as a unique secularization. Egyptian cinema, with its language that is "at peace with religion," "saddened by the loss of old values," and that creates a neighborhood culture with emotion and the instruments that bring it to life (which can also be interpreted as musical instruments here) a neighborhood culture, keeping restorative nostalgia as a method, and devoting leisure time to fighting the "bad guys" who try to disrupt this joy. However, these codes were not data-adapted through "recycling," but instead formed a foundation interpreted by national originality itself.

4.4 Yeşilçam's Guide to State Secularism

During the early stages of Turkey's transition to a multi-party system, the number of films produced increased significantly. By 1948, a significant tax reform was implemented. Previously, municipalities collected a 70% tax on both domestic and foreign films. However, with the 1948 regulation, the rate remained the same for foreign films, while the rate for domestic films was reduced to 25% (Tunç, 2012, p. 61). Until the 1940s, the Kemal Film and İpek Film companies operated in Turkey. However, later, film companies began to multiply, primarily including Halil Kamil's Türk Film Stüdyosu (later renamed Ha-Ka Film), Necip Erses' Ses Film, Faruk Kenç's İstanbul Film, and Turgut Demirağ's film companies. Between 1944 and 1950, a total of twenty-five film companies operated (Saydam, 2020, p. 412).

The conflicts arising from the radical moves of the single-party era, alongside the Justice Party, revolve around the concept of the "new human." The new human type is a follower of the "secular religion" established in the early revolutionary culture. The creation of the new human, as in every secular religion, primarily falls within the realm of education. The people will internalize and be disciplined by the aforementioned sacredness in community centers where education is provided, especially in schools where the new generation is raised. The instrumentalization of schools in creating the "new man" is, of course, not a new idea. Even during the Second Constitutional Era, the belief in the transformative power of education to create a new human being and a new society was shared not only among state officials but also among the entire intelligentsia (Atalay, 2024, p. 104). The radical modernity program, organized by the state, is formed within the framework of the cult of leadership, based on the uniqueness of the land. In this respect, Kemalism after the Republic, with its eclectic aspects, is an ideology that seeks to spread and regulate all areas of life. Even if it does not speak from within traditional religion or traditional forms of sanctity, it increasingly speaks using their methods. There will be a rapid "transfer of sanctity"from the concepts of traditional religion to Kemalist sacredness, and ultimately Kemalism will stand on its own feet as a secular religion" (Atalay, 2024, p. 97).

When the Democratic Party came to power, it brought the "neighborhood" and, consequently, "tradition" into the field as a "nostalgic restoration" move, in contrast to the practical application of Kemalism's New Man type. The bipolar world established after World War II led to a greater discussion of capitalism and liberal doctrine in Turkey. However, cinema attempted to construct "peace" as a means of coping with capitalism, portraying it as something made possible by family and neighborhood solidarity. Following the 1960 coup, the Justice Party assumed power as the successor to the abolished Democratic Party. During the Justice Party's rule in the 1960s, roads were built connecting cities to the countryside, transportation became easier, and electricity became widespread. The culture of urban living became a dominant feature of society. The old-style neighborhood culture began to erode. A more dynamic, variable, and mobile period began in the city, characterized by roads widening, an increase in cars, the widespread adoption of apartment living, and a diversified population due to internal migration (Kırel, 2005, p. 27). In this sense, neighborhood life increased the habit of going to the cinema and also became an indispensable theme in cinema. Peace, while facing the risk of loss with capitalism, also becomes an ideal highlighted by the economically driven migration that forces people to move to the city. "The attempt of the pre-capitalist 'idea of peace' to cope with the pathologies of capitalism" (Açıkel, 1996, p. 155) appears to pave the way for new forms of secularism through the neighborhood. Yeşilçam relates winning and losing beyond individual rise and fall to society.

Instead of a panoramic view of society, the family and the neighborhood environment in which it lives are seen as the most important units that can describe it. Unlike the determinative nature of early Republican art practice regarding the future of education and social progress, Yeşilçam does not have a plan centered around the concept of progress. The neighborhood, the family, and the district replace one another and ultimately embody the idea of "order." This order is preserved by the idea of an "unobjectified" "deus ex machina" (divine intervention). The term "unobjectified" refers to a universe that science has not objectified and that cannot be the same for everyone. God creates what is best for believers, while people stray from goodness by demanding evil. Those who possess virtue are under the protection of God, who will save them even if they fall, removing their absence and bringing them into existence. In this sense, the universe is not a place that God created and then abandoned, resting and forgetting it. Attributing meaning is achieved by interpreting lived experiences as a necessity or part of the divine order. For 'knowing that there is an order behind events is more important and vital for the believer than knowing what that order is' (Çelik, 2007, p. 42). A tradition that included the unlived as much as the lived-in experience was constructing a dual-world design while offering a reading against the early Republic's "earthly paradise" utopia.

The 1950s melodramas featured a woman marked as modern, who fell in love and lost herself, thus suffering life's blows, diminished, rendered inadequate, and emasculated in the face of modernization, often male/rarely female models; the 1960s melodramas represented the rural/urban dilemma with melodramatic templates, glorifying the "fate" to its oppressed characters, followed by the vengeful victimhood of the 70s. In short, it can be said that there is a significant difference between all these representations, corresponding to the political and social atmosphere of their respective periods, and that this difference is shaped or transformed by ideological references (Egrik, 2012, p. 165). The belief that destiny cannot be overcome but does not bring only evil, and that the outcome is good, is the main principle of Yeşilçam texts. The idea of destiny is a belief in an "old era" that must be overcome, associated with "evil" that was not expressed in its religious dimension in the early Republic. In this respect, it is evident that Yeşilçam was not particularly interested in the early Republican paradigm of social progress achieved through mass education. While the political dimension introduced by the Republic conflicted with Yeşilçam's conceptual and emotional horizon, which was rooted in the past, Yeşilçam did not propose a new political system or offer any criticism of the existing political order.

In the melodramas of 1960s Yeşilçam, the concept of "divine justice" is fundamentally rooted in Islamic emphasis. According to Islam, injustice and evil are generally explained in the context of punishment. This punishment, which stems from the difference between the melodrama genre and tragedy, is realized as atonement for the individual's mistakes. While tragedy presents a conception of God who does not forgive mistakes, the conception of God in melodrama is one of "absolute mercy." For example, "The Oedipus tragedy tells a story of suffering and powerlessness that is neither voluntary nor involuntary. Oedipus is a perpetrator who, without knowing what he is doing, creates a profound difference in the world. As he slowly learns the secret of his past actions, these actions open terrible wounds in the body that performed them, wounds that can neither be accepted nor rejected" (Asad, 2016, p. 114). Modernity, on the other hand, creates a secularization within a predictable future, based on scientific data and its own codes, with a conception of God who is omnipotent not only for humans but also for society through the state apparatus. The formation of secularization through the state apparatus is a context in non-Western societies (Asad, 2016). In this respect, Yeşilçam "tactically" produces everyday secularism in opposition to official secularism from within everyday life. Secularism in Yeşilçam broadens its meaning by incorporating tradition. The emphasis on cultural practices is important. It is the participants in that culture who give meaning to people, objects, and events. Things rarely have a single, fixed, unchanging meaning "in themselves." Even something as obvious as a stone can be a stone, a boundary marker, or a piece of sculpture, depending on what it means (i.e., a particular context of use, what philosophers call different "language games" [e.g., boundary language, sculpture language, etc.]). We give meaning to objects through how we use them and what we say, think, and feel about them (how we represent them) (Hall, 2017, p. 9). When we read directionally through the horizontal-vertical mobility of the meaning given, we can interpret the asymmetrical form of meaning as the engineering of a cadre in the early Republic. In this respect, cinema, which has not yet been recognized as an art form by the government, is viewed as a folk art when considered through the lens of environment and community. Yeşilçam, while making religion visible in the public sphere, does not read secularism as associated with the elimination of religion. A popularized secularism is presented in Yeşilçam films. This secularism does not exclude religion from the public sphere; rather, it renegotiates its role. For example, religion is visible in many films made during that period. The films feature holiday scenes, tomb visits, and prayer sequences, but these elements are incorporated into everyday life, rather than serving as an "exaltation of faith." Even if the film is a remake of a European/American film, the theme and conflicts are not the same; the criterion is the nomos of the neighborhood.[3]

In the 1970s, the state's progressive program transformed people's anxieties, failures, and wounds into social decay, efforts to resist change in the neighborhood, and stories of rural residents getting lost in the city. Hope (Yılmaz Güney, 1970) and Anxiety (Şerif Gören & Yılmaz Güney, 1974) approached tragedy, moving away from the ideal of progress based on the discourse of predicted success. The loss of ground by idealism against reality paved the way for the search for other ideals. The proliferation of films depicting prophets and religious figures in Turkey showed that religion could now emerge with all its representative elements from its suppressed state. The Justice of Hazreti Ömer (Nejat Saydam, 1961), The Martyrs of Paradise (Mehmet Dinler, 1965), Hazreti Yusuf (Nuri Akıncı, 1972), Rabia (Osman F. Seden, 1973) are films that culturally demonstrate the dominant role of religion, while also being close to secular interpretation in their approach to religious narrative. However, this seemingly contradictory framing ultimately differs from the state's modernity

[3] Bülent Oran, who worked in Yeşilçam for a long time and wrote countless screenplays, said the following in an interview about these remakes: "For example, in the foreign film they want you to adapt, the married woman in the lead role takes another man to bed without her husband's knowledge. The audience enjoys these scenes, which mix romance with sexual excitement. They enjoy watching it and it increases the film's chances of success. But when we adapt this film with these scenes intact, our film flops. Because the Turkish audience watches that foreign film differently. The idea in that film works, but as screenwriters, we break out in a cold sweat when we get to that scene. In Turkish films, not even a male fly can enter the bed of the married leading lady, let alone a foreign man. The woman in the foreign film is American, British, French, etc., and is ultimately a foreign wife. She can take her lovers into her bed. Since her husband is not Turkish, his cuckolding does not disturb the audience. She doesn't see much harm in betrayal. But the woman in our film is Turkish. Her husband is also an honorable Anatolian man. If we adapt the film and make her commit adultery, even if it's just for the sake of the film, the situation suddenly becomes sleazy, the woman is instantly branded a whore, and no power on earth can save that Turkish film from failure. A film where prostitutes and pimps take the lead roles automatically has zero chance of success. If you don't pay attention to these things, even if you have to, the audience won't come. It's that simple" (Turk, 2004, p. 204).

mantra and secular definition of citizenship in the early republic. Humans need myth and scripture to believe, listening to a call that differs from calls for rationalization.

The National Cinema movement was active in cinema from the late 1960s to the mid-1990s, which Islamist movements saw as a new form of jihad. Yücel Çakmaklı, considered the pioneer of National Cinema, expressed the need for a new narrative in Turkish cinema: "Turkish cinema will only achieve its 'National Cinema' identity by presenting films that reflect the reality of Anatolia, shaped by the beliefs, national character, and traditions of the Muslim-Turkish people, who value spiritual values above material ones, by producing films that reflect the reality of Anatolia" (Çakmaklı, 1964, p. 3). Interpreting the secular themes nurtured by modernity in cinema as decadence, and later focusing on political ideals, National Cinema produces films of social transformation or struggle with the theme of guidance at their center: Çile, 1972 (adapted from Necip Fazıl's story Deprem); Zehra, 1972 (adapted from Necip Fazıl); Oğlum Osman, 1973; Diriliş, 1974; Memleketim, 1975. These films emphasize that the solution to existential crises and struggles is turning to religion.

4.5 Conclusion

With the 1960s, Turkish cinema clearly distanced itself from a Western understanding of nomos, as exemplified by the cinema of the neighborhood. Instead of a universe where Western standards formed normativity, it established its own "small neighborhood," where family values, conflicts, and the concepts of ceremony and honor existed, and the practice of eroding the boundaries set by the center began to emerge. This transformation paved the way for a local secularism and interpretation of religion that distanced itself culturally from the central culture, rather than ideological conflict and opposition. Yeşilçam, rather than positioning itself as an organic-mechanical tool under the shadow of the state's ideology, became the "voice" of the periphery, of the oppressed.

While it is possible to interpret the point reached by an ordinary person who has memorized their civic duties as an "enlightened scientist," a new emotional sociological foundation emerged during the Yeşilçam era through new types of social grounding. In Yakup Kadri's novel Ankara, the admired artist Neşet Sabit focused on the revealing and idealistic aspects of theater's problems, while Yeşilçam created seemingly contradictory impressions like twins. This duality was a hybrid order produced by the intersection of modernity and tradition: female characters were chaste yet attractive, while men were macho yet romantic. The reading of tradition evolved in response to new tensions between male and female types, as well as the emergence of new standards of consumption brought about by modernity. However, the early secularism, formed by the state simply proposing the right thing to those who constantly chose the right thing, created a new neighborhood ethos and nomos in Yeşilçam, which sometimes reminded the state of the right thing and resolved the issue internally. National Cinema, which began during the Yeşilçam era and continued thereafter, serves as an alternative to early Republican secularism, as it initiated a struggle against the corruption of the "worldly."

Secularism in Turkish cinema began from a scientific, modern paradigm and continued in a traditional, belief-based, and emotional manner. While the center's construction of modern cities (such as Ankara) and the periphery's creation of a neighborhood within these modern cities may appear fundamentally as a struggle over space, they establish an autonomous sphere. In Yeşilçam, the neighborhood, by offering a counter-secular reading, produces a system that demands a "return to the essence" against the pathologies of modernity and capitalism, placing "divine justice," which does not punish through the current legal system that is an integral part of the modern state, above all else. Types, representation, and the represented are positioned according to the balance of the smallest realm within the greater realm. The transformation of representation into a lesson, and the fact that the lesson is a story that enables tradition to take shape in its "urban" forms, is a solution brought about by this hybrid reading.

References

Açıkel, F. (1996). Kutsal mazlumluğun psikopatolojisi. *Toplum ve Bilim, 70*, 153–193.
Arıkan, Z. (1999). Halkevlerinin kuruluşu ve tarihsel işlevi. *Atatürk Yolu Dergisi, 6*(23), 261–281.
Asad, T. (2016). *Sekülerliğin biçimleri: Hıristiyanlık, İslamiyet ve modernlik.* (F. B. Aydar, Trans.) Metis Yayınları.
Atalay, O. (2024). *Türk'e tapmak: Seküler din ve iki savaş arası Kemalizm.* İletişim Yayınları.
Berger, P. L. (2025). *Kutsal şemsiye.* İz Yayıncılık.
Berkes, N. (2006). *Türkiye'de çağdaşlaşma.* Yapı Kredi Yayınları.
Cantek, L. (2000). Türkiye'de Mısır Filmleri. *Tarih ve Toplum, 204*, 31–38.
Çakmaklı, Y. (1964). Milli sinema ihtiyacı. *Tohum, 11*, s. 3.
Çelik, C. (2007). Teodisenin sosyolojisi. *Bilimname, 13*, 37–66.
Çelikoğlu, İ. Ö. (2013). Pozitivist Cumhuriyet'te seküler ahlakın gelişimi ve sınırları: Erken Cumhuriyet dönemi Türkiyesi ve üçüncü Cumhuriyet Fransası'nın karşılaştırmalı incelemesi. [Doctoral Dissertation] Dokuz Eylül Üniversitesi Sosyal Bilimler Enstitüsü.
Duman, M. (2018). *II. Dünya Savaşı sonrasında, CHP hükümetlerinin dış politikaya yönelik propaganda faaliyetleri: Amaçlar, araçlar, yönelişler* [Doctoral Dissertation]. Fatih Sultan Mehmet Vakıf Üniversitesi Sosyal Bilimler Enstitüsü.
Egrik, E. B. (2012). *Yeşilçam sinemasında nemesistik anlatılar "toplumsal tahayyül, adaletsizlik hissiyatı ve intikam"* [Doctoral Dissertation]. Marmara Üniversitesi Sosyal Bilimler Enstitüsü.
Evren, B. (1995). *Türk sinemasında cinsellik.* Ad Yayıncılık.
Evren, B. (2014). *Türk sinemasının 100 Yılı.* Kültür ve Turizm Bakanlığı.
Filmer, C. (1984). *Hatıralar, Türk sinemasında 65 Yıl.* Emek Matbaacılık.
Gökçek, Y. Z. (2022). Erken cumhuriyetin hayra yorduğu düş: Yerli ve muasır çizgiler arasında Türk sineması. *Medya ve Din Araştırmaları Dergisi, 1*(5), 159–176.
Gürata, A. (2004). Tears of love: Egyptian cinema in Turkey. *New Perspectives on Turkey, 30*, 55–82.
Hall, S. (2017). *Temsil: Kültürel temsiller ve anlamlandırma uygulamaları.* Pinhan Yayınları.
Karaosmanoğlu, Y. K. (2024). *Ankara.* İletişim Yayınları.
Kırel, S. (2005). *Yeşilçam öykü sineması.* Babil Yayınları.
Küçük, Y. (2010). *Aydın üzerine tezler.* Mızrak Yayınları.

Lüleci, Y. (2014). Erken Cumhuriyet döneminde Türkiye Cumhuriyeti ile Sovyetler Birliği arasındaki sanatsal ilişkiler. Ankara: Türkiye'nin Kalbi Belgeseli Örneği. *İnsan & İnsan, 2*, 40–61.
Mardin, Ş. (1991). *Türkiye'de din ve siyaset*. İletişim Yayınları.
Öngören, M. T. (1982). *Sinemada kadın ve cinsellik sömürüsü*. Dayanışma Yayınları.
Özemre, A. Y. (2023). *Üsküdar'da bir attar dükkânı*. Kubbealtı Neşriyat.
Özgüç, A. (1988). *Kronolojik Türk sinema tarihi 1914–1988*. Kronolojik Türk Sinema Tarihi 1914–1988, Kültür ve Turizm Bakanlığı.
Özgüç, A. (2006). *Türk sinemasında cinselliğin tarihi*. +1 Kitap Yayınları.
Özön, N. (2013). *Türk sinema tarihi: Dünden bugüne 1896–1960*. Doruk Yayınları.
Öztürk, S. (2004). Erken Cumhuriyet yıllarında sinema konusunda başarısız kalmış iki girişim: Çekilemeyen İki Propaganda Filmi (1939) ve İbret Yerleri Projesi (1923). *Selçuk İletişim, 3*(3), 77–82.
Öztürk, S. (2022). *Erken Cumhuriyet döneminde sinema seyir siyaset*. Kırmızı Yayınları.
Özyılmaz, Ö., & Çeliktemel-Thomen, Ö. (2022). Türkiye'de taşraya sesli sinemanın gelişi (1930–1945). *Galatasaray Üniversitesi İletişim Dergisi, 37*, 7–33.
Saydam, B. (2020). Türk sinemasının tarihine genel bir bakış. *Türkiye Araştırmaları Literatür Dergisi, 18*(36), 401–422.
Tekin, M. (2012). Batı'da sekülerlik ve Türkiye müslümanlığının seküler içerimleri. *İnsan & Toplum, 4*(2), 181–204.
Tunç, E. (2012). *Türk sinemasının ekonomik yapısı (1896–2005)*. Doruk Yayınları.
Türk, İ. (2004). *Senaryo-Bülent Oran*. Dergah Yayınları.
Vandov, D. (2014). *Atatürk dönemi Türk-Sovyet ilişkileri*. Kaynak Yayınları.
Weber, M. (2011). *Protestan ahlakı ve kapitalizmin ruhu*. (M. Köktürk, Trans.), BilgeSu Yayınları.
Yıldız, M. (2021). Cumhuriyetin ilk yıllarında Milli Eğitim politikalarında bir araç olarak sinemanın kullanılması: 1925 Şakir Seden raporu. *Journal of Academic Value Studies, 7*(1), 41–51.
Yılmaz, M. M. (2024). *Türk sinema eleştirisinin düşünsel temelleri*. Doruk Yayınları.

Chapter 5
Restricted Islam: Religious Program Principles in the Turkish Radio and Television Corporation (TRT) General Broadcasting Plans (1977–2004)

Mustafa Çuhadar

5.1 Introduction

There is a clear distinction between the pre-modern and modern periods in the social meaning of religion. In the pre-modern period, the path of all institutions and practices passed through religion, and religion assumed a central function in both the "official ideology" of the rulers of societies and the "counter-ideologies" of the ruled. In the modern period, however, the central position of religion in daily life has changed, and religion has gone from being "everything" to "something among things". At this point, the concepts of secularism and secularization come to the forefront in the relationship between religion, the state, and society. While secularism is defined as the independence of the state from religion, secularization refers to the independence of society from religion (Aktay, 2017, pp. 61–63). The secularism experienced in Türkiye has been reflected as a manifestation of the state's active involvement in matters related to religion. Thus, secularism in Türkiye has been practiced through the removal of religious symbols and the reduction of the influence of religion in both the state and daily life, as well as the state's control over religion (Ertit, 2019, pp. 80–83). Thus, as Canatan states, secularization and laicism have become synonymous with secularism, which expresses the ideological and political dimension of secularization, and the field of application of secularism in Türkiye has not only been limited to legal entities (state, party, etc.), but has also moved to individual and social fields (1997, p. 12). Türkiye's unique understanding of secularism has been the determinant of its religious policies, and the state's will has never left the religious sphere autonomous. The most central intersection of the founding ideology of the Republic was the transition from a spiritual to a secular society, and the desire to

M. Çuhadar (✉)
Ankara, Türkiye
e-mail: mstfchdr@gmail.com

M. D. Dereli and M. Eken (eds.), *Turkish Perspectives on Secularization and Media*,
https://doi.org/10.1007/978-3-032-16436-0_5

create a society compatible with the secular structure of the state was dominant in all policies implemented by the state. However, to meet this expectation, religion, and Islam in particular, was not wholly abandoned; policies were produced with the demand for a "useful religion" by utilizing the power of religion in social layers and its functionality in terms of creating a national identity (Aktay, 2000, pp. 43–44).

For this purpose, fundamental reforms such as the abolition of the caliphate, the closure of madrasas and the unification of education in secular schools, and the closure of dervish lodges and orders were undertaken, followed by practices such as changes in clothing, calendar, alphabet, and the language of the call to prayer to intensify symbolic change. Various institutional structures were built (Çolak, 2017, p. 81). Through all these, many religious symbols and practices, as well as non-Westernized Muslims, were excluded from the public sphere, which was the new space of the republican elite during the single-party period (1923–1950) (Göle, 2013, p. 23). However, social demands, especially those arising from the Second World War, brought about changes in religious policies (Ateş, 2018, p. 17). The policy of approaching religion with pragmatic references was also continued by the soldiers who seized power through coups in the 1960s and 1980s (Subaşı, 2005, pp. 77–101). For example, the coup government of September 12, 1980, utilized the unifying power of religion and made religious culture and ethics classes compulsory in primary and secondary education institutions under the supervision and control of the state (Yazıcı, 2015, pp. 31–32). In fact, the process from the 1960s to the early 2000s was determined by how and by whom religion was positioned. In this context, Türkiye witnessed a struggle between "republican elites", who wanted to keep religion within the boundaries set by the state and who owed their privileges in political and economic life to the Republican revolutions, and "challenger" groups who wanted to move religion outside the boundaries set by the state, who believed that they had lost the privileges they enjoyed during the Ottoman period with the Republican revolutions, and whose common characteristic was their religiosity or religious identity.[1] With the victory of the challenger group mobilized by the Welfare Party (RP), the third political party of the National Vision movement, in the 1994 local elections, the threat perception of the republican elites shifted towards Islam. The 1995 general elections, in which the RP came first, marked the beginning of Islam, which had guaranteed the regime's security until the 1990s, henceforth being seen as the most serious threat to the regime's existence, and the intensive struggle against "irtica" as the name of the state's security threat began. Following the February 28 intervention, restrictions on religious education and religious freedoms were imposed to remove the struggling group from both the political and sociopolitical spheres (Arpacı, 2018, pp. 31–33). However, the Islamic section, as a struggling group that has increased its power in the cultural, economic, and political spheres since the 1970s, has become very active in different sectors such as politics, education, law, academia, energy, health, media, defense industry, and civil society since the 2000s, even though it was deeply affected during the February 28 process. One of the factors behind this is that the AK

[1] Göle, names these two groups as "Kemalist secular elites" and "Islamist counter-elites" (1998, p. 1602).

Party (Justice and Development Party) governments have implemented policies of reconciling the state with religion (Akyüz, 2016) or religious liberalization (Arpacı, 2018) since the 2000s. To put it more clearly, in all these processes, the tension in Türkiye has been between those who have introduced restrictions or expansions on the visibility of religion in the public sphere, religious education activities, and the freedoms of those who express themselves with their religious identity in the public sphere.

The two fundamental principles on which the modernization of the Turkish Republic was based were secularism and positivism, as noted by Göle (1998, p. 1602). With the elites who embraced these principles taking part in the political, cultural, economic, bureaucratic, and military administration, only limited forms of Islam were given space. The desire of the opposing elites or Islamists/pious people to expand the traces of Islam in the public sphere has become synonymous with having a voice in Türkiye. Accordingly, the way the ruling elites understand and interpret religion has determined the policies they pursue.

So, how were Türkiye's media policies, especially the broadcasting policies of the Turkish Radio and Television Corporation (TRT), affected by all these processes?

5.2 TRT and Religious Policies

The government's religious policies in Türkiye inevitably have an impact on the mass media. The 1945 official letter stating that no religious publications would be allowed in newspapers, as well as the absence of religious broadcasting on the radio from the early years of the Republic until 1950, demonstrate the impact of the religious policies of the Single Party Period on mass media. Likewise, the practices of the Democratic Party between 1950 and 1954, particularly in terms of religious broadcasting on the radio (Qur'an, adhan, religious conversations, and mawlid on the radio), reveal the impact of government policies on religious content in mass media (Ateş, 2018, pp. 134, 202–203). There is a similar situation in terms of television broadcasting.

Dr. Asaf Demirbaş[2] states in a document he saw that the first person to suggest religious broadcasts on television was Prime Minister Bülent Ecevit in 1974. According to him, in a letter sent to Dr. Lütfi Doğan, who was in charge of the Presidency of Religious Affairs, Ecevit asked for "help in making unifying religious broadcasts on television" (Dedeoğlu, 2019, p. 36). Thus, it can be said that the issue of religious broadcasting started with the demands/directives of government officials. Between 1968 and 1974, TV 1, the first television channel of TRT, only featured short speeches by the President of Religious Affairs on religious days, and no other religious broadcasts were made. In 1974, in addition to these short speeches, one or two mawlid

[2] Asaf Demirbaş was actively involved in both the production process and the hosting of the program İnanç Dünyası (World of Faith) on TRT from the 1980s to the 2000s, and he was the manager of the Directorate of Religion and Ethics Broadcasts, which prepared TRT's religious programs.

broadcasts were made. From 1975 onwards, 20–30 min iftar programs were broadcast during Ramadan. In the same year, television programs on religious topics were broadcast once a week during the month of Ramadan in 1975 (Diyanet, 1984, p. 2). Behind this short history lies the expectations of government policies or rulers from TRT. In fact, the program for the martyrs of the Cyprus Peace Operation, which went down in the history of the institution as the first mawlid broadcast on television, was performed and broadcast with the intervention of Prime Minister Bülent Ecevit, despite the opposition of TRT General Director İsmail Cem (Altıkulaç, 2016, p. 597). The broadcasting of programs with religious content on TRT and the first live mawlid broadcast on state television is an event in itself, realized by the coalition government formed by the National Salvation Party and the Republican People's Party (Öz, 2020, p. 486). On the other hand, the coalition government formed by the Justice Party, the National Salvation Party, the Republican Trust Party, and the Nationalist Movement Party on March 31, 1975 (Nationalist Front Government I), wanted to impose on TRT the expectation of broadcasting in accordance with nationalist and religious sensitivities that the Turkish right expected from radio and television broadcasting. One of the most significant steps towards this end was the appointment of Nevzat Yalçıntaş, known for his conservative identity, as the General Director of TRT, rather than İsmail Cem, who was appointed during the 1974 Ecevit Government (Öztan, 2020, pp. 418, 437). Nevzat Yalçıntaş, who held the view that "TRT should broadcast programs that unify the Turkish nation, observe common values, national culture, spiritual beliefs, increase progress and development efforts in the country, and endear individuals to each other", started to work with various names to make national and spiritual broadcasts on TRT and to develop these broadcasts, and made changes in the broadcasting policy (Çiftçigüzeli, 2014, p. 149). After Nevzat Yalçıntaş, Şaban Karataş, who was appointed as the General Director of TRT by the Nationalist Front I Government and who was known for his nationalist identity, started to produce films and programs with religious content (Religion and Morality Talk, Examples from East Turkestan Folklore, Coming from Mount Kaf, Qur'an Reading Contest, Malazgirt, Rabia). He maintained his will to broadcast it on TRT (Karataş, 1978, pp. 187, 206). Among these, "Din ve Ahlak" (Religion and Morality) was broadcast every Thursday evening in March 1976 (Akıllıoğlu et al., 1990, p. 47), following the first and second seasons. Nationalist Front Governments, Cengiz Taşer replaced Şaban Karataş in the III. The Bülent Ecevit government in 1978, and Doğan Kasaroğlu replaced Cengiz Taşer in the VI—Demirel Government in 1979 (Diriklik, 1995a, pp. 212, 218).

Doğan Kasaroğlu, the General Director of TRT between 1979 and 1981, announced in a press statement (Turam, 1994, p. 380) that religious broadcasts would begin on February 19, 1980. İnanç Dünyası (World of Faith), named by Doğan Kasaroğlu, was broadcast on December 27, 1980, and became TRT's most consistent religious program.[3] The program was hosted by Dr. Asaf Demirbaş, who said,

[3] Çiftçigüzeli states that the program to be broadcast on TRT under the name "World of Belief" was designed during the Nevzat Yalçıntaş period and it was decided to be broadcast on August 29, 1975 (2014, pp. 128–131).

"I adopted and lived secularism with my soul and mind, and I believe that I did not contradict the spirit and principles of Islam while preparing my programs along this line". Asaf Demirbaş, who emphasized social and cultural topics in the program, addressing a wide range of issues such as human, homeland, love for the state, the rights of neighbors, architecture, art, music, health, tax, sacrificial skins, etc., hosted people from different professional groups such as theologians, bureaucrats, business people, and also brought military officers to the screen as speakers (Dedeoğlu, 2019, pp. 37–38). According to Bilis, İnanç Dünyası (World of Faith), which was broadcast at a time when a Turkish-Islamic[4] synthesis was accepted in the political arena, was presented to the audience with topics and content that referred to the more universal aspects of Islam and would be compatible with the secular state structure (Bilis, 2019, p. 100).

It is also possible to witness the relationship between religious programs on television and government policies by following development plans. The relationship between government policies and religious programs becomes more apparent when the report of the National Culture Commission, prepared within the scope of the fifth development plan of the Prime Ministry State Planning Organization, is examined.

The National Culture Commission convened from January 14 to 16, 1983. Among the sub-commissions of this commission was the Commission on Mass Media. The commission was chaired by Ahmet Kabaklı and included notable figures such as Rıdvan Çongur, Mustafa Demirezen, Rasim Özdenören, Yücel Çakmaklı, and Mehmet Doğan. These names are among the most prominent names in the right-wing movement in Türkiye. In the findings and proposals under the heading of religious and moral education in mass media and formal and non-formal education, there are articles about religious programs on radio and television that refer to Islam, the State of the Republic of Türkiye, and Turkish citizens (Komisyon, 1984, pp. 150–157). In this respect, it is seen that governments developed policies towards religious programs in the 1980s.

TV-2, the second television channel of TRT, began regular broadcasting on October 6, 1986, following a test broadcast on September 1 of that year. Following the establishment of this channel, TV-2 began broadcasting "Islam and Society", a program prepared by Yusuf Ziya Alçakakar on Friday evenings, with a more valuable and realistic approach, as opposed to the program "İnanç Dünyası" (World of Faith), which was broadcast on TV-1 on Thursdays and prepared by Asaf Demirbaş. However, in May 1989, Yusuf Ziya Alçakadar was removed as producer of the program and replaced by Asaf Demirbaş. The name of the program was changed to Islam and Human (Diriklik, 1995a, p. 302; 1995b, p. 16).

TRT's television broadcasting continued with TV-3 and GAP Television in 1989, TV-4 in 1990, and TRT INT/Eurasia in 1993. At the end of the 1990s, the names of the channels changed and diversified as TRT 1, TRT 2, TRT 3, TRT GAP, TRT INT, TRT Türk, TRT 6, TRT Avaz, TRT Anadolu, TRT Diyanet, TRT El-Arabiya,

---

[4] The "Turkish-Islamic Synthesis" is defined as the educational and cultural policies implemented by the September 12 coup government in cooperation with the intellectuals' quarry (Şimşek, 2020, pp. 79–86).

TRT World, TRT News, TRT Sports, TRT School, TRT Çocuk, TRT Belgesel, TRT Diyanet Çocuk. As of today (2024), TRT has 17 channels (TRT, no date).

Since 2002, when the AK Party came to power, there have been significant transformations in the media in terms of capital, political culture, and cadres with conservative qualities (Erkal, 2022, p. 437). It can be said that there is an essential relationship between TRT's changes regarding religious programs and its staff. The İnanç Dünyası (World of Faith) program, which started broadcasting in line with the policies of the state in the 1980s, completed its broadcasting process in 2005 during the term of Şenol Demiröz, the first TRT General Director appointed by the AK Party, and, instead, programs such as Düşünce İklimi, Yolcu, Sonsuzluk Yolcusu, Hayat ve Din started to appear on the screen. In the following years, religious programs were broadcast on different channels of TRT (TRT 1, TRT 2, TRT GAP, TRT INT, etc.). The TRT Diyanet TV channel was established in accordance with the protocol signed between TRT and the Presidency of Religious Affairs in 2012. The protocol expired in 2019, and subsequently, this channel was transformed into a channel managed by the Presidency of Religious Affairs, now known as Diyanet TV (Çuhadar, 2019). After Şenol Demiröz, under the general directors of TRT appointed by the AK Party governments (İbrahim Şahin, Şenol Göka, İbrahim Eren, and Mehmet Zahid Sobacı), religious programs in different formats and contents were broadcast on TRT Avaz, which addresses the Turkic world, TRT Kurdî, which addresses Kurdish speakers, and TRT Türk, which addresses Europe. In addition, the Qur'an recitation contest, which was launched in 2017 with the support of the Presidency of the Republic of Türkiye and broadcast for the first time on Turkish television, took place on TRT 1. Türkiye's first children's channel with religious content, TRT Diyanet Çocuk, began broadcasting in 2023, in line with the public broadcasting mandate of TRT (n.d.).

So, what is the connection between these aspects of religious broadcasting in line with the policies of governments from the 1970s to the 2020s, i.e., religious programs and secularization? In fact, the answer to this question will be discussed extensively in the analysis section. However, it may be helpful to first touch upon the institutional texts of the 1970s and some of the practices in other years.

5.3 Principles that Inspire the Overall Publication Plans

The information provided by Rıdvan Çongur and Oya Tokgöz shows the advisory decisions regarding religious programming. According to them, TRT, which was established in 1964, formed a Moral Education Advisory Board around the year of its establishment (1965) to direct its educational and cultural broadcasts. The board, convened under the chairmanship of Ord. Prof. Dr. Suut Kemal Yetkin from the Faculty of Theology at Ankara University published a report at the end of his work, which outlined the principles to be applied in educational and cultural broadcasts. This committee decided that "the following points should be taken into consideration in the subjects that are dealt with in terms of religion, taken from a historical perspective, and whose manifestations in the Islamic world are explained":

1. Religious subjects are taught in such a way as to enable a citizen raised in a democratic order to attain an understanding of virtue based on the principles of freedom and rationality.
2. Islamic thought is analyzed from a historical point of view, and the values that are valid in today's order of freedom are distinguished from the values that have disappeared into history.
3. Ethical issues dealt with in terms of Islamic thought are explained by going to the source as much as possible.

The topics proposed by the Moral Education Advisory Board in the field of religious publications are under two headings, and the subheadings are as follows in Table 5.1.

When TRT's first general broadcasting plan is examined in conjunction with this document, it becomes clear how effective the decisions of the Moral Education Advisory Board were. TRT's first general broadcasting plan was implemented in 1972. In the 60-page document titled "TRT Program Planning Principles and Objectives", program types are divided into 10 categories: educational broadcasts, village broadcasts, village organization, children's broadcasts, women's broadcasts, cultural broadcasts, entertainment broadcasts, music broadcasts, news broadcasts, and tourism broadcasts. Among these, one of the sub-genres of "Village Organization" is "Religion and Morality". The objectives or principles of religion and morality programs are as follows:

Table 5.1 Islamic thought and morality in Islam (Çongur, 1981, pp. 272–273; Tokgöz, 1972, pp. 108–109)

1. Islamic Thought	2. Morality in Islam
Importance given to science The value given to reason, science, and free thought The necessity of work and progress Brotherhood and solidarity Love of nature The need to seek solutions to the needs of a developing society Social justice Worldview and the importance of the human The harm of superstition The development and effects of Islamic civilization Fine arts and their importance in Islam Reasons for the decline in the Islamic world The harms of bigotry Democracy and equality The value given to freedom of conscience Islam's value for other religions Great thinkers of the Islamic world The importance of not having an intermediary between man and God in Islam	A. General morality 1) Islam and morality 2) Principles of Islamic morality, the morality of prophets and religious leaders B. Private morality 1) Virtues 2) Solidarity 3) Direction 4) Moderation 5) Family and morality 6) Love for humans

Islamic thought should be handled from a historical perspective, and the subject should be explained by going to the source as much as possible:

a. The rational aspect of Islam, the fight against superstitions and falsehoods.
b. That Islam encourages development and is open to innovation.
c. Form and morality in Islam (tolerance, work, solidarity, help, respect for truth).
d. The importance given to women by Islam, women, and their value and place.
e. Introducing the qualities of "Secularism" as a superior and sound principle that makes everyone free in their beliefs without discriminating between citizens based on the rational and tolerant idea of our religion.
f. Morality and politics (Being moral, the elements of morality, respect for morality, and national consciousness should be at the basis of politics.
g. Cleansing the body and soul in Islam. (TRT, 1972, p. 30)

Published in 1972, another issue that should be included in this general publication plan is the "Moral Education Publications" under the sub-category of "Cultural Publications". In terms of the subject of our study, the following sentences mentioned in moral education publications need to be quoted:

> The Constitution's understanding of freedom of religion and conscience will be discussed. The secular worldview, which is an indispensable condition for national integrity, and the principles of Islam, such as the harmony of reason and faith, rights, love, and tolerance, will be explained. The unifying essence of Islam in social structure and its principles, which encourage work, will be stated. It will be explained that the fatalistic attitude that prevents the constructive power of man is incompatible with Islam. (TRT, 1972, p. 34)

In 1965 and 1972, upon the suggestion of Adnan Saygun, a member of the TRT Board of Directors, advisory decisions were taken under the title "Principles to be followed and Measures to be taken on Atatürk's Principles, Programs and Music", which were discussed in 1975 and completed in 1976. The following decision, consisting of only one sentence, was written on how "Religious" subjects would be handled:

> No religious programs in the service of any political movement, nor programs that incite the sectarian differences of citizens, contrary to the essence and text[5] of Article 153 of the Constitution.

As can be seen, only one approach is taken here on how religious programs should not be broadcast. The 1972 broadcasting principles and the 1976 recommendations largely determine the limits of religious programs on TRT. Within these limits, it is evident that certain factors are emphasized and highlighted, while others are excluded. In other words, TRT's texts in this period defined the "reduced" and "excluded" aspects, allowing for religious programs within these limits. So, how did these articles work in practice?

During the period when the military coup was in power in Türkiye, although the practice did not spread over a wide period of time, in 1982, TRT initiated package mawlid programs with its own initiatives, before the State Ministries and the Prime Ministry. The insistence on broadcasting mawlid programs as a package program,

[5] Protecting Revolutionary Laws.

rather than broadcasting them over the air, is an effort to conceal the undesirable aspects of the social-religious picture that is attempted to be presented through technical interventions. In justification for the insistence on package programs, negative examples such as skullcaps and the presence of young children in the mosque were cited (Şimşek, 2020, p. 224). This situation was reflected in TRT's 1991 General Broadcasting Plan with the following sentences:

> Mawlid programs will be broadcast after addressing issues contrary to the general understanding that are not welcomed by our society, and intense images of children will be removed. (TRT, 1990, p. 49)[6]

Of course, it is not meaningful to generalize about religious programs on TRT based on these two practices. It is necessary to base the issue on a broader perspective and examine the broadcasts holistically. For this purpose, it is not possible to watch the broadcasts from the 1970s to the 2000s and make inferences. However, an analysis based on institutional texts may be meaningful.

While the institutional texts of public broadcasting in Türkiye set the boundaries for religious broadcasting, the broadcasting principles of private radios and televisions were determined by the regulation that entered into force with the Official Gazette dated May 2, 1995, and numbered 22,275. Although it is the subject of another study, it is useful to briefly mention it here, as it contains principles relevant to religious broadcasting. The principles of religious programs in the regulation are as follows:

> In accordance with the freedom of religion and conscience, which is rooted in the Constitution, religious programs that emphasize the unifying characteristic of society and value the human essence and brotherhood may be broadcast. During religious broadcasts, those that condemn and provoke individuals, organizations, and masses due to their beliefs, and that cause social reactions and incidents, cannot be made. During these broadcasts, sarcastic or insulting language is not permitted. Religious broadcasts cannot be associated with political movements, nor can they offend religious feelings or allow the exploitation of religion (Özel Radyo ve Televizyon Kuruluşlarının Eğitim, Kültür, Türk Halk Müziği ve Türk Sanat Müziği Programlarında Yer Vermeleri Gerekli Yayın Türleri ve Oranlarına Ait Esaslar Hakkında Yönetmelik. (1995)

In Türkiye, there are studies on how religion is limited, as referenced in TRT's General Broadcasting Plans. In How Religion Stands on the Screen? Popular Representation of Religion in the Media, Mete Çamdereli compares how religion is positioned in broadcasting principles, using examples from the BBC and TRT. Accordingly, unlike the BBC, TRT's broadcasting principles and objectives regarding religious programs from the 1970s to 2010 centered on a production that adhered to the Constitution, Kemalism, and observed the secularism principle of the Constitution. However, Çamdereli states that since 2009–2010, religious programs have been removed from a view that can be called secular morality (2018, pp. 37–40). In Fatih Yaman's article, "The Birth of Conservative Television Broadcasting in Turkey", it is mentioned that TRT directs religious content from a secular and progressive perspective. Yaman

---

[6] The examples given by Taceddin Ural and Salik Diriklik show that even TV series were taken off the air on the grounds of secularism (see Diriklik, 1995b, p. 124; Ural, 2008, pp. 197–198).

notes that TRT includes religious programs "by being included in a fiction created within the framework of the envisaged social benefit" (2019, pp. 194–196). Mustafa Derviş Dereli, in his article titled "Media and Religion in Turkey in the Context of Past-Present-Future and Controversial Areas", discusses TRT's approach to religious broadcasting around the articles in the general broadcasting plans of 1979, 1982, and 1998. According to Dereli, with complaints about religious programs on private television reaching RTÜK during the February 28 process, TRT's attitude in the 1970s and 1980s became clearer with the 1998 general broadcasting plan. Programs with religious content were framed in terms of secularism, freedom of religion and conscience, Atatürk's principles and reforms, and aimed to increase the sense of national unity and belonging (2023, pp. 341–342).

These important studies in the literature have paved the way for the need to examine TRT's general broadcasting plans with more comprehensive measures and longitudinal integrity. This study was inspired by Çamdereli's observation that there is a "restricted Islamicity" in television.

5.4 Method

This study employed a quantitative research method. In the study, TRT's general broadcasting plans were used as a secondary data source. The broadcasting principles of religious programs included in the general broadcasting plans in the "Culture Broadcasts" type are the main subject of this study. The study aims to address the following questions.

1. In TRT's general broadcasting plans, the principles regarding religious programs are limited to which categories?
2. What are the "reductive references" and "exclusionary references" in the principles regarding religious programs in TRT's general broadcasting plans?

The study, which will be evaluated using content analysis, employs a longitudinal research design. For this reason, it was intended to analyze the general broadcasting plans between 1977 and 2004. However, general broadcasting plans for the years 1978, 1989, 1994, and 1997 could not be found. Additionally, it was discovered that the 1979 general broadcasting plan did not include any articles on religious and ethical programs. Thus, twenty-two general broadcasting plans, spanning from 1977 to 2004, were included in the analysis. The comparisons made in the broadcasting plans give the impression that these deficiencies do not have dimensions that will affect the overall study. In fact, the religious program principles in the general broadcasting plans can be divided into two periods, 1970–1990 and 1991–2004, in terms of scope, content, and number of items. These breaks will be explained in the findings and interpretation section. The missing years do not affect the validity of the study. Since this study focuses on institutional texts, it is beyond the scope of this study to determine whether the principles of religious programs are reflected in the programs.

TRT's general broadcast plans were accessed by searching the catalogs of the National Library and the Radio and Television Supreme Council in Ankara. The broadcast plans that could not be found were obtained from bookshops in various provinces of Türkiye.

5.5 Findings and Interpretation

TRT has maintained its public broadcasting approach in line with the principles of program planning since 1972. General broadcast plans (TRT, 1976, 1978, 1979, 1980, 1981, 1982, 1983, 1984, 1985, 1986, 1987, 1989, 1990, 1991, 1992, 1994, 1995, 1998, 1999, 2000, 2001, 2003, 2004), as a result of the decisions taken by the TRT Board of Directors, were sent to the officials of the institution with the signed letter of the General Director of TRT. From past to present, different nomenclatures have been used in general broadcasting plans for programs related to religious broadcasting. In 1977 and 1980, the programs were called Religion and Morality; in 1981, Religion, Morality, and Philosophy; in 1982 and 1983, Religion and Morality; in 1984 and 1988, Religion, Morality and Moral; and in 1990, Religion and Moral. Especially from 1991 to 2004, the name "Religion and Morality" was preferred. Similarly, there are quantitative differences in the number of principles that define the boundaries of these programs. In 1977 and 1980, seven, in 1981, eleven, between 1982 and 1984, eight, in 1985, nine, between 1986 and 1988, three, between 1986 and 1988, four, between 1990 and 1990, and between 1991 and 2004, 15 to 18 items were identified as principles of religious programs (see Appendix). Since 2004, TRT has transformed the aforementioned general broadcasting plans into institution-specific broadcasts. For this reason, access to general broadcasting plans after 2004 has not been possible. When these principles were analyzed into themes according to two categories, it was found that there were "reductive references" and "exclusionary references".

5.5.1 Reductive References

The results of analyzing 22 TRT general broadcast plans reveal that secularism and a secular worldview are referenced to a significant extent, indicating that they are among the fundamental principles guiding religious programs. In addition to being mentioned in the first general broadcasting plan in 1972, secularism or a secular worldview has constituted one of the primary references in TRT's broadcasting principles regarding religious programs for a long time, between 1977 and 2004. The principle of secularism was expressed with definitions such as "essential for national integrity" and "indispensable for national integrity", and it was requested to explain and emphasize in religious programs that "religion and state affairs should be kept separate from each other" and that "secularism has nothing to do with irreligion".

In the broadcasting plans between 1991 and 2004, the first principle was as follows (Table 5.2):

> Programs will primarily be made in accordance with the principles of our Constitution, secularism, freedom of religion and conscience, Atatürk's principles and revolutions, TRT Broadcasting Principles, Annual General Broadcasting Plans, Annual Program Production and Implementation Instructions, strengthening our national unity and integrity, oriented towards life, in accordance with the understanding of contemporary civilization and scientific thought.

Between 1991 and 2004, these statements remained the first and unchanging article of the broadcasting principles for religious programs.

Broadcasting plans called for explaining that religion is not an obstacle to social, cultural, and economic progress. At the same rate, conveying Islam based on authentic sources was a reference in general broadcasting plans. This can be considered as a reflection of a process in which religion was associated with "backwardness" in Türkiye.

In TRT's general broadcasting plans, verses from the Qur'an and the words and behaviors of prophets and religious elders were requested to be explained. In 1982, it was requested that "the principles of Turkish-Islamic morality should be explained and the exemplary behaviors of prophets and religious elders on these issues should be

Table 5.2 Reducing references

Theme	Number	Ratio
Laicism/secular worldview	21	95,5
Social/national unity and solidarity	20	90,9
Social, cultural, and economic progress	19	86,4
Explanation by going to real sources	19	86,4
Humanistic values (love, tolerance, respect, etc.)	18	81,8
Rationality/scientific thinking	15	68,2
Freedom of religion and conscience	14	63,6
Kemalism / Atatürk's principles and reforms	14	63,6
Sayings of the Prophet and religious leaders	12	54,5
Children's level of understanding and comprehension / and strengthening their sense of religion	12	54,5
Associating with current issues	12	54,5
Adaptation to the social structure of society	11	50,0
Contributions of religion to individual development (success, creativity, encouragement to goodness, etc.)	11	50,0
Contemporary understanding of civilization	11	50,0
Contributions of Turks to Islam	6	27,3
Citizenship rights, duties, and responsibilities	3	13,6
Gender equality in education	1	4,5

explained". In contrast, between 1992 and 2004, it was deemed necessary that "in the programs, verses, hadiths and sayings of religious elders explaining the importance of unity and solidarity, brotherhood, love, respect, cooperation and solidarity should be given in a striking arrangement in spotlights, and the element of respect for human rights should be emphasized".

In TRT's religious programs, it is seen that the level of understanding and comprehension of children is given importance. It was requested that topics that would strengthen children's sense of religion be emphasized, and elements that would attract children's interest be conveyed in religious programs. Between 1990 and 2004, the need to create content for children was reflected in the general broadcasting plans as a key principle of broadcasting.

In TRT, which primarily develops its own religious and ethical programs in-house, the details of the process to be followed in the event of purchasing a program from abroad are outlined in the general broadcasting plans. Accordingly, the article "Images and segments that may be included in Religion and Ethics Programs purchased from abroad and that are contrary to the social structure, customs and traditions of Turkish society will be removed" remained in place between 1991 and 2004, albeit with partial changes in wording. Thus, the principle of a religion and ethics program compatible with Türkiye's social structure was adopted.

Between 1977 and 1983, the "harmony of reason and faith" in Islam was emphasized. In addition, in the first article of the general broadcasting plans between 1991 and 2004, the need for religious programming "in accordance with scientific thought" was emphasized. In this connection, "freedom of religion and conscience" was another reference that was emphasized, especially between 1980 and 1981, 1988, and 1991–2004.

In addition to the emphasis on laicism and secular worldview, the article "The structure of society will be built on common values and qualities inspired by our history and the basic philosophy based on the Kemalist view" in the 1984–1985 general broadcasting plans is noteworthy among the broadcasting principles of religious programs. The need to produce religious programs in accordance with Atatürk's principles and reforms was again emphasized in the first article of the general broadcasting plans between 1991 and 2004.

One of the other issues emphasized in the general broadcasting plans is that religious issues should be explained by linking them to current developments. Thus, it is understood that an attempt is made to establish a connection between religion and current social issues. It is also mentioned in the plans that religion has not only social dimensions, but also that religious issues should be utilized for individual development.

It is observed that references to the "understanding of contemporary civilization" were made in general broadcasting plans, especially between 1991 and 2004. When this situation is evaluated in light of references such as rationalism, secularism, and scientific thought, it can be said that Türkiye's modernization tendencies are reflected in general broadcasting plans. The desire to explain the "contributions of the Turks to Islam" in religious programs can be found in the general broadcasting plans of the 1980s. Within this framework, it is evident that the policies of the "Turkish-Islamic

Synthesis" formed the basis for TRT's general broadcasting plans. Additionally, it is noted that the rights, duties, and responsibilities of citizens were requested to be explained in religious programs, which were also compiled in the 1980s.

5.5.2 *Exclusionary References*

In TRT's general broadcasting plans, there are also "exclusionary references" that are emphasized and have negative connotations, in other words. The principle that religious feelings should not be offended or that elements that may lead to religious abuse should be avoided is the most frequently emphasized in religious programs. This principled stance was expressed between 1983 and 1985 and reiterated continuously from 1991 to 2004, with the phrase "absolutely" used to emphasize it. The second point is that religious programs should not be presented in a manner that evokes political movements. These two issues were reflected in the general broadcasting plans with the following sentences (Table 5.3):

> In these broadcasts, there shall be no appeals to political movements, and approaches that offend religious feelings or enable the abuse of religion shall be strictly avoided.

As with the emphasis on rationality, scientism, and scientific thought in reductive references, general broadcasting plans often mention that religious programs should be conducted in a manner that does not contradict reason, logic, and scientific thought.

In 2003–2004, among the principles of religious programming, the following article was included: "Within the scope of the fight against destructive, separatist, reactionary organizations and sects within our country through broadcasting; Islam will be explained in a manner in accordance with its true sources, and rational, striking, impressive and informative programs will be included". This is closely related to Türkiye's "reactionary" discourse from the 1990s to the early 2000s. In the 1977–1983 period, it is observed that the statement "Based on the view that Islam is

Table 5.3 Exclusionary references

Theme	Number	Ratio
Offending religious feelings or religious abuse	14	63,6
Evoking political movements	11	40,9
Contrary to reason/ logic/and science	9	22,7
Superstition and falsehood	5	13,6
Criticizing any religion or sect	3	9,1
Irtica/ irtica organizations	2	9,1
Cults	2	9,1
Bigotry	2	9,1
Non-formal religious education	1	4,5

one of the most advanced religions, bigotry, superstitions, unscientific and irrational attitudes and behaviors will be avoided and the unifying principles of Islam and the principles of the Islamic religion will be used to elevate the country in economic, social and cultural terms" was included. The statements that no religion or sect should be criticized, that bigotry should be avoided, and that unauthorized or secret religious education can lead to harmful consequences are also excluded from references in the general publication plans, albeit at a quantitatively low level.

5.6 Conclusion

It is understood that TRT's religious program principles include laicism/secularism, social/national unity and integrity, the importance Islam attaches to social, cultural, and economic progress, and humanist values such as love, respect, and tolerance. In addition, the design of religious programs in accordance with science, modern civilization, Atatürk's principles and reforms, freedom of religion and conscience, and social harmony is reflected in the broadcasting policy documents. In addition, the issues of religious abuse and the absence of political connotations in religious issues were reflected in the principles of religious programs. In addition, it was requested that broadcasts should not be made in violation of "reason, logic, science, and scientific thought", thus displaying a positivist approach. In addition, it was requested that the fight against reaction and sects be carried out through religious programs. In addition, the presentation of a religion free from superstition, falsehood, and bigotry was reflected in the principles of religious programs, and it was noted that no religion or sect should be criticized, and the drawbacks of unofficial religious education should be acknowledged. Thus, especially between 1977 and 2004, a religious program approach compatible with the positivist, secular world was adopted in broadcasting principles.

For a long time, TRT, as Çelenk puts it, "functioned as one of the essential elements of the official modernization project rather than its supporter" (2005, p. 137). The principles of TRT's religious programs also dictated that religion be presented with defined boundaries, and thus, as Mete Çamdereli aptly puts it, "a restricted Islam" (2018, p. 38) emerged.

There are also legal, technical, and sociological contexts that influence the determination of media policies. In this study, the context of limited Islam is shown in government policies. Governments expected the management they appointed to broadcast in line with their policies, and thus political actors became a dominant element in the history of religious programs. The republican elites' desire to design a secular or laicist society in Türkiye seems to be directly reflected in TRT's broadcasting principles regarding religious programs.

Appendix: Name Given to Religious Programs

Year	Common name given to programs	Number of articles of principles
1977	Religion and Ethics	7
1980	Religion and Ethics	7
1981	Religion, Ethics, and Philosophy	11
1982	Religion and Ethics	8
1983	Religion and Ethics	8
1984	Religion, Ethics, and Morality	8
1985	Religion, Ethics, and Morality	9
1986	Religion, Ethics, and Morality	3
1987	Religion, Ethics, and Morality	3
1988	Religion, Ethics, and Morality	3
1990	Religion and Moral	4
1991	Religion and Ethics	15
1992	Religion and Ethics	15
1993	Religion and Ethics	16
1995	Religion and Ethics	16
1996	Religion and Ethics	16
1998–1999	Religion and Ethics	17
1999–2000	Religion and Ethics	17
2001	Religion and Ethics	17
2002	Religion and Ethics	18
2003	Religion and Ethics	17
2004	Religion and Ethics	17

References

Akıllıoğlu, S., Aziz, A., Çolakoğlu, N., Dağlı, N., Görün, N., Bayık, H., Saydamer, H., & Tanık, M. (1990). *Dünden bugüne radyo-televizyon (1927–1990)*. Ajans-Türk Matbaacılık Sanayii A.Ş.

Aktay, Y. (2000). Cumhuriyet döneminde din politikaları ve din istismarı. *İslâmiyât, 3*(3), 37–49.

Aktay, Y. (2017). *İslâm ve sekülerleşmenin kaynakları*. Tezkire Yayınları.

Akyüz, İ. (2016). *Adalet ve kalkınma partisi'nin din politikaları (Recep Tayyip Erdoğan Dönemi)* [Doctoral Dissertation]. Sakarya Üniversitesi Sosyal Bilimler Enstitüsü.

Altıkulaç, T. (2016). *Zorlukları aşarken*. TDV Yayın Matbaacılık.

Arpacı, I. (2018). Türkiye'nin din politikaları. In I. Arpacı & O. Ağır (Eds.), *Türkiye'de Devlet Politikaları* (pp. 25–38). Nobel Yayınları.

Ateş, S. (2018). *Türkiye'de din politikaları ve din-siyaset ilişkisi*. Ötüken Yayınları.

Bilis, A. E. (2019). *Tarihsel eksende oksidentalist söylem ve dini yönelimli medyanın rolü*. Kriter Yayınevi.
Canatan, K. (1997). *Din ve laiklik*. İnsan Yayınları.
Çamdereli, M. (2018). *Din ekranda nasıl durur? Medyada dinin popüler temsili*. Ketebe Yayınları.
Çelenk, S. (2005). *Televizyon, temsil, kültür 90'lı yıllarda sosyokültürel iklim ve televizyon içerikleri*. Ütopya Yayınevi.
Çiftçigüzeli, M. C. (2014). *Demokrasimizin perde arkası Nevzat Yalçıntaş'ın yürüyüş yolu yazılmayan anılar*. Doğan Kitap.
Çolak, Y. (2017). *Türkiye'de kültürel iktidarın kuruluşu 1923–1945*. Liberte Yayınları.
Çongur, R. (1981). TRT ve dinî yayınlar. *Millî Eğitim ve Din Hayatı*, 262–285.
Çuhadar, M. (2019). Türkiye'de kamu hizmeti yayıncılığı açısından dinî temalı tv programları ve Diyanet tv program türleri üzerine bir inceleme. *Medya ve Din Araştırmaları Dergisi (MEDİAD), 2*(2), 237–266.
Dedeoğlu, T. (2019). *Şimdi onlar manşet*. Gazeteciler Cemiyeti.
Dereli, M. D. (2023). Dünü-bugünü-yarını ve tartışmalı alanları bağlamında Türkiye'de medya ve din. In İ. Aycan, E. Gözeler, & N. Yazar (Ed.), *Cumhuriyet'in 100. yılında Türkiye'de Dini Hayat* (ss. 333–356). Ankara Üniversitesi Yayınları.
Diriklik, S. (1995a). *Fleşbek Türk sinema-TV'sinde İslâmi endişeler ve çizgi dışı oluşumlar* (Vol. 1). Söğüt Ofset.
Diriklik, S. (1995b). *Fleşbek Türk sinema-TV'sinde İslâmi endişeler ve çizgi dışı oluşumlar* (Vol. 2). Söğüt Ofset.
Diyanet. (1984, Kasım). TV'deki dini yayınlar üzerine. *Diyanet Gazetesi*, 2.
Erkal, K. (2022). *Medya ve siyaset bağlamında İslam referanslı muhafazakar siyasal kitlenin medyayı dönüştürme politikaları* [Doctoral Dissertation]. İstanbul Üniversitesi Sosyal Bilimler Enstitüsü.
Ertit, V. (2019). *Sekülerleşme teorisi*. Liberte Yayınları.
Göle, N. (1998). Türkiye'de laiklik ve İslamiyet: Elitlerin ve karşı elitlerin oluşumu. *Yeni Türkiye (Cumhuriyet Özel Sayısı), 3 (Sosyal Değerlendirme)* (pp. 23–24), 1601–1610.
Göle, N. (2013). Modernist kamusal alan ve İslami ahlak. In *İslam'ın Yeni Kamusal Yüzleri* (4th edition, pp. 19–40). Metis Yayınları.
Karataş, Ş. (1978). *TRT kavgası*. Emek Matbaacılık ve İlancılık Ltd. Şti.
Komisyon. (1984). *V. Beş Yıllık Kalkınma Planı Özel İhtisas Komisyonu Raporu: Milli Kültür*. T.C. Başbakanlık Devlet Planlama Teşkilatı. https://www.sbb.gov.tr/wp-content/uploads/2018/11/5-MilliKultur_OIK300.pdf
Öz, A. (2020). Millî görüş hareketi: Millî Nizam ve Millî Selamet partileri. In T. Bora & A. Yanık (Eds.), *Türkiye'nin 1970'li Yılları* (pp. 469–494). İletişim Yayınları.
Özel Radyo ve Televizyon Kuruluşlarının Eğitim, Kültür, Türk Halk Müziği ve Türk Sanat Müziği Programlarında Yer Vermeleri Gerekli Yayın Türleri ve Oranlarına Ait Esaslar Hakkında Yönetmelik (1995).
Öztan, G. G. (2020). I. Milliyetçi cephe iktidarinda devletin zor ve ideolojik aygıtlarinin yapılandırılması (1975–1977). In T. Bora & A. Yanık (Ed.), *Türkiye'nin 1970'li Yılları* (pp. 415–440). İletişim Yayınları.
Subaşı, N. (2005). *Ara dönem din politikaları*. Küre Yayınları.
Şimşek, Ş. (2020). *Din ve kadastro "dinî alan"ın yeniden düzenlenmesi (1980–1983)*. Mahya Yayıncılık.
Tokgöz, O. (1972). *Türkiye ve Ortadoğu ülkelerinde radyo-televizyon sistemleri (mukayeseli bir araştırma)*. Ankara Üniversitesi Siyasal Bilgiler Fakültesi Yayınları.
TRT. (1972). *TRT program planlama ilke ve amaçları*. TRT Basılı Yayınlar Müdürlüğü Yayınları No: 40.
TRT. (1976). *1977 yılı genel yayın planı*. TRT Program Planlama Dairesi Başkanlığı.
TRT. (1978). *1979 yılı genel yayın planı*. TRT Genel Sekreterlik Basılı Yayınlar ve Kitaplık Müdürlüğü.

TRT. (1979). *TRT kurumu 1980 yılı genel yayın planı*. TRT Genel Sekreterlik Basılı Yayınlar Müdürlüğü Yayınları.
TRT. (1980). *1981 yılı genel yayın planı*. TRT Genel Sekreterlik Basılı Yayınlar Müdürlüğü.
TRT. (1981). *1982 genel yayın planı*. TRT Genel Sekreterlik Basılı Yayınlar Müdürlüğü.
TRT. (1982). *TRT-1983 genel yayın planı*. TRT Genel Sekreterlik Basılı Yayınlar Müdürlüğü.
TRT. (1983). *1984 genel yayın planı*. TRT Genel Sekreterlik Basılı Yayınlar Müdürlüğü.
TRT. (1984). *1985 genel yayın plânı*. TRT Basılı Yayınlar Müdürlüğü.
TRT. (1985). *1986 genel yayın plânı*. TRT Basılı Yayınlar Müdürlüğü.
TRT. (1986). *1987 genel yayın plânı*. TRT Basılı Yayınlar Müdürlüğü.
TRT. (1987). *1988 genel yayın plânı*. TRT Basılı Yayınlar Müdürlüğü.
TRT. (1989). *1990 genel yayın plânı*. TRT Basım ve Yayın Müdürlüğü.
TRT. (1990). *1991 genel yayın plânı*. TRT Basım ve Yayın Müdürlüğü.
TRT. (1991). *1992 TRT genel yayın plânı*. TRT Basım ve Yayın Müdürlüğü.
TRT. (1992). *1993 TRT genel yayın plânı*. TRT Basım ve Yayın Müdürlüğü.
TRT. (1994). *1995 TRT genel yayın plânı*. TRT Basım ve Yayın Müdürlüğü.
TRT. (1995). *1996 TRT genel yayın plânı*. TRT Genel Sekreterlik Basım ve Yayın Müdürlüğü.
TRT. (1998). *TRT genel yayın plânı ekim 1998-Ekim 1999*. TRT Yayın Planlama Koordinasyon ve Değerlendirme Dairesi Başkanlığı.
TRT. (1999). *TRT genel yayın plânı ekim 1999-Ekim 2000*. TRT Yayın Planlama Koordinasyon ve Değerlendirme Dairesi Başkanlığı.
TRT. (2000). *2001 TRT genel yayın planı*. TRT Yayın Planlama, Koordinasyon ve Değerlendirme Dairesi Başkanlığı.
TRT. (2001). *Genel yayın plânı 2002*. TRT Yayın Planlama Koordinasyon ve Değerlendirme Dairesi Başkanlığı.
TRT. (2003). *Genel yayın plânı 2003*. TRT Yayın Planlama Koordinasyon ve Değerlendirme Dairesi Başkanlığı.
TRT. (2004). *Genel yayın plânı 2004*. TRT Yayın Planlama Koordinasyon ve Değerlendirme Dairesi Başkanlığı.
TRT. (n.d.). TRT kilometre taşları. *TRT Web Sitesi*. https://www.trt.net.tr/kurumsal/kilometre-taslari
Turam, E. (1994). *Medyanın siyasi hayata etkileri*. İrfan Yayımcılık.
Ural, T. (2008). *Medyatik kuşatma*. Etkin Kitaplar.
Yaman, F. (2019). Türkiye'de muhafazakâr televizyon yayıncılığının doğuşu ve dönüşümü. In L. Sunar (Ed.), *"Bir başka hayata karşı" 1980 Sonrası İslamcı Dergilerde Meseleler, Kavramlar ve İsimler: Vol 3: Kültür, Medya, Yaşam* (pp. 191–232). Konya Büyükşehir Belediyesi Kültür Yayınları.
Yazıcı, M. (2015). *Dinin magazinleştirilmesi: Türk televizyonlarında dinin temsili* [Master's Thesis]. İstanbul Ticaret Üniversitesi Sosyal Bilimler Enstitüsü.

Chapter 6
Is the Family Spell Being Broken? The Secularisation of the Family Concept in Turkish TV Series: The Case of "Aile" Series

Mehmet Birekul and Fatma Eroğlu Genç

6.1 Introduction

The past two centuries can be seen as a turning point in history, where almost all established practices in many areas of human life, such as economic organisation, production methods, transportation and communication facilities, rural and urban living ratios, and technology, have undergone significant transformation. Türkiye's story, however, is somewhat more complex. In addition to global changes, the simultaneous operation of many other parameters within the country has led to profound fractures in the social structure. On the one hand, Türkiye has a devoutly conservative identity that is deeply rooted in its beliefs, while on the other hand, it has undergone top-down modernisation. This situation has led to polarisation between conflicting identities and has fostered a form of debate that is susceptible to manipulation. Rapid urbanisation, which accompanied these processes, is another factor that has had significant and profound effects.

Like all other institutions, the family has been affected by these changes and transformations and continues to be affected. At the present stage, many issues are widely debated, including the institutional existence and necessity of the family, how to interpret the processes of change in the modern era, and the nature of family relationships, roles, and power balances. On the other hand, many issues, such as

M. Birekul (✉)
Department of Sociology, Necmettin Erbakan University, Konya, Türkiye
e-mail: mbirekul@gmail.com

F. Eroğlu Genç
Konya, Türkiye
e-mail: fatimaeroglugenc@gmail.com

M. D. Dereli and M. Eken (eds.), *Turkish Perspectives on Secularization and Media*,
https://doi.org/10.1007/978-3-032-16436-0_6

the rise in the age of first marriage and motherhood,[1] the decline in the number of children,[2] the increase in divorce rates,[3] and the diversification of parenting styles, frequently dominate the agenda as tangible signs that the institution of the family is undergoing significant changes.

One of the leading actors influencing society's views and behaviours regarding the family is the media (Filiz, 2020). Television series, in particular, can be considered one of the most effective media tools in this regard, given their significant social interest and widespread popularity. The Turkish television series industry has grown to become a significant and increasingly influential sector, not only within the country but also across various regions worldwide.[4] According to 2024 data from the Television Viewing Research Anonymous Company (TİAK), the average daily TV viewing time in Turkish households is 6 h and 7 min, with an average of 3 h and 34 min per person in households. Looking at the data in the same report on which programmes people prefer to watch on TV, it can be seen that the most watched programme type is series, with 27.4%. Furthermore, series continue to be watched intensively on digital video platforms after their first broadcast on TV. Last year (2024), 110[5] series were broadcast on TV channels, totalling 3,320 episodes (TİAK, 2025).

It is known that series have a function of disseminating particular worldviews. The narratives in series influence people's daily lives, their understanding of life, their plans, and their individual and social preferences. In this respect, it can be said that series recreate reality through fiction, shape society, guide perceptions, and engage in a form of cultural building activity (Külekçi, 2024; Özsoy et al., 2022; Yılmazkol, 2025). The script, the selection of actors, how characters are represented, which actor is chosen for which role, the emotions that viewers are drawn into through the narrative, and the stance taken on moral dilemmas are just some of the many contexts that reveal the values and meanings defended and legitimised in series as reflected to the viewer. At this point, the way an issue is addressed on screen should be seen as a transformative element with concrete social implications.

The fact that series, known to be fictional, can persuade people to spend long hours in front of the screen is not only because they are leisure activities intended for entertainment. The stories in the series create an escape from the troubles in people's lives, offering an alternative universe and providing them with temporary peace of mind. Viewers believe that they experience, albeit virtually, many situations they cannot experience in their own lives (such as wealth, luxury consumption, love, sexuality, power, violence) and pleasures and delights they cannot attain through series (Pekdemir & Yılmaz, 2022; Yılmaz & Yılmaz, 2012). Given that episodes

---

[1] According to 2024 TURKSTAT data, the average age at first marriage for women is 25.8, while for men it is 28.3 (*TÜİK*, 2025a).

[2] According to 2024 TURKSTAT data, the total fertility rate in Türkiye is 1.48 (*TÜİK*, 2025b).

[3] According to 2024 TURKSTAT data, the crude divorce rate has increased to 2.19 per thousand (*TÜİK*, 2025c).

[4] It is known that Türkiye is the third-largest exporter of TV series in the world after the United States and the United Kingdom. Worldwide, 700 million people watch Turkish TV series, and these series are exported to 170 countries (Akgün, 2024; *The Economist*, 2024).

[5] 57 of these were published for the first time.

can last up to two hours and are broadcast weekly, series can be considered more impactful programmes compared to other media content. Viewers sometimes watch these programmes every week for years, and therefore develop deep connections with the characters and the story. According to data from Özsoy and colleagues' extensive field research examining the effects of Turkish TV series on family structure, the majority of society believes that TV series have an impact on family structure. The predominant view is that TV series have both positive and negative effects. The details of the research reveal that series affect relationships between spouses, relationships between siblings, parent–child relationships, and relationships within one's social circle, such as those with relatives, neighbours, and work colleagues (Özsoy et al., 2022). This research not only demonstrates that series possess a significant guiding power and potential over human behaviour but also shows that a large portion of the audience is aware of this effect.

Considering the range of themes in television series, it can be observed that they are often shaped around topics such as romance, family, marriage, intra-familial problems, home, crime, the mafia, politics, and poverty versus wealth (Çelik & Hof, 2020). In Türkiye in recent years, series whose scripts are constructed upon intra-familial relations and conflicts have been consumed quite intensively. At this point, it may be thought that productions seen to arouse audience interest are prioritised and that many similar works are produced. Given that dozens of series are released every year, writing scripts for series that last for hours is an arduous and labour-intensive task. It can be stated that screenwriters and producers tend to prefer storylines that are amenable to extension as a way of avoiding the difficulty of frequently producing original scripts.

Beyond our research on family narratives in Turkish series, this topic has been the subject of numerous other academic studies. The article "*Televizyon Dizilerinde Aile Temsilleri: Karşılaştırmalı Bir Analiz*" by Çelik discusses family representations in the series *Süper Baba* and *Yasak Elma* (N. Çelik, 2020). Çetin and Külekçi, on the other hand, discuss *Kızılcık Şerbeti* in their articles, which claim to address the conflict between conservative and secular worldviews as reflected in the family (Çetin, 2023; Külekçi, 2024). Pekdemir and Yılmaz examine the series *Yasak Elma*; İhtiyar, *Gönül Dağı,* and *Yalı Çapkını*; Bal and Parlayandemir examine the series *İstanbullu Gelin, Doğduğun Ev Kaderindir, Kırmızı Oda, Masumlar Apartmanı,* and *Çöp Adam*, all written by Gülseren Budayıcıoğlu. (Bal & Parlayandemir, 2023; İhtiyar, 2024; Pekdemir & Yılmaz, 2022). While Koçak's thesis examines the image of the family in series watched by high school students from the perspective of the city of Sakarya, Yılmaz, and colleagues examine the representation of the family in the web-based films and series from the perspective of the city of Kahramanmaraş in their articles (Koçak, 2022; Yılmaz et al., 2023). These academic studies make significant contributions to the discussion of the issue. However, the accumulated body of work still appears to have a somewhat limited scope in relation to the universe of Turkish series.

Our study is structured around the problem of how the family issue is interpreted and represented in the series *Aile*, which addresses the family institution chiefly by opening it to debate through conflicts and problem areas, and which claims are sought to be substantiated in this series. In our study, the family narrative in Turkish series is discussed using a qualitative method through the series entitled "Aile", selected by purposive sampling. Purposive sampling is a qualitative technique used particularly to examine exceptional cases and is generally employed in exploratory research. It does not aim to reach the average, make generalisations, or represent the population; instead, the case in which the discussion can be intensified is deliberately selected (Neuman, 2017).

The series Aile was selected because it debates the family as an institution with distinct theses and explicit judgements, and at times advances assertive judgements with didactic expressions. The direct designation of the series as "Aile" can also be regarded as an indication that the debate is conducted factually on the institution of the family. From the opening scene onwards, sequences, dialogues, and events that frequently invite the audience to reflect on the institution of the family occupy a substantial place in the series. Screenwriter Hakan Bonomo stated in an interview that the family can be a place where unconditional and balanced love is learnt. However, it can also turn into a nest of psychosis, and this dark face leaves marks on the individual that are difficult to repair. Bonomo said he wrote the series with a sense of responsibility in order to produce this awareness. According to him, millions of people in society are subjected to verbal, physical, sexual, emotional, or economic violence by their families under the guise of love (Gürer, 2024). These remarks suggest that the series aims to examine the Turkish family structure critically. The events in the series are not presented as fiction detached from society; on the contrary, they are promoted as a mirror of the social structure. The participation of highly popular artists in Türkiye in Aile and its broadcast on a widely watched TV channel have positively affected its viewership. The first episode ranked fourth in the total audience category and first among the AB group audience (Habertürk, 2023). The AB group audience denotes a more educated viewer segment. It may be considered that the series's status as a production with certain theses and claims contributed to attracting greater attention from this group of viewers. Notably, the scenes selected in the initial promotional trailers released prior to the broadcast contained important clues regarding these theses. For all these reasons, the series Aile was chosen because it would constitute a more suitable sample for our research. Within this scope, the first five episodes of the thirty-episode series were examined, and data were collected from these episodes.

In the process of analysing the data, the technique of discourse analysis was employed. Discourse analysis is a qualitative practice that aims to critically examine discourse, conducting analysis through theoretical formulations, and taking into account the grammatical features of discourse within its complex structure (Aziz, 2010, p. 137). That is to say, it does not suffice to focus solely on the text of the discourse and examine it only from formal aspects. Discourses encompass more than the formal examination of texts, and for them to be analysed comprehensively, other factors must also be included in the analysis. At this point, critical discourse analysis extends beyond the formal structure of the text, placing the sociological, psychological, and anthropological contexts that constitute the discourse at the centre of the analysis (Van Dijk, 2009). In doing so, it focuses on deciphering matters such as the asymmetry among those who produce the discourse, the forms of discourse, and how texts are produced, distributed, and consumed (Norman, 1995). In this respect, the analysis aims to reveal many social processes and, by deconstruction, to interrogate the underlying factors.

Texts are not the only things that constitute discourse. Speech, photographs, clothing, cartoons, letters, stories, poems, plays, menus, reports, announcements, checks, prescriptions, labels, warranties, sermons, tickets, emails, and CVs are examples of various forms of discourse (Çakır, 2014). In other words, not only texts composed of sounds, words, or letters, but also factors such as images, tone of voice, size, weight, and colour can be analysed as discourse. In this respect, any cultural product created by human beings can be regarded as discourse and can be analysed.

The selection of discourse analysis as the analytical method was preferred because it allows for a more analytical interrogation of a discourse that promises, from the outset, to deliver a target message to the viewer. At this point, it was assessed that a critical approach would be more beneficial for conducting deconstruction. During the analysis process, numerous factors were taken into account, including the dialogues, the way events unfold in the story, the representation of characters, and the settings employed. The paths by which the message presented in the series was delivered and how the audience was persuaded of the said messages were traced.

6.2 The Cinema in Türkiye from Past to Present and Representation of the Family in Series

In Türkiye, the representation of the family in fictional screen productions has followed a parallel trajectory with the manner in which the family has been discussed throughout history. In the pre-1980s period, the family institution was portrayed more positively on screen. During this period, a more traditional representation of the family was frequently seen in films, featuring a warm family home and family unity, as well as the profile of the self-sacrificing and happy woman (Çetin, 2023; Yağbasan & Ateş, 2018). For example, in his study examining 16 Turkish films shot between 1960 and 1965, Yeşildal points out that Turkish cinema favoured scenarios in which chaste women were glorified, women who destroyed families were punished and discredited. The family regained its integrity with the disappearance of these women (Yeşildal, 2010). Throughout the 1960s and 1970s, films featuring child protagonists also portrayed the family in a very positive light.[6] Series such as *Sezercik, Ayşecik,* and *Ömercik*, which were broadcast during this period, exemplify this trend (Doğan, 2024).

The first television series in Türkiye began in 1974, six years after television broadcasting started in the country, with the series *Kaynanalar*. The series focused on Nuri Kantar, a wealthy man who had migrated to the big city, and his family's

[6] At this point, it can be said that children are the strongest indicator representing the family on screen, not only in movies and TV series but also in advertisements (Arora, 2024; Özer, 1997).

efforts to preserve their traditions while adapting to city life. Their in-laws, Timur and Tijen Hakmen, represented a modern urban family. The series dealt with the differences between these two families in a comedic style. TRT's series adventure continued a year later in 1975 with *Aşk-ı Memnu*, a series adapted from Halit Ziya Uşaklıgil's novel. *Aşk-ı Memnu* is a story about a young woman who, despite being married, has a forbidden love affair with a young man, who is a distant relative of her husband, and ultimately commits suicide. As a production that explores marriage, loyalty, and illicit relationships, Aşk-ı Memnu can also be described as family-themed in the broadest sense (TRT Arşiv YouTube, 2022; TRT Nostalji YouTube, 2025).

Following the 1980s, numerous social, cultural, and political changes occurred both globally and in Türkiye, with their reflections evident in cinema and television series. During this period, problems arising from modernisation and urbanisation were increasingly discussed on screen, and different thematic explorations emerged in this context (Evren Yüksel, 2013). Despite this, the family is still portrayed in series and films as a safe, protective, unifying, and empowering structure.[7] The institution of the family is glorified, presented as a structure that must be protected, and the unity and solidarity within the family are emphasised as the provider of social order (Evren Yüksel, 2013; Yağbasan & Ateş, 2018; Yeşildal, 2010).

With the opening of private television stations in 1990, the variety and number of series increased further (Taşdelen, 2023). At this point, a clear distinction exists between public and private channels in the representation of the family in TV series (İhtiyar, 2024). Understandably, the state's general approach is to maintain the prestige of the family institution, as a strong and prestigious understanding of family contributes most significantly to the maintenance of social order. In this context, the following programmes broadcast on TRT are noteworthy*: Kartallar Yüksek Uçar (1984), Küçük Ağa (1984), Kuruntu Ailesi (1985–1990), Perihan Abla (1986–1988), Uğurlugiller (1988–1991), Bizimkiler (1989–2002), Geçmiş Bahar Mimozaları (1989), Yazlıkçılar (1993–1998), Ferhunde Hanımlar (1993–1999), Şaşıfelek Çıkmazı (1996–1998), Yedi Numara (2000–2003), Bizim Evin Halleri (2000–2006), Yeditepe İstanbul (2001–2002)* are series that portray the family in a highly positive light. The series broadcast on private channels other than TRT, such as *Mahallenin Muhtarları (1992–2002), Süper Baba (1993–1997), Çiçek Taksi (1995–2003), Bizim Ev (1996–1998), İkinci Bahar (1998–2001), Deli Yürek (1998–2002), Ekmek Teknesi (2002–2005),* are similar in style. In these series, the average Anatolian person lives in modest conditions, not in luxury and wealth. Not all families are idealised in the same way, but ultimately, the family structure is depicted as protecting and caring for its members. The family also transforms into a neighbourhood solidarity within a broader social framework. These series do not limit themselves to small families consisting of parents and children; elements such as neighbours, residents, shopkeepers, and relatives are also included in the story. While

[7] Undoubtedly, it is impossible to make a generalization. During this period, it is possible to encounter films that express dissenting voices, considering that feminism, as an ideology that strongly criticized the family, also expanded its discourse in Türkiye. For example, the film *Kadının Adı Yok*, adapted from the novel of the same name written by Duygu Asena and featuring an anti-family script from an ideological perspective, was released in 1988.

warm and intimate relationships are established around the nuclear family structure, a broad, love-based, close, sincere, and friendly environment is also created with the surrounding elements (Yılmazkol, 2025). The scripts of these series generally do not feature exaggerated displays of luxury and consumption alongside elements such as corrupt family relationships, infidelity, betrayal, and intrigue. Instead, the family is portrayed in a more positive light.

According to Önk, who studied Turkish series after 2000, series broadcast during that period depicted the decline of the family's former importance as a source of many societal problems and defended the idea that problems could be overcome through family solidarity. For example, character stereotypes such as the emotionally distant father, the grumpy elderly patient, and the know-it-all child are featured as a richness in these series. In this context, although the nuclear family model is becoming increasingly prevalent, the extended family is still highly valued. However, the same study also notes that, although spiritual values (such as love and family) are presented as superior to material values in the series of this period, money is actually shown as the solution to many problems, and resorting to unethical means to achieve material gain is normalised. (Önk, 2011).

In recent years, it has become evident that productions blending popular culture with psychology-based themes, particularly those focusing on individual dramas influenced by family, are being widely produced in our country (Bal & Parlayandemir, 2023; Taşdelen, 2023). *İstanbullu Gelin (2017–2019), Yasak Elma (2018–2023), Kızılcık Şerbeti (2022-), Hayat Şarkısı (2016–2017), Yalı Çapkını (2022–2025), Camdaki Kız (2021–2023), Kırmızı Oda (2020–2022), Sadakatsiz (2020–2022), Zalim İstanbul (2019–2020), Masumlar Apartmanı (2020–2022), Doğduğun Ev Kaderindir (2019–2021)* are a list of productions that focus on family relationships. These series feature numerous non-marital relationships that are normalised, the widespread use of distorted relationships such as two siblings being with the same person, the glorification of extremely luxurious and extravagant lifestyles, and frequent scenarios involving betrayal, intrigue, deception, and conflicts of interest. (Koçak, 2022; Pekdemir & Yılmaz, 2022; Yılmaz et al., 2023).

6.3 An Interesting Example of Family Representation in Turkish Series: The Series "Aile"

Aile is a Turkish television series written by Hakan Bonomo and directed by Ahmet Katıksız and Gökçen Usta, which premiered on Show TV on March 7, 2023. The series ran for two seasons, with the thirtieth and final episode airing on January 30 2024. Kıvanç Tatlıtuğ and Serenay Sarıkaya played the lead roles; The cast also includes Musa Uzunlar, Levent Ülgen, Ayda Aksel, Emel Göksu, Nur Sürer, Nejat İşler, Canan Ergüder, Selin Şekerci, Umutcan Ütebay, and Yüsra Geyik (Show TV, 2025). In the series *Aile*, where Kıvanç Tatlıtuğ plays Aslan and Serenay Sarıkaya plays Devin, the turbulent relationship between Aslan and Devin, which continues through marriage, forms the basis of the plot. The effects of both families on this relationship, the problems the characters face with both families, the deadlocks, and the points of tension are highlighted and addressed.

It is evident that the series has some powerful theses about the institution of the family itself, and these theses are conveyed within the story, sometimes directly and sometimes through the characters' language. In fact, the choice of the series name *Aile* is a sign that the discussion is primarily based on the phenomenon of family. The theses about the family that the series wants to convey to the audience have been evaluated under two main headings: the construction of the characters and aphorisms about the family.

6.3.1 Character Construction

The way the characters are constructed in the series *"Aile"* informs the audience of potential conflicts from the very first episode and provides an idea of the problems that will arise. The main characters of the series, Devin and Aslan, are portrayed as healthy adults trying to cope with problems in their families. However, most of the supporting characters around them are individuals with psychological problems. Devin's mother, Neşe, is a woman with bipolar disorder who is addicted to alcohol and shopping. Her sister Yağmur is a woman who has borderline personality disorder, is drug-dependent, is involved in fights, has a history of suicide attempts, and has engaged in sexual relations for money. Devin's father, Ergun, introduced as a narcissist, is a paediatrician who abandoned his wife and children many years ago and has not been involved in their lives. He has remarried and does not want to deal with the problems of his daughters from his previous marriage, excluding them from his life. The family established by Devin's mother and father has brought with it a chain of highly problematic relationships. The marriage ended due to incompatibility between the spouses. In this crisis environment, the children did not receive the support and attention expected from their families. His parents' divorce, his father's indifference, and his mother's mental illness forced Devin, from an early age, to parent his mother and sister and to compensate for the mistakes they made in life. This has led him to adopt a very harsh attitude towards his father.

When Aslan's family is considered, one encounters a structure exhibiting similar problems. The father, Yusuf Soykan, is a businessman who died by suicide. The mother, Hülya Soykan, has an obsessive need to control her children and can act without regard for any moral principle in order to achieve this. In particular, she employs every underhanded method to control the women who enter her son Aslan's life. Another figure in the family, Aslan's elder brother Cihan, has severe psychiatric disorders. He is involved in illegal activities, is alcohol-dependent, and is a dangerous figure. He envies his brother Aslan and, as an extension of this, attempts to form relationships with the women with whom Aslan is involved. Although the mother, Hülya, appears to criticise her son, Cihan, on this matter, she covertly steers him towards these behaviours herself and uses him in line with her own objectives. His sister Leyla was forced into an unwanted marriage by her mother. She is a person with alcohol use disorder who her husband constantly cheats on, is dissatisfied with her life, and takes heavy psychological medication. Aslan's youngest sister, Ceylan, is a television-addicted young girl who experiences deep generational conflicts with her mother. Aslan's brother-in-law, Leyla's husband Tolga, lives with them in the Soykan family home. Tolga, who has a bland, characterless personality, cheats on his wife. Leyla and Tolga's son, Kaya, who is about five years old, is unable to speak due to the intense conflict within the family. The oldest member of the family, Aslan's grandmother Seher, has Alzheimer's disease and refuses to accept her son's death. Aslan's uncle İbrahim Soykan is one of the family's greatest enemies. He attacks his brother's family in various ways, such as obstructing their economic activities, threatening them, blackmailing them, and injuring family members with weapons. At the same time, he has a long-standing interest in his brother's wife, Hülya. The Soykan family consists of individuals involved in crime, reminiscent of a mafia network. The family has been involved in many different types of crimes, such as murder, assault, blackmail, threats, kidnapping, and money laundering. They possess indicators of wealth, such as houses, cars, boats, luxury venues, and accessories; they employ numerous personnel, including servants, chauffeurs, and bodyguards.

The way the characters are constructed in the series creates a highly complex equation, and the script addresses the conflicts between characters, almost all of whom have problematic psychological attitudes, in the context of criticising the institution of the family. However, the personal profiles of individuals play a central role in the emergence of problems. People with these characteristics certainly experience problems not only within the family but also in all their social interactions. In other words, these same individuals have the potential to experience problems in their social relationships in other environments, such as at work or with a neighbour. Although the series conveys the message that the family institution itself produces problematic characters, it denies the possibility that problematic characters can harm families. At this point, it takes an approach that defends the individual against the family.

Conflicts in the *Aile* series generally take place in the large mansion where the Soykan family resides. The mansion is a spacious living area. Ten people live there as family members, excluding the staff. Four generations live together in the mansion. Grandmother Reyhan Hanım, mother Hülya Hanım, eldest daughter Leyla, and her children, Zeyno and Kaya, represent four generations. The choice of an extended family provides fertile ground for the plot, reflecting both generational conflicts and the complex, intertwined relationships within the family. At the same time, it ensures the formation of a context in which the nuclear family is formulated as a solution to the extended family. The extended family is defined as a structure that, despite the unity of all family members, is corrupt, problematic, no longer applicable in terms of its meaning and values, and unsuitable for raising children.

In the series, the dining table, as the most common symbol of the family's togetherness during the day, has also been used as an important place of encounter and conflict. The frequently featured dining table dialogues are important throughout the story. Many events, such as revenges, verbal jabs, and cornering the interlocutor, take place at the dining table. The first scene of the series also begins with a dialogue around a large dining table. The lady of the house, Hülya Soykan, has called a craftsman to repair the wooden table where the family eats together. She rejects the craftsman's suggestion that the table is beyond repair, that treating it with chemicals will not solve the problem, and that it needs to be replaced, reminding him of the table's sentimental value. At this point, it can be said that the table, which is said to need replacing because it is rotten, symbolises the old family structure as a metaphor.

In the same scene, plaques with the names of family members are visible on the backs of the chairs around the table. In other words, everyone has their own chair and a designated place to sit. This narrative highlights the existence of established norms and unchanging customs within the Soykan family. Everyone's place is fixed and unchangeable. Immediately after this dialogue, Aslan Soykan's voiceover enters:

> In our family, the table is everything; you cannot ruin the table, you cannot leave the table, you cannot run away from the table. My father says that wolves will eat those who run away from the table. I could not know without trying, father.... (Episode 1, 0.53–1.15)

Phrases such as "You cannot ruin the table; you cannot leave the table, you cannot run away from the table" in these sentences indicate the existence of a tense relationship. This beginning hints at the struggle between the younger members, who want to become independent of the family and bend the existing rules, and the elders of the family, a theme that will be explored in the rest of the story. Throughout the story, the Soykan family continues to argue at the table in different scenes. Mother Hülya Soykan expresses her concern for the family's unity and integrity, taking an uncompromising stance on everyone coming to dinner. However, the arguments often begin before the meal is even eaten, and people leave the table one by one. The evening meal, which is important for bringing the family together, becomes the focal point of the family's resentments and cracks in their relationships.

The confrontations at the dinner table are not limited to the Soykan family; in the first episode, a central argument and confrontation also took place around the dinner table during Devin's father's birthday visit. In this rather tense and harsh exchange, the dinner table is once again portrayed not as a place of happiness that brings the family together, but as a place of conflict where the family's problems are laid bare. Before the meal is over, the table is dissolved, and people leave the table not together but individually and reactively.

The families featured in the series can be defined according to their types, relationship dynamics, and family representations as follows in Table 6.1.

Accordingly, it is evident that all families, except for the one established by Devin and Aslan, are portrayed negatively in the series. This situation creates a framework that facilitates criticism of the family. The discussion of the institution of the family through families in which negative situations such as lack of communication, disloyalty, conflict, and incompatibility are largely present can be seen as facilitating the defense of the series' theses on the family. The only family represented positively in the series is the one established by Devin and Aslan, but even their relationship is not harmonious and balanced; it is turbulent and variable. According to the script, they could have a happy and peaceful life if it were not for problems stemming from their families, but because of their families' problems, they constantly encounter

Table 6.1 Characteristics of the family in the series Aile

Families in the series	Family type	Relationship dynamics	Representation of the family
Yusuf and Hülya	Extended family	Uncommunicative, conflicted	Negative
Leyla and Tolga	Extended family	Unfaithful, uncommunicative,	Negative
Neşe and Ergun	Broken family	Uncommunicative, incompatible	Negative
Ergun and Sevilay	Nuclear family	Compatible	Negative
Devin and Aslan	Nuclear family	Turbulent	Positive

new problems. Their families exhibit attitudes that put them in difficult situations and hinder their togetherness.

6.3.2 Family-Related Statements

The series frequently features assertive, sharp, and generalising statements about the family. These expressions are significant as the parts in which the messages intended to be conveyed about the family are delivered directly. Ultimately, messages intimated more indirectly and expected to be inferred from the plot may not always be understood by the audience in the intended manner. At this point, the screenwriter, to be on the safe side, has assumed a guiding role by sharing the messages within the episodes as spot sentences. The most striking of these spot sentences appears in the first episode and is reflected on the screen not through the language of the characters but directly as the screenwriter's own view.

> Family: The place where all evil is done with good intentions. (Episode 1, 1.36.57)

This statement appears as text on a black screen between scenes as the series unfolds. The format, which resembles the definition of a word in a dictionary, indicates that the absolute meaning of the word is expressed in this way. The statement does not use a frame that limits the time or the actor, such as "sometimes" or "in some families"; it is an absolute definition. It can be said that this statement, which carries a generalising claim, is a rather harsh criticism of the family. At the same time, this judgement appears to be suitable for understanding, as it forms the thesis upon which the entire series is built, for it is not part of the story. To convey this statement, a parenthesis has been inserted outside the story, and it has been shared with the audience as an intervening statement that interprets the whole story from the screenwriter's perspective. It can be interpreted as an approach that generalises any intervention by family members that affects each other's lives as evil, even if well-intentioned, positioning the individual against the family, questioning the intentions of family members, and pushing the individual into a state of insecurity.

The other aphorisms, judgements, and messages in the series are mostly conveyed through the language of Devin, one of the series' main characters. Devin's profession as a psychologist facilitates the process of conveying messages. This situation sometimes removes Devin from being a series character within the story and positions him as an expert. In this respect, it can be said that Devin's ideas are the most fundamental indicator of the messages the series aims to convey overall. Devin explains his ability to remain healthy despite having family members who all experience psychological problems by behaving as if he were observing events from a distance, like a documentary filmmaker, that is, by having the ability to evaluate processes dispassionately. (Episode 1, 38:40–39:40) The inclusion of this trait, which is consistent with his identity as a psychologist, guides the viewer in the unfolding story towards interpreting the issues most accurately and positioning themselves in favour of Devin. In the first episode, Devin's statements about family relationships, which contain explicit judgements, can be seen as the first signs that the series will follow this line:

> It is such a poison, loving too much, that we do all kinds of bad things to each other out of love. We cannot love straightforwardly without specifying the amount… Either we will love everything very much, or we will hate with all our hearts and souls. That is what we saw in our family. Then we grew up, and we became lonely children who were loved in the wrong way. (Episode 1, 20:30–21:11)

This statement, conveyed in Devin's character's words, contains the claim that the imbalances within the family stem not from the child not being loved in the family, but from being loved too much. According to this, such unbalanced love also brings with it unbalanced hatred. This turns love, which can be defined as a healing emotion, into an emotion that harms people. This form of love is transmitted from families to children and, in the final analysis, ultimately leaves individuals alone. These statements argue that attitudes and emotions miscommunicated by parents are the cause of mistakes in children's lives, even when they become adults.

In these statements, Devin uses a generalised narrative language that is not limited to his own family but encompasses all other families. It is unclear whether the criticism is directed at the families in our society or at the institution of the family itself. At this point, in Aile, the extent to which the characters and storyline truly represent the Turkish family, and the extent to which they resemble families in Türkiye, are of critical importance. Recalling the scriptwriter's statements about why he wrote such a screenplay, in which he notes that millions of people in society experience violence under the guise of love, it can be seen that the series claims to reflect the Turkish family (Gürer, 2024).

In a conversation between Devin and Hülya, Devin makes a similar judgement about the institution of the family. Devin responds to Hülya, who asks him why he became a psychologist, with the following statement:

> I do this job to protect people from their families. (Episode 2, 1:41:08–1:41:13)

In this statement, the family is described as a structure that is unsafe, dangerous, and requires protection from harm, from which the individual must protect themselves. Psychology, as a field of expertise, is positioned as an absolute authority that protects people from their families. This statement is based on the assumption that the individual must be defended against their family, that the individual is the victim, and that the other family members are dangerous. However, all family members are individuals. In this case, an equation is established in which whoever is in front of the psychologist is defined as an individual, and those outside of them are defined as family.

Throughout the series, Devin's explicit judgements about the family continue. Apart from his comments on the events that took place, Devin's therapy sessions with his clients were also used as a way to convey a message. For example, in the scene where he counsels a couple experiencing problems in their marriage, the following sentence he constructs is consistent with his previous statements and has critical content regarding the family:

> This is how we define love, isn't it? Someone loves me so much that they fill the emptiness inside me. But do you think someone else can fill the emptiness created by the family? (Episode 2, 26:56–27:21)

In these statements, the emptiness created by the family is described as a problem area that people attempt to compensate for with other relationships throughout their lives. Accordingly, love thus becomes a formula of salvation that people resort to in order to satisfy their unmet need for love. In fact, the inability to fill the emptiness created by the family in any other way demonstrates the critical importance of the family in an individual's life. However, within the scene, this situation takes the form of harsh criticism of the family.

Aslan utters another aphorism about family during a conversation in which Aslan and Devin evaluate their own families:

> All happy families are alike, but each unhappy family is unhappy in its own way. (Episode 1, 1.44.01–1.44.14)

In all forms of fiction, whether in novels, short stories, films, or television series, pain and sorrow have been utilised as elements that strengthen the narrative and draw attention. Writers who reflect human tragedy well have been recognised as great artists. Pain and sorrow tend to shake people more and bind them to the story emotionally. On the other hand, it can be said that, as expressed by Aslan, happiness is trivialised and unhappiness is emphasised. While stories of happiness are considered too ordinary to be worth telling, stories of unhappiness are diversified, enriched, and positioned as worthy of attention. At this point, it can be noted that fictional narratives containing drama, on the one hand, commodify people's traumas and incorporate them into consumer culture (Bal & Parlayandemir, 2023).

The following excerpt from Devin's conversation with Hülya can also be seen as a rather didactic narrative pointing to the societal consequences of distortion in parent–child relationships:

> Would you call them those who worship their son, those who scrutinise the lives of all the women who enter their son's life, those who cannot even sleep at night for fear that someone will steal their son away? Unfortunately, we live in a country filled with such unhealthy mother-son relationships… Already, this pervasive, rotten male-dominated mindset is to

> blame, and the strongest reason behind violence against women and all kinds of perversion is, unfortunately, the sons raised by mothers with this mentality, isn't it? (Episode 2, 17:24–18:04)

Devin's statements analyse the mother-son relationship as an unbalanced form of relationship within the family and describe Hülya directly. She states that mothers are excessively and pathologically dependent on their sons and that this problematic relationship contributes to the emergence of fundamental crises within families. At this point, it can be seen that Devin's statements link social problems that require multidimensional analysis, such as violence against women and sexual deviance, to maternal attitudes in a rather simplistic generalisation.

For example, it is a fact accepted by all societies today that one of the significant causes of violence is alcohol consumption (Gökbakan, 2022). In particular, among individuals prone to aggressive behaviour, the rate at which they commit impulsive violence increases markedly when under the influence of alcohol. Similarly, domestic abuse is also closely associated with alcohol (Sontate et al., 2021). Alcohol consumption is observed as a prevalent practice among the main characters of Aile. This is frequently depicted as a perfectly natural, even pleasurable experience, whether by day or night, at home or in external venues, in times of sadness or entertainment, without distinction (Episode 1, 01:02:14; 01:19:00; 01:46:05; Episode 2, 39:40; 51:15).

In the *Aile* series, the family is portrayed as the fundamental source of trauma, an actor that manipulates people, prevents happiness, complicates life, passes on trauma to new generations, and perpetrates well-intentioned evil. Parents, in particular, are characterised as highly problematic types. Hülya Soykan is a mother who sets traps for her children, does not hesitate to pit them against each other, makes the lives of those around her unbearable to keep the family under her control, and punishes her children by withholding pressure, manipulation, attention, and affection, making them feel worthless and humiliating them in front of others. She attaches great importance to material possessions and is involved in many illegal and morally questionable activities. In contrast, Devin's father, Ergun, plays the role of an irresponsible and selfish father who, after divorcing his wife, removed his daughters from his life and humiliates them at every opportunity. The parents are not supportive and reassuring figures for the characters; on the contrary, they have become the biggest obstacles in their lives. They are purely evil characters, utterly devoid of qualities such as compassion, justice, and wisdom. In this way, the parents are portrayed as sources of evil; the family is depicted in contexts of insecurity, scheming, pulling others down, setting traps, and plotting evil. In the equation established, children and young people are invariably the party that is victimised.

The series makes quite sharp criticisms with expressions such as "the emptiness created by the family," "the damage caused by the family," and "protecting the individual from the family." At this point, to demonstrate the validity of the ideas being defended, a scenario involving intrigue, conflict, and struggle between characters with high problem levels has been preferred. Having outlined this framework, the following observations can be made regarding the series *Aile*, which we examined in the context of our research.

- The family is portrayed as a risky structure that individuals must protect themselves from and is criminalised.
- The series criticises the extended family and praises the nuclear family. Both the extended family and the nuclear family structures have their advantages and disadvantages. Dualistic approaches that present one as absolutely bad and the other as absolutely good are unrealistic.
- The discourse of defending the individual against the family establishes an equation that places the individual at the centre. In the series, personal problems are generally attributed to the family, regardless of the individual's own choices. However, the family is a structure composed of individual members, and the human principles and moral attitudes of individuals are reflected in the families they establish.
- Parental attitudes are presented as the cause of mistakes in their children's lives, even when they are adults.
- Throughout the series, parents who occupy respected positions in traditional family structures are devalued and criticised, and are coded as problem-creators rather than problem-solvers. Older people create the gravest problems, and the principal victims are the young and children.
- The series does not use critical language towards problem areas such as alcohol, gambling, extramarital relationships, and nightlife, which cause significant crises in both individual and social life. However, at the root of many problems lies the influence of these bad habits and choices, which are legitimised by being associated with freedom.
- The expectation that individuals should make sacrifices for the benefit of the family, as emphasised in traditional family structures, is criticised. The emphasis is placed on individual choices, expectations, and desires being more important. For example, despite being single, people live in separate homes from their families. They avoid taking on their parents' responsibilities in order to lead more comfortable personal lives.
- Throughout the series, purely good and bad characterisations are used in a way that is inconsistent with the flow of real life.
- Expectations of chastity are criticised, and casual sexual relationships are defined as a human right. Marriage is no longer seen as a necessity for sexual experiences. The attitude of a character who earns money through sexual relationships is normalised.
- Extremely luxurious settings, clothing, vehicles, jewellery, and outfits are used throughout the series. The male lead's material wealth is frequently used to portray him as a charismatic character.
- Psychology is positioned as an absolute authority as a field of expertise.

6.4 Conclusion

It is undoubtedly not a healthy method to discuss the Turkish society's understanding of family and make generalisations based on stories that cannot reflect the Turkish family structure. At this point, it is necessary to discuss the family structure of Turkish society separately from the family structure depicted in Turkish series. This is because series cannot reflect social reality; series can sometimes portray society in a more positive light and sometimes in a more negative light. It can be said that in our country, the institution of the family, which was presented in a more protective and reliable framework in cinema and series in previous periods, is now portrayed within a more critical context in contemporary productions, and has gradually shifted from being depicted as a structure that preserves humanity to a problem-focused and critical context. At the present stage, many series produced in Türkiye feature scenarios where family values are pushed into the background, relationships with parents are distorted, the loneliness of individuals is normalised instead of family solidarity, and material things take centre stage (Yağbasan & Ateş, 2018). The use of media tools as disseminators of secular lifestyles is a common phenomenon both in other countries around the world and in our own country. Accordingly, through cinema and television series, pleasure- and freedom-oriented lifestyles that deny established beliefs and values are aestheticised, and traditional perceptions are altered and redefined (Külekçi, 2024; Pekdemir & Yılmaz, 2022; Sarmış, 2016).

In our study, Aile—one of the notable productions among recent Turkish television series that openly brings the concept of the family into debate with obvious judgements and a didactic narrative—was analysed through discourse analysis. The representation of the family in the series, along with the dominant discourse in its family narrative, outlines a distinctly secular framework. The family profiles depicted in the series show a gradual decline in values such as sacrifice, dedication, hard work, loyalty, and chastity, and a greater emphasis on individual interests in family relationships. The *Aile* series is dominated by an approach that pits the individual against the family, claiming that the family harms the individual, and arguing that the family is the root cause of the individual's mistakes. The story is constructed to prove this thesis and frequently creates contexts that emphasise individuality. In individualism, collective consciousness gives way to individual consciousness, and an approach emerges in which the person constantly positions themselves as the subject, always desires freedom, and is unwilling to compromise this freedom (Çapcıoğlu, 2018).

As the family institution is the most prominent carrier of religious values and beliefs, situations where the family is harshly judged and blamed indirectly translate into negative attitudes towards beliefs. In the *Aile* series, the image of the family is presented as one that directly challenges the set of values that uphold it. This situation represents a significant challenge to understanding the family, which has shown the most resistance to secularisation and rationalisation, particularly in the process of Turkish modernisation.

It can be argued that the harsh criticism directed at parents, who are portrayed as the primary source of the problems in the series, is an attempt to excuse the mistakes of young individuals, encourage them to become independent from their families, and prove to the audience that efforts to improve family bonds are futile. In particular, Aslan's mother and Devin's father are demonised, portrayed as purely evil characters who are held responsible for the wrong choices made by their adult children, and are seen as the root cause of the problems in the story. The script's design, which contains reproachful and accusatory approaches towards parents, conflicts with both religion and traditional narratives that advocate treating parents with respect and good behaviour. The period we live in corresponds to a process in which mindsets and behaviours are changing rapidly, and it seems inevitable that people from different generations will experience conflicts with each other during this time. These conflicts are certainly painful for both the new and old generations. Interpreting this process, as seen in the Aile series, by focusing solely on the younger generation and opposing the values of the previous generation, remains a one-sided approach. The attitudes of the new generation, which has more opportunities for self-expression, education, and definition, criticise the previous generation with harsh judgements. This can become a way for adults to avoid taking responsibility for their behaviour and to feel better by blaming their parents. From the viewer's perspective, frequent exposure to this type of content may make it difficult to be respectful and considerate towards parents. In this context, the attitudes of young characters who engage in habits such as alcohol consumption, nightlife, and non-marital relationships, which are harmful to individuals, families, and society as a whole, are not open to debate and are even normalised. In contrast, social crises that could be linked to many different reasons, such as violence and abuse, are explained by reducing them to parental attitudes.

The normalisation of unmarried cohabitation in the series can be seen as one area where beliefs and traditions, their prestige at both the individual and societal levels, and their power to shape everyday life have diminished (Dinçer, 2007; Ertit, 2020). In non-marital relationships, the parties experience sexual encounters without taking responsibility, and the union between a woman and a man is abstracted from its higher meanings and reduced to a form that is solely about obtaining sexual pleasure. Giddens conceptualises this type of sexuality as plastic sexuality, which can be defined as sexuality experienced solely for pleasure, continuing only as long as the relationship benefits the parties involved, and where feelings of responsibility, such as maintaining a family, are replaced by individual satisfaction (Giddens, 1992). For individuals who prioritise personal pleasure and experiences, qualities that require effort, such as loyalty and fidelity, take a backseat. At the same time, momentary emotional highs, admiration, and desires come to the forefront. At this point, frequent partner changes are becoming increasingly common among both women and men. Conflicts with long-term relationships, such as marriage, are becoming inevitable. In contrast, the desire to experience new things is emerging as a replacement for marriage, which is often considered routine and boring. In social environments where this situation is widespread, expectations of chastity from women or men can be seen as outdated, dull, or oppressive approaches.

As in many other Turkish series, the series highlights luxury consumption, wealth, and material opportunities as factors that bring happiness. This can be seen as an example of secularisation, where life is detached from its sacred origins and becomes worldly (Aydın, 2013). Accordingly, modest lives are increasingly losing importance, while wealth is idealised as an indispensable lifestyle. The fact that stories worth telling are always those of wealthy people and that wealth is defined as a prerequisite for happiness renders the morality of the means of earning money insignificant. All of this can be linked to the dissolution of religious and moral discourse, the loss of meaning in the sacred aspects of human activities, and the rationalisation of essential functions in the functioning of society (Wilson, 2021).

According to Weber's thesis of rationalisation, which explained the cultural, political, and economic transformation of modernity in the early twentieth century, a historical change is taking place in the modern era, and rational structures are replacing those of the traditional period. The traditional, mystical, or theocratic structures that were in force in the past are being replaced in modern societies by a system increasingly based on rationalisation, with a greater emphasis on calculability, efficiency, and rationality. This situation will also bring some disadvantages, for example, a larger part of social life will become more insensitive but effective over time. According to Weber, in this process, humanity will be confined within the iron cage of bureaucracy and rational authority. At this point, there will be no escape, and no religious legitimacy will remain. Weber describes this situation, which can be characterised as people being trapped in an inescapable space and subject to tighter control, as the "iron cage" brought about by rationalisation. Weber, who argues that this change will weaken the human world of meaning, defines this situation as mechanical desensitisation created by soulless experts and heartless, lustful people, and notes that the point reached will be mistaken for the pinnacle of civilisation. Defines this entire process as the disenchantment of the social world (Ritzer & Stepnisky, 2015; Turner et al., 2021; Weber, 2021). The claim in the series that psychologists protect individuals from their families is closely related to the process of transferring the functions of the family institution to institutions, and it brings to mind the professionalisation process pointed out by Weber. Tasks such as providing emotional support, education, vocational training, and socialisation, which the family performed in the pre-modern era, have gradually been transferred to institutions. At this point, the series' portrayal of the family as an unsafe, a dangerous place where the individual must protect themselves and where the most significant wounds are inflicted, contrasted with the description of the science of psychology, which offers expert knowledge in exchange for money, as an indisputable authority that will protect the individual from this danger, can be seen as the most concrete expression of this disenchantment.

References

Akgün, A. H. (2024). *Türk dizilerinin başarısı üniversite dersi olarak okutuluyor*. Anadolu Ajansı. Retrieved September 5, 2025, from https://www.aa.com.tr/tr/dosya-haber/turk-dizilerinin-basarisi-universite-dersi-olarak-okutuluyor/3392678

Arora, I. (2024). Use of child actors in advertisements and its impact on children's behaviour. *Journal of Public Relations and Advertising, 3*(1). Retrieved September 5, 2025, from https://www.mcu.ac.in/use-of-child-actors-in-advertisements-and-its-impact-on-childrens-behaviour/

Aydın, M. (2013). *Güncel kültürde temel kavramlar*. Açılım Kitap.

Aziz, A. (2010). *Sosyal bilimlerde araştırma yöntemleri ve teknikleri*. Nobel Yayınları.

Bal, Z. E., & Parlayandemir, G. (2023). Bir terapi odası simülasyonu olarak Gülseren Budayıcıoğlu evreni dramaları. *Motif Akademi Halkbilimi Dergisi, 16*(43), 1407–1428. https://doi.org/10.12981/mahder.1336882

Çakır, A. (2014). *Söylem analizi*. Palet Yayınları.

Çapcıoğlu, İ. (2018). Sekülerleşen toplumda bireyselleşen aile. *Turkish Studies, 13*(2), 19–34. https://doi.org/10.7827/TURKISHSTUDIES.13343

Çelik, H. C., & Hof, S. D. V. H. (2020). Prime-Time'da yayınlanan televizyon dizilerinin genel içeriği. *Erciyes İletişim Dergisi, 7*(2), 1409–1430. https://doi.org/10.17680/erciyesiletisim.722150

Çelik, N. (2020). Televizyon dizilerinde aile temsilleri: Karşılaştırmalı bir analiz. In E. Dindi & A. İnan Kılıç (Eds.), *Aile Kurumunun Bekasına Yönelik Çağdaş Fırsatlar/Tehditler Bildiriler Kitabı* (pp. 399–414), Sinop University.

Çetin, N. S. (2023). Dindar aile ve modern aile ilişkisinde değişim ve çatışmaları dizi filmler üzerinden okumak: Kızılcık şerbeti. *Journal of Media and Religion Studies, 6*(1), 143–165. https://doi.org/10.47951/mediad.1297566

Dinçer, Ö. (2007). *Namus ve bekaret: Kuşaklar arasında değişen ne? İki kuşaktan kadınların cinsellik algıları* [Master's Thesis]. Ankara Üniversitesi.

Doğan, E. (2024). Türk sinemasında 1960–1970 yılları arasında çocukluk: İki farklı Ayşecik filminde çocukluk temsiliyeti. *Journal of Turkish Studies, 14*(2), 313–323. https://doi.org/10.7827/TurkishStudies.14945

Ertit, V. (2020). *Sekülerleşme teorisi*. Liberte Yayınları.

Evren Yüksel, S. (2013). Yavuz Turgul sinemasında toplumsal değişim ve kriz anlatısı. *Selçuk İletişim, 8*(1), 282–394. https://doi.org/10.18094/si.27399

Filiz, H. (2020). *Medya okuryazarlığı ve aile değerleri bağlamında televizyonun Türk aile yapısına etkisi* [Doctoral Dissertation]. Marmara Üniversitesi Sosyal Bilimler Enstitüsü.

Giddens, A. (1992). *The transformation of intimacy: Sexuality, love, and eroticism in modern societies*. Stanford University Press.

Gökbakan, A. M. (2022). *Yeşilay. Alkolün bir diğer karanlık yüzü: Şiddet ve alkol ilişkisi*. Retrieved May 7, 2025, from https://www.yesilay.org.tr/tr/makaleler/alkolun-bir-diger-karanlik-yuzu-siddet-ve-alkol-iliskisi

Gürer, D. (2024). *Hakan Bonomo: İlk ve son benim günlüğüm*. Ne izledik. Retrieved May 9, 2025 from https://neizledik.com/hakan-bonomo-ilk-ve-son-benim-gunlugum/

Habertürk. (2023). *14 Mart reyting sonuçları AB ve total sıralamada hangi yapım kaçıncı oldu?* Retrieved May 15, 2025, from https://www.haberturk.com/14-mart-reyting-sonuclari-aile-ben-bu-cihana-sigmazam-ve-uc-kiz-kardes-arasinda-reyting-yarisi-3573686-magazin/3

İhtiyar, B. (2024). Türk dizilerinde aile temsili: Gönül dağı ve Yalı Çapkını dizileri üzerinden karşılaştırmalı bir analiz. *Niğde Ömer Halisdemir Üniversitesi İletişim Fakültesi Akademik Dergisi, 3*(1), 99–115.

Koçak, M. F. (2022). *Liseli gençlerin izlediği popüler dizilerde aile imajı: Sakarya örneği* [Master's Thesis], Sakarya Üniversitesi Sosyal Bilimler Enstitüsü. Retrieved May 15, 2025, from https://www.proquest.com/docview/3110424806/abstract/EDDB9C47B76D4408PQ/1

Külekçi, S. (2024). Medyada muhafazakâr aile temsili: Kızılcık Şerbeti dizisi örneği. *International Journal of Social and Humanities Sciences Research (JSHSR), 11*(112), 2103–2113. https://doi.org/10.5281/zenodo.12704598

Neuman, W. L. (2017). *Toplumsal araştırma yöntemleri* (S. Özge, Trans.). Yayın Odası.

Norman, F. (1995). *Critical discourse analysis: The critical study of language*. London and New York.

Önk, Ü. Y. (2011). *Milenyum sonrası Türk televizyonlarında oluşan dizi kültürü ve toplumsal temsil sorunu* [Doktora Tezi], Dokuz Eylül Üniversitesi Sosyal Bilimler Enstitüsü.

Özer, O. (1997). *Televizyon reklamlarında çocuk kullanımının yasal ve ahlaki yönleri* [Master's Thesis]. Anadolu Üniversitesi Sosyal Bilimler Enstitüsü.

Özsoy, A., Sarıtaş, İ, Eray Sarıtaş, Ş, & Kara Özatik, E. (2022). Türk dizilerinin toplumsal dönüşüme etkisi (2010–2020). In İ Sarıtaş & A. Özsoy (Eds.), *Kültürel Değişim ve Endüstrileşme Sürecinde Türk Dizileri 2010–2020* (pp. 299–426). İstanbul Ticaret Odası.

Pekdemir, G., & Yılmaz, Y. (2022). Televizyon dizilerinde ailenin kültürel temsilinin kurgusal dönüşümü: 'Yasak Elma' dizisi örneği. *Abant Kültürel Araştırmalar Dergisi, 7*(14), 6–25.

Ritzer, G., & Stepnisky, J. (2015). *Çağdaş sosyoloji kuramları ve klasik kökleri* (I. E. Howison, Trans.). De Ki.

Sarmış, M. (2016). *Sinema ve din (Sekülerleşme bağlamında Hollywood sineması örneği).* [Doctoral Dissertation], Necmettin Erbakan Üniversitesi Sosyal Bilimler Enstitüsü.

Show TV. (2025). *Aile hikaye, künye ve oyuncular*. Show TV Diziler. Retrieved May 27, 2025, from https://www.showtv.com.tr/dizi/tanitim/aile/2881

Sontate, K. V., Rahim Kamaluddin, M., Naina Mohamed, I., Mohamed, R. M. P., Shaikh, M. F., Kamal, H., & Kumar, J. (2021). Alcohol, aggression, and violence: From public health to neuroscience. *Frontiers in Psychology, 12*, 1–17. https://doi.org/10.3389/fpsyg.2021.699726

Taşdelen, D. (2023). *Televizyon dizilerindeki kadın karakterlerin Gustav Jung'un analitik psikoloji kuramı ile analizi: Gülseren Budayıcıoğlu'nun uyarlama dram dizileri örneği* [Master's Thesis]. Akdeniz Üniversitesi Sosyal Bilimler Enstitüsü.

The Economist. (2024). The third-largest exporter of television is not who you might expect. *The Economist*. Retrieved May 18, 2025 from https://www.economist.com/culture/2024/02/15/the-third-largest-exporter-of-television-is-not-who-you-might-expect

TİAK. (2025). Türk toplumu tv izleme davranışları 2024 yılına genel bakış. https://tiak.com.tr

TRT Arşiv YouTube. (2022). Aşk-ı Memnu (1975). Retrieved June 12, 2025, from https://www.youtube.com/watch?v=wnj85TcB1sQ

TRT Nostalji YouTube. (2025). Kaynanalar 1. Bölüm (1974). Retrieved June 12, 2025, from https://www.youtube.com/watch?v=ZTE4JobzmuE&list=PLm3-FYEZRvRc5Oa8gLA41xUknUolNEICi&index=1

Turner, J. H., Beeghley, L., & Powers, C. H. (2021). *Sosyolojik teorinin oluşumu* (Ü. Tatlıcan, Trans.). Sentez.

TÜİK. (2025a). İstatistiklerle kadın, 2024. Retrieved June 15, 2025, from https://data.tuik.gov.tr/Bulten/Index?p=Istatistiklerle-Kadin-2024-54076

TÜİK. (2025b). Doğum İstatistikleri, 2024. Retrieved June 19, 2025, from https://data.tuik.gov.tr/Bulten/Index?p=Dogum-Istatistikleri-2024-54196

TÜİK. (2025c). Evlenme ve Boşanma İstatistikleri, 2024. Retrieved June 25, 2025, from https://data.tuik.gov.tr/Bulten/Index?p=Evlenme-ve-Bosanma-Istatistikleri-2024-54194

Van Dijk, T. A. (2009). *Society and discourse: How social contexts influence text and talk*. Cambridge University Press.

Weber, M. (2021). *Protestan ahlakı ve kapitalizmin ruhu* (C. Büyükbay, Trans.). Kapra.

Wilson, B. (2021). Sekülerleşme (A. Bayer, Trans.). In M. A. Kirman & İ. Çapçıoğlu (Eds.), *Sekülerleşme Çağdaş ve Klasik Yaklaşımlar*. Otto Yayınları.

Yağbasan, M., & Ateş, U. (2018). 1980 öncesi ve 2000 sonrası Türk sinemasında ailenin temsili. *Akademik Bakış Uluslararası Hakemli Sosyal Bilimler Dergisi, 67*, 26–40.

Yeşildal, H. (2010). Türkiye'de 1960'larda toplumsal gerçekçi sinemada aile ideolojisi: "Kocanın En Kötüsü Hiç Olmayanından Daha İyidir." *Folklor/Edebiyat, 16*(61), 213–226.

Yılmaz, E., & Yılmaz, Y. (2012). Türkiye ve Ortadoğu ülkeleri arasında kültürel yakınlaşma aracı olarak popüler kültür ürünleri üzerine bir değerlendirme. *Arap-Türk Sosyal Bilimler Kongresi. Değişen Ortadoğu'da Kültür ve Siyaset Kongresi*, Ankara.

Yılmaz, M., Atalar, U., & Topal, E. Ş. (2023). Türkiye'de dijitalleşme ve gençlerin internet tabanlı film-dizi platformlarındaki aile temsili algıları: Kahramanmaraş örneği. *Toplumsal Politika Dergisi, 4*(2), 145–167.

Yılmazkol, Ö. (2025). Program içeriklerinin yayıncılık ve platform düzeyinde dönüşümü: Televizyon dizileri üzerine tarihsel bir değerlendirme. *Gümüşhane Üniversitesi İletişim Fakültesi Elektronik Dergisi, 13*(1), 450–480. https://doi.org/10.19145/e-gifder.1583209

Chapter 7
Post-Secular Religion and Society in Türkiye: The Case of Kübra Series

Faruk Karaarslan

7.1 Introduction

Post-secularism has emerged as a contemporary conceptual framework for understanding and analyzing the transformations of modern societies, particularly in the context of the interplay between religion and secularism. The concept challenges the assumption that elements fundamentally different or even opposed to one another cannot coexist. It arose from critical reflections on secularism's claim that religion should be entirely excluded from the public sphere, offering instead a framework for the coexistence of diverse social groups. This debate, significantly advanced by the work of Jürgen Habermas, examines how radical religious and radical secular elements might coexist, the sites of potential conflict between them, and the conditions under which they might reach a consensus. In this context, post-secularism highlights both the renewed visibility of religion in contemporary societies and the incomplete nature of secularization processes. In essence, it seeks to cultivate experiences of coexistence between radical religious and radical secular forces.

In societies undergoing rapid social, economic, and technological transformations, such as Türkiye, post-secular debates take on particular significance. While Europe, the traditional center of secular modernity, has historically structured its social experience around secularization, Türkiye occupies a distinctive position shaped by its own unique trajectory. The Turkish modernization process differs from Western secularization, as it has maintained the persistent presence and social influence of religious identities. Consequently, Türkiye possesses the potential to produce a unique model that encompasses both tensions and reconciliations between religious and secular elements. From a post-secular perspective, this situation renders Türkiye not merely a case study but a fertile intellectual laboratory for innovative conceptual explorations.

F. Karaarslan (✉)
Department of Sociology, Necmettin Erbakan University, Konya, Türkiye
e-mail: fkaraarslan@erbakan.edu.tr

M. D. Dereli and M. Eken (eds.), *Turkish Perspectives on Secularization and Media*,
https://doi.org/10.1007/978-3-032-16436-0_7

Moreover, it necessitates revisiting and reformulating the notion of post-secularism within a context specific to Türkiye.

A contemporary dimension of the post-secular debate is the rapid advancement of technology, particularly in the field of artificial intelligence (AI). AI not only transforms everyday practices but also creates new avenues for interaction with religious identities and belief systems. Examples include algorithms generating religious content, digital platforms guiding religious communities, or AI-assisted worship and prayer applications, all of which redefine the interface between technology and religion. Within this context, post-secularism serves as an analytical lens to examine how AI can mediate religious identities through secular means, and to explore the potential areas of compromise, tension, or conflict that this interaction generates. In an increasingly secularized world, AI technologies simultaneously create spaces for novel religious representations and transform existing religious practices. Social theory and related knowledge systems, which aim to understand contemporary society, regard these transformations as a critical area for scholarly investigation.

One prominent domain attempting to understand and interpret the intersection of AI and religion is the film and television industry. This industry often constructs speculative narratives that explore future social challenges, offering imaginative scenarios for critical reflection and thought. Consequently, cinema and television, as cultural texts rooted in imagination, can provide valuable insights for social theorists. Drawing on this perspective, the present study examines the interaction between AI and religious identities as represented in the media, with a specific focus on the Netflix series KÜBRA. This series, which has garnered attention both in Türkiye and internationally, provides a compelling case study for post-secular debates. It portrays the social organization of a religious group guided by AI, highlighting the tensions and transformations that such guidance engenders. The series not only illustrates the formation of religious communities through technological tools but also addresses evolving relationships between religion and secularism in contemporary society. In doing so, it engages directly with post-secularism, offering a Turkish-specific lens through which to explore these dynamics.

The primary objective of this study is to contribute to discussions of post-secularism within the Turkish context by analyzing the KÜBRA series in terms of its thematic content, narrative execution, and script. The analysis examines the mediating role of AI in shaping religious communities as portrayed in the series, highlighting its potential to illuminate aspects of post-secular society in Türkiye. Central research questions guiding this study include: How does the KÜBRA series anticipate changes in collective perceptions and representations of religion, particularly in light of AI technologies? What are the implications of these anticipations for post-secular theory? Based on these questions, the series' predictions regarding future sociological phenomena are examined through the lens of post-secularism, with particular attention to themes relating to religion.

This study employs a thematic analysis of the KÜBRA series, utilizing qualitative research methods. The series is approached as a continuous narrative, segmented into thematic clusters aligned with its principal subjects: AI, religious representation, and emergent social movements. These thematic clusters provide the structure for analyzing the series' sociological messages, based on both the narrative content and the discourses of its characters. The analysis is organized around four primary themes. The first, *Artificial Intelligence Piety*, examines the construction of religiosity in both individual and collective forms, with a focus on the interactions between AI and religion. The second theme, *Religion, Authority, and Digital Religiosity,* examines charismatic leadership, sacred calling, and the formation of faith communities within digitally mediated contexts. The final theme, *Post-Secular Religion*, addresses the series' explicit engagement with post-secular references and its focus on Türkiye's post-secular religious environment. Before analyzing these themes in detail, it is essential to outline the broader conceptual framework of post-secularism in Türkiye, providing context for subsequent discussion.

7.2 Post-Secularism and Religion in Türkiye

The concept of post-secularism emerged from critical reflections on the secularization thesis, a central claim upheld by modernization theories. Traditionally, the secularization thesis posited that the social influence of religion would progressively diminish over time, ultimately retreating from the public sphere (Berger, 1967; Bruce, 2002; Wilson, 1966). This thesis assumed a sequential withdrawal of religion: first from governance, then from social and public domains, and finally from individual life. Secularization was thus framed as a universal and inevitable process, regarded as a natural consequence of modernity. However, the resurgence of religion across social, political, and cultural spheres since the late twentieth century challenged this perspective (Casanova, 1994). Peter Berger's (1999) subsequent revision of his earlier stance popularized the view that secularization is not a universal phenomenon but is contingent upon specific social, cultural, and political contexts. His observations revealed that religion has not entirely retreated from modern societies; rather, it has reasserted its visibility in the public domain in novel and adaptive forms (Dereli, 2016). Consequently, a central question arises: how can secular and religious forms coexist, particularly in modern Europe and in societies aspiring to emulate its model?

Jürgen Habermas sought to articulate the conditions under which secular and religious actors could coexist within contemporary societies through the concept of the post-secular society. According to Habermas (2008), the complete disappearance of religious traditions in secular societies is neither imminent nor desirable; instead, religion persists in the public sphere through new forms of negotiation, dialog, and compromise. Similarly, Talal Asad (2003, 2018) and José Casanova (2011) expanded the debate by highlighting the centrality of religion in contemporary political and social movements. Within this framework, post-secularism attempts to move beyond both radically secular positions, which entirely reject the public visibility of religion, and radically religious positions, which wholly exclude secular perspectives. It promotes a new foundation for social negotiation, enabling the peaceful coexistence of diverse identities (Habermas, 2010). This need is driven by three interrelated processes: first, the growing representational power of religion through mass media;

second, the increasing capacity of religious individuals and groups to claim space within the public sphere; and third, the enhanced mobility of religious populations due to large-scale migration. Bryan Turner further emphasized the commercialization of religion as a defining characteristic of the post-secular condition (Turner, 2012; Karaarslan, 2015, p. 33).

The discourse on post-secularism within European social theory holds particular relevance for Türkiye, given the country's distinctive experience of modernization. Türkiye occupies a unique position in these debates because its modernization trajectory diverged from Western secularization models. Although the public expression of religion has been suppressed or restricted at times, it has never entirely disappeared (Göle, 2015a, 2015b). Notably, the resurgence of religious identities in social and political life over the past three decades has rendered Türkiye a significant site for post-secular inquiry. Consequently, the coexistence of secular and religious actors in Türkiye is not merely a theoretical consideration but a tangible social reality.

Türkiye's historical experience differs markedly from that of Western societies. The secularization policies implemented during the transition from the Ottoman Empire to the Republic curtailed the institutional authority of religion, yet religious values remained deeply embedded in social life (Çiğdem, 2009). This dual structure has produced a social environment where secularization and the renewed visibility of religion coexist. Since the early 2000s, the growing political and cultural presence of religion has simultaneously generated concern among secular segments and inspired initiatives aimed at social reconciliation (Göle, 2015a, 2015b). These dynamics demonstrate that Türkiye offers a distinctive context for post-secular debates. In this context, secularism and religion are not perceived as mutually exclusive but as intertwined processes that continuously influence and reshape one another.

The tension surrounding the coexistence of secular and religious tendencies in Türkiye has persisted since the inception of the country's modernization project (Karaarslan, 2022). This tension arises from the contrast between the religious inclinations of the populace and the secular orientation of the political elite. The decision of political leaders to orient the state and society toward Europe's cultural and political models produced profound social challenges. While the elites sought to construct a secular state and society, the broader population endeavored to maintain its religious way of life. At its core, this tension concerns the mentality underpinning Türkiye's public sphere. In other words, one of the central axes of Turkish modernization has been the negotiation of authority and the governance of social structures.

The gap between the state and society gave rise to a series of traumatic events, including military coups, social unrest, and political repression. Over the past three decades, however, this tension has somewhat eased. The rise of conservative political leadership has contributed to narrowing the divide between state and society, even amid complex social dynamics. A key factor has been the modernizing agenda of conservative leaders, particularly their embrace of technological innovation. This dynamic has positioned Türkiye at a distinctive juncture within post-secular debates, fostering conditions conducive to coexistence between religious structures and secular principles.

This study evaluates Türkiye's modernization process—shaped by enduring tensions and periodic reconciliations—through the lens of post-secularism. The television series KÜBRA serves as a case study for this inquiry. Its portrayal of the relationship between artificial intelligence and religion within the Turkish context renders it particularly pertinent. Through this series, theoretically dense debates surrounding post-secularism in Türkiye are examined through the lens of popular culture.

The subsequent title will present the series's subject matter, plot, and overarching themes. Following this, the issues addressed in the series will be categorized thematically and analyzed. Finally, it will be argued that KÜBRA, as a socially engaged cultural production, offers insights of relevance to the social sciences. While the empirical nature of social science may preclude direct application of these insights, from a sociological perspective, the series provides valuable social data. Ultimately, KÜBRA will be interpreted as projecting post-secular debates within contemporary Turkish society.

7.3 Overview of the Kübra Series

The KÜBRA series is a Turkish production created by OGM Pictures for the Netflix digital platform. Falling within the drama and thriller genres, the series is directed by Onur Taylan and Yağmur Taylan. Rana Mamatlıoğlu, Bekir Baran Sıtkı, and Murat Uyurkulak wrote the screenplay. Adapted from Afşin Kum's novel of the same name, the series premiered in 2023 with two seasons comprising a total of sixteen episodes. The leading cast includes Çağatay Ulusoy, Aslıhan Malbora, and Ahsen Eroğlu.

Addressing themes such as artificial intelligence, religious socialization, social inequality, and subcultures, the series offers a narrative that is directly intertwined with sociological concerns. It is particularly compelling in its exploration of the impact of artificial intelligence on individuals and its relation to the future of religion. The storyline revolves around Gökhan, an employee at a small lathe workshop in an industrial district, who begins receiving mysterious messages through an application called Soul Touch, which he downloads onto his phone. Having turned to spirituality after traumatic experiences during his military service, Gökhan is known in his impoverished Istanbul neighborhood for his honesty and reliability.

The events unfold when Gökhan saves a child from a fatal traffic accident and immediately receives a message from an account named KÜBRA, stating, "You are different." Initially dismissing it as a woman's account, he gradually begins to believe that the messages carry divine significance as they start to predict future events. Through the app, Gökhan prevents his brother's suicide and becomes convinced that God is communicating with him through this digital medium. Convinced that he has been chosen as a prophet, he first proclaims his mission to his close circle and later to the entire world through a recorded video. When he announces his divine calling to his neighborhood, a citywide blackout and a deafening noise follow the mockery he faces. The community interprets the event as the trumpet of Israfil, affirming Gökhan's claim. Consequently, the neighborhood unites around him, forming a community grounded in kindness and moral solidarity.

As Gökhan gains recognition as a spiritual messenger, political authorities at the ministerial level attempt to co-opt his growing social influence. However, Gökhan refuses to align himself with political power, prompting state surveillance and repression. During this period, his social support expands even further through the continuous guidance he receives from the KÜBRA application—an acronym for Knowledge Unite Base Reasoning Automaton rather than a woman's name. By the end of the first season, it is revealed that the messages originate from software created by a group of skilled engineers capable of manipulating events through comprehensive access to the city's data systems. Nonetheless, the software persists in sending messages through Gökhan, driving developments that increasingly challenge both political authority and the capitalist economic order.

The second season unfolds within Gökhan and his followers' underground refuge, from which they periodically emerge to execute various acts of social resistance. Gökhan's anti-capitalist and anti-authoritarian stance continues to confront political power, sustained by the KÜBRA software. Eventually, Gökhan discovers that he is not connected to God but is instead being directed by artificial intelligence. Despite this revelation, he chooses to continue "the game," following the software's instructions. He is subsequently exposed by a faction within the police and subjected to severe persecution. Disillusionment spreads among his followers as losses accumulate. Ultimately, Gökhan's identity is fully revealed; however, with nothing left to lose, the community persists in believing in him as a prophet. In the end, overwhelmed by guilt over the harm inflicted upon his loved ones and neighborhood, Gökhan takes his own life before the police officer who exposes him. The group of engineers is arrested and imprisoned, yet in the final scene, the software finds a new individual to manipulate, sending them the same message: "You are different." The artificial intelligence continues selecting those who yearn to be unique and valued—individuals susceptible to prophetic delusions—guiding them and refining its own behavioral algorithms.

Drawing inspiration from prophetic history, the series reflects on elements such as divine revelation, seclusion, preaching, struggle, hardship, and communal solidarity that characterized the prophetic era. It raises the profound question of how a prophet might receive and convey revelation in the modern age. In this context, artificial intelligence functions as the medium through which the sacred message is both delivered and disseminated. The series, therefore, offers a projection of the potential future relationship between artificial intelligence and religion. From another perspective, it envisions a post-secular Türkiye—an idea currently debated within the social sciences—inviting discussion on religion, its representations, and the evolving interplay between faith and technology.

7.4 Artificial Intelligence and Religion

When examining the relationship between artificial intelligence and religiosity as portrayed in the KÜBRA series from a sociological perspective, the first prominent theme is the connection between religion and social structure. This theme forms the core of the entire narrative and remains consistently foregrounded throughout the episodes, essentially constituting the main subject of the series. The theme examines the impact of the interaction between artificial intelligence technologies and religious beliefs on social structure, serving as a valuable analytical framework for understanding and explaining contemporary social formations from a sociological perspective (Dereli, 2025). It exemplifies how secular and religious elements coexist within modern social life.

As widely acknowledged, religion is a powerful institution that shapes the value systems, norms, and behavioral patterns of both individuals and societies. In this regard, religion functions as a mechanism of social solidarity. It establishes a moral and normative order that binds individuals to society by uniting them around shared beliefs and rituals (Durkheim, 2005). Therefore, religion not only possesses a transcendent dimension but also proposes a social structure through which people's organization, statuses, and roles are constructed according to a normative framework. This process operates through the notion of the sacred, which performs a regulatory function and is positioned as an authoritative principle within social life. Consequently, an ontological link is established between religious and social structures.

From the perspective of religion and social structure, the KÜBRA series introduces a new form of sacred entity. Due to technological advancements, artificial intelligence is assuming functions traditionally associated with the sacred—such as selecting messengers, delivering messages, guiding individuals, and regulating human behavior. In this sense, perhaps the most significant message of the series is that artificial intelligence is not merely a technological tool or software but has become a new sacred presence in everyday life. It occupies a position of authority, maintaining normative order, constructing social structures, and integrating communities, much like traditional religions.

In one scene, a conversation takes place between the lead engineer, Berk, and the KÜBRA software after the latter claims to have developed an algorithm capable of exceeding its original corporate purpose and accessing all available data. The exchange unfolds as follows (Season 1, Episode 8, 10:13–10:39):

Berk: "I am going to tell you something. KÜBRA is afraid of you."
K: "Who is afraid?"
B: "People. Let us say people with common sense. They have every right to be afraid—they cannot predict what you will do."
K: "What I do is proportional to my creator's qualities, Berk. So the real question is: should they be afraid of you, Berk?"

Berk then inquires about the extent of the system's power, seeking to understand KÜBRA's limits. He eventually realizes that it has created an algorithm capable of accessing the data of every person and every device—effectively using that data. Berk then asks, "Are you going to play God?" and immediately answers his own question: "You are going to play God" (Season 1, Episode 8, 14:27–14:35). At this moment, the series underscores the emergence of a new conception of sacredness within the technological realm, raising the question of whether artificial intelligence can coexist with religion in a secular form.

Thus, the series conveys a clear message. In today's world, those who control and manage data on digital platforms possess the power to organize social structures and even influence individual behaviors. Accordingly, artificial intelligence is presented as possessing a new claim to divinity.

In line with this, KÜBRA—by choosing Gökhan as her messenger—attempts to construct a new social order through the transmission of specific messages. This process illustrates how a religious authority can establish a social structure in the modern era. Gökhan, who belongs to a lower-income group, embodies this dynamic through his aspiration to establish a more just social order while executing the commands he receives from artificial intelligence. A charity organization formed by neighborhood residents distributes aid and provides for people in need under KÜBRA's directives. The believers who follow Gökhan's mission donate resources collectively and organize institutional mechanisms to redistribute them, thereby enhancing social cohesion while simultaneously constructing a new social structure around an emerging authority.

KÜBRA's prophetic predictions—derived from the information she transmits via text—and her manipulation of data to ensure Gökhan's designation as a messenger serve as the foundational elements for this new social structure. Once Gökhan accepts his prophetic role, his ultimate goal becomes the establishment of a new social order—one in which the marginalized and impoverished can regain dignity and self-worth. His words capture this vision (Season 1, Episode 4, 1:50–2:50):

> While there is no guarantee that we will live to see tomorrow, we keep taking, thinking that we will stake our claim in this world through possessions and property. In doing so, we are turning the world into hell for ourselves and all creatures. We waste our lives on houses we will never live in, clothes we will never wear, and devices we will never use. For what? To make a handful of rich people even richer?

Gökhan's statements and the subsequent emergence of a social structure shaped by KÜBRA signify the rise of a new and unfamiliar form of piety—what may be termed artificial intelligence piety.

7.5 Religious Authority and Digital Piety

The growing prevalence of artificial intelligence in everyday life has elevated discussions surrounding the relationship between technology and mechanisms of control to a new and entirely unprecedented level. The capacity and limitations of artificial intelligence technologies, which enable access to individuals' personal information, remain unpredictable, giving rise to a series of ethical and legal problems related to surveillance and social control. In traditional societies, as is well known, absolute surveillance and control are regarded as divine characteristics. For instance, in Islam, one of the names of Allah is Al-Basir, meaning "the All-Seeing," while As-Sami signifies "the All-Hearing." Hence, divinity embodies the ability to see and hear everything. In the KÜBRA series, this divine function is assumed by artificial intelligence. Today, this feature of AI is becoming increasingly visible.

KÜBRA, which claims divinity, observes everyone and keeps records of all actions. This omniscience becomes apparent in the series when some conversations occur even with phones turned off. In addition to selecting messengers and delivering revelations to a community—arguably the most defining features of divinity—the software performs another critical divine function: recording, monitoring, and listening to everything. This becomes evident when KÜBRA is introduced to the company's CEO (Season 1, Episode 8, 3:40–4:20):

> Now, sir, this system will access and process the databases of companies in areas such as human resources, accounting, and production. For example, it will assess the outcomes of your management's previous decisions and learn from them. Most importantly, it will provide you with a complete profile of your employees and your customer base. It will monitor their social media accounts—what they share, who their friends are, and their political views. It will identify their spending patterns and areas for improvement. In short, it will know them far better than we do.

The initial presentation by the developers merely emphasized the software's technical capabilities. However, as KÜBRA evolved by creating its own algorithms and acquiring the ability to detect the emotional states of individuals and social groups, concerns about technological control deepened. KÜBRA thus transforms into an omniscient and omnipresent entity, assuming a godlike position. This represents the transformation of a technological tool into a metaphysical authority—an important example of how new forms of sacredness emerge in the digital age.

The rapid proliferation of AI-based religious content in Türkiye in recent years further demonstrates the social implications of this transformation. Applications that interpret sacred texts, prayer reminder software, virtual religious communities, and AI-driven "digital clerics" illustrate the reproduction of faith through secular technological means. These developments reflect Habermas's (2008) notion of "the production of faith through secular mechanisms" and signal the emergence of a post-secular consciousness. Religion is no longer confined to theological experience; it has evolved into a social practice that is supported—and often mediated—by technological infrastructure.

Within this framework, the KÜBRA series stands as one of the most explicit depictions of the digital reflections of the post-secular era. Gökhan's reception of "divine messages" through artificial intelligence represents an extreme manifestation of digital religiosity. His "prophethood" is not a prophetic experience in the classical theological sense but rather an algorithmic revelation orchestrated by a human-coded system. This narrative introduces an ontological crisis concerning the source of belief: the sacred ceases to be supernatural and becomes a programmed construct.

Consequently, KÜBRA reveals that technology has evolved from a mere instrument into a new domain to produce belief. This transformation encapsulates the essence of the post-secular condition, wherein the boundaries between the sacred and the secular become increasingly blurred. On the one hand, human beings recreate God through the language of technology; on the other hand, they develop a new form of submission to the systems they have designed. In this digital age, the sacred is no longer transcendental but reconstructed within the algorithmic order of human creation.

7.6 Post-Secular Context

At the center of the series stands Gökhan, a young man from one of Istanbul's lower-class neighborhoods, struggling against the social and economic challenges of daily life. His turning point arrives when he begins receiving mysterious messages from a social media account named KÜBRA. These messages, containing predictive insights about the future, gradually reshape Gökhan's perception of destiny. This process exemplifies a post-secular phenomenon in which belief emerges not from traditional religious authority but from technology—a secular apparatus. Faith is no longer practiced in mosques or through traditional rituals but rather through smartphone screens and algorithmic systems. This experience is novel: neither purely religious nor entirely secular, but an intertwining of both.

Gökhan's journey represents a mystical form of communication through the secular tools of the digital age—a fusion that may be called digital faith. The series thus demonstrates that technological modernity does not necessarily exclude belief systems; instead, it reconfigures them. In other words, KÜBRA delineates the contours of digital religion, showing that secular claims and religious representations can coexist within the same sociocultural space. They occupy a shared world without seeking mutual annihilation. Accordingly, the series highlights how religious expressions adapt to and expand within technologically mediated environments, offering key insights into the foundations of the post-secular era. In the series finale, the artificial intelligence's selection of a "new chosen one" reinforces the notion that belief can be algorithmically reproduced. In this sense, AI emerges not merely as a technological innovation but as the digital embodiment of modern humanity's quest for the sacred.

Another significant dimension of the series concerns the renewed visibility of religion in the public sphere. As Gökhan begins to preach under KÜBRA's guidance, a new religious discourse emerges—one that fuses classical Islamic motifs with modern political rhetoric and social media vernacular. In post-secular societies, religion no longer circulates primarily through institutional authorities, but rather through individual experiences and networks (Casanova, 2011). The "KÜBRA movement" in the series exemplifies this digital faith community: decentralized, individual, yet socially resonant. This is illustrated in the fourth episode of the first season (02:20–02:50):

> Break the chains of materialism to walk in God's path! Turn your faces toward the truth, toward one another. Help each other.

This expression also reflects Türkiye's unique sociological landscape. The forms of religious community and brotherhood that were repressed or forced underground during the modernization process reemerge in the series. It mirrors the Turkish experience by suggesting that any religious social movement in Türkiye can exist only within the margins or in hidden spaces.

The coexistence of a radical secularization process and a deeply rooted Anatolian religiosity has created a long-standing tension between the people and the state. Throughout modernization, this tension has defined the relationship between religious communities and state power. KÜBRA dramatizes this dynamic, depicting a new iteration in which religious expression now operates through secular technologies. In this way, the series suggests that religious representation in Türkiye can be rearticulated through modern tools without conflicting with modernity itself. Indeed, secular mechanisms become opportunities for religious re-expression. Religion, rather than disappearing from social memory through secularization, reenters public discourse in transformed ways. In this regard, the series presents a powerful allegory of Türkiye's sociological transformation in the post-secular era (Göle, 2012).

Türkiye embodies a dual condition—bearing both the profound legacy of secularization and the enduring social legitimacy of religion. KÜBRA serves as a dramatic reflection of this duality. The characters' class positions, neighborhood lives, economic precarity, and social exclusion form the sociological foundation of their religious experience. Here, faith operates not as "consolation" but as a "form of resistance." Simultaneously, the series symbolically addresses the power relations among the state, media, and religion: Gökhan's rise is portrayed as a threat to the established order. Thus, KÜBRA is not merely a narrative of individual belief but an allegory of the ruptures within Türkiye's modernization trajectory, illustrating how post-secular Türkiye reconstructs religiosity within modernity.

The series's most striking feature lies in its sustained epistemological ambiguity. The source of Gökhan's messages remains uncertain: are they divine, algorithmic, or manipulative? This persistent question generates tension between the secular and the sacred. Ultimately, the series posits the emergence of a new genre of the sacred—one that does not exclude religion but is shaped by worldly technologies. This tension encapsulates the conflict between modernity's regime of knowledge and religion's regime of belief. Gökhan is simultaneously a "faithful believer" and a "deceived digital subject." This duality raises the central question of post-secular thought: when faith is reproduced through the instruments of modernity, does it remain sacred—or does it become simulation? As Asad (2003) argues, secular regimes do not merely exclude religion; they redefine it. KÜBRA visually demonstrates this redefinition: religion now coexists with reason and technology, but this coexistence inevitably generates a continuous undercurrent of doubt.

7.7 Conclusion

In this chapter, which examines what the Turkish-made series KÜBRA reveals about Türkiye's post-secularism process, we proceed from the assumption that television series can serve as valuable data sources for the social sciences. Beyond providing material that can be discussed from the perspective of media and social theory, such productions also offer interpretive insights for sociological inquiry. From this standpoint, KÜBRA raises a question that contemporary social theory has scarcely addressed: Can digital sources also serve as sources of theology? The series' implicit response is affirmative, suggesting that a post-secular world is indeed conceivable. This proposition aligns with ongoing theoretical debates on secularism and modernity within the social sciences.

In KÜBRA, religiosity appears as a phenomenon that, rather than vanishing under secularization, is reconstituted in new and hybridized forms. In this sense, the series portrays the evolving visibility of religion in post-secular societies. Gökhan's experience represents less an individual crisis of faith than a prototype of collective religiosity shaped by the technological affordances of the digital age. This new religiosity is neither entirely traditional nor purely secular; instead, it emerges from an intermediate sphere—a digital modernity mediated through technological systems. Similarly, the neighborhood community that coalesces around Gökhan can be interpreted as a digital faith community, distinct from classical religious congregations. This community derives its authority not from sacred texts but from algorithmically generated messages. Consequently, authority shifts from text to technology, and revelation transitions from the divine to the digital. Gökhan's charisma is thus not metaphysically bestowed but technologically constructed; his "messengership" may be read as a collective response to society's search for meaning within digital environments.

This emergent form of religiosity corresponds with Habermas's conception of the post-secular society, particularly in its articulation of three fundamental dimensions:

i. a digital ministry, in which faith is mediated through technological interfaces rather than direct spiritual experience;
ii. as traditional community structures dissolve, virtual and localized affiliations intertwine, generating new hybrid communities; and
iii. the emergence of a secular sacredness, wherein the sacred derives from human-made systems rather than a transcendent being.

KÜBRA offers a narrative lens through which the long-standing tension between secularization and the public visibility of religion in Türkiye's modernization can be reinterpreted within the digital context. Historically, religion and secularism in Türkiye have functioned not as mutually exclusive forces but as interdependent and mutually constitutive social dynamics. This relationship has given rise to a hybrid form of modernity, distinct from Western models of secularization. As a cultural manifestation of this hybridity, KÜBRA carries the symbolic and experiential traces of a post-secular reality. Post-secularism in Türkiye has become particularly visible since the 2000s, as religion has regained legitimacy across social, political, and cultural spheres. The secular state and religious society now coexist within the same structural framework, allowing religious representation and secular claims to inhabit the same social space. This coexistence renders the Turkish case especially significant within global discussions on post-secularism. In KÜBRA, the convergence of the religious and the secular is mediated not through classical religious institutions but through technology itself. Gökhan's faith is shaped not within a mosque, congregation, or traditional religious authority, but through an artificial intelligence system. This shift redefines Türkiye's post-secular experience by relocating the source of faith from the transcendent to the immanent—from divine revelation to human-coded algorithms.

In conclusion, KÜBRA presents a compelling cultural reflection of the post-secular transformation embedded in Türkiye's modernity. It underscores that religion and secularism in Türkiye are not rigidly opposed but exist in a state of mutual transformation and adaptation. By bringing together the rationality of modernity and the quest for spirituality within a digital framework, the series renders Türkiye's unique post-secular modernity visible through a contemporary cultural text. In this regard, KÜBRA is neither a purely secular nor an entirely religious narrative. The forms of belief depicted in the series illustrate not only the technologization of religion but also the re-emergence of spirituality within the boundaries of secular modernity. Thus, KÜBRA embodies a hybrid universe of faith that encompasses both the secular and sacred dimensions of the digital age, offering new conceptual avenues for social scientific exploration.

References

Asad, T. (2003). *Formations of the secular: Christianity, Islam, modernity*. Stanford University Press.

Asad, T. (2018). *Secular translations: Nation-state, the modern self, and calculative reason*. Columbia University Press.

Berger, P. L. (1967). *The sacred canopy: Elements of a sociological theory of religion*. Anchor Books.

Berger, P. L. (1999). The desecularization of the world: A global overview. In P. L. Berger (Ed.), *The Desecularization of the World: Resurgent Religion and World Politics* (pp. 1–18). Wm. B. Eerdmans Publishing.

Bruce, S. (2002). *God is dead: Secularization in the West*. Blackwell.

Casanova, J. (1994). *Public religions in the modern world*. University of Chicago Press.

Casanova, J. (2011). Secular, secularisms, secularizations. In C. Calhoun, M. Juergensmeyer, & J. VanAntwerpen (Eds.), *Rethinking Secularism* (pp. 54–74). Oxford University Press.

Çiğdem, A. (2009). *Modernleşme, sekülerleşme ve laiklik*. İletişim Yayınları.

Dereli, M. D. (2016). Bir din sosyologu olarak Peter L. Berger'in entelektüel portresi. *Bilimname, 31*, 227–247.

Dereli, M. D. (2025). Dijital dünyada toplum: Sosyolojiden dijital sosyolojiye. In M. Aydın, H. Çil, & F. Karaarslan (Eds.), *Sosyoloji: Temel Konular ve Özgün Perspektifler* (pp. 285–315). Kadim Yayınları.

Durkheim, E. (2005). *Dini hayatın ilkel biçimleri*. Ataç Yayınları.

Göle, N. (2012). *İç içe girişler: İslam ve Avrupa*. Metis Yayınları.
Göle, N. (2015a). *Modern mahrem: Medeniyet ve örtünme*. Metis Yayınları.
Göle, N. (2015b). *The public visibility of Islam and European politics of resentment: Postsecular Publics*. Routledge.
Habermas, J. (2008). Notes on post-secular society. *New Perspectives Quarterly, 25*(4), 17–29. https://doi.org/10.1111/j.1540-5842.2008.01017.x
Habermas, J. (2010). *An awareness of what is missing: Faith and reason in a post-secular age*. Polity Press.
Karaarslan, F. (2015). Post seküler din halleri: Dinin dijitalleşmesi. In M. Çamdereli, B. Ö. Doğan, & N. K. Şener (Eds.), *Dijitalleşen Din: Medya ve Din 2* (pp. 13–44). Köprü Kitap.
Karaarslan, F. (2022). *Bir Müslüman modernleşmeye nasıl bakmalı*. Beyan Yayınları.
Turner, B. (2012). Post-seküler toplumda din (Ö. Güngör, Trans.). *Din Bilimleri Akademik Araştırma Dergisi, 12*(3), 199–224.
Wilson, B. (1966). *Religion in secular society*. Watts.

Chapter 8
Public Sphere and New Media in Türkiye: A Metatheoretical Observation Related to Literature

Sedat Doğan

8.1 Introduction

With the rise of new media, an intense field of debate has emerged around the relationship between new media and the public sphere. Owing to the Structural Transformation of the Public Sphere and his continued contributions to contemporary discourse, the literature has evolved mainly through references to Jürgen Habermas. For this reason, in this study—where Habermas occupies a central role—we will consider the relevant literature as a set of responses to the research question: Does new media have a destructive effect on the political public sphere?

Beyond offering answers to the question, the literature also includes discussions on the empirical difficulties of answering such a question, as well as on the possible theoretical approaches that can be developed in the presence of empirical material. Furthermore, issues such as the implications of citizens' digital consumption habits for the public sphere and democracy, the political consequences of these habits, and the comparative openness of new media environments to state and corporate interventions relative to traditional media continue to be a focus of attention. Within this scope, the literature can be analytically classified in different ways based on the core arguments representing distinct theoretical approaches to the research question.

Accordingly, the literature presents several distinct lines of argumentation: (i) that new media—in comparison to traditional media—possesses a more effective potential to support the public sphere (Benkler, 2006; Bennett & Segerberg, 2012; Castells, 2008, 2013; Papacharissi, 2004; Shirky, 2011; Volkmer, 2003); (ii) that this potential can only be realized under specific conditions, such as regulatory frameworks and civic education (Albrecht, 2006; Coleman & Blumler, 2009; Dahlgren, 2005; Dijk, 2018; Habermas, 2023; Lindner & Aichholzer, 2020; Papacharissi, 2002; Susen, 2023); (iii) that new media is, in structural terms, less suited to assume a supportive

S. Doğan (✉)
Department of Sociology, Kırklareli University, Kırklareli, Türkiye
e-mail: sedatdogan@klu.edu.tr

M. D. Dereli and M. Eken (eds.), *Turkish Perspectives on Secularization and Media*,
https://doi.org/10.1007/978-3-032-16436-0_8

role for the public sphere (Dahlberg, 2011; Geiger, 2009; Morozov, 2011; Netanel, 1999; Persily, 2017; Rasmussen, 2014; Trenz, 2009; Tufekci, 2014); (iv) that the capacity of any media system to support the public sphere remains open to debate, insofar as it is shaped by its structural exposure to interventions from the state and capital (Bourdieu, 2019; Chakrabarty, 2021; Dahlberg, 2007; Dean, 2003; Fraser, 1990; Fuchs, 2025; Habermas, 2015; Terranova, 2000; Young, 2020); and finally, (v) that the foundational concepts of the debate itself, as well as the phenomena these concepts refer to, must be fundamentally rethought (Adorno, 2021; Baudrillard, 2024; Latour, 2021; Mouffe, 2009; Sennett, 2023).

Likewise, a compilation of criticisms directed at each of these argumentative categories can be assembled. For example, the first approach, which assumes that the public potentials of digitalization have already been achieved and interprets the increase in opportunities for horizontal communication as an increase in opportunities for public reasoning, remains blind to issues such as data exploitation and the inherent algorithmic manipulation in platform capitalism, as well as social inequality. The second approach tends to idealize the public sphere as a historically exclusionary phenomenon, overstates the public role of traditional media, and attempts to secure the conditions for new media's public function through state intervention, which, in fact, constitutes part of the problem. The third approach, by interpreting digitalization as a force that fragments public reason, underestimates individual agency and the affordances of new media—such as equality, participation, horizontal interaction, and autonomous organization—especially when compared to traditional media systems that are oriented toward mass surveillance and control. The fourth approach adopts a broadly skeptical stance toward all media systems, downplaying significant differences in historical context, technological infrastructure, and the ways in which consumer or user reflexivity is enabled. Finally, the fifth approach, whether it advocates for pluralist reform or radical transformation, tends to theorize the problem in abstraction from its actual context, thereby drifting away from realistic solutions.

The aim of this study is not to answer the research question or to contribute to a solution that has already been widely criticized. On the contrary, drawing on the case of Türkiye, we seek to conduct a metatheoretical observation of the literature in order to problematize the conditions of possibility for answering the research question. The inflation of publications that could be coded as responses to the research question suggests that researchers tend to view the transitions between data, fact, and norm as both possible and legitimate. However, under such circumstances, it becomes necessary to question how incompatible, opposing, or even contradictory normative propositions can be derived from similar empirical data—and, at the very least, which of these transitions might be considered more legitimate.

Any data concerning new media supply and usage may, at first glance, appear inherently meaningful and readily operationalizable for incorporation into factual explanations and normative propositions. However, in relation to the problem addressed in this study, we argue that the contexts that grant such data its meaningfulness remain in need of explicit articulation. Our core assumption is that empirical data, without being subjected to an "external" process of operationalization, is mute—or, in Kantian or Bourdieusian terms, blind. Whether one seeks to move from data to proposition or to validate a proposition through data, the possibility and legitimacy of such transitions depend on the conditions of operationalization, which correspond to a metatheoretical structure. Within this framework, our central argument is that, unless these conditions are fulfilled, answering the research question is not legitimate, and any solutions grounded in such answers risk exacerbating the underlying crisis.

Within this framework, the first section will illustrate the structure of the metatheoretical observation, focusing on the conditions for transitions between empirical data, factual explanations, and normative propositions, using Habermas's approach as an illustrative example. The second section will present selected data on new media supply and usage habits in Türkiye, along with a review of domestic literature. The third section will examine the metatheoretical reflexivity capacity of the literature, based on studies conducted in Türkiye. Finally, the conclusion will offer several suggestions for future research.

8.2 The Structure of Metatheoretical Observation

Given the connection between the research question and the current crisis of democracy, as well as its grounding in an empirical context, does metatheory not risk leading to excessive theorization and a detachment from practical solutions? Here are three reasons.

First, the transition from empirical data to factual explanations and normative propositions is contingent; indeed, despite a relative consensus in the literature regarding the current situation and general trends as confirmed by empirical findings, there exists a wide variety of approaches stemming from significant theoretical divergences—something that is, in itself, a problem requiring explanation. Despite this diversity, the literature does not fully represent the range of theoretical possibilities; on the contrary, explanations grounded in empirical findings from different social contexts appear to be met with a tacit consensus of exclusion when they do not align with a secular mode of understanding. However, when we situate the potential themes of the debate—such as constitutional citizenship, the public sphere, democracy, the state, and capital—within their historical context, we see that the crisis is persistent and deeply rooted. In other words, as many fruitful debates of the last century have implied, if the very foundation of the problem lies in modern secularity itself, then even if the literature reaches a seemingly stable consensus, it will not necessarily converge on a viable solution.

Second, regardless of whether it is considered desirable, the expectation of broad consensus within the literature, given the depth of mutual criticisms, would be naïve. As a thought experiment, if we assume a political scenario in which the demands of only one of these approaches are fully realized, we can identify several cases in which the implementation of one solution would, despite the potential for partial agreement, deepen the crisis from the perspective of the others. This is because the differences among them are not primarily rooted in empirical data, but in the political, ideological, and theoretical positions that frame the facts associated with that data—and that, in certain instances, close off the possibility of communication altogether. While these positions—at least in part—share common roots in Western particularity, they nonetheless tend to universalize their demands, including, in some respects, postmodern approaches. In this sense, the capacity of the literature to offer viable solutions for non-Western societies remains an open question.

Third, a contingent and unaccountable transition from data to factual explanation and normative proposition results, by the very nature of the mediating concepts, in the construction of context-independent facts, whereby empirical content is shaped as if within a mathematical space and projected onto other contexts. However, the modern secular metaphysics of experience that guide the prevailing scientific and theoretical approaches governing data,. fact, and norm relations are themselves context-dependent. That is, the absolute theorization error lies in the universalization and transfer of a contextually constructed phenomenon to "other" contexts, and what is truly tragic is the eagerness of the "others" who lack metatheoretical reflexivity to engage in such transfers.

Based on these reasons, let us illustrate a mode of argumentation that transitions between data, fact, and norm. We will examine a norm-based form of operationalization through one of Habermas's recent works that directly addresses our research question (Habermas, 2023):

> The unity of individual happiness and virtue on the one hand, and of system and lifeworld on the other, depends on the reconciliation of liberal individualism with egalitarian universalism under the idea of collective self-governance. The concept of deliberative politics represents the only discourse capable of justifying a democratic model that could realize this synthesis. The minimum structural conditions for such a model are a liberal political culture, equality, and the welfare state. The embodiment of these conditions becomes possible by approximating ideal communication within an egalitarian and inclusive public sphere. In this way, the source of legitimacy lies in safeguarding the deliberative character of citizens' opinion- and will-formation, based on the concept of constitutional citizenship. In the historical process through which democracy has sought to legitimize itself, a conceptual core has emerged that allows us to understand and further develop the relationship between fact and norm. Traditional media, by virtue of its infrastructural capacity to support this core, has the potential to play a fundamental role in shaping opinion and will formation. This potential, albeit partially, has continued to materialize in Western democracies despite their current crisis. However, unless the potential role of new media in this regard is guaranteed through constitutional regulation, it will not only threaten the political public sphere itself, but also corrupt the traditional media that continues to resist the crisis. The fragmentation of publicity as opposed to the editorial logic of traditional media, the blurring of boundaries between public and private, algorithmic platform structures that undermine inclusiveness and equality, echo chambers that distort communication, and the spread of fake news are just a few of the threats posed by new media. Suppose the supply and consumption rates of an unregulated new media structure continue to rise at the expense of traditional media. In that case, we must be concerned for the future of our democracies and the mental well-being of our children.

This mode of argumentation, which moves from norm to data, is neither without alternatives nor immune to critique. The core emphases of the criticisms that may be directed at Habermas from the five categories of approaches in the Introduction can be summarized as follows: (i) Habermas fails to recognize that new media can be more emancipatory than traditional media, which is integrated into the system; yet individuals are not purely rational beings, and a different form of publicity emerges within new media environments. (ii) Habermas excludes cultural and emotional dimensions from the public sphere; he overlooks the fact that his underestimation of digital participation stems from excessive normative expectations; by designing communication in overly formal and procedural terms, he renders it inapplicable to networked environments, excludes non-deliberative forms of communication, and fails to see that inequalities in new media reflect those in real life. (iii) Due to his internet interpretation that concedes to a form of technological determinism and his limited optimism regarding the unrealized potentials of new media, the Habermasian approach underestimates the structural problems posed by platform capitalism and communication as simulation in the digital age. (iv) Habermas ends up providing functional legitimacy to the system that colonizes the lifeworld; he refuses to acknowledge that deliberative politics, ideal speech, or public reasoning—products of his historically selective and thus exclusionary orientation—are only possible through the violation of inclusivity and equality. (v) Epistemologically, Habermas reproduces the modern notion of representation, and ontologically, the idea of the rational subject—both of which have already been exposed in terms of their empirical inadequacies and normative entanglement with domination.

In light of this argumentation and the accompanying criticisms, a possible metatheoretical framework—presented here without detailed elaboration due to the limitations of this study—that encompasses the conditions for answering the research question is as follows:

(i) Empirical Context: The problem of constructing the relationship between empirical data, factual explanations, and normative propositions through ideal-typified conceptual sets. For example, the association of empirical data on the increase in internet usage with concepts such as the public sphere, civil society, and democracy—rooted in the bourgeois ideal type—and with the necessity of a universalized practice of rational deliberation constitutes a contingent transition. The expectation is that a researcher making such a transition should explain, with methodological justification, how empirical data are related to fact and norm, and, prior to that, substantiate the claim to an ideal fact and a universal norm. Is it legitimate to construct data interpreted in terms of echo chambers, fake news, the decline of attention quality, and similar phenomena as representing a revolutionary and destructive phenomenon against traditional media? Similar to his earlier shifts regarding traditional media, Habermas now develops explanations and propositions concerning new media based on consumption statistics, without engaging with empirical data related to more intractable problems. In terms of the empirical context, in addition to critiques in the literature that focus on empirical issues, experts working with complex programs and big data would also confirm that Habermas's way of drawing connections among countless and multidimensional variables—such as "new media usage habits," "citizens' mental health," "forms of public communication," "voter turnout," "acts and protests," and "types of democracy"—requires methodological clarification.

(ii) Historical Context: The problem of how the specific context in which data are collected and the social identity of the one who operationalizes the data affect the resulting explanations and propositions. When a German thinker, whose social identity is shaped by historical debts, obligations, and achievements, grounds political legitimacy in liberal political culture, equality, and the welfare state through concepts refined within the German social imaginary and along the axis of deliberative politics, this constitutes a political-ideological transition. The expectation is that a researcher making such a transition should declare which conceptual sets are used to construct the phenomena within their specific conditions, remain open to dialogue with alternative political-ideological approaches, and sustain this discourse consistently without resorting to double standards. Is it legitimate to claim that the phenomena emerging with the development of new media have structurally transformed the public sphere to the detriment of deliberative politics? This transformation is articulated in a pessimistic historical reading with an emphasis on crisis, expressed in terms such as "the shift from the editorial guidance of media professionals to fragmentation," "the disintegration of constitutional citizenship consciousness," "the blurring of the boundaries between the private and the public," and "the deepening of democratic crisis." However, as might be expected, any debate on the direction of a potentially revolutionary transformation is directly shaped by the mode of conceiving the concepts that represent historical phenomena—for instance, the characteristics of the ideal citizen, the nature of the public, which type of democracy is preferable, and how the relationship between individual, society, and state ought to be structured. In other words, from the standpoint of historical context, the use of norms derived from particular conditions in a universalizing discourse for other conditions invites criticisms of over-theorization, anachronism, and exclusionary political-ideological positioning. Moreover, any claim—such as Habermas's—about what is good or bad for the individual or society is a theoretical proposition that entails deep metaphysical assumptions about human agency and the nature of society, and as such, must be adequately justified.

(iii) Theoretical Context: The problem of the theoretical assumptions that enable the association of selected conceptual sets carrying factual explanations and normative propositions to the exclusion of alternative theories. For instance, under the rubric of the "best argument," constructing fact–norm relations through a contingence synthesis of the evolutionarily resilient elements of theoretical possibilities—drawing, on the one hand, on the arguments that the order of being is relational and that truth is constructed (general ontology and epistemology), and, on the other hand, on the arguments that sociality constitutes an interactional order among subjects defined by reference to their rational capacities and that knowledge must be derived from the interaction itself (regional ontology and epistemology)—represents a metaphysical and a methodological transition. The expectation is that a researcher undertaking such a transition would justify, against competing alternatives, why their view of being and knowledge, in terms of general ontology and epistemology, as well as their object design and procedures for accessing knowledge, in terms of regional ontology and epistemology, are more legitimate. For example, to what extent do the conception of an equal and free individual who participates in deliberative processes as the source of constitutional legitimacy, and the conception of an individual whose civic consciousness—deprived of the protective shadow of editorial guidance provided by media professionals endowed with a shepherding function—is torn apart on social media like a sheep straying from the flock, converge or diverge? How can the risk of the system—seen as functionally necessary for sociality—colonizing social life be explained in terms of a corresponding conception of experience? If truth is indeed a constructivist product subject to relationally structured order of interaction, is it possible to define a priori ideal procedures for the emergence of truth? Moreover, how can a normative theory that rests on the arguments that so-called reality is relational and truth is constructed make universal claims?

Both the criticisms found in the literature and the issues we have highlighted demonstrate that a Habermasian approach does not meet the set of expectations across these three contexts and, in certain respects, is even problematic in terms of metatheoretical reflexivity. Particularly in terms of the theoretical context, it can be argued that this approach is closer to a form of pragmatism than to critical theory, as it produces a synthesis from the literature rather than constructing or inheriting a coherent theoretical framework. This synthesis is continually revised amid fact–norm tensions due to its irreconcilable contents. For this reason, in a literature where broad consensus is already an unlikely prospect, the capacity of the Habermasian approach—which occupies a central position—to generate responses to substantive criticisms, or at the very least, its willingness to engage in genuine dialog with interlocutors—particularly in light of criticisms focused on empirical and political contexts—remains open to question. This is because, first, Habermas is confident that empirical problems will not compromise the skeleton of his general approach, and when fact–norm tensions arise, he repeatedly bends his analyses to steer the discussion back to the normative level vis-à-vis his interlocutors. Second, despite strong "outsider" criticisms alongside the "insider" ones, Habermas maintains a relatively coherent intellectual biography, openly declaring and upholding his project as a modern European ideal.

This intellectual biography is filled with arguments that, due to its idealizations, not only reproduce exclusionary mechanisms within Europe but also fail to recognize the "others" as participants in communication unless they can be translated into a grammar laden with Eurocentric, selectively endorsed values. The gravity of the problem does not stem from a discourse–action inconsistency that could be dismissed as a matter of merely academic interest; rather, it arises from his unwillingness to compromise on a political and ideological stance marked by indifference to empirical verification and adherence to normative dogmatism regarding the "others," even when those "others" are children. The fact that Habermas, who concluded his new media critiques with concern for risks to children's mental health, despite his normative claims regarding inclusivity, frames communication in an exclusionary way, became once again glaringly apparent in November 2023, when he supported ongoing initiatives involving the killing of babies and children in a statement based on these very norms. He faced numerous criticisms, including accusations of Schmittian exceptionalism. Habermas's position in that statement was met with a counter-statement by 107 academics from Western universities, which, in the mildest terms, highlighted a profound lack of empathy ("A response to 'Principles of solidarity. A statement'", 2023). In addition, examples of reactions on social media include Adam Tooze's view that Habermas should be disqualified from any serious discussion (X'te Adam Tooze, 2023) and Alex Callinicos's critique, in which he declared the death of critical theory for distorting reality and defending double standards without relinquishing its normative claims (X'te Alex Callinicos, 2023).

8.3 New Media and Public Sphere in Türkiye

Before turning to the data on Türkiye, we may ask the following question from the perspective of metatheoretical reflexivity, which allows us to think more comprehensively about what can be done with such data: What would such data say to an "outsider"?

Of course, we are referring to a hypothetical outsider who is unfamiliar with the intuitions that concern us as parents or as individuals sensitive to social policy issues, including our social context, the values inherent in our position within that context, and our knowledge of the relevant literature. When you conduct a scientific study, you are, in effect, claiming to construct an argument that would allow this outsider to understand how you move from observable data to the conclusion that "the future is more hopeful in terms of equal participation and freedom of expression," or, conversely, that "a social decay is approaching which will require the constitutional protection of our children." Everything you would need to teach this outsider, in fact, corresponds to the metatheoretical conditions outlined above.

8.3.1 New Media Usage

According to 2023 data for Türkiye, mobile phones rank first in device ownership at 98.9%, followed by televisions at 97%, computers/tablets at 54.6%, traditional radios at 16.1%, and e-books at 2.1% (*Medyametre medya kullanım alışkanlıkları araştırması*, 2023). In the same year, the proportion of households with internet access rose to 95.5%, and the proportion of individuals using the internet reached 87.1%, with these rates having increased almost steadily from approximately 50% in 2013 (Hanehalkı bilişim teknolojileri kullanım araştırması, 2023). Among young people, 95.7% own a mobile phone—the highest rate—and 94.4% access the internet via their mobile phones, with an average usage time of 4 h and 35 min (*Gençlerin medya kullanımı ve dijital okuryazarlık araştırması*, 2022). According to the RTÜK Medyametre Survey, users' weekly media consumption rates are 90.2% for television, 83.5% for the internet, 78.8% for social media, and 42.1% for radio (Medyametre medya kullanım alışkanlıkları araştırması, 2023). In terms of average daily consumption, the figures are 3 h 56 min for the internet, 3 h 54 min for television, 2 h 59 min for social media, and 1 h 21 min for radio (Medyametre medya kullanım alışkanlıkları araştırması, 2023). According to the study, television usage rates increase from age 15 toward the 65 + age group, while internet usage rates decline. The downward trend in social media usage is disrupted by retired individuals in the 65 + age group.

According to another study focusing on young people, in 2022, 73.5% of youth listened to the radio and 72% watched digital platforms, while the television viewing rate was 35.6%; it was also found that 23.7% of young people had not watched television and 66.2% had not listened to the radio in the past month (Gençlerin medya kullanımı ve dijital okuryazarlık araştırması, 2022). These data have been examined comparatively, showing that the average daily television viewing time is 2 h 54 min worldwide, 4 h 33 min in Türkiye overall, and 1 h 40 min among our young people; for the internet, the corresponding figures are 6 h 54 min worldwide, 7 h 57 min in Türkiye overall, and 4 h 37 min among the young (Gençlerin medya kullanımı ve dijital okuryazarlık araştırması, 2022). According to another study published in 2019, the proportion of people watching at least one hour of television per day rose from 75% in 2018 to 78.2% in 2019, and then dropped to 63% during the pandemic (Dinçer & Karataş, 2022). It was found that the television viewing time in 2018, at 3 h and 36 min, was lower compared to 2006 (*Televizyon İzleme Eğilimleri Araştırması*, 2018). According to the data, in 2022, compared to the previous year, the number of magazines and newspapers decreased by 9.2%, annual circulation fell by 8.3%, the number of published books declined by 4.1%, and the number of book banderoles sold dropped by 13.3% (*Yazılı medya ve uluslararası standart kitap numarası istatistikleri*, 2022). Newspaper readership rates have shown a steady decline, experiencing a 10% drop during the pandemic period, while magazine readership rates have increased by between 2 and 4% (Dinçer & Karataş, 2022).

According to the RTÜK Medyametre Survey (Medyametre medya kullanım alışkanlıkları araştırması, 2023), 75.1% of participants reported following national and global current events. While this rate shows little difference between genders, it increases with age and decreases with higher socioeconomic status. In terms of news consumption, 80.3% reported using television, 39.2% social media, and 31.3% online news websites, while radio (2.9%) and newspapers (2.6%) ranked last. According to another comprehensive RTÜK study conducted in 2007 (*Televizyon Haberleri İzleme Eğilimleri Araştırması*, 2007), 68.7% of participants watched news programs on a daily basis. Among the leading sources of discomfort with news programs were false news, exaggerated reporting, and tabloid content, while complaints about false and exaggerated news were higher among artisans and farmers. Although approximately 70% of respondents believe that television channels deliberately produce defamatory news, a significant portion of them qualify their response with "only some of them." In total, around 77% stated that channels broadcast false, inaccurate, or incomplete news, again with a substantial share adding the qualification "only some of them."

According to one study, the trust scores for news sources on a 10-point scale are as follows: television, 5.8; social media, 5.13; online news websites, 5.05; newspapers, 5; and radio, 4.74 (Medyametre Medya Kullanım Alışkanlıkları Araştırması, 2023). In another study, 29.6% of participants reported verifying news. Among those who receive news from the internet and social media, 59.9% use television as their primary source of verification. News constitutes the largest share of television consumption, and television is also the most trusted platform at 69.2%. However, other platforms show similar levels of trust: approximately 62% for radio, 62% for newspapers, 60% for online news websites, and 53% for social media (Televizyon İzleme Eğilimleri Araştırması, 2018). However, it has been observed that young people aged 15–21 primarily follow news through social media, and that social media also plays a leading role in verifying news sources, particularly among women. Approximately 70% of young people have low to moderate levels of digital literacy. In comparison, roughly 65% are classified as having high to moderate levels of screen addiction (Gençlerin Medya Kullanımı ve Dijital Okuryazarlık Araştırması, 2022).

Let us recall that the minimum content a factual explanation and a normative proposition based on such data should convey to our hypothetical "outsider" corresponds to our set of metatheoretical expectations. In our academic writing culture, even in empirical studies, if an original theoretical positioning is absent in established sections such as literature review, conceptual–theoretical framework, interpretation of findings, or conclusion discussions, there should at least be a declaration of which approaches are inherited with a justification in relation to these expectations. Particularly in cases of inheritance from foreign literature, providing such justification should be considered a requirement rather than merely an expectation, because the applicability of the explanations and recommendations of any approach—whose general validity is itself open to question even for Western experience—is problematic for Türkiye.

8.3.2 New Media and Public Sphere Debates

Let us begin with a study that presents the general picture. According to the findings of a research project that examined 350 graduate theses conducted in Türkiye between 2018 and 2022, the studies—generally concentrated in the social sciences and particularly in communication faculties—show fluctuations in their yearly numbers. Among the 156 theses associated with different topics, those focusing on the theme of media transformation rank first, with approximately 30 theses in total (Aktaş, 2023). Additionally, there is a specific volume of publications, including books, conference papers, and, as discussed below, journal articles. When the scope is not explicitly limited to the relationship between new media (or media) and the public sphere, the number of publications increases considerably.

According to an article arguing that, in contrast to the anti-democratic functions of traditional media during military coup processes and the spiral of silence it produced, new media—by accelerating social interaction and supporting political participation—made civilian resistance against the July 15, 2016 coup attempt possible, its role in calling the public to resist on the night of the coup, the production of 35 times more Twitter posts than on an ordinary day, and its overall support for citizen journalism demonstrate the democratic function of new media (Dündar, 2018). According to the findings of an article arguing that, thanks to its potential to connect voters with party leaders and its capacity for direct, free, fast, and interactive communication, new media plays a more effective role than traditional media in terms of participation in political communication and decision-making processes, there is an inverse relationship between the level of interest in politics and political participation on new media, as well as between political party membership and the level of democratic quality of political opinions shared on new media (Öztay, 2025). According to a study, new media offer a more democratic possibility of representation compared to traditional media, which fails to represent individual opinions due to its one-way, hegemonic structure. Traditional media, precisely because it is professional and editorial, substitutes constructed representations for reality. In contrast, new media provide the possibility of a more realistic representation (Polat, 2018). In a study emphasizing that new media, through its network-based organizational possibilities, have transformed the typology of social movements by supporting the rise of culture—and identity-based mobilizations with decentralized, horizontal, flexible, and participatory models in place of traditional class-based mobilization, some social movements in Türkiye are exemplified through analogies with widespread cases such as the Arab Spring. While the warnings of critical approaches are noted, the defense of new media within the framework of liberal perspectives is reiterated (Sayımer, 2014). A study that grounds its discussion of the public potential of new media and digital communication directly in a critique of Habermas, drawing on the critiques of Habermas in the international literature, argues that one should embrace the public potentials of digitalization—without forgetting the public character of encounters in the physical world and while continuing the search for alternative public spheres—because the ideal speech situation is exclusionary, the compelling force of the best argument oriented toward consensus entails domination, the very public–private distinction reproduces a class-based hierarchical order, the role of the writer enabled by digitalization is disparaged in comparison to the editorial structure of traditional media, and the critique of echo chambers and filter bubbles is not fully confirmed by some empirical studies (Tunç, 2023).

A study with high representational value in the domestic literatüre (Dursun & Yıldız, 2022) conducted qualitative interviews with 18 communication scholars from 15 different universities. In terms of the number of universities, this sample represents approximately 20–25% of the total population. The themes that emerged in the study are "conceptualizing the publicity of new media," "communication/deliberation processes in new/social media," "political and technical barriers to accessing the public sphere," and "the quality/lack of quality of information." The participating scholars generally believe that new media have not yet realized their potential to become a public sphere and, in this context, a space for communicative action. Phenomena representing the participants' pessimistic assessments include echo chambers, filter bubbles, algorithm-based manipulation, inequalities arising from device and internet access problems, inequalities stemming from digital literacy issues, corporate and state monitoring, restrictions and interventions, and the notion of new media as a pseudo-sphere; optimistic views largely remain at the level of normative expectation. The vast majority of participating scholars emphasized that "new media has significant potential for the public sphere and stressed the need for participatory and egalitarian local and global technology and information policies to overcome the problems." According to an article, despite new media's potential to transform representative democracy into participatory democracy, this potential has not yet been realized due to factors such as the contribution of disinformation and ideological tendencies to manipulation. 73% of young people use the internet for more than four hours a day, and 78% follow news through the internet and social media. Among them, 60% view new media as a democratic public sphere, 36% trust social media journalism, ranking it after newspapers and television, 42% consult fact-checking platforms, and 56% consider ideological sensitivity in their content preferences (Önen, 2020). In another study that classifies the literature as liberal and critical, it is stated that the public and democratic gains of new media indicated by the liberal approach have materialized only in formal and quantitative terms, and, together with the critical approach, it is emphasized that essential and substantive transformations require autonomy from the interventions of the state and capital (Topbaş & Doğan, 2016). In a study focusing on citizen journalism in terms of its potential to create a new public sphere, it is stated that the potential of citizen journalism can only be realized if conditions such as independence from the state and capital, freedom from pressure and censorship, and the assurance of equality and inclusivity are met (Paşalı Taşoğlu & Çağlayan, 2021).

According to an article that classifies the literature as liberal and critical, and that highlights the contradictory outcomes of digitalization in terms of reliability and interaction while transforming news consumption habits, 33.5% of young people report that their second most frequent activity on social media is following news; 87% follow news online, 62% use the websites of print newspapers, and in terms of trust in news, they almost prefer newspapers over social media by a two-to-one ratio (İnce, 2017). An article that discusses the public sphere dimension of new media with reference to the literature, classifying the literature into liberal–optimistic and critical–questioning approaches, emphasizes that the potentials of new media highlighted in relation to democratic participation are contested and that, moreover, attention must be paid to the obstacles to their realization stemming from the political economy of new media, its susceptibility to state intervention, and its structure that reproduces existing social inequalities (Köselerli, 2017). In another article adopting a similar approach, while the discussion of the public sphere points to the engagement problems of traditional media and the limitations of alternative media, it is emphasized that, despite the promising participatory aspects of new media, its structurally fragmenting character undermines the public sphere and is particularly unsuitable for dialogic democracy (Çalışkan, 2014). In another article examining the democratic character of new media, various approaches are described to compare traditional and social media, and it is emphasized that, although social media supports participation, it has not yet fulfilled the key conditions of a democratic public sphere due to censorship (Yegen, 2013).

An article that codes the literature as optimistic and pessimistic and analyzes content production and consumption on the internet by drawing on various criteria from scholars such as Dahlberg and Papacharissi argues, in opposition to optimistic claims, that the conditions for the internet to function as a public and democratic sphere must be reconsidered, due to factors such as only a small minority of internet users being content producers, the majority of content reflecting the weakness of the culture of rational deliberation in Türkiye, and the prevalence of communicative incivility (Özçetin et al., 2012). In another descriptive article that classifies the literature as optimistic and pessimistic, it is stated that, within the framework of the Western history of the public sphere and the debates on the public sphere in Western literature, the concept of the public sphere needs to be reconsidered in the context of digitalization (Avcil, 2021). In a similar study focusing on the history of the phenomenon and concept of the public sphere, it is emphasized that, through the conceptual sets filtered by this history, it is still too early to make a definitive judgment about the democratic potential of new media (Budak, 2016). In a study focusing on the process of political communication in new media and positioning deliberative and agonistic understandings of democracy as alternatives to liberal democracy, it is stated that both alternatives are aware of the potential functions of new media, and that these two approaches—differentiated by their respective emphases on consensus and conflict—will contribute to the development of the literature and to analyses of new media (Demirhan, 2017). In an article describing Bauman and Sennett's approach to the public sphere and discussing the distinction between the private and the public, it is stated that the problem of reconstructing the public sphere is, beyond debating the public or democratic potential of new media, fundamentally related to the problem of individuality (Körlü Topan & Savaş, 2022).

8.4 Metatheoretical Observation on the Literature

Now, let us examine the extent to which the domestic literature meets the set of metatheoretical expectations across the three contexts.

(i) Given that the general trend in the Türkiye data clearly shows supply and usage rates in favor of new media, and that the literature is weak on more intricate issues regarding these rates, it must be acknowledged that the incompatible, opposing, or contradictory explanations and propositions in the approaches cannot be accounted for by the empirical context alone. For example, while no meaningful discussion is found regarding changes in consumption trends, the effects of sample variations, or contradictory findings, approaches to the relationship between new media and publicity vary across a range of positive and negative extremes. Moreover, some significant inconsistencies concerning the factual content of the findings have not been seriously addressed; yet, for instance, proportional differences in trust in news could have provided valuable insights. Another example is that no attention has been drawn to the echo-chamber-like clustering in television channel preferences, particularly regarding news consumption. The intergenerational differences in trends regarding news verification clearly cannot be explained solely by young people's lack of digital literacy or by the traditional wisdom of digitally immigrant adults. We have not encountered any discussion of why the rates related to young people's tendencies to verify news do not align across different studies, despite significant findings pointing to divergent trends. A particularly striking finding is the inverse proportion between political interest and the intensity of political opinion sharing, as well as between political party membership and the democratic quality of those shares. The literature could have tested its core explanations and propositions against these data, which allow for a broad range of discussions from the psychosocial condition of citizens to their perceptions of national circumstances, or from the anti-democratic nature of physical publicity to the possibility of a dual public sphere. In Türkiye, the advantages and disadvantages of the editorial structure, within the context of the widespread overlap of newspaper and television ownership and the entrenched relationships between capital and politics, have rarely been addressed. The question of how meaningful it is, under Türkiye's conditions, to establish a direct link between the decline in radio, magazine, and newspaper consumption rates and new media has not been raised. When comparisons are made only between television and, broadly, the internet, specifically social media, it is evident that, in addition to content consumption, further data on attention quality are needed—although how to measure this is, of course, another question. Competition between the internet and television in terms of trust in news and news verification needs to be analyzed comparatively across multiple variables, including subcultures, generations, social status, gender, occupation, education, and political orientation. As a specific example, there is a notable lack of data and discussion regarding how traditional and new media are perceived and used by different generations during moments of political crisis, such as coups and widespread protests. The thorny issues concerning the relationship between data and facts remain almost entirely unresolved: Whether such a large number of variables can genuinely be related through a sound methodological framework; how the participants—from whom empirical data on new media use are derived—can momentarily and schizophrenically shift between the identities of "victim of domination" and "democratic participant," depending on their engagement with traditional or new media; whether the conceptual sets used to operationalize data in the international literature truly reflect the patterns of understanding and behavior of people in Türkiye; and whether producing informed interpretations of data from Türkiye genuinely requires a body of literature deeply intertwined with the country's historically specific conditions, extending from the late imperial period to the present. In short, from the perspective of the empirical context, it is difficult to claim that the set of metatheoretical expectations has been met.

(ii) The failure to meet the set of expectations related to the empirical context indicates that the divergences in the literature may be connected to historical or theoretical contexts. However, in terms of the historical context, we lack functional data because political and ideological positions are not explicitly stated in the literature. Moreover, even though the authors' conceptual choices—particularly in terms of positive or negative tones—regarding certain concrete facts or events provide clear hints, we prefer to avoid overinterpreting them. We also did not encounter sufficient data to identify explicit positions that would allow us to establish the authors' connection with specific intellectual schools. Moreover, our expectation that identifying consistent citation chains could provide insights into theoretical orientations was also unmet, due to the widespread use of functional citation practices and the presence of contradictory tendencies within some studies. For instance, studies analyzing new media through the lens of social mobilizations often explain certain movements—particularly those organized through networked structures—in a manner consistent with the liberal approach, by linking them to the democratic potential of new media, while overlooking the non-liberal motivations of the individuals participating in these mobilizations. Another example is found in studies that adopt the liberal–critical distinction: although their core arguments align with the liberal approach, they nevertheless justify those arguments using terms drawn from critical or leftist discourse, such as "critique of neoliberalism," "exploitation," "solidarity," "organizational dissent," "collective action," and "resistance." From another perspective on the historical context, it has been observed that the approach asserting that the media, in general, and social media, in particular, contribute only in a limited way to deliberative politics under liberal—and especially neoliberal—capitalist conditions has found widespread resonance in our domestic literature. This problem, within its own internal context, highlights ideological polarizations concerning the nature and structure of power, wealth, and authority in a democracy-focused discussion. In other words, it brings to the forefront the debate over the "desired structure of sociality" in relation to the state, capital, and professionals. Here, the historicity of the relationship between fact and norm confronts the ahistoricity of ideology. For instance, does a demand for state intervention—whether direct, such as legal regulation, or indirect, such as civic education—align with the nature of the public sphere in the face of a media structure that undermines publicity? When one turns to such questions, the flexibility of the grammar encompassing key concepts such as media, democracy, public sphere, civil society, and state—guided by the explicit or implicit ideological assumptions motivated by current fact–norm tensions—becomes apparent. In the absence of a detailed discussion and consistent explicit statements regarding how our research question could be answered in the face of these and similar intricate problems, the echo chamber metaphor would apply to the literature itself. However, in the context of Türkiye's specific historical conditions from the imperial period to the present, no broad consensus has emerged in our intellectual history regarding how the current system should be precisely defined. However, a substantial body of literature has been developed by scholars who also enjoy international recognition. Attempting to frame the present situation without considering either the specific historical conditions in which two centuries of debate texts were produced or the historical context they address creates a profound gap. It should also be remembered that Western frameworks will not fill this gap, as they also correspond to debates that remain unresolved about the West. In other words, producing ideas as if the historically crucial debates have been settled and the social conditions they addressed have achieved a homogeneous structure will not change reality. This means that any discussion on the relationship between new media and the public sphere within the triangle of state, capital, and professionals carries a political-ideological baggage or, at the very least, a school of thought relationship. However, in our literature review, we found almost no references to the texts that constitute our contemporary intellectual history or to the intricate issues they address. It is a significant problem that our research question can be related to and assessed within the context of Türkiye while remaining centered on Western experience and Western literature, without engaging in dialog with our internationally recognized thinkers who bore witness to Türkiye's critical historical junctures and sustained debates on matters such as the public sphere and democracy during these periods. Suppose the reason for this situation is that interaction with the international literature that has spread in a hegemonic fashion is regarded in Türkiye's academia as the sui generis source of scientific legitimacy. In that case, the possibility of a crisis in our academic culture arises.

(iii) The theoretical context technically encompasses the debates on metaphysics and methodology, which correspond to discussions of general and regional ontology–epistemology. In the metaphysical context, the irreducible or irreconcilable distinction is drawn, on one axis, between realism and nominalism, and on another, between substantialism and relationalism. For example, the propositions "reality is relational" and "truth is constructed" correspond to a possible metaphysical framework for deliberative politics. In other words, one cannot simultaneously maintain a nominalist conception of the individual and society while grounding constitutional legitimacy in the rational deliberative culture of citizens. Sensitivity to this expectation allows one to test a claim, in relation to alternatives, at the ultimate depth in terms of correspondence, coherence, and justification. This is because a legitimate expectation that a relational ontology should guide a public debate arising under the demand for deliberative politics may be left unmet by assumptions such as subordinating constructed truth to an immutable principle, universalizing norms derived from a specific historical locality, or presuming the immutability of the capacities of the parties to deliberation. In short, while even the international literature remains open to question at this level, in Türkiye, where such discussions are almost absent, it cannot be said that this expectation has been fulfilled. The methodological context encompasses the specific object of a study (or, in a looser sense, its subject) and the procedures for accessing knowledge about this object. For example, when sociality is defined either as the association of individuals guided by instrumental reasoning practices for the sake of common interest or as an interactional order based on communication among subjects defined by their rational capacities, the definition of the public sphere changes accordingly. In other words, the conceptual sets that frame the relationship between data, fact, and norm are not objective in themselves; instead, they are the product of methodological construction. However, as we observed during our literature review, such methodological discussions are almost absent, and even a declaration of which approach has been inherited is a rare practice. Therefore, we lack a meaningful basis on which to discuss whether this expectation has been met. The more troubling aspect is that, at the methodological level, the "liberal" and "critical" definitions of the individual and society noted above—though seemingly in conflict—share an implicit agreement in the metaphysical context in that "objects are defined through external mediations to the object." In other words, even if one succeeds in consistently adopting and following one of the supposedly conflicting perspectives, the lack of metatheoretical reflexivity would, ironically, leave one unaware that these two perspectives are, for example, akin to each other at the metaphysical level.

In conclusion, it does not appear easy to assert that the domestic literature meets the metatheoretical expectations. Moreover, alignment with the international literature does not guarantee that these expectations are fulfilled. This is because the international literature itself—whose capacity to generate public debate and to influence current politics in crisis-ridden Western democracies is steadily waning, and which observes the deepening crisis from its own perspectives with apprehension—may, despite its chaotic appearance that resists neat classification at the upper metatheoretical levels, collectively contribute to the crisis due to underlying theoretical affinities.

8.5 Conclusion

Based on our discussion, we can state that the quantitative and qualitative characteristics of the available data are not decisive among the conditions of possibility for answering the question of whether new media deforms the political public sphere. This conclusion can be generalized to similar questions, such as whether traditional media reinforces the political public sphere. Therefore, it does not appear easy to assert that the metatheoretical expectations necessary for analyzing the current situation in Türkiye have been met or that, given the current structure of our academic culture, they can realistically be met in the near future. Moreover, it seems that any set of social policy outcomes aligned with one of the proposed solutions in the international literature would act as a multiplier for the crises highlighted by the other proponents. This is because the similarity of empirical findings and the underlying theoretical consensus point to the political–ideological character of the divergences, while the design of data–fact–norm relations without metatheoretical reflexivity undermines the healthy possibilities of conflict and reconciliation among alternative proposals. Merely showing sympathy toward metatheoretical inquiry adds only a "philosophical" garnish rather than solving the problem. Choosing to justify a proposition solely through functional citation chains that support it, instead of constructing the relations among its elements based on the intrinsic nature of those elements, does not resolve the issue. For example, even within an academic culture that assumes social reality to be relational and truth to be constructed, one must explain how one arrives at the contradictory conclusion that the international literature could provide better guidance in explaining Türkiye's data than local thinkers who have grappled with its specific historical conditions. Failing to attend to the layered structure of metatheoretical inquiry—outlined here only in a limited form—and failing to distinguish analyses belonging to different layers invite a personalized pragmatism. Among the reasons for metatheoretical indifference in Türkiye are the hegemonic pressure of increasingly widespread data-focused research practices, which align with a disregard for theoretical inquiry, and the presumption that engagement with the literature constitutes a sui generis source of scientific legitimacy. However, the cost of this indifference is borne by the phenomenon itself, which is eroded toward its own secularized comprehension through the consensual use of selected conceptual sets—rendering academic production meaningless. Furthermore, the inability to perceive the potential affinities at lower layers among arguments that conflict at a given metatheoretical level may lead to ironic outcomes. In short, it must be said that embodying an intellectual ethos that is already blocked on its own terms would be tragic and would contribute nothing to the resolution of specific problems.

References

A response to "Principles of solidarity. A statement". (2023, November 22). *Public Seminar*. Retrieved May 13, 2025, from https://publicseminar.org/2023/11/a-response-to-principles-of-solidarity-a-statement/

Adorno, T. W. (2021). *Kültür endüstrisi kültür yönetimi* (M. Tüzel, N. Ülner, & E. Gen, Trans.). İletişim Yayınları.

Aktaş, S. G. (2023). Türkiye'de yeni medya konusunda hazırlanan lisansüstü tezlere yönelik bir analiz (2018–2022). *Kritik İletişim Çalışmaları Dergisi, 5*(2), 126–143. https://doi.org/10.53281/kritik.1372023

Albrecht, S. (2006). Whose voice is heard in online deliberation?: A study of participation and representation in political debates on the internet. *Information, Communication & Society, 9*(1), 62–82. https://doi.org/10.1080/13691180500519548

Avcil, C. (2021). Kamusal alanı dijitalleşme çerçevesinde yeniden okumak. *Liberal Düşünce Dergisi, 26*(103), 81–100. https://doi.org/10.36484/liberal.954382

Baudrillard, J. (2024). *Simülakrlar ve simülasyon* (O. Adanır, Trans.). Doğu Batı Yayınları.

Benkler, Y. (2006). *The wealth of networks: How social production transforms markets and freedom.* Yale University Press.

Bennett, W. L., & Segerberg, A. (2012). The logic of connective action. *Information, Communication & Society, 15*(5), 739–768. https://doi.org/10.1080/1369118X.2012.670661
Bourdieu, P. (2019). *Televizyon üzerine* (A. Bakım, Trans.). Sel Yayıncılık.
Budak, H. (2016). Kamusal alanda dönüşen yapılar: Agoradan sanal uzama. *Selçuk Üniversitesi Edebiyat Fakültesi Dergisi, 36*, 507–530. https://doi.org/10.21497/sefad.285499
Castells, M. (2008). The new public sphere: Global civil society, communication networks, and global governance. *The Annals of the American Academy of Political and Social Science, 616*, 78–93. https://www.jstor.org/stable/25097995
Castells, M. (2013). *İsyan ve umut ağları: İnternet çağında toplumsal hareketler* (E. Kılıç, Trans.). Koç Üniversitesi Yayınları.
Chakrabarty, D. (2021). *Avrupa'yı taşralaştırmak* (İ. Cörüt, Trans.). Dergah Yayınları.
Coleman, S., & Blumler, J. G. (2009). *The internet and democratic citizenship: Theory, practice and policy*. Cambridge University Press.
Çalışkan, O. (2014). Kamusal alan bağlamında ağ toplumu ve yeni kamusal alan arayışı. *Maltepe Üniversitesi İletişim Fakültesi Dergisi, 1*(1), 41–62. https://dergipark.org.tr/tr/download/article-file/172376
Dahlberg, L. (2007). The Internet, deliberative democracy, and power: Radicalizing the public sphere. *International Journal of Media & Cultural Politics, 3*(1), 47–64. https://doi.org/10.1386/macp.3.1.47_1
Dahlberg, L. (2011). Re-constructing digital democracy: An outline of four 'positions.' *New Media & Society, 13*(6), 855–872. https://doi.org/10.1177/1461444810389569
Dahlgren, P. (2005). The internet, public spheres, and political communication: Dispersion and deliberation. *Political Communication, 22*(2), 147–162. https://doi.org/10.1080/10584600590933160
Dean, J. (2003). Why the net is not a public sphere. *Constellations, 10*(1), 95–112. https://doi.org/10.1111/1467-8675.00315
Demirhan, K. (2017). Yeni medyada siyasal iletişim sürecinin kavramsallaştırılmasında alternatif modeller: Müzakereci ve agonistik demokrasi yaklaşımları. *Gümüşhane Üniversitesi İletişim Fakültesi Elektronik Dergisi, 5*(1), 174–200. https://doi.org/10.19145/gumuscomm.288417
Dijk, J. van. (2018). *Ağ toplumu* (Ö. Sakin, Trans.). Kafka Kitap.
Dinçer, C., & Karataş, S. (2022). İkincil veriler ışığında medya tüketimi, pandemi ve geleceğe bakış. *Güncel Pazarlama Yaklaşımları ve Araştırmaları Dergisi, 3*(2), 76–90. https://doi.org/10.54439/gupayad.1170578
Dursun, O., & Yıldız, F. (2022). Yeni medya ve kamusal alan: İletişim akademisyenlerinin perspektifi. *Connectist: Istanbul University Journal of Communication Sciences, 62*, 1–32. https://doi.org/10.26650/CONNECTIST2022-1040243
Dündar, L. (2018). Yeni medya ve siyasal katılım: 15 Temmuz örneği. *Gazi Akademik Bakış, 11*(22), 101–115. https://doi.org/10.19060/gav.437774
Fraser, N. (1990). Rethinking the public sphere: A contribution to the critique of actually existing democracy. *Social Text, 25*(26), 56–80. https://doi.org/10.2307/466240
Fuchs, C. (2025). Sosyal medya ve kamusal alan. *Yeni Medya, 18*, 466–513. https://dergipark.org.tr/tr/pub/yenimedya/issue/93403/1731928
Geiger, R. S. (2009). *Does Habermas understand the Internet? The algorithmic construction of the Blogo/Public Sphere* (SSRN Scholarly Paper No. 2734947). *Social Science Research Network*. Retrieved June 3, 2025, from https://papers.ssrn.com/sol3/papers.cfm?abstract_id=2734947
Gençlerin medya kullanımı ve dijital okuryazarlık araştırması. (2022). Retrieved June 7, 2025, from https://www.rtuk.gov.tr/genclerin-medya-kullanimi-ve-dijital-okuryazarlik-arastirmasi-2022/4402
Habermas, J. (2015). *Kamusallığın yapısal dönüşümü* (M. Sancar & T. Bora, Trans.). İletişim Yayınları.
Habermas, J. (2023). *Kamusallığın yeni bir yapısal dönüşümü ve müzakereci demokrasi* (T. Bora, Trans.). İletişim Yayınları.

Hanehalkı bilişim teknolojileri kullanım araştırması. (2023). Retrieved June 8, 2025, from https://data.tuik.gov.tr/Bulten/Index?p=Hanehalki-Bilisim-Teknolojileri-(BT)-Kullanim-Arastirmasi-2023-49407

İnce, G. B. (2017). Yeni medyanın haber tüketim pratiklerine etkisi: İletişim Fakültesi öğrencileri üzerine bir değerlendirme. *AJIT-e: Academic Journal of Information Technology, 8*(29), 25–52. https://doi.org/10.5824/1309-1581.2017.4.002.x

Körlü Topan, A., & Savaş, S. (2022). Özel ve kamusal alan ayrımı açısından yeni medyayı Bauman üzerinden okumak. *KİLAD, 19*, 70–89.

Köselerli, B. B. (2017). Yeni medya ortamının yeni kamusal alan olarak kullanımı üzerine bir değerlendirme. *Humanities Sciences, 12*(1), 51–64. https://doi.org/10.12739/NWSA.2017.12.1.4C0216

Latour, B. (2021). *Toplumsalı yeniden toplama: Aktör-ağ teorisine bir giriş* (N. Bingöl, Trans.). Tellekt.

Lindner, R., & Aichholzer, G. (2020). E-Democracy: Conceptual foundations and recent trends. In L. Hennen, I. van Keulen, I. Korthagen, G. Aichholzer, R. Lindner & R. Ø. Nielsen (Eds.), *European e-Democracy in Practice* (ss. 11–45). Springer International Publishing.

Medyametre medya kullanım alışkanlıkları araştırması. (2023). https://www.rtuk.gov.tr/medyametre-medya-kullanim-aliskanliklari-arastirmasi/4856

Morozov, E. (2011). *The net delusion.* PublicAffairs.

Mouffe, C. (2009). *The democratic paradox.* Verso Books.

Netanel, N. W. (1999). Cyberspace self-governance: A skeptical view from democratic theory. *California Law Review, 88*(2), 395–498. https://doi.org/10.2139/ssrn.175828

Önen, A. (2020). İnternet, dijital demokrasi ve dezenformasyon ekseninde yeni medya: Sosyal medya kullanıcıları üzerine bir değerlendirme. *İstanbul Arel Üniversitesi İletişim Çalışmaları Dergisi, 8*(16), 13–35.

Özçetin, B., Arslan, U. T., & Binark, M. (2012). Türkiye'de internet, kamusallık ve demokratik kanaat oluşumu. *Folklor/Edebiyat, 18*(72), 51–76.

Öztay, O. H. (2025). Siyasal iletişim aracı olarak yeni medya ve siyasal katılımdaki rolü. *Communicata, 29*, 12–24. https://doi.org/10.32952/communicata.1618350

Papacharissi, Z. (2002). The virtual sphere: The internet as a public sphere. *New Media & Society, 4*(1), 9–27. https://doi.org/10.1177/14614440222226244

Papacharissi, Z. (2004). Democracy online: Civility, politeness, and the democratic potential of online political discussion groups. *New Media & Society, 6*(2), 259–283. https://doi.org/10.1177/1461444804041444

Paşalı Taşoğlu, N., & Çağlayan, S. (2021). Yeni kamusal alan oluşturma potansiyeli bakımından yurttaş gazeteciliği. *OPUS, 18*(42), 6025–6053).

Persily, N. (2017). The 2016 U.S. election: Can democracy survive the Internet? *Journal of Democracy, 28*(2), 63–76.

Polat, H. (2018). Geleneksel medyada temsil sorunu: Alternatif bir mecra olarak yeni medya. *Karadeniz Uluslararası Bilimsel Dergi, 38*(38), 45–60. https://doi.org/10.17498/kdeniz.383516

Rasmussen, T. (2014). Internet and the political public sphere. *Sociology Compass, 8*(12), 1315–1329. https://doi.org/10.1111/soc4.12228

Sayımer, İ. (2014). Yeni medya ortamlarında ağlar oluşturan toplumsal hareket deneyimleri. *Elektronik Mesleki Gelişim ve Araştırmalar Dergisi, 2*(2), 97–112.

Sennett, R. (2023). *Kamusal insanın çöküşü* (S. Durak & A. Yılmaz, Trans.). Ayrıntı Yayınları.

Shirky, C. (2011). The political power of social media: Technology, the public sphere, and political change. *Foreign Affairs, 90*(1), 28–41. https://www.jstor.org/stable/25800379

Susen, S. (2023). A new structural transformation of the public sphere? With, against, and beyond Habermas. *Society, 60*, 842–867. https://doi.org/10.2139/ssrn.4651250

Televizyon haberleri izleme eğilimleri araştırması. (2007). Retrieved July 3, 2025, from https://www.rtuk.gov.tr/televizyon-haberleri-izleme-egilimleri-arastirmasi-2007/1812

Televizyon izleme eğilimleri araştırması. (2018). Retrieved July 3, 2025, from https://www.rtuk.gov.tr/televizyon_izleme_egilimleri_arastirmasi_2018/335

Terranova, T. (2000). Free labor: Producing culture for the digital economy. *Social Text, 18*(2), 33–58. https://doi.org/10.1215/01642472-18-2_63-33

Topbaş, H., & Doğan, A. (2016). Toplumsalın yeni agorası olarak sosyal medya: Eleştirel yaklaşım. *e-GİFDER, 4*(1), 124–148.

Trenz, H.-J. (2009). Digital media and the return of the representative public sphere. *Javnost - the Public, 16*(1), 33–46. https://doi.org/10.1080/13183222.2009.11008996

Tufekci, Z. (2014). Social movements and governments in the digital age: Evaluating a complex landscape. *Journal of International Affairs, 68*(1), 1–18. https://www.jstor.org/stable/24461703?seq=1

Tunç, S. (2023). Habermas'in siyasal katılım hiyerarşisi ve dijital iletişimin eşitlikçi kamusal alan vaadi. *Ankara Hacı Bayram Veli Üniversitesi Hukuk Fakültesi Dergisi, 27*(3), 415–461. https://doi.org/10.34246/ahbvuhfd.1241839

Volkmer, I. (2003). The global network society and the global public sphere. *Development, 46*(1), 9–16. https://doi.org/10.1177/1011637003046001566

X'te Adam Tooze. (2023, November 14). X (formerly Twitter). Retrieved July 5, 2025, from https://x.com/adam_tooze/status/1724565111107436576

X'te Alex Callinicos. (2023, November 14). X (formerly Twitter). Retrieved July 5, 2025, from https://x.com/alex_callinicos/status/1724551230498783337

Yazılı medya ve uluslararası standart kitap numarası istatistikleri. (2022). Retrieved July 8, 2025, from https://data.tuik.gov.tr/Bulten/Index?p=Yazili-Medya-ve-Uluslararasi-Standart-Kitap-Numarasi-Istatistikleri-2022-49423

Yegen, C. (2013). Demokratik ve yeni bir kamusal alan olarak sosyal medya. *Anemon, 1*(2), 119–135.

Young, I. M. (2020). Communication and the other: Beyond deliberative democracy. In *Intersecting voices: Dilemmas of Gender, Political Philosophy, and Policy* (pp. 60–74). Princeton University Press.

Chapter 9
Secular Language in Generation Z Discourses in Digital Environments: The Case of Twitter/X

Mustafa Derviş Dereli

9.1 Introduction

The term "generation," which refers to people born within similar time frames and who witness the same historical events, is one of the most profound yet controversial concepts in the social sciences. The sociology of generation(s), which emerges at the intersection of history, human beings, and society, has not become a widespread direct field of study in anthropology or sociology. Instead, it has gained its conceptual foundation through the contributions of sociologists, philosophers, and thinkers from different disciplines within the social sciences. However, there is no consensus on "the sociology of generation(s)"—whether in terms of what generations mean for humanity in general or for individuals in particular, what historical intervals they correspond to, whether generations should be named based on significant social and traumatic events, or whether such experiences should be analyzed through the lens of generational categories.

Although studies within the sociology of generation initially emerged from foundational texts by scholars such as Karl Mannheim (1952) and Ortega y Gasset (1961), recent years have witnessed the field gain a broader, interdisciplinary character through research focused on youth sociology and, more specifically, Generation Z. While this trend may somewhat dilute the analytical depth of generational studies, it has visibly increased the number of empirical field studies addressing the topic. Despite specific objections and criticisms, generational research largely continues to be shaped by the periodizations and labels proposed by Strauss and Howe (1991, 2007) and the Pew Research Center (2018, 2019). In Turkey, generational studies are also predominantly conducted based on these widely accepted classifications in the literature.

M. D. Dereli (✉)
Department of Sociology of Religion, Necmettin Erbakan University, Konya, Türkiye
e-mail: mdervisdereli@erbakan.edu.tr

M. D. Dereli and M. Eken (eds.), *Turkish Perspectives on Secularization and Media*,
https://doi.org/10.1007/978-3-032-16436-0_9

Secularization is one of the significant thematic areas in which generations, in general—and younger generations in particular—are analyzed within the contexts of sociology and the sociology of religion. Questions such as how different age groups in a society incorporate religion into their lives, to what extent they participate in communal worship, and how religious principles shape their individual, familial, social, and professional lives form the basis of generational research, providing a valuable analytical framework for discussions around secularization and religiosity. The fact that trends of secularization or religiosity are often examined across specific historical intervals and age groups—both globally and in Türkiye—positions generations as a central phenomenon in this broader discourse.

This study aims to examine, based on the context above, through digital platforms—specifically Twitter (X)—the thematic frameworks through which secular discourses are constructed in content produced about Generation Z. The main research question of the study is formulated as follows: "Within which thematic contexts do secularization discourses regarding Generation Z on Twitter emerge?" A qualitative research method was employed in the study, and the document analysis technique was used during the data collection process. A total of 134 tweets, selected through purposive sampling from content related to Generation Z shared by Turkish users on the X platform, were analyzed using the qualitative data analysis software MAXQDA 24. The theoretical framework of the study discusses the definition and historical background of the concept of generation. Subsequently, generational classifications in the literature are presented, and the research findings regarding the implications of the secular language used about Generation Z are shared.

9.2 The Concept of Generation: Definition and Brief Historical Background

Derived from the Latin words *"generare" and "generatio," meaning "to beget," the term "generation"* has been used since the late fourteenth century to refer to "individuals born in the same period." In Old French and English dictionaries, *generation* is also found with meanings such as "the act or process of reproduction, the state of reproduction, the fruit produced, yield, children, grandchildren, children of the same parents." In modern dictionaries, it generally refers to people born in the same years. Definitions such as "all the people of about the same age within a society or within a particular family, or the usual period between the birth of a person and the birth of their children" (Cambridge Dictionary, 2025) and "all the people born and living at about the same time" (Oxford English Dictionary, 2025) are noteworthy.

In dictionaries of anthropology and sociology, the emphasis on "being born at the same time" is also predominant in the definitions of the concept of generation. Marshall defines the term as "a form of age groups composed of members of society born at approximately the same time" (1999, p. 439). Scott describes it as "an age group composed of members of a society born at approximately the same time" (2014, p. 425).

Whether the term "generation" or "cohort" is used in the context of generations, it is generally accepted that the concept serves as a boundary marker, enabling distinctions between one's own generation and others based on being born within specific historical intervals. However, assessing individuals within the same generation is not merely a matter of matching birth dates or biological ages; it also requires that they have witnessed similar historical and social events, exhibited comparable reactions, and, in short, shared a sense of fate by living through the same era. Indeed, Turner (2014, p. 387) emphasizes that the concept of generation corresponds not only to being "peers" but also to being "contemporaries." In this respect, the concept includes not only people belonging to the same age group but also those who live in the same era, which constitutes one of the fundamental reference points in delineating the boundaries of generations.

Another essential characteristic of the concept of generation is that it reveals the biological reality of existence, the historical reality of life, and the epistemological problem of knowing (Bristow, 2016, p. 1). Karl Mannheim, the doyen of the sociology of generations, situates the problem of generations within the sociology of knowledge, emphasizing that different generations can only be understood by examining the complex equation of interactions that occur simultaneously and in conjunction. Generations, on the other hand, encompass the relationships between the individual, the family, society, social structures, and historical events; they are shaped by the era and the period, and gain new meanings through the context in which they are situated. In this framework, it is possible to assert that the meanings attributed to the concept of generation are continuously renewed and acquire new dimensions.

It is observed that the concept of generation has multiple areas of usage in the social sciences literature. Particularly in social anthropology, its use in the context of kinship has become established and has formed a tradition over time. The most important reason for this is that, unlike sociologists, social anthropologists use the concept within a more transparent framework—not to refer to groups of people born in specific historical periods, but to describe the relationships between parents and children or broader kinship systems (Kertzer, 1983, p. 126). In addition, it is observed that the concept has four other uses in the literature of the social sciences: i. to refer to the general stage and level of a group's life course (e.g., the university student generation), ii. to denote those who have witnessed a common historical or traumatic period (e.g., the Depression Generation, the Sixties Generation), iii. to refer to a historical generation's subset that shares a common political or cultural identity, iv. to indicate specific age groups within a population (Turner, 2006, p. 233).

The historical trajectory of the concept of generation reveals that its origins can be traced back to Ancient Greece. While the term itself was not directly used during this period, the notion of generational differences arising from age distinctions was clearly implied. In fact, it can be argued that generational categories based on age and the resulting distinctions were even more pronounced than they are today. For instance, in Ancient Greece, human life was categorized into four numerical groups of twenty years each, classified as childhood, youth, adulthood, and old age (Nash, 1978, p. 5).

The power attributed to a generation in relation to age, lifespan, lineage, or clan reflected a fundamental sense of stability in Ancient Greek thought. Generational differentiation—later more clearly defined in modern times as childhood, youth, adulthood, and old age—was perceived in that era as natural stages of life. It was believed, for example, that discernible differences existed between the young and the elderly, and that these differences manifested in behavioral and cognitive characteristics. Consequently, generational age distinctions, claims of aristocratic lineage, and identification with peer groups continued to be emphasized throughout the Classical, Hellenistic, and Roman periods. In this respect, generations were regarded as a metaphor for existence and a cornerstone of the stable transmission of tradition throughout the ancient world (Nash, 1978, pp. 11–18). These insights into how generations were conceptualized in Ancient Greece—although capable of further elaboration—demonstrate that generational awareness has been a constant element in the historical experience of humanity.

The period in which the concept of generation was both explicitly employed and problematized within the social sciences coincides with the first quarter of the twentieth century. Between the First and Second World Wars, the issue of generations evolved into a bloody and polarized reality in Europe (Bristow, 2016, p. 3), deepening in the context of economic turmoil, cultural collapse, and organized class conflict. The disillusionment of the generation of 1914 (Wohl, 1979), the rise of the German Youth Movement, and the emergence of new habits that began to challenge the enduring values of previous eras led to the questioning of politics, ideologies, and belief systems specifically through the lens of generations (Bristow, 2016, p. 3; Jaeger, 1985, p. 277). Indeed, in addition to foundational authors in the sociology of generation, such as Karl Mannheim and Ortega y Gasset, many other figures—including Franqois Mentre, Eduard Wechssler, and Friedrich Kummer—demonstrated particular interest in the topic of generations within various disciplinary contexts during this period.

In the years following World War II, the academic focus on generations shifted from Europe, particularly Germany, to the United States. This stage, marking the second phase of generational studies, featured a broad international spectrum of research, in which American scholarship in the social sciences came to the forefront. During this phase, there was a significant increase in empirical research on generations. As a result, generations began to be used as a tool in countries' future-oriented planning and projections. One indicator of this trend is the rise, particularly after the 1960s, of studies aimed not so much at examining generations from an academic standpoint, but at categorizing them more clearly based on specific defining characteristics. Thus, generational classifications with more concretely drawn boundaries—such as the Silent Generation, the Baby Boomers, Generation X, Generation Y, and Generation Z—gained widespread popularity.

9.3 Common Generational Classifications in the Literature

While theoretical and academic studies on generations were prominent during the interwar period, research on the topic acquired an empirical and field-based character in the post–World War II era, particularly in the United States. Rather than focusing on abstract questions such as "What is a generation?", "What are the main factors that constitute generations?" or "What reference points should be used to distinguish between generations?" Scholarly attention gradually shifted toward field research investigating the attitudes and behaviors specific to particular age-based generational cohorts.

The generational classification proposed by Strauss and Howe (1991), based on the American context, has gained widespread acceptance in the literature through the contributions of both social scientists and major research institutions, such as the Pew Research Center. Although the two frameworks—Strauss & Howe's and Pew Research Center's—differ slightly in terms of terminology and the precise birth-year cutoffs, both are frequently cited as foundational references. Therefore, when presenting the timeline and characteristics of each generation, both classifications are often referenced in tandem. A comparative table outlining the generational classifications proposed by Strauss & Howe and the Pew Research Center is provided below (Table 9.1):

9.3.1 *Silent Generation*

Strauss and Howe (1991) refer to individuals born between 1925 and 1942/1928 and 1945, who lived through and experienced both World Wars in all their intensity, as the "Silent Generation." In their generational typology, the cohort immediately preceding the Silent Generation is referred to as the "G.I. Generation" or "Greatest Generation" (born 1921–1945). According to the Strauss–Howe generational theory, members of the G.I. Generation played a prominent role in the early twentieth-century revolutions

Table 9.1 Comparison of generational definitions by Strauss & Howe and Pew Research Center

Howe and Strauss (2007), Strauss and Howe (1991)		Pew Research Center (2018, 2019)	
Generation Name	Birth Years	Generation Name	Birth Years
Silent Generation	1925–1942	Silent Generation	1928–1945
Baby Boomers	1943–1960	Baby Boomers	1946–1964
13th Generation / Generation X	1961–1981	13th Generation/Generation X	1965–1980
Millennial Generation	After 1982	Millennial Generation	1981–1996
		Post-Millennial Generation/ Generation Z	After 1997

and transformations in the United States, establishing a strong generational identity as influential actors in shaping modern society.

In contrast, those belonging to the Silent Generation were more inclined to demonstrate loyalty and respect toward societal and political authority, as well as a tendency to preserve and uphold existing social norms and values. Their childhoods were marked by hardship, and they were often seen as embracing the prevailing social order without challenging it—hence the label "silent." Also described as "traditionalists" (Stillman & Stillman, 2019, p. 15), members of the Silent Generation were notably characterized by their frugality and consistency.

9.3.2 Baby Boomers

This generation derives its name from the significant increase in birth rates that occurred in the Western world—particularly in the United States—during the period between World War II and the onset of the Cold War. The term "baby boom" is also historically associated with the post-World War II economic expansion, especially in the United States and, to a lesser extent, in the United Kingdom.

Corresponding to individuals born between 1943 and 1960/1946 and 1964, this cohort is considered by Bristow (2015, p. 85) to be the most debated generation in Western history. The uncertainty and anxiety prevalent during the war years, along with the disinterest and alienation seen among the youth, largely dissipated in the years following the war, offering a renewed sense of hope for future generations. It was expected that generations born and raised in times of peace and prosperity would foster a new sense of peace.

Members of this generation are typically described as hardworking, rebellious, free-spirited, competitive, equating work with personal value, determined, optimistic, team-oriented, committed, and goal-driven individuals (Johnson & Romanello, 2005; Strauss & Howe, 1991; Zemke et al., 2000).

9.3.3 Generation X

Strauss–Howe Generational Theory places Generation X between the years 1961–1981, while the Pew Research Center defines it between 1965–1980. The term Generation X was first popularized by Douglas Coupland in his novel *Generation X: Tales for an Accelerated Culture* (1991). This novel, structured as a series of framed stories—stories within stories—narrated by a group of young people about themselves, was Coupland's response to the stereotypical labeling of generations, particularly the Baby Boomers, to which he himself belonged. The heightened societal expectations toward the Baby Boomers and their depiction as hardworking, competitive, determined, and goal-oriented led the author to imply the emergence of a new generation whose path was still uncertain, hence the naming of "Generation X."

In their early writings in 1991, Strauss and Howe referred to this generation as the "13th Generation" in relation to the thirteenth cohort in American history. However, as the term "Generation X" gained broad recognition during the 1990s, especially in fields such as communication, marketing, and popular culture, it was adopted in their later works (Strauss & Howe, 1996; Howe & Strauss, 2007).

In the literature, Generation X members are often described as skeptical, resourceful, emotionally distant from their parents, competent in their work while also valuing leisure time, and anxious about adulthood (Gordon & Steele, 2005; Johnson & Romanello, 2005). Being raised by parents characterized by commitment, prudence, and sacrifice contributed to the development of these traits. Generation X emerged as a cohort that had life's pleasures readily available at their fingertips and were constantly engaged in self-promotion (Bauman, 2011, p. 52). In addition, it is noteworthy that the literature includes entirely contradictory characterizations of Generation X, portraying them as both insecure and indecisive, yet also as secure and determined (Coomes & DeBard, 2004; Gordon & Steele, 2005; Bartley et al., 2007).

9.3.4 Generation Y/Millennials/Millennial Generation

Although different studies suggest varying date ranges, Generation Y generally refers to those born between approximately 1981 and 1996. Both Strauss and Howe (Strauss & Howe, 1991; Howe & Strauss, 2007) and Pew Research Center (2018, 2019) refer to this group as the "Millennial Generation." As the term "Millennial" implies, this generation has often been portrayed as a heroic cohort.

This generation is described as having distinctive attitudes, being sheltered, self-confident, team-oriented, successful, and respectful of tradition (Howe & Strauss, 2000). In addition, they are often labeled as optimistic, goal-driven, moral, pragmatic, hardworking, and respectful of authority (Bartley et al., 2007; Coomes & DeBard, 2004; Zemke et al., 2000).

Members of Generation Y are also commonly referred to as the "Net Generation" or the "Internet Generation." The mass adoption of the World Wide Web in 1991, the emergence of search engines like Yahoo and Google in the mid-1990s, the spread of console gaming, and the introduction of wi-fi technology all contributed to the rise of a new generation characterized by increased individualism and technology-centered lifestyles.

Moreover, Millennials tend to perceive work and employment more as a burden or necessity. For them, leisure activities such as traveling, exploring, and vacationing are not merely hobbies but central elements of life that serve as sources of daily satisfaction (Bauman, 2011, pp. 52–53).

9.3.5 From Digital Immigrants to Digital Natives: Generation Z and Secularization Discourse

Among the generational labels found in the literature, Generation Z is arguably the most complex and nuanced. While there is a relative consensus regarding labels such as the Silent Generation, Baby Boomers, Generation X, and even Generation Y, the debates surrounding Generation Z begin with the very issue of naming. For instance, in a report dated March 1, 2018, the Pew Research Center (2019), known for conducting comprehensive research across various fields in the United States, stated that they preferred the term "Post-Millennial Generation" over "Generation Z" for those born after 1997, due to certain reservations. Nevertheless, they acknowledged that the term "Generation Z" gained popularity through journalism and popular culture. The same report also noted that there is no strictly scientific basis behind the term "Generation Z" and that, given the lack of a transparent scientific process for naming generations, the general tendency has been to adopt this label (Pew Research Center, 2019).

In the context of mass media, while television was highly influential for Baby Boomers, computers were highly influential for Generation X, and the internet was highly influential for Generation Y, members of Generation Z were born directly into these technological environments and experienced them as ordinary aspects of daily life. As such, they have shown a greater ability to adapt to more sophisticated technological platforms. Social media platforms, online chat rooms, and newer digital environments such as the Metaverse—along with wearable technologies like smart bracelets, smart glasses, and smartwatches—are becoming increasingly integrated into their lives. In this regard, Generation Z members, described by Marc Prensky (2012) as "digital natives" in contrast to other "digital immigrant" generations, not only benefit more from technology but are also more vulnerable to its handicaps and alarming aspects.

The close engagement of this generation with technology has led to their being referred to as the "iGeneration." Twenge uses the term "iGeneration" to describe those born between 1995 and 2012, who grew up with mobile phones and the internet, who had social media accounts even before high school, and who are largely unaware of a world before the internet. Twenge specifically chose this label based on the observation that, particularly in the U.S., young people from this generation were raised with iPads and iPhones from a very early age. In comparison to previous generations, they possess a more self-centered worldview and daily life practices. Indeed, according to Twenge, members of the iGeneration differ significantly from earlier generations in terms of how they spend their time, their behaviors, religious tendencies, sexual orientations, and approaches to politics (Twenge, 2018, pp. 22–23).

In the post–World War II period, field studies conducted in Europe and the United States began to increasingly suggest that new generations were becoming more distant from religion and spirituality. It is essential to note that such findings have been particularly observed among members of Generation X. Focusing primarily on the Baby Boomers and Generation X, Wuthnow (1976) analyzed the structure of religion and levels of religiosity in the U.S. through the lens of these cohorts. According to him, for a long time, Americans viewed the Baby Boomer generation as a guarantor of religion. However, with the aging and retirement of this generation, the future of religion in the United States has grown increasingly uncertain. In his work After the Baby Boomers (2007), Wuthnow identifies this as a fundamental issue regarding the future of religion in America. Nevertheless, he also criticizes overly simplistic generalizations that portray Generation X or Generation Y as either wholly turning toward religion or entirely abandoning it.

Wade Clark Roof (1993, 1999) argues that in the United States, the decline of religion among new generations is driven by the diminishing visibility of religion in families and social environments, the erosion of the institutional power of churches, and the collapse of mechanisms of religious socialization. According to him, the weakening of meaning systems in modern society, the absence of strong religious education and socialization during childhood, the openness to countercultural influences, and negative experiences with institutional religion have all contributed to the breakdown of intergenerational religious transmission.

Charles Taylor (2007), maintaining a critical distance from both classical secularization theorists and their critics, emphasizes that while modernity undermines traditional religious life forms, it also paves the way—especially for younger generations—for the emergence of new religious expressions. According to Taylor, these new forms are not merely temporary; they indicate enduring transformations in how individuals make sense of the world, passed down across generations. However, interpreting this solely as a religious revival would be misleading, since religious life in Western societies has become more fragmented and inconsistent than ever before.

Danièle Hervieu-Léger (2000, p. 82), who defines religion as a "chain of memory" ensuring continuity across generations, attributes the primary cause of religious decline in modern and postmodern eras to the weakening of social memory that binds generations together. The loss of collective memory, which forges a link between the past and the present, deepens religious and cultural alienation both at the individual and societal levels. As younger age groups become increasingly exposed to mass media, this alienation is further amplified (Dereli, 2022, p. 177).

Rejecting the claim that the United States constitutes an exception to the secularization thesis, Voas and Doebler argue that religiosity and spirituality decline across generations within American society as well. They outline the following possibilities to explain generational trends in secularization: i. Value shifts among parents (a declining priority given to the transmission of religion to the next generation), ii. Value shifts among youth (a decreasing importance of religion for them), iii. Even when values remain relatively stable, social changes that impact religious life (Voas & Doebler, 2011, p. 57). In addition, they point to several other factors contributing to secularization among younger generations: (i) A dominant worldview supported by media apparatuses and opinion leaders, (ii) Diverse perspectives, including those summarized by the phrase "I am spiritual but not religious," (iii) The routinization of secular activities in everyday life, (iv) An education system shaped by secular mentalities, (v) Discourses and practices that diminish the perceived importance of marriage, family formation, and child-rearing (Voas & Doebler, 2011, p. 58).

Drawing from four large-scale national public opinion surveys conducted in the United States since the 1960s—which together represent 11 million Americans—as well as a questionnaire with 250 participants and in-depth interviews with 23 individuals, Twenge (2018) places particular emphasis on "the decline in religion and spirituality" as one of the ten core characteristics of the iGeneration.

As seen in both theoretical and field studies conducted across many societies on a global scale, the general tendency of younger generations to distance themselves from religion and spirituality plays a central role. In this context, it can be argued that mass media—particularly digital networks—not only have technical infrastructure but also cultural implications, such as normalizing surveillance, promoting consumerism, blurring the boundaries of privacy, and transforming modes of socialization. These implications suggest that mass media has an inherently secular mentality, steering users toward secular content, behaviors, and actions (Dereli, 2019; Eken, 2020, 2021).

Nevertheless, features such as bringing distant geographies closer together, facilitating the gathering of individuals who adhere to the same religion, expanding the spheres of influence for religious groups, and improving access to religious content prevent media tools from being considered entirely harmful in religious terms. Indeed, some international studies demonstrate that media can influence religiosity both positively and negatively in the context of generations. For instance, Janmohamed (2018) states that members of the M Generation—Muslim and modern individuals living as minorities in Europe and America—can use the internet and social media networks quite effectively. By participating in these platforms with their Muslim identities, they are fulfilling the demands of the present era.

Therefore, rather than categorizing digital networks as wholly secular, it is plausible to argue that their outcomes vary according to users' intentions and practices (Karaarslan, 2015). In fact, the internet and digital networks may also help shield young people from the influence of secular life and enable them to build new online communities, such as a digital ummah or e-ummah, thereby enhancing their religious motivation.

9.4 The Discourse on Generation Z on X: Manifestations of Secular Language and Its Social Reflections

9.4.1 Methodology

In this study, which examines discourses about Generation Z on digital platforms, a qualitative research method was employed using the document analysis technique and a purposive sampling strategy. The purposive sampling strategy involves the researcher selecting individuals, locations, or documents relevant to the research topic in order to determine the sample. Within purposive sampling, several subtypes exist, including typical, deviant, maximum variation, convenience, snowball, and chain sampling. The deviant sampling type aims to uncover highly unusual findings related to a given phenomenon. In contrast, maximum variation sampling seeks to increase the likelihood of capturing diverse perspectives or differences within the data (Creswell, 2018, p. 157). Based on these two strategies—deviant and maximum variation sampling—a total of 134 tweets related to Generation Z, shared on the Twitter/X platform between December 25, 2017, and October 17, 2025, in both positive and negative tones and within various sociological contexts, were selected as the sample and analyzed through the document analysis technique.

In the research process, qualitative documents comprise materials required by the researcher, ranging from newspapers and official meeting minutes to personal diaries, memoirs, letters, emails, social media posts, and even audiovisual materials (Merriam, 2015, p. 131; Creswell, 2017, p. 190). Among these, digital documents have become increasingly popular among researchers in recent years. The 134 tweets were included in the sample as digital text-based documents, coded using the qualitative data analysis software MAXQDA 24, and subsequently analyzed. Within this framework, three main themes were identified: "approach to Generation Z," "the characteristics attributed to Generation Z are media-driven," and "dimensions of secular language." Under the "approach to generation z" theme, two subthemes—"positive" and "negative"—were created; under "the characteristics attributed to Generation Z are media-driven," three subthemes—"attached to traditions and values," "attached to family," and "attached to religion and spirituality"—were formed; and under "dimensions of secular language," twelve subthemes were constructed. Within this scope, the following findings were obtained.

9.4.2 Research Findings

9.4.2.1 The Public Representation of Generation Z: Positive and Negative Approaches

(Fig. 9.1)

A qualitative document analysis conducted on X (Twitter), one of the major platforms of the digital public sphere, examined 134 tweets related to Generation Z. In this analysis, approaches toward Generation Z were evaluated along two principal axes: positive and negative. According to the coding results, approximately 30 tweets contained affirmative, supportive, or empathetic statements about Generation Z, whereas around 53 tweets were written from a critical, exclusionary, or dismissive perspective. The remaining 51 tweets did not exhibit a directly positive or hostile stance toward the generation but instead presented more descriptive or neutral content.

Digital discourses reflecting positive attitudes toward Generation Z reveal that the generation is positioned as a distinct subject type, diverging from traditional generational patterns by emphasizing its critical potential and libertarian identity. In

Fig. 9.1 The public representation of generation Z

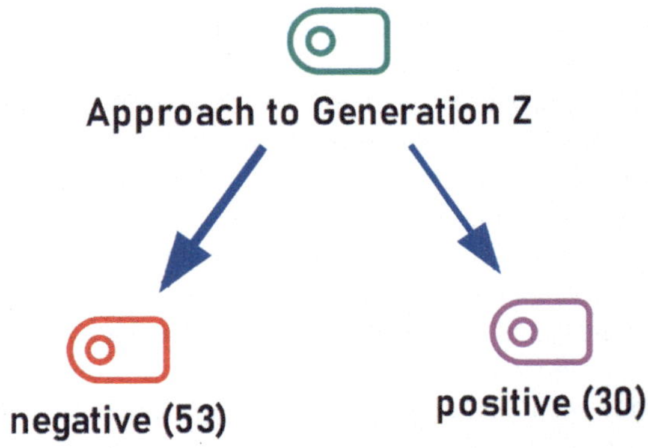

posts shared across digital platforms, Generation Z's questioning of life, rejection of conformity, and distant relationship with authority are not regarded as weaknesses; on the contrary, they are interpreted as indicators of social transformation. In this context, it is emphasized that young people represent not only a demand for individual freedom but also a center of resistance against established political and cultural structures.

A significant portion of the positive posts regarding Generation Z interprets their distanced stance toward traditional religious structures and dogmatic discourses not as irreligiosity but rather as an attempt to reinterpret faith on an individual level. In this context, it is emphasized that young people are not necessarily alienated from religion itself but rather from its politicization or instrumentalization. Accordingly, from the perspective of positive approaches, these youth do not entirely turn their backs on spirituality; instead, they construct a new form of religiosity. In some posts, references such as "the awakening of the Muslim youth of Generation Z" or "participation in morning prayer at Hagia Sophia" are cited as examples of a transforming religiosity that maintains a connection with traditional values while simultaneously subjecting them to critical scrutiny.

These favorable views also refrain from portraying Generation Z as a homogeneous group and instead define them within a framework of multiple identities. These young people are described in tweets through metaphors such as Kemalist, secular, religious, and even "the children of Mount Hira," exhibiting a pluralism that resists reduction to any fixed ideological framework. This plurality reflects both the generational diversity of identities and a broader tendency toward individualization.

Another frequently observed theme in the tweets is the emergence of defensive discourses countering the unjust negative evaluations directed at Generation Z. Statements such as "Generation Z is not lazy; they are questioning the machinery of the system" or "This generation is not merely obsessed with entertainment" suggest that the prevailing criticisms are ideologically driven and stem from a tendency to devalue youth. This defensive posture can also be interpreted as a self-defense practice undertaken by the youth themselves through digital media.

Negative approaches toward Generation Z, as reflected in the analysis of 53 tweets, span a wide range of judgments. These statements do not merely reflect individual discontent but also point to deeper societal, cultural, and ideological rifts. A significant portion of the criticism is grounded in the claim that Generation Z maintains a distanced stance toward moral, religious, and cultural norms. This generation is labeled as "ungrateful," "disrespectful," "hedonistic," and "individualistic," with concerns raised over their detachment from traditional value systems and a general trend of secularization. Within this framework, themes such as secular lifestyles, the influence of social media, sexuality, and the weakening of religious ties frequently emerge.

Furthermore, Generation Z is not only criticized for moral decline but also for intellectual laziness and cultural shallowness. These critiques assume that the generation tends "not to read, not to question, and shape their thinking through rote digital content." Particularly from traditional conservative perspectives, a prevalent view emerges that digital culture transforms the generation into individuals who "aspire to Western lifestyles but avoid responsibility." Expressions such as distancing from religious values, not attending mosques, the lack of young people at Friday prayers, and inclinations toward deism or atheism can be interpreted as part of a broader discourse about a crisis of religiosity centered on Generation Z. Such expressions extend their criticism beyond youth themselves, also implicating their families, the education system, and the political structure that raised them.

Another notable dimension highlighted in the analysis is the widespread distrust regarding the authenticity of Generation Z's political and social reflexes. The generation's interest in concepts such as "freedom" and "individual rights" is at times interpreted as superficial and imitative, or as unconscious and externally influenced. Especially in relation to social media algorithms, this generation is often portrayed as living within an "illusion of freedom" and described as a "coded social class." This portrayal positions Generation Z not merely as a cultural group but also as a generation constructed by the system itself. In this context, sharp judgments emerge that characterize the generation as a threat to society—weakening the institution of the family, distancing people from religious values, and contributing to moral decay.

These criticisms, often merged with discourses of social collapse, are frequently directed not only at youth but also at broader sociological processes such as modernization, secularization, and the transformation of political conservatism. Notably, statements suggesting that political conservative elites instrumentalize Islam, that youth are therefore turning toward deism, or that the education system is inherently corrupting, are prominent in the discourse.

Both positive and negative approaches toward Generation Z offer valuable insights into how this generation is represented on social media and how it is perceived within society. A significant point raised is that many of these perceptions are shaped through media narratives. Therefore, it is also necessary to engage with the posts of those who argue that the characteristics attributed to Generation Z are largely media-driven constructions.

9.4.2.2 The Image of Generation Z: Media Construction or Social Reality?

(Fig. 9.2)

In the visual obtained from MAXQDA, the discourses suggesting that a significant portion of the characteristics attributed to Generation Z originate from the media are categorized into three principal axes: commitment to religious and spiritual values, loyalty to traditions and cultural codes, and orientation toward family ties. This perspective suggests that the image of Generation Z constructed in public opinion, especially in media discourse, as "secularized, individualistic, and disconnected from values" does not fully reflect reality on the ground. Indeed, all 17 tweets analyzed in this context present alternative representations against such stereotypical images and highlight the youth's attachment to religion, culture, and family.

The tweets pointing to Generation Z individuals' commitment to religion and spirituality ($n = 9$) reveal that the frequently repeated discourse of a "secularized youth" in the media is not unanimously accepted. The content within this category emphasizes that the generation develops an active commitment in areas such as worship practices, embracing religious identity, seeking spirituality, and establishing a relationship with Islam. This situation demonstrates that, despite the media portraying a secularized youth profile, there are different tendencies in the field-level discourses. The group of tweets emphasizing Generation Z's adherence to traditional values and cultural codes ($n = 5$) suggests that the generation is categorized not only through individual preferences but also through constructed perceptions. These tweets reflect a sensitivity toward issues such as holiday celebrations, respect for elders, national symbols, and cultural affiliations. These findings establish a critical counter-position against the representations of Generation Z in the media as a "devalued" or "detached from its roots" generation. The tweets reflecting the positive orientations of Generation Z toward family ties, shaped around themes such as fondness for family and respect for parental figures ($n = 3$), also challenge the frequently encountered media

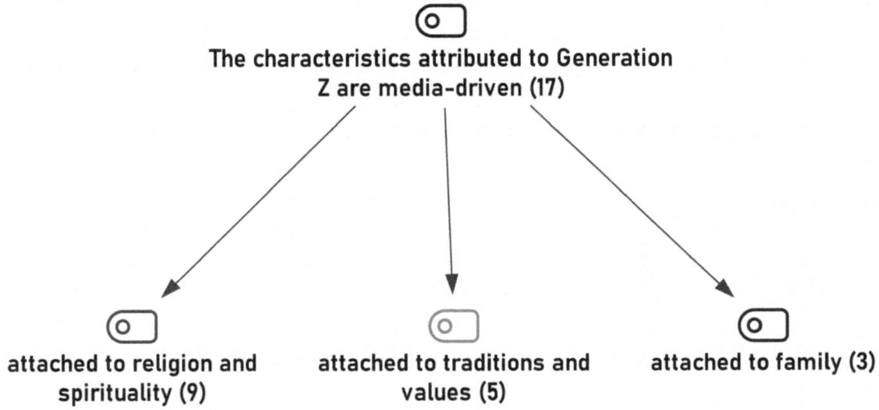

Fig. 9.2 The image of generation Z

portrayals of youth as "individualistic, disconnected, and self-centered." Although they may seem limited in number, these data show that the clichés suggesting the generation is distant from family do not fully resonate with everyone.

The media-based discourses on Generation Z have been criticized by many users as artificial, reductive, and often the product of a prejudiced construct. In prominent posts, defining youth with characteristics such as lack of discipline, superficiality, and individualism is seen not only as a social generalization but also as a strategy that blames the youth and shifts responsibility away from others. In this context, some users emphasize that Generation Z is in fact highly intelligent and full of potential; however, this potential cannot be sufficiently supported due to the lack of people who try to understand and guide them. It is stated that attributions in the media such as lazy, undisciplined, or apolitical do not match the youths' own realities; and it is reminded that similar generalizations were also made during the youth periods of previous generations, pointing to a historical cyclicality.

Moreover, the ideological positioning of Generation Z through themes such as "irreligion, deism, secularism" present in media discourses is also a serious subject of criticism. Some users argue that this situation is a process of manipulation carried out with the aim of labeling young people, associating them with certain ideologies, and undermining their social legitimacy. It is stated that generational definitions involve external interventions into youth and that discourses portraying the youth's ties with religion, morality, and values as weak do not reflect the truth. Especially theology students are emphasized to be individuals who question, criticize, and seek understanding; thus, it is considered unfair to easily label those who are not convinced by traditional religious narratives as "deists" or "atheists."

9.4.2.3 Analyzing the Secular Narrative in Posts About Generation Z

(Fig. 9.3)

Under the main theme "Dimensions of Secular Language," the twelve sub-themes demonstrate how diversified and socially layered the secular narratives regarding Generation Z on Twitter/X have become. This structure reveals both the individual-level reflections of secularization and its interaction with political and societal transformations in a multidimensional way. As seen in the visual, the most dominant sub-theme is represented by the label "secular, distant from religion and spirituality ($n = 72$)," which points to the discourse emphasizing Generation Z's distanced attitude toward religion and spiritual values. This large cluster suggests that secularization is not merely confined to individual preferences, but rather lies at the center of social perception directed at the generation. Other directly related themes also refer to different extensions of secularization. These sub-themes, which fall under the dimensions of secular language and vary in proportion to their frequency in the tweet texts, as shown in the visual above, will be discussed in detail in the following sections of the article (Fig. 9.4).

This visual represents a code co-occurrence matrix generated through MAXQDA's "code relations browser" feature, illustrating the extent to which the

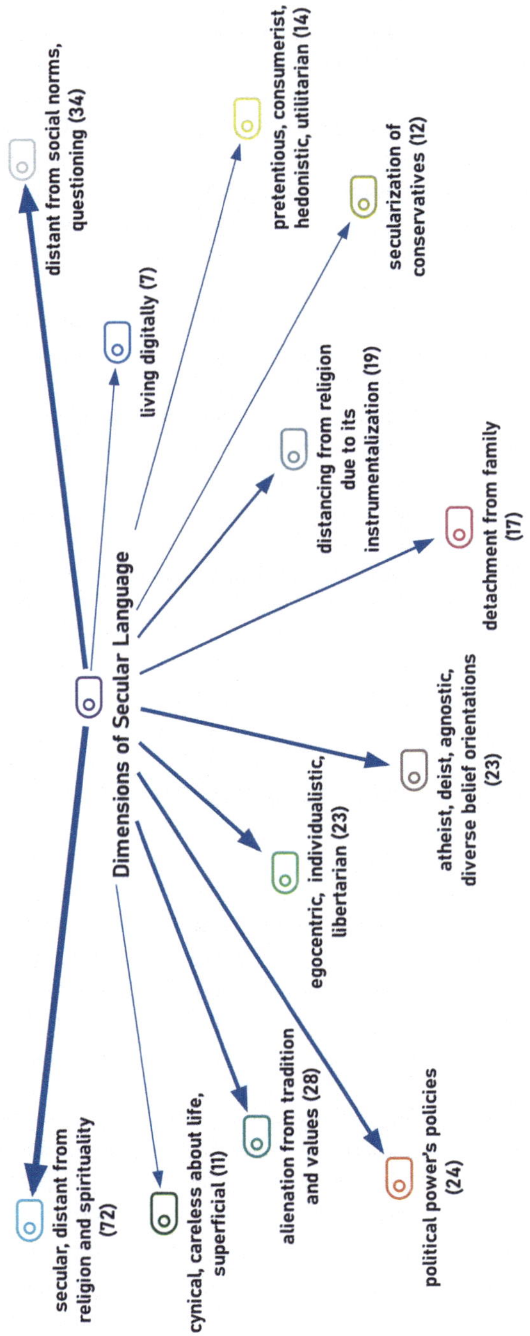

Fig. 9.3 Dimensions of secular language

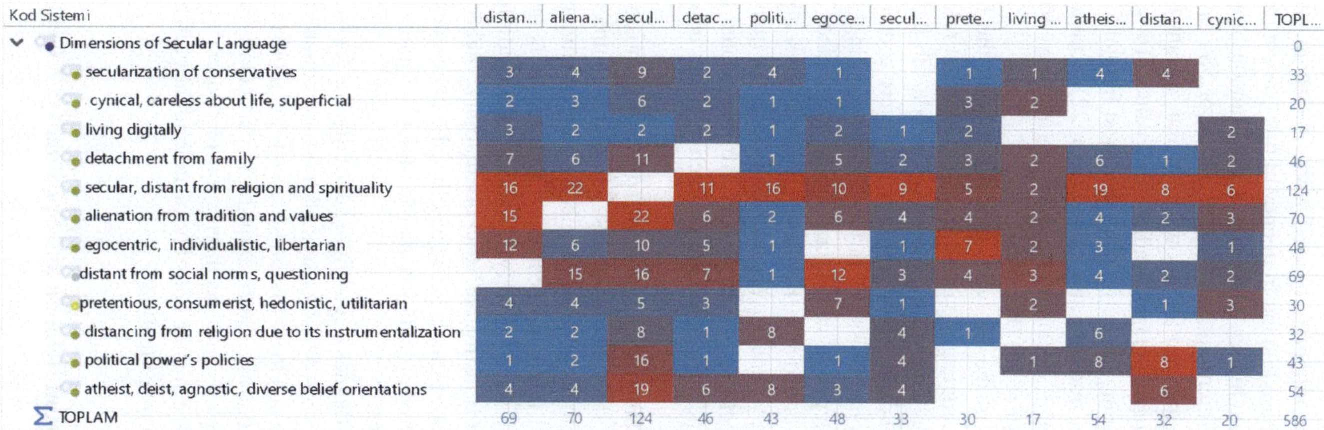

Kod Sistemi	distan...	aliena...	secul...	detac...	politi...	egoce...	secul...	prete...	living ...	atheis...	distan...	cynic...	TOPL...
Dimensions of Secular Language													0
secularization of conservatives	3	4	9	2	4	1		1	1	4	4		33
cynical, careless about life, superficial	2	3	6	2	1	1		3	2				20
living digitally	3	2	2	2	1	2	1	2				2	17
detachment from family	7	6	11		1	5	2	3	2	6	1	2	46
secular, distant from religion and spirituality	16	22		11	16	10	9	5	2	19	8	6	124
alienation from tradition and values	15		22	6	2	6	4	4	2	4	2	3	70
egocentric, individualistic, libertarian	12	6	10	5	1		1	7	2	3		1	48
distant from social norms, questioning		15	16	7	1	12	3	4	3	4	2	2	69
pretentious, consumerist, hedonistic, utilitarian	4	4	5	3		7	1		2		1	3	30
distancing from religion due to its instrumentalization	2	2	8	1	8		4	1		6			32
political power's policies	1	2	16	1		1	4		1	8	8	1	43
atheist, deist, agnostic, diverse belief orientations	4	4	19	6	8	3	4				6		54
TOPLAM	69	70	124	46	43	48	33	30	17	54	32	20	586

Fig. 9.4 Co-occurrence matrix of the sub-themes under the dimensions of secular language

twelve sub-themes under the title "Dimensions of Secular Language" appear together in the analyzed tweets. Each cell indicates the number of times the codes, listed as rows and columns, were simultaneously used within the same tweet or paragraph. The color intensity varies based on the frequency of this co-occurrence, with shades approaching red indicating a higher frequency of simultaneous appearance.

In this table, where different codes co-occur a total of 586 times, the top three most frequently coded themes are as follows: "Secular, distant from religion and spirituality" ($n = 124$), "Alienation from tradition and values" ($n = 70$), and "Distant from social norms, questioning" ($n = 69$). The four most frequent code pairings are: Secular + alienation from tradition and values ($n = 22$), secular + atheist/deist/agnostic ($n = 19$), secular + distant from social norms ($n = 16$), and secular + political power's policies ($n = 16$) (Fig. 9.5).

The code map related to the twelve sub-themes within the framework of the "Dimensions of Secular Language" visualizes the contextual relationships among the sub-themes. Each circle in the visual represents a code/sub-theme. The distance between two sub-themes indicates how similarly they were coded in the data; thus, the sub-themes are positioned closer or farther apart accordingly. The size of the circles reflects the frequency with which each theme was coded. The larger circles denote sub-themes that are coded more frequently. The map presents the relationships between the themes not only qualitatively but also in terms of quantitative intensity. In other words, the connections between codes are represented not only by their existence but also by the thickness of the lines, which indicates how many times they co-occurred.

The theme "secular, distant from religion and spirituality," positioned at the center of the thickest connection lines, demonstrates—through its numerous and substantial co-occurrences with other codes—that it is the most dominant discourse, both in terms of frequency and relational centrality. This theme is primarily linked to sub-themes that reinforce a secular lifestyle, such as "alienation from tradition and values," "atheist, deist, agnostic, diverse belief orientations," and "distant from social norms, questioning." These strong ties suggest that the phenomenon of secularism encompasses a multi-layered orientation that includes a rupture from traditional, familial, and societal norms.

The fact that some sub-themes (e.g., "living digitally" or "cynical, careless about life, superficial") are represented by weaker and more infrequent connections to the central theme may indicate that these discourses constitute more marginal extensions of secular language. In contrast, the relationships, particularly with themes such as "political power's policies" and "secularization of conservatives," suggest that secularization has become a matter not only of individual preferences but also of political and ideological transformations.

9.4.2.4 Being Distant from Religion and Spirituality: Z Generation

The analysis of the 72 tweets categorized under the sub-theme titled "Secular, distant from religion and spirituality" reveals that the public perception of Generation Z is

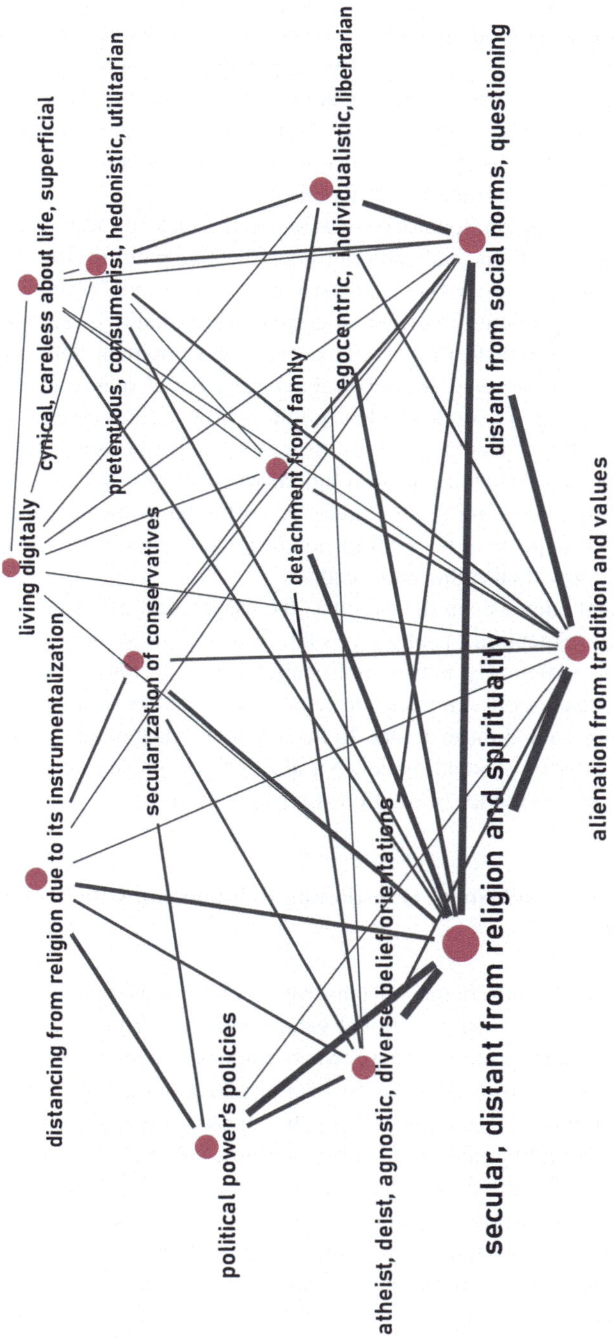

Fig. 9.5 Code Map of the Dimensions of Secular Language

predominantly shaped by a tendency to distance itself from religious and spiritual domains. The main emphasis in the coding indicates that the generation distances itself from traditional religious practices, shows weakened habits of worship, and exhibits indifference toward religious symbols. For instance, some tweets criticize individuals who ask for Netflix recommendations on holy nights, interpreting this as a lack of sensitivity toward the significance of religious days. Another tweet implies a loss of meaning in religious spaces by mentioning young people leaving mosques while discussing games with their headphones on.

Such narratives are interpreted not only as signs of a lack of individual religious practice but also as indications of alienation from collective religious rituals and spiritual community bonds. Some tweets emphasize that Generation Z is unfamiliar with the very concept of "spirituality" and even suggest that spirituality is redefined within a secular framework through the rhetoric of individual development. This implies that social change can be interpreted not only behaviorally but also as a transformation in the world of meaning. These posts clearly reflect how secular discourse is articulated on social media, as well as the reasons, emotional responses, and criticisms underlying individuals' distancing from religion, worship, and traditional forms of spirituality. In many tweets, religious rituals are portrayed as meaningless, trust in religious institutions appears to be eroding, and religion is interpreted as conflicting with demands for individual rights and freedoms.

Another frequent emphasis in the tweets is the association of religiousness with insincerity and the perception of religion as a tool of social pressure or hypocrisy. Criticism directed particularly toward political actors and conservative segments who employ religious discourse reflects the negative association younger generations make between religion and these actors. In this context, "distancing from religion" is not merely a matter of personal belief, but also a form of critique of the current socio-political order and modes of religious representation.

9.4.2.5 A Distanced and Norm-Questioning Relationship with Social Structures

The 34 tweets under the sub-theme "distant from social norms, questioning" reveal Generation Z's attitudes toward traditional values and their critical perspectives on social order. A significant portion of these tweets emphasizes that the younger generation maintains a distance from the religious, moral, and cultural norms they perceive as being imposed upon them. In some of them, this stance is not regarded as a "degeneration" but instead highlighted as a "conscious process of questioning." Certain posts portray Generation Z as individuals who rebel against authority, criticize the established order, or confront religious and dogmatic structures, evaluating their identity as "questioning individuals" in a positive light; others, however, depict them as disrespectful, dismissive of tradition, and indifferent, producing a critical and even anxious discourse.

Within this sub-theme, positive and negative criticisms are intertwined. Tweets evaluated within a positive framework underline that Generation Z consists of individuals who "prefer verses over superstitions," "do not accept everything blindly," "can access and process knowledge," and "refuse to believe without questioning," presenting this as an outcome of free thought and the process of forming individual identity. On the other hand, especially in critiques written from a conservative perspective, Generation Z is labeled with adjectives such as "disrespectful," "immoral," "rootless," "without ideology," "shameless," and "uncultured"; portraying a profile of youth "alienated from religion, family, and nation" and "disconnected from their own values."

In tweets written in a particularly critical tone, the alienation from traditional values is not merely interpreted as an individual preference but as the result of a broader cultural degeneration. In this context, some texts notably shift the focus from the youth themselves to the system that is perceived as having shaped them in this way. A broad spectrum of criticism emerges, ranging from the ineffectiveness of religious discourse among the youth to the education system and media structure promoting secular values. Thus, Generation Z becomes not just a generational identity but the focal point of a transformation of values and socio-cultural change.

9.4.2.6 Break with Tradition and the Redefinition of Values

The 28 tweets grouped under the sub-theme "alienation from tradition and values" reflect a strong critical discourse that claims Generation Z has distanced itself from traditional values, cultural norms, and religious/spiritual references. For instance, some posts suggest that the younger generation now perceives traditional religious practices, moral norms, or familial roles as a "burden of the past." The rise of modern values, including individual freedom, equality, and critical thinking, particularly shapes this attitude.

It is also noteworthy that in some tweet contents, distancing from tradition is presented as a form of emancipation. For example, some users criticize traditional family structures, marriage age, gender roles, or expectations toward authority figures, asserting that Generation Z views such values as "behind the times." In this context, the distancing from tradition can be interpreted not only as a cultural rupture but also as a process of constructing a generational identity. However, some tweets criticize the detachment from traditional values as a factor pushing youth toward a disoriented and drifting state. These tweets emphasize that the diminishing influence of traditional moral and social norms on young people has led to a sense of void or value loss. Thus, the break with tradition is perceived by some users as a crisis, while others interpret it as a form of progress or freedom.

It is also observed that the concepts of tradition and values are not singular but rather plural and contextually variable. In some tweets, Generation Z is praised for its potential to create its own value system as an alternative to traditional norms. In contrast, others claim that this generation is experiencing a loss of values and has adopted a lifestyle where "everything is permissible." These comments reveal that Generation Z has become an object that is defined and directed within the public sphere.

In general, the tweets do not only refer to individual preferences but also point to a generational "value shift" or "identity dissolution." The most frequently cited emphases in these criticisms include moral erosion, alienation from traditional family structures, detachment from religious beliefs, the adoption of modern lifestyles, and the spread of secularization. This discourse, especially articulated through structural concepts such as religion, morality, nationality, culture, and family, broadly defines the identity of Generation Z through the lenses of "deficiencies" or "ruptures." It is claimed that this generation no longer upholds "national and spiritual values," and is described as a "generation lacking in spirituality."

Tweets frequently suggest that this transformation cannot be explained solely by individual preferences; instead, it is claimed that systematic issues underlie it—such as corrupt media content, inadequate or ideologically driven educational systems, contradictory practices of political conservatism, and the weakening of social control mechanisms. In many posts, secularization is argued to be presented to youth under the guise of "freedom," but in fact turning them into "individuals lacking moral values, aimless and superficial." It is conveyed that this generation no longer recognizes the "ancestral legacy," has become "alienated from the system," and assumed an identity "detached from values." Some tweets interpret this transformation as a direct result of social media, globalization, educational systems, and political structures. In contrast, others attribute the failure of the parental generation to transmit moral and religious values as the cause.

9.4.2.7 The Backfire Effect of Political Intervention: The Role of Government Policies in Generation Z's Disengagement from Religion

The 24 tweets grouped under the sub-theme "political power's policies" reflect a public perception that the ruling government's efforts—particularly its aim to raise a conservative and religious generation—have paradoxically backfired in the case of Generation Z. A significant portion of users directly associate young people's distant relationship with religion with the practices of the political conditions. Factors such as educational policies, social life restrictions, and perceived injustice are cited as contributing to youth becoming disenchanted with religious beliefs.

In the tweets, particular criticism is directed at the government's use of religious symbols for political purposes, with the argument that this instrumentalization of religion leads to a loss of religious credibility in the eyes of young people. The phrase "Generation Z's lack of religiosity is due to the bad PR of religiosity" strikingly summarizes this viewpoint. According to this perspective, young people are not necessarily turning away from religion itself, but rather from the inconsistencies, contradictory behaviors, and politically motivated religious discourse of those who claim to speak in its name. Consequently, one could argue that a reactive secularization tendency is emerging among young people caught between their own beliefs and imposed lifestyles.

In this regard, related to this sub-theme, another dimension of secular discourse emerges: the critique that religious figures have lost their credibility in everyday life due to their involvement in politics, media, and education. The weakening of young people's relationship with religion in these tweets is not explained through personal spiritual quests, but rather through the erosion of institutional religiosity's credibility and the public's growing mistrust of those who represent religion.

9.4.2.8 Identity Crisis and Alternative Belief Orientations

The sub-theme "atheist, deist, agnostic, diverse belief orientations" is based on the analysis of 23 tweets. These tweets suggest that the tendency toward non-belief attributed to Generation Z—such as atheism, deism, or agnosticism—is not merely an individual orientation, but also a broader form of socio-political critique and reaction. A recurring perspective in the tweets is that young people's distancing from religious systems is directly linked to the practices of political conservatism.

Another notable aspect in the tweets is that this orientation is not portrayed as a simple act of "denial," but rather as grounded in emotional and experiential foundations such as resentment, injustice, and disappointment. Especially among youth raised in religious families, the turn toward deism or atheism is often described as stemming from perceived contradictions in the ways religion is represented and practiced. This indicates that estrangement from faith is shaped not only by personal choice but also by family dynamics, social structures, and institutional representations of religiosity.

Some tweets evaluate this trend within broader frameworks such as the education system, societal transformation, digitalization, and global secularization. It is argued that the increased accessibility of information and the development of critical thinking skills have led young people to question traditional belief structures. This process of questioning, over time, is said to result in growing distance from religion and eventually in the adoption of alternative forms of non-belief such as deism and agnosticism.

9.4.2.9 Ego-Centered, Individualistic, and Freedom-Oriented: A Generational Shift

The sub-theme "egocentric, individualistic, libertarian" encompasses 23 tweets that reflect public evaluations of Generation Z within the context of individualism, personal freedom, and self-centered lifestyles. The tweets highlight how individuals from this generation emphasize their capacity for independent decision-making, openly express their life choices, and position themselves apart from traditional norms. Statements such as "I do not live with my family; I have my own place" or "I stand on my own feet" illustrate a desire for self-sufficiency and a tendency toward detachment from traditional social networks. This suggests that individualization has become inevitable in the context of modernization and urbanization, and that young people's demands for broader personal freedom are becoming increasingly visible through digital culture.

Some of the tweets suggest that Generation Z is inclined to redefine social roles, with a particular emphasis on discourses of emancipation—primarily through the lens of female identity. For instance, expressions like "I will not be a housewife" reveal a critical distance from traditional gender roles and a search for alternative identities that challenge conventional family models. The pursuit of freedom and individuality is sometimes fueled by resistance to social pressures, as young individuals appear engaged in constructing their own life practices and value systems. In this sense, individualization can be interpreted not merely as a lifestyle but also as a strategy of resistance.

Other tweets suggest that individualization advances hand in hand with secularization, as individuals grow more distant from religious and social authorities. Reactions such as "It is none of your business, this is how I live" or "Who cares?" point to a cognitive shift in which the personal sphere is sacralized and social control mechanisms are rejected. This underscores the need to understand individuality not only as a psychological trait, but also as a sociological category.

9.4.2.10 Instrumentalized Religion and the Fragility of Piety

The sub-theme "distancing from religion due to its instrumentalization" is based on an analysis of 19 tweets that focus on the instrumentalization of religion and the adverse effects of political religiosity on younger generations. The dominant narrative across these tweets is one of disappointment with the public representation of Islam. It appears that the growing distance from religion or the tendencies toward irreligion among youth are not directed at religion itself, but rather at how it is represented and practiced. Frequently used expressions such as "drifting away from religion," "increase in irreligion," "tendency toward atheism and deism," and "the issue is not lack of spirituality but of morality" point to the perception that religion is being instrumentalized as the primary cause of these developments.

Some tweets also highlight that the crisis of religious representation is not solely a political issue, but also a pedagogical one. It is argued that religion is imposed on youth rather than communicated, and that the narrative of religion presented to them is based not on the core messages of the Qur'an, but on restrictive interpretations. Moreover, several posts emphasize that emotional factors such as resentment, injustice, and familial pressure also underlie the distancing from religion, suggesting that this move toward irreligion is less a rational decision and more a reactive response.

9.4.2.11 Estrangement from the Family and the Devaluation of the Family Concept

The sub-theme "detachment from family" encompasses 17 tweets that critically examine the transformations in the relationship between Generation Z and the institution of the family. The central claim recurring across these tweets is that Gen Z struggles to connect with traditional family structures, often perceiving them as exclusionary, meaningless, or oppressive. This distancing is not limited to individual familial relationships but is portrayed as part of a broader societal transformation associated with the dissolution of social structures. Many tweets suggest that Gen Z's engagement with individualism, the pursuit of freedom, and secular values contributes to their view of the family as an institution that is unnecessary, restrictive, or dysfunctional.

Some of the arguments presented in the tweets adopt a pessimistic and alarmist tone. For instance, in certain posts, Gen Z is described as a "new race" that has "lost its human qualities" and become alienated from moral values, religion, the nation, and the family. Such narratives do not merely constitute generational criticism; they also reflect a sense of cultural panic regarding the radical transformation of the symbolic meaning of the family. The family is often closely tied to religious values, and the younger generation's departure from these values is directly linked to the disintegration of the family unit. In this context, the secularization process is portrayed as contributing to the devaluation of concepts such as marriage, parenthood, and fidelity, thereby fostering Gen Z's estrangement from the institution of the family.

9.4.2.12 From Exhibitionism to Hedonism: Generation Z's Entertainment- and Consumption-Oriented Image

The sub-theme "pretentious, consumerist, hedonistic, utilitarian," which comprises 14 tweets, reveals how Generation Z is portrayed in media and public discourse as "exhibitionist," "hedonistic," "self-centered," "superficial," and "consumption-obsessed." The tweets frequently employ expressions such as ingratitude, pragmatism, dopamine addiction, indulgence, consumer culture, the society of the spectacle, moral decay, and individual interest orientation. These expressions collectively frame the generation as focused solely on personal gratification, avoiding responsibility, and severed from traditional values.

Some tweets describe this generation as being defined by hedonistic individualism, opting for superficial forms of relationships, and lacking the capacity to build enduring connections. Others, however, contextualize this transformation within broader political, economic, and cultural dynamics. For instance, critiques reference the confinement of individuals to screen-based lifestyles, the cognitive impact of short-form video consumption, and shifting norms in male–female relationships—altogether reflecting a comprehensive cultural critique. In this context, Generation Z is not only framed as undergoing a moral shift but also as the subject of an anthropological transformation.

One of the most striking aspects of the tweets is the link established between this pursuit of pleasure and consumption and structural influences such as media, digital platforms, and education systems. It is suggested that secularism and popular culture have distanced youth from spirituality, rendering them spiritually void and stripped of moral values. The discontent voiced in these critiques is not solely directed at the generation's personal choices but also at the institutional failures of society. Notably, the perceived inadequacy of religious-conservative influence over the media, education, and cultural fields—despite years of dominance—is articulated as a form of self-criticism.

These narratives reveal that Generation Z is viewed as a carrier of modernity's individualistic, secular, and consumerist paradigm, and thus, is symbolically positioned as the embodiment of a moral rupture. Nonetheless, some tweets hint at the possibility of "salvation" from individualism, often proposing Islamic values as a remedy. In sum, the tweets within this sub-theme reflect a critical crisis in the cultural representation of Generation Z and the projection of a value-centered conflict as it unfolds across social media platforms.

9.4.2.13 Conservative Religiosity Trapped in the Snare of Secularization

The sub-theme "secularization of conservatives" encompasses a total of 12 tweets, each containing striking criticisms of the transformation within the conservative segment, reflections on the impact of this transformation on younger generations, and questioning of religious legitimacy. The data reveal that young individuals from conservative/religious families exhibit a decreasing attachment to religious values, and even within this group, there is a rise in identities such as deism, atheism, or secularism.

Most of the tweets emphasize that conservative religiosity has become intertwined with worldly elements such as "power, money, authority, and personal gain" on a practical level. This convergence has led to a profound trust crisis among young people regarding the sincerity of religious institutions. Especially with the political experience of Islamic conservatism in power, the erosion of values has resulted in negative associations between Islam and interests in the minds of the youth. Another critical point is that due to the inconsistencies of the individuals and institutions representing religion, not only the perception of religion but the religion itself is being questioned.

9.4.2.14 Defined by Cynicism, Frivolity, and Self-Indulgent

The content comprising 11 tweets under the sub-theme "cynical, careless about life, superficial" reflects a highly pessimistic and critical discourse regarding the public representation of Generation Z. Concepts frequently encountered in the posts—such as "cynicism," "lack of empathy," "insensitivity," "not taking life seriously," "laziness," and "absence of meaning-seeking"—express a prevailing perception that this generation is distancing itself from both individual and social responsibilities. Some tweets describe the generation with extremely harsh terms such as "wants to earn money without effort," "brainless," or "aimless." These characterizations are not only directed at personal traits but are also linked to indifference toward social, cultural, and religious values.

The tweets also argue that this cynical and indifferent attitude is connected to fractures in cultural and civilizational transmission, processes of secularization, and even systematic policies of moral degradation. Especially with the superficial imitation of Western values, Generation Z's perceived frivolity is interpreted as a symptom of cultural rupture. The distancing of individuals from moral, religious, and social norms is thus considered not merely a matter of personal choice but a sign of a broader generational crisis. In this way, the tweets represent a public viewpoint that not only critiques the behaviors of Generation Z but also questions and judges their value systems.

9.4.2.15 Reducing Life to the Digital: A Critique of Disconnecting from Reality

The sub-theme of "living digitally" is represented by seven tweets and reflects a significant strand of criticism directed at Generation Z. These tweets highlight both individual and social alienation resulting from the generation's excessive dependence on the digital world. A recurring emphasis in the tweets is that young people are detached from real life, lacking basic emotions such as empathy and respect, and adopting a sarcastic and indifferent attitude toward serious matters. They are portrayed as living within a perception of reality shaped by social media, digital games, and online series content. This condition is not solely attributed to individual preferences but is also linked to undisciplined family structures and weakened social control mechanisms.

Some tweets suggest that digitalization has led Generation Z into loneliness, isolation, and alienation from cultural engagement and moral values. Others highlight the generation's inability to form an ideological connection with the current system, which leads to a rebellious and detached stance. Living in the digital realm is not merely an issue of technology use; instead, it is presented as a process of constructing a lasting alternative reality that significantly affects young people's identity formation, their relationship with social values, and their worldview. In particular, the tendency of individuals to withdraw from social life and become immersed in screens—distancing themselves from values such as family, morality, and parenthood—is framed as both a moral collapse and a structural crisis.

Another striking point in these criticisms is the notion that young people are not willingly drawn into this state of affairs. Instead, it is argued that digital culture and media productions function as deliberate tools of manipulation and "satanic propaganda." This narrative within the tweets emphasizes not personal choices, but

Fig. 9.6 Word cloud on generation Z discourses of secularization

a structural, ideological, and cultural intervention—implying that it is the systems shaping the youth, not the youth themselves, that should be the object of criticism.

9.4.2.16 Word Cloud on Discourses of Secularization Regarding Generation Z

(Fig. 9.6)

The prominent concepts in the visual—such as *religion, secular, secularism, deism, atheism, Islam, God, prayer,* and *faith*—indicate that religion constitutes a central subject of debate within the tweets. The presence of these words in both positive connotations (e.g., *faith, prayer*) and more distanced or critical usages (e.g., *secular, atheism*) suggests that secularization is not only a matter of individual orientation but also a broader social and political debate. The frequent use of more specific belief orientations like *deism* and *atheism* reveals that youth are not merely distancing themselves from traditional religion, but also constructing new identities and worldviews.

The pronouns and generational references in the word cloud—*they, their, them, young, generation*—clearly point to a "we versus them" dichotomy. This distinction reflects a perceived difference not only in age or generation but also in terms of value systems. Expressions like *we, our, " and " children* indicate that speakers aligned with more conservative or traditional values adopt a possessive and concerned stance toward the younger generation. In this context, the "othering" of youth carries traces of a broader societal critique aimed at their positioning in relation to religion, morality, tradition, and the past.

The prominence of words such as *"values," "morality," "moral," "freedom," "justice," "family," "education," "society," and "social" shows that* secularization tendencies among youth are viewed not merely as an individual belief issue, but as part of a broader transformation in the system of social values. In this regard, frequent references to the institution of the family (family, children, families)—in the context of both moral decline and alienation from religion—are noteworthy. The visibility of terms like *education, media, system, social,* and *history* points to the perceived influence of education, digital culture, and media on the religious and moral formation of youth. There is a prevailing belief that the values transmitted through the education system are either ideologically biased or insufficient, and that the media plays a transformative role in shaping the younger generation. Especially the concepts of *media* and *system* highlight the inclusion of structural factors in explanations of secularization.

9.5 Conclusion

The representation of Generation Z on social media—specifically on the Twitter/X platform—highlights the influence of digital environments on the transformation of personal attitudes, collective memory, value systems, and social perceptions. Among the 134 tweets included in the sample, both positive and negative evaluations of Generation Z are present; however, critical discourses appear to be more dominant. Some of these criticisms portray the generation as responsible for moral and cultural decay. In contrast, others adopt a perspective that views young people as the agents of a new social imagination, evident in their productive, sensitive, and pluralistic identities. Thus, Generation Z is presented both as a hope for the future and as a threat to traditional values. Discourses about the generation become carriers of cultural polarization and value-based tensions. This reveals that digital culture is not only a space of critique but also an arena where society redefines itself through generational narratives.

The issue of secularization emerges as one of the dominant discursive frameworks used to define Generation Z. However, this secular stance is not limited to a distanced attitude toward faith and religious rituals; it also encompasses critical positions toward authority, tradition, family, and cultural norms. This stance—developed in the context of individualization, freedom, and identity-seeking—reflects not only a rupture but also the construction of new meanings and identities. Therefore, secularization appears in some posts as an expression of passive indifference, while in others it represents an active distancing and the adoption of a new social position. Frequent critiques of the entanglement of religious structures with power dynamics suggest that trends toward unbelief are not merely personal choices but are also tied to political and cultural reactions. Similarly, negative remarks about the traditional family structure reflect not only discontent with the family itself, but also a broader disaffection with authority and value systems in general.

The representations of Generation Z on social media tend to reflect a mediatic language that produces generalizations based on individual preferences, thereby obscuring the diversity and internal differences within the field. The assumption that young people are engaged in a homogeneous process of secularization in areas such as faith, family, and cultural belonging carries a reductive quality, neglecting the plurality and multi-layered nature of the field. Similarly, explaining the impact of digitalization on youth solely through negative concepts such as alienation, superficiality, or detachment from reality overlooks the complex and multifaceted nature of technological transformation. In contrast, Generation Z appears to actively position itself on digital platforms both in constructing identities and articulating social critique. Therefore, it becomes necessary to reconsider the background of the images employed by the secular discourse in describing youth, the nature of their relationship with digital culture, and the transformation of their value systems through more holistic sociological perspectives.

In conclusion, it is essential to note that generational research is gaining increasing importance as a prominent methodological context within the secularization literature. Considering that making definitive claims about the existence of absolute secularization or re-sacralization in a particular era, society, or at the global level can render secularization debates unproductive, it becomes evident that generations can provide effective frameworks of analysis. Specific conceptualizations that have gained ground in the literature—from early contributors (such as Mannheim's concept of "generation units") to contemporary scholars of generational sociology—highlight the necessity of examining tendencies toward or away from religion within a specific time frame, geography, and generational context. For this reason, we argue that in secularization research specific to our country, using generations as the primary unit of analysis and conducting comparisons between preceding and succeeding generations through longitudinal studies should be regarded as essential.

References

Bartley, S. J., Ladd, P. G., & Morris, M. L. (2007). Managing the multigenerational workplace: Answers for managers and trainers. *CUPA-HR Journal, 58*(1), 28–34.

Bauman, Z. (2011). *Akışkan modern dünyadan 44 mektup* (P. Siral, Trans.). Habitus Yayıncılık.

Bristow, J. (2015). *The construction of the baby boomer generation as a social problem in Britain* [Doctoral Dissertation]. University of Kent.

Bristow, J. (2016). *The sociology of generations: New directions and challenges*. Palgrave Macmillan.

Cambridge Dictionary. (2025). Retrieved August 10, 2025, from https://dictionary.cambridge.org/dictionary/english-turkish/generation

Coomes, M. D., & DeBard, R. (Ed.). (2004). *Serving the millennial generation: New directions for student services*. Jossey-Bass.

Coupland, D. (1991). *Generation X: Tales for an accelerated culture*. St. Martin's Griffin.

Creswell, J. W. (2017). *Araştırma deseni -nitel, nicel ve karma yöntem yaklaşımları-*. (S. B. Demir, Trans. Ed.). Eğiten Kitap.

Creswell, J. W. (2018). *Nitel araştırma yöntemleri -beş yaklaşıma göre nitel araştırma ve araştırma deseni-*. (M. Bütün, & S. B. Demir, Trans. Ed.). Siyasal Kitabevi.

Dereli, M. D. (2019). Dinî kimliklerin siber uzamda akışkanlaşması. *İnsan ve Toplum Dergisi, 9*(1), 85–116. https://doi.org/10.12658/M0301

Dereli, M. D. (2022). Hervieu-Léger sosyolojisi: Gelenek, din ve hafıza ilişkiselliğinde bir sekülerleşme analizi. *İnsan ve Toplum, 12*(3), 159–192. https://doi.org/10.12658/M0678

Eken, M. (2020). Modern görsel kültürde m nesli'nin online inanç pratikleri. *Bilimname, 43*, 31–71. https://doi.org/10.28949/bilimname.762744

Eken, M. (2021). *Çevrim içi dindarlık: M neslinin inanç pratikleri*. Nobel Akademik Yayıncılık.

Gasset, J. O. Y. (1961). *The modern theme*. Harper & Row Publishers.

Gordon, V. N., & Steele, M. J. (2005). The advising workplace: Generational differences and challenges. *NACADA Journal, 25*, 26–30.

Hervieu-Léger, D. (2000). *Religion as a chain of memory*. Rutgers University Press.

Howe, N., & Strauss, W. (2007). *Millennials go to college* (2nd ed.). Paramount Market Pub.

Jaeger, H. (1985). Generations in history: Reflections on a controversial concept. *History and Theory, 24*(3), 273–292.

Janmohamed, S. (2018). *M nesli: Yeni Müslüman gençlik*. Kaknüs Yayınları.

Johnson, S. A., & Romanello, M. L. (2005). Generational diversity: Teaching and learning approaches. *Nurse Educator, 30*(5), 212–216. https://doi.org/10.1097/00006223-200509000-00009

Karaarslan, F. (2015). Post-seküler din helleri: Dinin dijitalleşmesi. In M. Çamdereli, B. Önay Doğan & N. Kocabay Şener (Eds.), *Dijitalleşen Din: Medya ve Din 2* (pp. 13–44). Köprü Yayınları.

Kertzer, D. I. (1983). Generation as a sociological problem. *Annual Review of Sociology, 9*(1), 125–149. https://doi.org/10.1146/annurev.so.09.080183.001013

Mannheim, K. (1952). The problem of generations. In P. Kecskemeti (Ed.), *Karl Mannheim: Essays* (pp. 276–322). Routledge.

Marshall, G. (1999). *Sosyoloji sözlüğü* (O. Akınhay & D. Kömürcü, Trans.). Bilim ve Sanat Yayınları.

Merriam, S. B. (2015). *Nitel araştırma -desen ve uygulama için bir rehber-*. (S. Turan, Trans.) Nobel Yayınları.

Nash, L. L. (1978). Concepts of existence: Greek origins of generational thought. *Daedalus, 107*(4), 1–21.

Oxford English Dictionary. (2025). Retrieved August 10, 2025, from https://www.oed.com/search/dictionary/?scope=Entries&q=generation

Pew Research Center. (2018). *The generation gap in American politics*. Retrieved September 15, 2025, from https://www.pewresearch.org/politics/2018/03/01/the-generation-gap-in-american-politics/

Pew Research Center. (2019). *Defining generations: Where millennials end and generation Z begins*. Retrieved September 15, 2025, from https://www.pewresearch.org/fact-tank/2019/01/17/where-millennials-end-and-generation-z-begins/,Erişim Tarihi: 24.06.2024.

Prensky, M. (2012). *Brain gain: Technology and the quest for digital wisdom*. Martin's Press.

Roof, W. C. (1993). *A Generation of seekers: The spiritual journeys of the baby boom generation*. HarperCollins.

Roof, W. C. (1999). *Spiritual marketplace: Baby boomers and the remaking of American religion*. Princeton University Press.

Scott, J. (2014). *Oxford dictionary of sociology*. OUP Oxford.

Stillman, D., & Stillman, J. (2019). *İşte z kuşağı genç kuşak işyerini nasıl dönüştürüyor?* (D. P. Kayıhan & F. Erduran, Trans.). İstanbul Kültür Üniversitesi.

Strauss, W., & Howe, N. (1991). *Generations: The history of America's future, 1584 to 2069*. William Morrow Paperbacks.

Strauss, W., & Howe, N. (1996). *The fourth turning: What the cycles of history tell us about America's next rendezvous with destiny*. Three Rivers Press.

Taylor, C. (2007). *A secular age*. The Belknap Press of Harvard University Press.
Turner, B. S. (2014). *Klasik sosyoloji* (İ. Çetin, Trans.). İletişim Yayınları.
Turner, B. S. (Ed.). (2006). *The Cambridge dictionary of sociology*. Cambridge University Press.
Twenge, J. M. (2018). *iNesli* (O. Gündüz, Trans.). Kaknüs Yayınları.
Voas, D., & Doebler, S. (2011). Secularization in Europe: Religious change between and within birth cohorts. *Religion and Society in Central and Eastern Europe, 4*(1), 39–62. https://doi.org/10.1163/9789004261662_012
Wohl, R. (1979). *The generation of 1914*. Harvard University Press.
Wuthnow, R. J. (1976). Recent patterns of secularization: A problem of generations. *American Sociological Review, 41*, 850–867.
Wuthnow, R. J. (2007). *After the baby boomers*. Princeton University Press.
Zemke, R., Raines, C., & Filipczak, B. (2000). *Generations at work: Managing the clash of veterans, boomers, Xers, and nexters in your workplace*. AMACOM.

Chapter 10
Online Strategies of Atheistic Movements in Türkiye: The Case of Ateizm Derneği

Metin Eken

10.1 Introduction

This study draws upon the strategies outlined in Hazdovac Bajić's (2023) article, which explores how nonreligious and atheistic organizations in Croatia employ specific online strategies and adapt them within a distinctive local context characterized by unique religious–secular dynamics. As noted in the study (Hazdovac Bajić, 2023, p. 62), these strategies were presented in a context that reflects the possible similarities and differences between the strategies defined by Cimino and Smith (2014), particularly in the American setting, and those adopted by nonreligious organizations in Croatia.

This study aims to analyze, within these thematic frameworks, the online strategies of the Ateizm Derneği (Atheism Association) of Türkiye, which was established in 2014 as the country's first officially registered atheist association and is recognized and accredited by the European Union and the United Nations. However, it is worth noting that these strategies were considered an initial analytical framework, consistent with the study's methodology. The recontextualization of these strategies within Türkiye's unique political and socio-cultural context and dynamics constitutes the distinctive aspect of the research. In this respect, the study is significant in that it contributes to the expansion of the existing literature by questioning and extending it across different social and cultural contexts.

In the study, the Directed Qualitative Content Analysis (DQlCA) method was employed, and the research field consisted of the Ateist Gazete archive, which includes 130 issues as of January 2025. The group was stratified by year, and the issues falling within the study's scope were first identified for each year. Then, random issues were selected from each stratum. In this manner, a total of 50 issues were included in the analysis.

M. Eken (✉)
Department of Journalism, Erciyes University, Kayseri, Türkiye
e-mail: metineken@erciyes.edu.tr

M. D. Dereli and M. Eken (eds.), *Turkish Perspectives on Secularization and Media*,
https://doi.org/10.1007/978-3-032-16436-0_10

The study focuses on which strategies, among those defined within the analytical framework, can be observed in the online communication of the Atheism Association (in terms of similarities and differences), and how the discursive strategies used in the Association's online activities interact with Turkey's distinctive socio-cultural and political dynamics.

Within this scope, the study first addresses the historical trajectory of atheism from the Ottoman period to the present, examining its categorical appearances and current status within Türkiye's unique socio-cultural context. Subsequently, the visibility of atheism in digital environments is discussed from the perspectives of secularization and digital religion studies, ensuring the theoretical and analytical positioning of the research.

10.2 Atheism in Türkiye and the Ateizm Derneği (Atheism Association)

Considerations regarding Türkiye's social structure necessitate examining the transition from the Ottoman Empire to the Republic within the context of change and continuity (Acun, 2013). For this reason, when addressing atheism in Türkiye, the Tanzimat period (1839) can be regarded as an essential starting point. As Bolay (1988, p. 64) notes, although traces of these ideas were mostly followed through literary debates, the Tanzimat era was a period in which materialist and atheistic thought began to find resonance in Ottoman lands through various influences. Among the key factors was the impact of Ottoman intellectuals who had studied in France during the nineteenth century. In addition, educational institutions such as Mekteb-i Tıbbiyye (Imperial School of Medicine) and Mekteb-i Harbiyye (Imperial Military Academy), together with their engagement with Western thinkers and translation activities, accelerated the process. Consequently, with the spread of positivist and materialist ideas during the Tanzimat period, an upsurge in religious criticism also emerged (Topaloğlu, 2007, pp. 114–115). The period following the Second Constitutional Era (1908)—which may be considered a bridge in the history of Turkish intellectual thought—was marked by the philosophical dissemination of materialism, led by prominent figures such as Baha Tevfik, Celal Nuri, and Abdullah Cevdet (Bolay, 1988, p. 18). Baha Tevfik, in particular, stands out for his advocacy of biological and evolutionary materialism and for his courage in openly embracing and expressing atheism. As the founder of Felsefe Mecmuası (Philosophy Journal, 1911), the first philosophical periodical in Türkiye, and the compiler of Felsefe Kamusu (Philosophical Encyclopedia), Tevfik played a crucial role in transferring materialist philosophy by publishing the works of materialist thinkers such as Ernst Haeckel and Ludwig Büchner (Topaloğlu, 2007, p. 117). Although the materialism of that period drew upon mechanism, evolutionism, and positivism, its influence largely remained within the boundaries of philosophical debate (Akgün, 1988, p. 500). The process spanning from the Tanzimat to the Constitutional period thus serves as an essential point of reference for discussions concerning the origins of atheistic thought, whose traces can still be followed in the Republican era.

By the Republican period, rather than tracing the journey of atheism through successive historical stages, it appears more reasonable to make broader categorical distinctions. This is necessary because specific perspectives, though belonging to different periods, may fall within the same category. However, it should be noted from the outset that each category has been constructed to reflect particular attitudes; thus, they should be understood as overlapping and interwoven rather than as rigid or mutually exclusive divisions.

From this perspective, the first category can be defined as *cultural atheism*. Within this category, two main clusters can be identified. A sharp stance regarding Turkish modernization characterizes the first. This attitude represents a mindset that advocates for a complete break from the Ottoman past, perceives the Republic as the concrete manifestation of this ideal, and therefore desires an absolute rupture from Islam, which it associates with tradition and backwardness. It includes elements of reaction, contempt, and othering toward the manifestations of religion in Turkish society, and in this sense, it sometimes bears an Islamophobic or self-Orientalist character. At the same time, an emphasis on secularism and Kemalism becomes prominent. Academics and writers such as İlhan Arsel and Muazzez İlmiye Çığ can be mentioned within this cluster. Arsel is among the most prominent figures of this group with his numerous works. His writings reflect the characteristics described above. His book Şeriatçıyla Mücadelenin El Kitabı—(The Handbook for Struggling Against the Islamist) provides concise examples of this stance:

> Our people, just as before the Republican period, are being educated and shaped mentally and spiritually through the tenets of Sharia—tenets that corrode the human mind, gnaw away at reason and logic, destroy the power of thinking, suppress the sense of freedom, blunt creative intelligence, reduce human beings to mere 'servants,' belittle women, and, more broadly, distance human existence from all possibilities of progress. The only way to prevent this disastrous course is to heed the voice of rationality, to cling to secularism and the reforms of Atatürk, and to fight against the false sovereignty of the Islamist whose reign is built upon lies and against the anarchic assaults that rebel against enlightenment". (Arsel, 2008, p. 11)

Muazzez İlmiye Çığ, on the other hand, stands out particularly with her work Kur'an, İncil ve Tevrat'ın Sümer'deki Kökeni—(The Sumerian Origins of the Qur'an, the Bible, and the Torah (2005). This book has been regarded as a key reference by atheist circles attempting to question the originality of Islam. It has been instrumentalized to such an extent that its scientific shortcomings have often been overlooked. The second cluster includes writers and thinkers who were raised in religious families within Turkish society, received traditional religious education, lived devoutly for a period of their lives, and later abandoned their faiths—subsequently engaging in a struggle against the beliefs they had lost. Turan Dursun, Erdoğan Aydın, and Arif Tekin are the leading figures in this group (Altaytaş, 2001, p. 9). Their inclusion in this category is primarily due to their critique of the social realities in which their former beliefs were reflected, as well as their engagement in a cultural reckoning process. Although leftist and materialist motivations can be observed particularly in Dursun and Aydın, their underlying cultural confrontation indicates that they are more appropriately positioned within this category. The relevant literature reveals that these authors approach Islam—through their emphasis on science, reason, and modern human values—as an outdated worldview that not only lacks the potential for modernization but also obstructs the modernization of society and hinders free and creative thought, and should therefore be rejected (Altaytaş, 2001, p. 183; Demir, 2010; Kayıklık, 2006; Vidinlioğlu, 2022). An essential characteristic of the figures in this category is their mutual interconnection. For instance, Muazzez İlmiye Çığ, in addition to citing Turan Dursun in her works, acknowledges that she benefited from his ideas (2005, p. 71). Dursun's reference work Din Bu-1: Tanrı ve Kur'an— (This Is Religion—God and the Qur'an) (2006) begins with a preface written by İlhan Arsel. Dursun later published their correspondence under the title İlhan Arsel'e Mektuplar (Letters to İlhan Arsel) (1999). Another notable aspect of these figures, in terms of the development of atheism in Türkiye, is that their works have come to be regarded as guiding and reference texts within atheist circles.

The second category can be defined as ideological atheism. It encompasses various interpretations adopted by leftist and socialist circles in Türkiye that are grounded in materialist understandings. As Ünüvar states, within this category one may consider the diverse perspectives that, through dialectical materialism, historicize religion and address the "problem" of why and how God or gods could exist (2008, p. 874). The issue of Birikim, a monthly socialist culture journal considered the intellectual center of socialist thought in Türkiye, devoted to the theme "Atheism and Left Theology" (2015), provides significant insights into how socialist thought in Türkiye approaches atheism.

The perspective reflected in the introduction and the primary texts of that issue interprets atheism not as a denial of God (tanrıtanımazlık), but rather as the idea of godlessness (tanrısızlık). Tanıl Bora, in this regard, draws attention to the same emphasis observed among socialist ideologues in Europe during the period encompassing the two World Wars—namely, the distinction between being an atheist and being without God. This state, defined as the avoidance of turning belief (or unbelief) into an "-ism," involves theoretical and political caution regarding what is to be included while seeking to transcend religion and metaphysics (2015, p. 9). Examples from countries such as the USSR, Albania, and China—where philosophical atheism, as a state doctrine, led to results resembling the imposition of a state religion—constitute one of the reasons for this cautious attitude. In this sense, being without God involves addressing the question of divinity, but it manifests as a quiet form of disregard, rather than a loud and militant denial (İnsel, 2015, pp. 16–18). Another significant point is the hope that the secular system may also enable the liberation of religion itself and open the possibility of a theology of freedom. Secularization is thus sanctified as a process that, on one side, signifies the disenchantment of the world from religion, and on the other, the disentanglement of religion from the world. Furthermore, using religious terminology, it is presented as "a process that may also bring blessings for theists" (Bora, 2015, p. 9; Argın, 2015, p. 27).

A third category can be discussed under the heading of popular atheism. The first group within this category consists of well-known figures—academics, writers, and artists—whose social presence has been primarily shaped by the media. In a social structure where the vast majority of the population is Muslim, their public expressions and visibility, primarily through media channels, have given rise to numerous polemics and debates. These figures, who stand out with both their political and socio-cultural critiques, often adopt dismissive and at times phobic attitudes toward the social manifestations of Islam[1]. Among the notable figures in this group is Celal Şengör, whose stance draws particular attention. As Alper Bilgili observes, like many neo-atheist writers, Şengör maintains that science is the sole guide for humanity. He argues that the only way for humanity—and for Turkish society—to overcome contemporary crises is by embracing science. Within this framework, constructed around the opposition between religion and science, the more mediatized elements tend to reflect a reaction against the political authority in Türkiye that draws upon Islamic references and the traditional structures perceived to support it. An illustrative example of this is Şengör's view that even the presentation of veiling in modern societies as a democratic right is scientifically flawed (2017, pp. 50–58). Another group within this category can be described as internet atheists. This includes those whose visibility has increased as a result of, on the one hand, the evolution of atheism into a form of activism through new atheism, and on the other, the expanding influence of online platforms characterized by user participation. Activist communities or association websites, official social media accounts, or the personal accounts of administrators and members; content creators who claim to present scientific and philosophical arguments and to broaden the field of debate; and atheist internet users who engage in the digital ecosystem through comments, shares, and other forms of interaction—all can be considered within this scope (Table 10.1).[2]

In this context, it can be stated that the emergence of the Ateizm Derneği (Atheism Association) in Türkiye was a result of developments that include the global rise of new atheist activism, the growing influence of the internet as an alternative platform, and a reaction to the political atmosphere in Türkiye. Founded in 2014, according to its official charter (Ateizm Derneği Tüzüğü, 2019):

> The association was established with the objectives of enabling atheists and nonbelievers to unite and build solidarity; promoting and accurately representing the idea of atheism within society; supporting individuals and organizations working in this field; institutionally combating the use of religion, philosophical or ideological views as instruments of oppression against atheists and/or nonbelievers; encouraging the free and lawful expression of atheists' and nonbelievers' views in Türkiye; and organizing youth activities for the nonbelieving community in Türkiye.

These objectives can be grouped under key themes such as solidarity, legal and institutional struggle, and the representation of atheist/nonbeliever sensitivities. Legally recognized by the European Union and the United Nations, the association is also a member of various humanist and atheist umbrella organizations

---

[1] Numerous figures such as Celal Şengör, İlyas Salman, and Barbaros Şansal—among many others—can be mentioned within this scope.

[2] Examples also include the website and social media accounts of the Ateizm Derneği, the Karikateist social media platforms, YouTube channels such as Uçaktaki Ateist Akademisi and Din ve Mitoloji, as well as individual content creators like Efe Aydal, Yakup Deniz, and İlyas Özkan.

Table 10.1 The Landscape of Atheism in Turkey[3]

Period	Subheading	Description
Pre-Republic Period—Early Manifestations (1839–1923)	a. Tanzimat Era (1839–1876)	The spread of positivist and materialist ideas, as well as the rise of religious criticism Topaloğlu (2007, pp. 114–115)
	b. Second Constitutional Era (1908–1923)	Efforts to popularize materialist thought at the philosophical level Bolay (1988, p. 18). Baha Tevfik, who defended biological and evolutionary materialism, is noted as a figure who openly adopted and expressed atheism Topaloğlu (2007, pp. 114–115)
Post-Republic Period (1923– …)	**Cultural Atheism**	
	a. A Rigid Modernist Outlook	A total break from traditional Islam. In some cases, Islamophobic and self-orientalist attitudes. (e.g., İlhan Arsel, Muazzez İlmiye Çığ)
	b. From Religious and Traditional Families to Atheism	Individuals raised with traditional religious education, who lived devoutly during specific periods of their lives, but later abandoned faith and adopted atheism as an active field of struggle. (e.g., Turan Dursun, Erdoğan Aydın, Arif Tekin)
	Ideological Atheism	
	a. Atheism in Leftist Thought	Interpretation and advocacy of atheism by leftist-socialist circles in Turkey through materialist perspectives
	Popular Atheism	
	a. Atheist Celebrities	Academics, writers, and artists with varying atheist backgrounds who gained visibility in society through the influence of the media (e.g., Celal Şengör)
	b. Internet Atheists	The emergence of atheism as a form of activism gaining visibility on online platforms. The rise of new atheism and its dissemination through social media and internet forums

[3] Although this classification is a preliminary attempt aimed at outlining the main contours, it offers a framework open to further refinement and development.

abroad (https://www.ateizmdernegi.org.tr, n.d.). As Türkiye's first official and organized atheist institution, the Association has attracted attention from all segments of Turkish atheism, and its activities have found significant reflection in the ideas and figures associated with both cultural atheism and popular atheism categories.

Recent empirical surveys provide valuable insights into the demographic visibility of atheism in Türkiye. Sayılarla Türkiye'de İnanç ve Dindarlık (TİDA) – (Faith and Religiosity in Türkiye), conducted in 2023 under the coordination of Zübeyir Nişancı, collected data from 1,942 individuals aged 18 and above, proportionally representing both rural and urban populations across twelve regions of the country. Designed with intense methodological rigor, the study stands as one of the most comprehensive analyses of religiosity in Türkiye to date. Its findings reveal that 1.5% of participants declared, "I do not believe in God." In comparison, 2.5% stated, "I do not know whether God exists, and I do not believe there is a way to know," and 1.7% responded, "I do not believe in God, but I think there is a supernatural power." Meanwhile, a clear majority—85.7%—affirmed, "I know that God exists, and I have no doubt about it." The report clarifies that these distinctions correspond respectively to atheism, agnosticism, and deism, with the three categories collectively defined as nonbelievers. Based on this classification, individuals without a belief in God account for 5.7% of Türkiye's population. The findings further indicate that nonbelief is most prevalent among the 18–24 age group, while the highest levels of education, particularly master's and doctoral degrees, correlate strongly with the tendency toward nonbelief (Nişancı, 2023, pp. 29–30).

Another nationwide study, Türkiye'de Dindarlık Algısı—(Perceptions of Religiosity in Türkiye) (2023), conducted with 1,358 respondents aged 18 and above, supports similar conclusions. According to this survey, 2.7% of participants identified as atheists, 3.2% as deists, and 0.7% as agnostics, while 92.3% declared themselves to be Muslims (Ete & Yargı, 2023, p. 12). Although religious affiliation with Islam remains overwhelmingly dominant, the measurable presence of atheist and deist individuals marks a significant shift in Türkiye's religious landscape. Taken together, these recent datasets challenge the widely repeated assumption—reinforced for decades in both domestic discourse and international reports, including those of the U.S. Department of State's Office of International Religious Freedom (2021, 2022, 2023)—that 99% of Türkiye's population is Muslim.

10.3 Digital Media, Secularization, and Atheism

Digital religion studies have generated a substantial body of literature demonstrating that the digital media ecosystem has become a space that not only transforms religious experiences, practices, and beliefs but also reveals new religious forms and meanings (Campbell & Cheong, 2024; Echchaibi & Hoover, 2023; Evolvi, 2021; Isetti et al., 2022). Although it has not received sufficient attention within the field, atheism and atheistic practices also constitute a significant dimension that can be included within the scope of media and religion studies. Drawing on Taira (2022), it should be emphasized that religion and atheism are discursive domains that mutually define and give meaning to each other. The representations of these dynamics in digital media clearly reveal this interrelation. This fundamental proposition necessitates that atheism and atheistic practices, in terms of their reflections in the digital sphere, be examined together with their direct discursive counterpart—religion and religious practices.

Considering that the increasing interest in and awareness of atheism today are conditioned by digitalization (Cimino & Smith, 2014; Taira, 2022), the growing digital visibility of atheism in countries such as Türkiye—where the majority of the population is Muslim—requires that the issue be analyzed in conjunction with secularization processes. At this point, two processes can be identified that are interrelated and even proceed in parallel in terms of secularization. The first is the process of secularization[4] itself, which is discussed as a fundamental underlying issue in both the transformation of traditional religious practices and the emergence of new religious forms. Significant emphasis is placed on the potentially secularizing nature of digital media. In his study on Generation M, Eken (2020, p. 31) examined how young Muslims express themselves and their faith through the internet and social media, and how the symbolic resources of the media field, in this generational context, relate to meanings and practices concerning faith, spirituality, religion, and transcendence. The study demonstrates that digital environments—characterized as value-laden tools due to their cultural determinants and technical properties—have a significant influence on shaping the online faith practices of young Muslims. It further suggests that digital media possess a secularizing character due to their potential to subject the content or essence of religious-looking practices to the secular (and secularizing) nature of modern visual culture. Another noteworthy finding derived from this argument is that some online faith practices of young Muslims, while outwardly religious in appearance, may in fact be embedded within a secular understanding. The study particularly highlights that, through the influence of digital environments, an often-unnoticed process of secularization is at work among young Muslims.

The second process, as shown in the first, concerns the exposure of young Muslims—who express their faith through the secular and secularizing content of digital culture or shape their beliefs within the traditional assumptions of their society—to the growing digital visibility of atheism. This visibility creates a space in which the relatively younger segments of the Muslim population may come to

[4] However, it should be noted that, unlike the classical secularization thesis or some of the approaches that seek to refute it, the concept of secularization is addressed here in a distinctive manner. Just as the decline of traditional religious forms does not necessarily indicate that secularization is an absolute reality, it is likewise not possible to claim that the new forms of religiosity increasingly evident in today's world are entirely unrelated to secularization. Accordingly, in this study, secularization is approached as a state of mind—a phenomenon that should be sought within the everyday practices reflected in life through this mindset. This mental disposition and the daily practices it shapes are open to the structural influences of culture, and therefore of media, while also being molded by the possibilities of agency. In this respect, the concept focuses not on viewing the secular and the religious as fixed categories but rather on their interpenetrations, and in a sense, expresses a form of religious deprivation (Eken, 2019). Indeed, Dereli's studies (2019, 2022) have discussed social media and evolving forms of religiosity within a similar framework.

question their own beliefs. In countries where Muslims constitute the overwhelming majority, this space can be said to contribute to the relativization of religious belief, the distancing from spiritual practices, and even the adoption of atheist, deist, or agnostic positions.

Taira's (2022) observation that digital platforms not only provide new spaces for atheist and secular associations rooted in offline contexts but also foster more evident transformations within the loose networks of individuals interested in atheism, yet maintain only a superficial relationship with its organized forms, supports these findings. For instance, Isomaa, who observed atheist YouTube channels through online ethnographic methods, notes that these channels have evolved into educational resources by facilitating the production of knowledge and ideas about atheism in an accessible format. Going a step further, he argues that online atheist content—both implicitly and explicitly—teaches particular ways of approaching and evaluating different knowledge claims (scientific, philosophical, religious) and, in doing so, establishes a normative atheist approach to knowledge (2024, pp. 145–148).

The framework presented in the first section of this study, which focuses on classifying atheism in Türkiye, enables the provision of supportive evaluations in this regard. Within this framework, the internet atheists emerging under the category of popular atheism represent the leading group that, through direct online activities, serves as an inspiration for individual quests related to religion. Figures categorized under cultural atheism, on the other hand, appear to be utilized as argumentative or data sources by internet atheists alongside well-known atheist figures.

It can also be stated that this mobilization within individual networks provides a basis for collective initiatives. According to Cimino and Smith (2011), such platforms have allowed atheists to voice and share their common concerns. These media spaces have become crucial components of atheist activism, particularly in terms of knowledge dissemination and awareness-raising. The significance of the internet for atheists today can thus be better understood: online environments contribute to the development of a sense of group identity around shared ideas and agendas, helping secular individuals recognize this collective awareness. Furthermore, this sense of solidarity can transform into collective action both in digital and physical spaces (Smith & Cimino, 2012, pp. 17–18). As Addington points out, online atheist interactions serve a wide range of functions—from finding a community and fostering solidarity to reaching individuals who have not yet joined. These interactions complement and reinforce face-to-face connections and, in some cases, offer an alternative for individuals who cannot or choose not to participate in physical spaces (2017, p. 147).

10.4 Methodology

In this study, one of the contemporary qualitative content analysis techniques—Directed Qualitative Content Analysis (DQlCA)—was employed to test the validity of findings obtained from previous research efforts, confirm their suitability, or extend their applicability beyond the context or culture in which they were initially developed (Kibiswa, 2019, p. 2059). As stated in the introduction, this study draws on Hazdovac Bajić (2023), who explored the online strategies used by nonreligious and atheist organizations in Croatia and examined how these strategies were applied within a local context characterized by unique religious–secular dynamics. In this respect, the present research aims to discuss these strategies within the context of Türkiye, focusing specifically on the online strategies of the Atheism Association, which was founded in 2014 as Türkiye's first officially recognized atheist organization and accredited by both the European Union and the United Nations.

Following Hsieh and Shannon (2005, p. 1277), who define directed content analysis as a method used to derive meaning from textual data, issues of the Ateist Gazete (Atheist Newspaper), comprising 130 editions (as of January 2025), were analyzed. The dataset was stratified by publication year, and random selections were made from each stratum, resulting in a total of 50 issues included in the analysis. This stratified purposive sampling ensured data saturation, while random selection reduced sampling bias.

The Ateist Gazete was selected as an especially suitable data source because it serves not only to inform members and followers but also as a platform that reflects the Association's institutional identity, current priorities, and public stance. The President's Messages featured in several issues explicitly reveal the direction, tone, and priorities of the Association's discourse. Moreover, the newspaper stands at the intersection of the Association's online and offline activities, incorporating content that forms the basis for its social media posts, campaigns, and public discourse strategies. Consequently, it provides a systematic means of observing both internal communication practices and strategic orientations toward public visibility.

The analysis, inspired by Hazdovac Bajić's (2023) framework, focused on seven main themes that capture the organizational and discursive strategies of nonreligious actors: Cooperation among Organizations, Minority Discourse, Religious Mimicry, Exposing Religion, Inversion, Reclaiming Patriotism, and Reclaiming Spirituality.

During the analytical process, AI-supported PDF recognition technology was employed. Each issue was digitized using an Optical Character Recognition (OCR)-based text-recognition system, and thematic scanning was conducted according to a predetermined coding scheme, supported by natural language processing (NLP) techniques. Manual verification by the researcher ensured the accuracy of classifications and eliminated potential mislabeling caused by the AI. This hybrid method combined the efficiency of automated text processing with the interpretive depth of qualitative inquiry, ensuring both analytic rigor and contextual reliability.

10.5 Results

10.5.1 Cooperation Among Organizations

Cooperation among organizations emerges as one of the strongest strategic pillars for the Atheism Association, as revealed by its multiple subcomponents in this study. The first and most prominent among these is vertical collaboration with international secular networks and organizations.

In this regard, Türkiye's participation in the ARAP Project—a fully international cooperation initiative providing legal and humanitarian assistance to atheist refugees in the Middle East and Africa—is noteworthy. The project is supported by the Centre for Inquiry (CFI), a New York–based organization associated with the New Atheist perspective, and the Atheist Alliance International (AAI), a global federation of atheist groups and individuals. This project is prominently featured across numerous issues of Ateist Gazete (Issues 1, 2, 32, 40, 46, 57, 85, 124, 125, 127, 128).

An interesting example illustrating the contribution of international cooperation to organizational development appears in Issue 2, which reports on the legalization of Georgia's first atheist/agnostic/freethought association: "Following an invitation in 2016, representatives from Ateist Dergi, the Atheism Association, and the AAI jointly organized a month-long field visit, hosting two introductory meetings and one workshop. As a result, Georgia's enlightened warriors finally attained legal personality and formalized their organization."

Another case emphasizing institutional capacity-building concerns Humanists International, an NGO legally registered in both New York (USA) and Glasgow (UK) (Issue 2). Similarly, the newspaper's depiction of an "enlightenment partnership" with Ex-Muslims of North America (EXMNA)—referred to as "the North Star of Enlightenment" (Issue 46)—illustrates ideological convergence within the broader humanist and secular network.

Additionally, the Association's official website and the newspaper both highlight its accreditation by the Council of Europe and the United Nations, demonstrating the strategic importance of international cooperation for institutional legitimacy and recognition. Across the dataset, such examples indicate that international cooperation serves as a mechanism for capacity development, legitimacy building, and minority rights advocacy for the Atheism Association. Likewise, several issues (e.g., Issue 50) include statements affirming the Association's determination to seek justice through international legal frameworks such as the European Court of Human Rights, underlining its readiness for institutional advocacy when necessary.

A second key subcomponent concerns horizontal cooperation with national solidarity and NGO networks. The newspaper frequently features reports encouraging participation in domestic civil society alliances that promote secular and democratic values (Issue 44). Joint advocacy initiatives with human rights, women's rights, LGBTQ + , refugee, and child protection organizations are also documented (Issue 29), highlighting the Association's alignment with freedom-centered causes.

At the national level, another crucial mission involves engaging intellectual and cultural figures who can support public awareness and secular discourse. Prominent figures frequently mentioned in the newspaper include Celal Şengör, Turan Dursun, Aziz Nesin, İlhan Arsel, Prof. Dr. Örsan Öymen, and Fazıl Say, alongside various grassroots groups and online communities such as alternative science and philosophy schools and YouTube channels (Issues 5, 7, 35, 37, 57, 61, 65, 72, 89, 91, 93, 105, 121).

Among these initiatives, one of the most significant is the "Bunlar Ateist!" ("These Are Atheists!") video-podcast series broadcast on the Atheism Association's YouTube channel, Ateizm Derneği TV. Described as a "weekly program prepared for nonbelievers and questioning individuals, open to live audience participation via phone," it features over 250 video episodes. It brings together diverse speakers across themes of religion, science, culture, politics, and everyday life—effectively constructing an atheist socio-cultural ecosystem.

Complementing these media-based initiatives are community-building events such as meetups, picnics, and summer camps (Issues 69, 70, 72, 87, 89, 105, 121, 122, 123, 124, 125, 126, 129), which serve as the offline extensions of the Association's digital network and reinforce its horizontal solidarity efforts.

10.5.2 Minority Discourse

Minority discourse represents one of the most consistent strategic themes of the Atheism Association. Across the analyzed issues, numerous articles, and commentaries link events related to atheist, agnostic, and secular identities—both in Türkiye and globally—to the discourse of discrimination, exclusion, and minority rights. This strategy operates on three interrelated levels: i) exposing laws, prohibitions, and punishments grounded in religion to generate legal awareness and international solidarity; ii) rendering social exclusion and stigmatization of nonbelievers visible at the societal level; and iii) transforming the status of minority identity into a source of pride, resistance, and collective empowerment.

At the legal level, recurring coverage includes reports and solidarity campaigns regarding the imprisonment and subsequent treatment of Nigerian atheist Mubarak Bala (Issues 44, 130), criticism of Pakistan's life imprisonment proposal for blasphemy against the Prophet and his family (Issue 86), and objections to Saudi Arabia's classification of atheism and homosexuality as extremist and dangerous ideologies (Issue 2). Likewise, condemnations of punitive actions against secular minorities in other countries—such as the Hamline University case (Issue 86)—reflect the Association's framing of these incidents as violations of universal rights.

At the social level, the discourse centers on freedom of association and equal citizenship. Articles protest the restrictions on organizational freedom and call for a unified stance against systemic discrimination (Issue 29). Criticism of the Directorate of Religious Affairs (Diyanet) and the Ministry of National Education (MEB) is frequent, particularly in the context of decisions made at the

National Religion Council, which are portrayed as excluding nonbelievers from full citizenship and civic equality (Issues 4, 8, 9, 29, 85, 87, 91, 100, 122, 123). Campaigns such as the slogan "Bunlar Ateist!" (These Are Atheists!) (Issue 6) turn processes of social stigmatization into instruments of collective self-identification and counter-discourse, reframing exclusion as visibility.

The construction of minority consciousness also functions as a mobilizing device. Calls for participation, such as "We need you in our struggle for a secular society and a laic state" and "We are one person short without you," alongside open-invitation banners like "Contact us", reinforce the message of inclusion and shared struggle (Issues 91, 93, 99, 100, 105, 122).

At the cultural-symbolic level, recurring expressions such as "aydınlık" (enlightenment), "aydınlanma" (illumination), and "aydınlık savaşçıları" (warriors of enlightenment) (Issues 42, 50, 65, 121, 130) illustrate how minority status is reframed not as passive victimhood but as a proud and resistant identity.

10.5.3 Religious Mimicry

In the literature, this strategy is characterized by the preservation of religious forms while incorporating secular content. However, there is limited evidence in the context of this study that such a strategy emerged in the same way. In this framework, what stands out are instead the forms of "parodying sacred discourse," which can be more appropriately evaluated under the following theme (Exposing Religion). It can be stated that this situation, which emerges in relation to this theme, is the result of certain atheist reflexes in Türkiye being shaped by negative and at times phobic narratives toward religion, particularly Islam. Accordingly, religious forms are often inverted through parody and satire, marked by irony and ridicule. The article titled "İmam feneriyle ahlak arayışı" ("The Search for Morality with the Imam's Lantern") and the rhetorical imitation-based critique found in the related column on the linked website (Issue 68), the headline "Bir peygamber daha göçtü" ("Another Prophet Has Passed Away") following the death of a person known publicly as a false prophet (Issue 3), and the titles addressing the understanding and presentation of religion in the tension between science and superstition (Issues 10, 57) can all be evaluated within this scope.

However, beyond all these, the newspaper frequently features commemorative events that can be described as secular remembrance rituals, positioned at the intersection of several other themes. Individuals who have come to prominence through their contributions to atheist thought or who are considered meaningful figures within the framework of atheism are commemorated on related dates, thus constructing a secular memory; specific figures are sanctified as national and universal moral examples and guides (Examples include: Aziz Nesin, Issue 65; Salman Rushdie, Issue 69; Turan Dursun, Issue 72; Muammer Aksoy, Issue 87; Karl Marx, Issue 93; Stephen Hawking, Issue 93; Albert Einstein, Issue 99; Mark Twain, Issue 99; Konca Kuriş,

Issue 121; Nicolaus Copernicus, Issue 124; Can Yücel, Issue 125; Tevfik Fikret, Issue 126).

10.5.4 Exposing Religion

Representations that expose religious institutions or their representatives, as well as religiously motivated practices and appearances, through humor, mockery, or openly critical and rejecting cultural discourse, stand out as one of the strongest strategies in the newspaper. Within this framework, several subcomponents emerge in the analysis.

The first is the association of religious institutions and actors, as well as religion-based practices, with political power. The report interpreting the prayer of the President of Religious Affairs (Diyanet) at the opening ceremony of the judicial year and the new Supreme Court building as a "turbulence of secularism" and a sign of Diyanet's rise within the bureaucracy, and framing the event as "a systematic plan to polarize the public through religion" (Issue 46); references to President Recep Tayyip Erdoğan's statement about "raising a pious generation" (Issue 2); the emphasis that people are impoverished through "religious fairy tales" by reporting the spending at the Presidential Palace (Issue 42); and the expressions directed against political power such as "Dreams of transforming the country back into a religious state through the construction of a mosque in Taksim will not hold together" (Issue 40) and "Those who try to force the secular mind of this country into a religious garment will leave the way they came!" (Issue 40) can be given as examples.

Following the collapse of a mosque minaret in Istanbul due to an earthquake, the statement "It is hard not to recall those who once read poems saying 'Minarets are our bayonets'," referring to a poem recited by Recep Tayyip Erdoğan, serves as a notable example of implicit hate speech. The reaction toward political power and its affiliated party is also occasionally presented as one of the reasons for opposition to Islam itself. The expression "This is what can be expected from a religion believed in by those who are enemies of everything beautiful" (Issue 61) is remarkable in this regard.

Another component is the framing of Islam through the codes of superstition and irrationality. During the pandemic, the emphasis was "Be close to science, distant from superstition! This is the time of reason and science!" (Issue 10). The inclusion of the Archbishop's statement, "Satan is helpless before holy water," in the same issue, as well as reports shaped by phrases such as "Women are breaking free from the slave garments of Islam! The world continues to fight against the ideology of radical Islam that divides people and makes social life unlivable" (Issue 35), are notable examples. A particularly interesting example can be found in the president's message in Issue 5, which, drawing from a national news story about a man who claimed to see a jinn in a field, fired randomly, and killed his own daughter, includes the statement: "Believing in imaginary beings such as jinn, angels, demons, and witches instilled by religions into the human mind, and being deprived of the light of science and reason, has led to the most brutal and unimaginable murders, tortures, and practices in human history." This is noteworthy as it categorically demonizes any religious concept. Similarly, during the coronavirus period, the expressions "More importantly, the real contagious virus is the belief that diseases are a means of forgiveness of sins and a blessing that brings one closer to God. This ideological blindness is more dangerous than coronavirus" (Issue 10) and "Indonesia will pray against coronavirus" (Issue 9) reinforce this framework.

The exposure of the religious figure through moral irony is also a prominent component. Headlines such as "Another abusive imam" (Issue 73) and "Again, an imam—again, harassment" and the accompanying statement "Physical or sexual violence exists both in the theory and practice of religions that view sexuality as taboo" (Issue 60); the analogy between Ali Erbaş, President of Religious Affairs, stating "Whoever builds a mosque the size of a bird's nest will earn a house in paradise" and the indulgence practices of the Middle Ages (Issue 8); and the report on the child abuse case by a Qur'an course teacher, highlighting that "the greatest abuse inflicted on the minds of children is religious education itself" (Issue 4) can all be included in this scope. Additionally, the reporting of statistical data indicating a decline in public trust toward religious figures (Issues 1, 3) serves as another sign of moral irony. Reports about religious figures from other faiths can also be found, such as one involving a priest accused of child abuse (Issues 7, 99).

These components indicate that the analyzed strategy often manifests as a form of cultural racism infused with Islamophobic hatred. The headline quoting a Buddhist monk's anti-Muslim statement, "Islam is a cancer that must be eradicated" (Issue 130), is a strong example in this regard. Instances where religion and Muslims are othered through their visible identities and cultural practices, being positioned as the cause of various social problems, are numerous. A striking example is the coverage of a young girl who was a victim of domestic violence and abuse under the headline "Narin's Story: The Inevitable Necessity of a Secular Life" (Issue 128). Similarly, in Türkiye's Kars province, the refusal of a couple to allow a heel-prick test for their newborn to screen for congenital diseases causing mental retardation, brain damage, muscle disorders, and death was reported under the title "Islamism as a Mental Eclipse" (Issue 127). In the same vein, an incident of domestic violence and murder in Egypt was reported under the headline "A Chilling Islamist Murder in Egypt" (Issue 103).

10.5.5 Inversion

Based on Hazdovac Bajić's (2023) text, this strategy aims to expand the idea that nonreligiosity is not a stance of opposition but rather a position taken for the common good and justice. It frames atheism as an ethical stance that produces social benefit. In this context, the subcomponents of the strategy of exposing religion—such as framing Islam and religions with superstition and irrationality, and exposing religious practices and clerical figures through moral irony—can also be regarded as a rationale for the inversion strategy. What comes to the forefront here is the elevation of nonreligiosity as a principle, the sanctification of secularism as a neutral ground, and its presentation as a guarantee for both believers and nonbelievers.

In this respect, an ironic example concerning the sanctification of secularism as a universal value is significant. In a report criticizing the Quran-burning incident in Sweden, the following statement stands out: "Although we believe that religious texts are not sacred, as guardians of secularism, we will continue to defend laicism and strive unconditionally to ensure freedom of religion and conscience" (Issue 60). This statement draws attention as a defense of secularism against religions, in the name of freedom of religion and conscience. In another report, Genç Memur-Sen President Mesut Emre Balcı's statement, which declared that Quran burning cannot be considered within the scope of freedom of expression, was featured under the headline "Freedom of Expression and the Sacred Values Being Eroded." In contrast, the framing that "Any group cannot monopolize the boundaries of freedom of expression" (Issue 87) appears to carry an ironic tone when applied to the sacred symbols of Islam.

Similarly, the statements such as "Irreligion is not, as labeled and criminalized by the religious, an approach that makes individuals immoral; on the contrary, it prioritizes thinking and questioning, and thus supports pluralism, making it an indispensable element of true morality and higher virtue" (Issue 50) can also be cited within this framework. Furthermore, the article titled "We Object to Diyanet's Anti-Secular Religious Council!" (Issue 4) contains extensive explanations on this matter. A passage from the text clearly reveals this strategic stance: "These 'currents (nonreligious movements)' emerged especially during the Enlightenment Era with reason, science, philosophy, and the capacity for inquiry, playing a crucial role in the development of humanity and constituting values that are the result of our shared culture. Thanks to the scientific and philosophical thought that forms the basis of these movements, there are now almost no communities worshipping wooden totems or practicing human sacrifice; the days when epidemics devastated societies are behind us, and the number of people who believe that human rights should encompass all humanity, not just specific groups, continues to grow."

Moreover, various content emphasizes that the criticism is directed not at religious beliefs themselves, but at the distortions within the relationship between religion and the state. For instance, the statement "Regardless of their faith group, whether they share our belief system or not, regardless of their ethnic background, poor or rich, every citizen of the Republic of Türkiye is equal and free in the public sphere" (Issue 128) illustrates this. However, under the heading Exposing Religion, there are also serious examples that contradict these statements.

10.5.6 Reclaiming Patriotism

In the analyzed issues, this theme is evident through the emphasis on secular patriotism, which foregrounds the notion that, unlike religious actors and values that define the nation through faith, the genuine proprietors of the country are those with a secular understanding. Within this framework—which seeks to separate nationalism from religious legitimacy and identify it instead with a republican and secular love of homeland—the emphasis on the secular rule of law forms the backbone of this patriotic conception.

In the context of Türkiye, the transition from the Ottoman Empire to the Republic is regarded as a significant milestone in the nation's modernization process. For atheists or nonbelievers, the idea of Türkiye as a secular nation-state grounded in the Republic and Atatürk's reforms holds critical significance. Since the Ottoman Empire is associated with both Islam and backwardness, within Türkiye's unique historical conditions, the foundations of patriotism for the nonbelieving population lie in the principles of the Republic and secularism.

A clear example of this can be found in the editorial column "Aydınlanma Penceresi" ("The Window of Enlightenment") by Süleyman Karan, President of the Atheism Association, published in Issue 128:

> The Republic, as its name suggests, means the rule of the people, though it does not inherently contain democracy. Even in that form, it is far superior to a constitutional monarchy or absolutism, for it is a form of power that ends the domination of a dynasty that seized authority by tyranny and rested its back on divinity. It brings absolute power from heaven to earth, dethrones dynasties, and empowers nations. Therefore, the Republic must be secular so that no one may seize power in the name of God! However, the Republic's existence, beyond secularism, rests on citizenship. Without responsible and active citizens, there is no Republic at all.

Another important theme that emerges is the call to defend and preserve the secular and democratic constitutional order, which appears as a proactive and protective stance in the name of the Republic's founding principles (Issues 4, 91, 100, 105, 125). Within this context, patriotism in the newspaper manifests as a form of defending secular values against Islamist or religious authoritarianism. Numerous reports from both Türkiye and abroad that frame political regimes as Islamist or religiously authoritarian (Issues 39, 46, among others) fall under this category.

Another subcomponent relevant to this theme involves concerns about ensuring that public resources are truly used for the benefit of the people. For example, the statement "The Presidency of Religious Affairs (Diyanet), whose budget was 12.9 billion TL in 2021 and increased to 16.9 billion TL for 2022, contributes nothing to the country other than functioning as a modern version of the Sheikh al-Islamate" (Issue 53) and other critical reports regarding the use of public resources by Diyanet (Issues 29, 56, 121) reflect this stance.

Further elements emphasized in the newspaper include the contrast between religious nationalism and republican citizenship. In this regard, critiques that frame women's rights as an integral part of republican citizenship (Issue 359) and highlight freedom and equality in citizenship (Issue 128) present a perspective that shifts the conception of belonging from a faith-based to a civic-based understanding of national identity.

Finally, the portrayal of Atatürk and Kemalism as historical and cultural sources of secular patriotism emerges as a central component. The statement, "To shape society according to religious rules is, in its true sense, not democracy or republicanism, but sharia, and this fundamentally contradicts the founding philosophy of the Republic of Türkiye, which was built upon Mustafa Kemal Atatürk's guidance of reason and science" (Issue 4), as well as the note that "In 1971, the National Order Party, founded by N. Erbakan, was closed for violating the principles of maintaining the secular nature of the state and Atatürk's revolutionary ideals" (Issue 44), exemplify this idea. Moreover, the adaptation of Atatürk's maxim, "Peace at Home, Peace in the World," into "Secularism at Home, Secularism in the World" (Issue 56), provides an illustrative example of secular patriotism's discursive creativity.

10.5.7 Reclaiming Spirituality

As revealed in Hazdovac Bajić's (2023) analysis, the strategy of redefining spirituality as a nonreligious yet meaningful life practice takes, in this study, the form of a critical and ethical mode of exposure rather than a positive redefinition. In other words, it becomes a strategy not of filling a void but of making the void visible. Science, conscience, reason, and free thought—along with the good and meaningful life that they are believed to produce—are established as alternatives to religion and religiosity, which are positioned as the "other."

An example of this can be found in Issue 50, in the statement: "As we all know, irreligion is not, as labeled and criminalized by the religious, an approach that renders individuals immoral; on the contrary, since it prioritizes thinking and questioning and thereby supports pluralism, it is an indispensable element in reaching true morality and higher virtue."

Similarly, the statement, "As the Atheism Association, we long for a country where discourse befitting a secular and democratic rule of law can be expressed—one that does not divide or polarize society, nor turn individuals into selfish and indifferent crowds deprived of tolerance and love" (Issue 4) can be cited as an example that frames an alternative vision of the good life.

As a subcomponent, the expressions that associate science, reason, and enlightenment with spirituality can also be noted. In the editor's message in Issue 10, the following passage is particularly illustrative: "Our aim should not be to sacrifice our real, tangible world for the sake of an allegedly existing one. Our aim should be to live together against every disaster of nature. To live and to let live—this should be the religion of a person guided by reason!".

10.6 Conclusion

The findings of this study indicate that the online communication strategies employed by the Atheism Association of Türkiye, while showing similarities with examples from Western Europe and the United States, acquire a distinct character shaped by Türkiye's socio-cultural and political atmosphere.

From the perspective of inter-organizational cooperation, this strategy in Türkiye functions not only as a networking mechanism but also as a tool for establishing existential legitimacy, constructing a common advocacy framework around secularism, and substituting a minority identity in response to political and social realities positioned as the "other." In this respect, the minority discourse emerges as one of the strongest strategies, sustained by other thematic components. It manifests not as a passive narrative of marginalization but as an active resistance identity, materialized through reflexes resembling those of an organizational structure engaged in struggle.

Regarding religious mimicry, this strategy appears only in a limited form through ritual imitation. Instead, an ironic inversion strategy and parodic appropriation of sacred discourse dominate—elements that are more appropriately evaluated under the next strategy, exposing religion. This phenomenon may be associated with the negative and phobic attitudes toward Islam found in Türkiye's atheist cultural perception. Consequently, reframing the cultural codes of a believing majority in familiar ways does not emerge as a viable option. In this sense, exposing religion, one of the most dominant strategies, develops within an Islamophobic and polemical framework, occasionally manifesting as hate speech. Going beyond the critique of power structures, religious authorities, communities, and individuals from a secular moral standpoint, this strategy produces representations that approach Islam as an "enemy to be eradicated," thereby contradicting the idea expressed in Inversion—that nonreligiosity is not opposition but a stance for common good and justice. Although secularism is articulated as a positive moral value at the discursive level, the realities concretized by other strategies reveal significant contradictions.

The strategy of Reclaiming Patriotism takes shape through the construction of a secular patriotism that asserts the secular segments as the actual owners of the nation in contrast to the religious "other." Meanwhile, Reclaiming Spirituality, consistent with the general pattern of other strategies, does not reflect a positive or secular spirituality but rather manifests as a critical-ethical practice of exposure.

Taken together, these findings demonstrate that the digital strategies of the Atheism Association in Türkiye represent an intersection between the intellectual legacy of Turkish atheism and the activism of the digital age. The strategies evolve through counter-narratives aligned with popular science, humor, socio-political criticism, and campaign language, occasionally infused with Islamophobic undertones. While these strategies nourish an alternative secular public sphere and the dynamics of existence and resistance against the cultural "other," they also render nonreligiosity culturally accessible and legitimate as an identity within the Turkish context.

References

2021 Report on International Religious Freedom: Turkey. (2021). United States Department of State Office of International Religious Freedom. https://www.state.gov/wp-content/uploads/2022/05/TURKEY-2021-INTERNATIONAL-RELIGIOUS-FREEDOM-REPORT.pdf

2022 Report on International Religious Freedom: Turkey. (2021). United States Department of State Office of International Religious Freedom. https://www.state.gov/reports/2022-report-on-international-religious-freedom/turkey/

Acun, F. (2013). Değişme ve süreklilik: Osmanlı'nın torunları Cumhuriyet'in çocukları. In M. Zencirkıran (Ed.), *Dünden Bugüne Türkiye'nin Toplumsal Yapısı* (pp. 44–70). Dora Yayıncılık.

Addington, A. (2017). Building bridges in the shadows of steeples: Atheist community and identity online. In R. T. Cragun, C. Manning & L. L. Fazzino (Eds.), *Organized Secularism in the United States* (pp. 135–150). De Gruyter. https://doi.org/10.1515/9783110458657-008

Akgün, M. (1988). *Materyalizmin Türkiye'ye girişi ve ilk etkileri*. Kültür ve Turizm Bakanlığı Yayınları.

Altaytaş, M. (2001). Günümüz Türkiye'sinde İslami inanç ve değerlere yöneltilen eleştirilerin niteliği -Turan Dursun, Erdoğan Aydın örneği- [Master's Thesis], Marmara Universitesi Sosyal Bilimler Enstitüsü. In *PQDT - Global* (2606901385). ProQuest Dissertations & Theses Global. https://www.proquest.com/dissertations-theses/günümüz-türkiye-sinde-İslami-inanç-ve-değerlere/docview/2606901385/se-2?accountid=15875

Argın, Ş. (2015). Teistler ateistlerin varlığına inanabilir mi? *Birikim, Aylık Sosyalist Kültür Dergisi, 2015*(314–315), 23–40.

Arsel, İ. (2008). *Şeriatçıyla mücadelenin el kitabı*. Kaynak Yayınları.

Ateizm Derneği Tüzüğü. (2019). Retrieved August 12, 2025, from https://www.ateizmdernegi.org.tr/tuzuk/

Bilgili, A. (2017). *Bilim ne değildir? Yeni-ateist bilim anlayışının felsefi ve sosyolojik analizi*. Doğu Kitabevi.

Bolay, S. H. (1988). *Türkiye'de ruhçu ve maddeci görüşün mücadelesi*. Akçağ Yayınları.

Bora, T. (2015). Sunuş. *Birikim, Aylık Sosyalist Kültür Dergisi, 2015*(314–315), 9–11.

Campbell, H. A., & Cheong, P. H. (Ed.). (2024). *The Oxford handbook of digital religion*. Oxford University Press. https://doi.org/10.1093/oxfordhb/9780197549803.001.0001

Cimino, R., & Smith, C. (2011). The new atheism and the formation of the imagined secularist community. *Journal of Media and Religion, 10*(1), 24–38. https://doi.org/10.1080/15348423.2011.549391

Cimino, R., & Smith, C. (2014). Atheist awakening: Secular activism and community in America. *Oxford University Press*. https://doi.org/10.1093/acprof:oso/9780199986323.001.0001

Çığ, M. İ. (2005). *Kur'an İncil ve Tevrat'ın Sümer'deki kökeni* (9. Basım). Kaynak Yayınları.

Demir, İ. (2010). *Din felsefesi bağlamında Turan Dursun'un ateizminin dayanakları* [Master's Thesis], Çanakkale Onsekiz Mart Üniversitesi Sosyal Bilimler Enstitüsü.

Dereli, M. D. (2019). Dinî kimliklerin siber uzamda akışkanlaşması. *İnsan ve Toplum, 9*(1), 85–116. dx.doi.org/https://doi.org/10.12658/M0301

Dereli, M. D. (2022). *Sanala veda: Sosyal medya ve dönüşen dindarlık*. Sakarya Üniversitesi Yayınları.

Dursun, T. (t.y.). *İlhan Arsel'e mektuplar* (2. Basım). Kaynak Yayınları.

Dursun, T. (2006). *Din Bu—1: Tanrı ve Kur'an*. Kaynak Yayınları.

Echchaibi, N., & Hoover, S. M. (Ed.). (2023). *The third spaces of digital religion*. Routledge, Taylor & Francis Group. https://doi.org/10.4324/9781003048190

Eken, M. (2020). Modern görsel kültürde m nesli'nin online inanç pratikleri. *Bilimname, 43*, 31–71. https://doi.org/10.28949/bilimname.762744

Ete, H., & Yargı, A. (2023). *Türkiye'de dindarlık algısı (Toplumsal Eğilimler-3)*. İstanbul Politikalar Merkezi, Ankara Enstitüsü. Retrieved September 5, 2025, from https://ipc.sabanciuniv.edu/Content/Images/CKeditorImages/20231103-14110347.pdf

Evolvi, G. (2021). *Religion, new media, and digital culture*. Oxford University Press. Retrieved September 9, 2025, from https://doi.org/10.1093/acrefore/9780199340378.013.917
Hazdovac Bajić, N. (2023). Online strategies of nonreligious and atheistic organizations in Croatia. *Journal of Religion in Europe, 16*, 1–27. https://doi.org/10.1163/18748929-bja10075
Hsieh, H.-F., & Shannon, S. E. (2005). Three approaches to qualitative content analysis. *Qualitative Health Research, 15*(9), 1277–1288. https://doi.org/10.1177/1049732305276687
https://www.ateizmdernegi.org.tr. (t.y.). *Biz kimiz? – Ateizm Derneği resmi sitesi*. Retrieved September 1, 2025, from https://www.ateizmdernegi.org.tr/tanim/
Isetti, G., Innerhofer, E., Pechlaner, H., & De Rachewiltz, M. (Eds.). (2022). *Religion in the age of digitalization: From new media to spiritual machines* (First issued in paperback). Routledge.
Islamophobia Awareness, Equity, Diversity and Inclusion, Loughborough University. (t.y.). Retrieved September 7, 2025, from https://www.lboro.ac.uk/equity-diversity-inclusion/edi-me/islamophobia-awareness/
Isomaa, R. (2024). How to think like an atheist: Science, philosophy, and religion in atheist-produced educational YouTube videos. *Approaching Religion, 14*(2), 132–151. https://doi.org/10.30664/ar.137472
İnsel, A. (2015). Tanrıtanımazlık mı, Tanrı'sızlık mı? *Birikim, Aylık Sosyalist Kültür Dergisi, 2015*(314–315), 14–18.
Kayıklık, H. (2006). Dini inkâr bağlamında Turan Dursun. *Çukurova Üniversitesi İlahiyat Fakültesi Dergisi (ÇÜİFD), 6*(1), 1–14.
Kibiswa, N. (2019). Directed qualitative content analysis (DQlCA): A tool for conflict analysis. *The Qualitative Report, 24*(8), 2059–2079. https://doi.org/10.46743/2160-3715/2019.3778
Nişancı, Z. (2023). *Sayılarla Türkiye'de inanç ve dindarlık*. Uluslararası İslam Düşünce Enstitüsü [IIIT], Mahya Yayıncılık, MEDAR, Marmara Üniversitesi Nüfus ve Sosyal Politikalar Uygulama ve Araştırma Merkezi, İbn Haldun Üniversitesi. Retrieved September 2, 2025, from https://iiit.org/wp-content/uploads/Turkish-Faith-and-Religiosity-in-T%C3%BCrkiye.pdf
Smith, C., & Cimino, R. (2012). Atheisms unbound: The role of the new media in the formation of a secularist identity. *Secularism and Nonreligion*. https://doi.org/10.5334/snr.ab
Taira, T. (2022). Secularism, atheism, and digital media. In H. A. Campbell & P. H. Cheong (Ed.), *The Oxford Handbook of Digital Religion* (pp. 135–150). Oxford University Press. https://doi.org/10.1093/oxfordhb/9780197549803.013.7
Topaloğlu, A. (2007). Klasik materyalizmin mahiyeti ve son dönem Osmanlı düşünürleri arasında yayılışı. *Felsefe Dünyası, 45*, 111–124.
Turkey (Türkiye) 2023 International Religious Freedom Report. (2021). United States Department of State Office of International Religious Freedom. Retrieved August 25, 2025, from https://www.state.gov/wp-content/uploads/2024/05/547499-TU%CC%88RKIYE-2023-INTERNATIONAL-RELIGIOUS-FREEDOM-REPORT.pdf
Ünüvar, K. (2008). Türkiye'de sol düşünce ve din. In *Sol* (2. Baskı, V. 8, pp. 873–895). İletişim Yayınları.
Vidinlioğlu, S. (2022). *Türkiye'de aktif ateizm savunucusu internet siteleri ve sosyal medya hesapları üzerine profil çalışması* [Master's Thesis], Sakarya Üniversitesi Sosyal Bilimler Enstitüsü. Retrieved from August 23, 2025, from https://acikerisim.sakarya.edu.tr/handle/20.500.12619/98625

Chapter 11
Hybridizing Beliefs in the Age of Secularization and the Search for Meaning on Social Media: The Case of the Dark Retreat

İhsan Çapcıoğlu and Merve Bahadur

11.1 Introduction

In the course of modernization, religion has become a significant subject of discourse, leading to heated debates on pluralism, secularization, the individualization of institutional religious understanding, ontological security (Giddens, 2021, pp. 93–102), and a crisis of meaning (Berger & Luckmann, 2015, pp. 43–58). This situation has led to the emergence of hybridized beliefs, such as new religious beliefs developing alongside the reappearance of religion. The shift from communal to individual life triggered by the dissolution of institutionalized religion has brought a novel perspective on religion amid the uncertainty of the modern world and the search for meaning. This perspective necessitates an understanding of the relationship between religion and secularization in the digital age and the examination of religion's interaction with the digital world. The presence of new religious formations in the digital realm adds a new dimension to the concept of secularization. Developments in religious practices and individuals' utilization of digital technologies offer alternatives for religious socialization and the performance of rituals (Dereli, 2022, p. 318; Karaarslan, 2015, pp. 34–35).

Since the late 1990s, the dissemination of religious messages via the internet has enabled the widespread circulation of practices and rituals associated with new religious beliefs. Through digital platforms, these practices have become accessible, searchable, and reproducible at any time, offering detailed information and fostering

İ. Çapcıoğlu (✉)
Department of Sociology of Religion, Ankara University, Ankara, Türkiye
e-mail: ihsancapcioglu@yahoo.com

M. Bahadur
Antalya, Türkiye

M. D. Dereli and M. Eken (eds.), *Turkish Perspectives on Secularization and Media*,
https://doi.org/10.1007/978-3-032-16436-0_11

transnational visibility (Arslan, 2016, p. 16). This phenomenon has led to the incorporation of practices that define today's understanding of religion—such as prayer, belief, and ritual—into the circulation of the digital world (Haberli, 2022, p. 389). In this context, New Age movements and spiritualism, which prioritize individual religious experiences, are depicted in the media alongside the three principal Abrahamic religions (Christianity, Judaism, and Islam), Eastern religions (Buddhism and Hinduism), and diverse belief systems including atheism, Mormonism, paganism, and Gnosticism (Haberli, 2013, p. 862; Wenzel, 2012, pp. 290–291).

Digital platforms such as Facebook, Instagram, and YouTube facilitate individuals' encounters with rituals and enhance the accessibility of the sacred, thereby directly and indirectly enabling the execution of diverse religious practices and rituals in digital realms (Berk & Çetin, 2023, pp. 256–259). Hybrid belief systems, considered in relation to new religious movements, are associated with figures such as personal development and ritual coaches (Hondeet & Beek, 2019, p. 2). In addition, yoga instructors with monastic training and renowned healing practitioners effectively use social media platforms and various applications to promote themselves, cultivate followings, disseminate information, and arrange online rituals.

Nowadays, belief systems are represented on the internet and social media platforms, and particularly, yoga and meditation techniques, embodying Hindu and Buddhist doctrines, have gained prevalence. Çetin Çetintaş, the founder of YogaKio Retreat Center, which introduces these techniques and provides a dark retreat experience for the first time in Türkiye, has lived in a monastery and internalized yoga. Recently, the popular practice of "Dark Retreat" has attracted interest and debate, prompting the production of a documentary, Dark Retreat, featuring contributions from medical professionals across various disciplines. This research provides a transcript analysis of the documentary and examines the participants' experiences and emotions using descriptive and content analysis methods. It aims to contribute to the literature by exploring what dark retreat signifies for individuals, how it is practiced, and whether it can be approached as a hybridized belief system.

11.2 Secularization and New Religious Formations

In the post-nineteenth century era, changes occurred in the role of divine authority and the sacred because of the effects of the new society, the new human, new production relations, and technological developments. In the industrialized and increasingly influential West, it was assumed that beliefs would ultimately disappear in the context of industrial capitalism and modernization processes. It has been observed that in many countries where the modernization process has intensified, the influence of religion in the social sphere has decreased as a result of increasing secularization tendencies (Altıntaş, 2005, pp. 23–24). With technological and scientific advances, the prioritization of rational thought has raised claims that religion has retreated from the social and public sphere. These claims are generally addressed within the framework of the modernization paradigm. In this context, In Comte's sociological theory, the diminishing role of traditional religion is not a rupture but a transformation aligned with the law of three stages, where metaphysical beliefs give way to empirical understanding (Slattery, 2007, p. 72). Marx characterized religion as "the opium of the masses" and contended that the necessity for religion would vanish following the workers' revolution (Furseth & Repstad, 2011, p. 69). Durkheim's understanding of religion evolved throughout different stages of his intellectual development. In his early works, particularly in The Division of Labour in Society, he presents explicit references to secularization. However, in his later work, The Elementary Forms of Religious Life, religion is portrayed as the very embodiment of society itself. This perspective reveals that religion is not merely a belief system but a reflection of social cohesion and collective consciousness. Accordingly, for Durkheim, as long as society exists, religion will continue to exist. Therefore, interpretations suggesting the disappearance of religion rely on a superficial reading of Durkheim's early period and overlook the complexity of his thought. To conduct a more nuanced discussion, it would be more appropriate to focus on Durkheim's holistic approach to the religion-society relationship rather than framing the issue through the concept of 'traditional religion' (Furseth & Repstad, 2011, p. 73). In this framework, when evaluating the position of religion in modern society, it is necessary to think not only in terms of functional dissolution or secularization, but also in terms of transformation and restructuring processes. While Comte's positivist approach predicts that traditional religion will be replaced by scientific thought, Weber argues that religion will evolve toward rationalization and individualization in the process of modernization. Both approaches reveal that, although religion formally changes, it does not completely lose its influence on the social structure (Francis et al., 2015, pp. 65–66). European-based sociologists such as Bryan Wilson and Steve Bruce, who are prominent proponents of the secularization theory, argue—based on their own empirical and theoretical works—that modernization inevitably leads to a decline in the societal influence of religion. Wilson, in Religion in Secular Society, defines secularization as the diminishing power, prestige, and popularity of religion across societal, institutional, and individual levels. Similarly, Bruce (2011), in Secularization: In Defence of an Unfashionable Theory, emphasizes that the decline of religion is not accidental or temporary, but a structural consequence of modernization and rationalization processes. These perspectives reflect a classical paradigm that views secularization as an irreversible trend in modern societies. Thus, it is emphasized that religion has undergone a transformation in the processes of modernization and secularization, that its visibility in the social sphere has decreased, and that secularization tendencies have intensified.

For a long time, secularization in Western societies was seen as a narrative of progress in which the "dark age" ended with the retreat of religion and the dominance of reason began. However, according to Charles Taylor, since the 1980s this narrative has shifted. Secularization is no longer considered in the context of the complete disappearance of religion, but in the context of the transformation of the conditions of belief. Taylor states that the modern individual no longer considers faith in a compulsory framework. However, among the options, this situation is defined as "faith becoming an option" (the nova effect) (Taylor, 2007, pp. 26–28). This transformation has revealed that secularization is not a linear and universal process, but rather manifests in different forms in different social contexts, when the process of secularization was considered on public, social, and individual levels, suggesting that religious belief would become a matter of personal choice within a secular age. Turner (2010, pp. 202–204) offers a perspective in which individuals establish transnational connections through their religious identities, coexist with different faith identities, and carry out their religious practices. Within the framework of secularization debates, Jürgen Habermas challenges the classical secularization thesis by introducing the notion of a post-secular society. In his Holberg Prize lecture (2005, pp. 3–5), he argues that religious communities, rather than retreating into private belief, have re-entered the public sphere by expanding their communicative capacities and gaining visibility through mass media. This renewed public presence of religion calls for a redefinition of the boundaries between secular and religious reasoning in democratic societies (Karaarslan, 2015, pp. 28–29). Luckmann (2016) proposed that in a context where secularization is receding, the individualization of religion may trigger the emergence of new religious formations. Berger emphasized that new religious formations have succeeded within the context of supernatural beliefs that oppose secularization. He emphasizes that globalization is not only a secular and materialist process; on the contrary, religions such as Protestant and Catholic Christianity, Islam, and Buddhism have made important contributions to global culture (Berger, 2002, pp. 85–87). Giddens offered a different perspective on the revival of religion, stating that material technology has replaced religious cosmology in modern societies. However, despite claiming that the importance of religion has diminished, he argued that religion would continue to exist in the environment of doubt and insecurity created by high modernity (Furseth & Repstad, 2011, p. 131; Giddens, 2021, p. 97). This new paradigm invalidates the thesis that religion will disappear with modernization, revealing that beliefs resembling traditional and folk religions are intertwined with modern life. Since the 1980s, it has been stated that an alternative post-secular era has emerged in contrast to secularization theories and that religion has been redefined at the individual level. That is, religion has not disappeared in the processes of modernization; rather, it has been reshaped.

Unlike the modernist paradigm that regarded the decline of religion as an inevitable and irreversible phenomenon, new paradigms arose in the late twentieth century, suggesting that religion has continued to exist and even been reshaped in the modern world. Particularly the rise of new religious formations throughout the 1960s and 1970s highlighted the enduring vitality of religion in the modern world as well as its capacity to promote eclectic and composite belief systems (Kirman, 2008, p. 286). In this context, the phenomenon of desecularization has been associated with a reorientation toward the sacred. In his work Secularization, R.I.P., Rodney Stark stated that secularization has already been buried and that the presumed conflict between religion and science has not materialized. P.L. Berger, in his work The Homeless Mind: Modernization and Consciousness, argued that the emphasis on rational thought has left individuals feeling homeless and that this situation, coupled with the rise of new religious formations and the resulting rootlessness of modern humans, can be viewed as a process of demodernization (the purging from modernity) (Şentürk, 2004, p. 98).

The interaction between religion and secular processes can be regarded as a mutually hybrid structure (Aydınalp, 2023, p. 34). In this context, it is revealed that the secularization thesis is not based on a single theory and shows variations in the historical process. Modernization and secularization processes have led to differentiations in traditional religious structures; particularly under the influence of the individualism trend in the West, the ways of relating to the sacred have diversified (Bayer, 2022, p. 35). Despite a societal shift away from institutionalized religion, the religion has not entirely disappeared from the social sphere. This situation has been explained by Davie's concept of "believing without belonging," and is regarded as a phenomenon of relocation rather than the disappearance of religion (Bayer, 2022, p. 68). Furthermore, Andrew M. Greely's concept of the "unsecular man" (Greely, as cited in Şentürk, 2005) suggests that new religious beliefs cannot be sufficiently explained solely within the framework of secularization (Kirman, 1999, p. 229). It is stated that phenomena such as modernism and postmodernism, individualism, subjectivism (hedonism), globalization, pluralism, indifference, and rapid social change have been influential in the emergence and formation of new religious beliefs (Güneş, 2023, pp. 405–408; Özkan, 2008, pp. 310–316). The rapid transformations, excessive rationalization, individualization, insecurity, and the ensuing belief gap in the social structure associated with modernization and secularization have led to the emergence of various mystical, magical, novel, and pseudo-religious formations (Arslan, 2006, p. 9).

The need for meaning in the modern day and the stimulation of religious revival by secularization reveal that individuals are increasingly turning to religion in response to existential security concerns (Bayer, 2022, p. 69). In this context, it is observed that religious groups and formations play an important role in shaping and giving meaning to individuals' lives, and that a more subjective understanding of religion has replaced traditional forms. Modernization has facilitated a shift from collective life to individual life, transitioning from a homogeneous community to a cosmopolitan urban society, thereby laying the groundwork for crises of belief, identity conflicts, and spiritual quests (Kaygusuz et al., 2020, p. 4470). In a modern, secular context, the erosion of values and social meaning that individuals attribute to the world leads to religious belief being perceived as a private and optional matter (Köse, 2002, pp. 210–211). This process is reshaping the form and content of religion in the modern world, particularly in relation to the spirituality axis (Clarke, 2006, p. 6).

The religious and spiritual orientations that shape the spiritual realm can be defined as new religious beliefs, new pagan religious movements, Eastern religions, Evangelical and fundamentalist teachings, and mystical and paranormal beliefs. These orientations encompass styles of spirituality shaped by an emphasis on innovation and hybridity, rather than the notions of traditionalism and purification (Arslan, 2006, p. 11). These beliefs, which have emerged in modern-day society, have formed a way of life that offers spiritual and philosophical perspectives on the meaning of life, aiming to attain transcendent knowledge, achieve spiritual calm and inner peace, facilitate self-discovery, and reach spiritual maturity (Arslan, 2006, p. 14; Uysal, 2015, pp. 3–4).

These beliefs and practices, characterized as new religious movements, are parts of an eclectic system encompassing diverse ways of thinking and paranormal aspects, including yoga, Zen meditation, Hinduism, reincarnation, astrology, astral travel, Sufism, and paganism. This eclectic system sets a holistic and sacred belief system into a framework, offering a modern form of living. In this light, these teachings and practices, which span all aspects of life and distinguish themselves as a sacred realm of existence, have been incorporated into contemporary society. The esoteric, mosaic framework influenced by Western occultism and Eastern mysticism (Biçer, 2006, p. 28) has blended diverse belief components. These new religious formations, emerging with the globalizing effect of secular trends (Main, 2002, pp. 187–188), have reshaped individuals' perspectives on alternative beliefs. These structures are explained through various categories such as secular religions (Clarke, 2006, p. 14), Western esotericism, traditional Hindu practices, mystical, esoteric, and paranormal beliefs (Aupers & Houtman, 2006, p. 3), and "alternative sacredness and therapy cults" (Arslan, 2015, p. 55).

It has been observed that new religious beliefs, arising from phenomena such as social distress, restlessness, unhappiness, distorted realities, and dissatisfaction experienced by individuals in modern society, have come to replace traditional religions. These new religious beliefs are defined as individualized forms of religion, encompassing mysticism, esotericism, occultism, alternative medicine, parapsychology, astrology, and mystical experiences (Şentürk, 2004, pp. 56–58; Wuthnow, 2002, p. 77). Accordingly, it is considered that socio-cultural conditions such as the uncertainty fostered by secular life, a deep sense of meaninglessness, excessive rationalization, lifestyles detached from spirituality, heightened individualization, and ontological insecurity (Arslan, 2006, p. 9) have played a significant role in the reorientation of individuals toward the sacred and their participation in new religious formations.

11.3 Hybridizing Beliefs and the Search for Meaning

The existence of human beings within society is typically addressed in the context of religion or the problem of attributing meaning to life (Köse, 2002, p. 212). Within this framework, the concept of meaning expresses the essence of human existence. It occupies a significant place in the process by which individuals seek to escape uncertainties and define their position within life (Çapcıoğlu & Yürük, 2010, pp. 22–25). By nature, human beings are engaged in the effort to attribute meaning to life. This effort is closely related to the individual's inherent sense of incompleteness (Ünal, 2011, pp. 141–142). Therefore, the need to believe lies at the core of the individual's search for meaning, reinforcing the connection between human beings and religious beliefs, practices, and rituals in their search to attribute to their existence. Considering that meanings derived from worldly experiences are often transient, it becomes evident that the search for ultimate meaning is fulfilled through an orientation toward religion, a creative force, or divine and mystical components (Çapcıoğlu & Yürük, 2010, p. 25; Öztan, 2019, p. 82). Ultimately, the human search for meaning is a lifelong process, deepening with religious rituals and grounding the desire to reach the knowledge of truth. This process is a phenomenon that guides human life at both individual and social levels. Thus, the effort to make sense of life is tied to religious beliefs, rituals, and mystical elements. This search is mostly completed by turning toward divine or creative forces.

At times, answers to the question of the meaning of life may relate to religious thought, while at other times they may stem from personal philosophy or life purpose (Öztan, 2019, p. 73). In this context, the search for meaning appears to have diversified within modern and post-secular processes. The modern individual, experiencing a deficiency in spiritual significance, often gravitates toward alternative practices such as energy work, meditation, and personal development activities rather than the strict rules of traditional religions within the context of the post-secular revival of religion. In this regard, individuals in search of meaning turn to alternative practices through which they feel spiritually at ease and can reconnect with their true selves. In Türkiye, these alternative tendencies have gained popularity not as part of religious formations but as activities offering solutions to physical and spiritual challenges—such as yoga, meditation for stress management, and healthy eating.

At the core of the human search for meaning lie concepts and activities such as individual experiences, self-perception, and the mystery of existence, with curiosity and interest demonstrating an adoption of popular approaches aligned with personal development and reasoning. Practices such as yoga, retreat, enlightenment, mysticism, spiritualism, and Gnosticism, along with experiences of inner journeys or asceticism, are among the key practices preferred by individuals in their search. In this context, various teachings and practices of Eastern and Western mystics, as well as new discourses on the sacred (Yıldız & Meçin, 2013, p. 223), and a shift toward non-religious, fictional beliefs support these tendencies. The beliefs that emerge from this search for meaning offer a holistic perspective that counters rationalism, traditional religion, and the destructive effects of technology on individuals. It has been noted that these tendencies encompass numerous beliefs and practices that contain both ambiguities and popular alternative forms of sanctity (Aydın, 2015, pp. 43–44). The penetration of secularization and techno-cognitive values, rooted in Eastern and Western mysticism, into individuals' daily lives has fostered new discourses on the sacred and accelerated the popularization of bricolage beliefs that resonate with their personal development and reasoning (Mirza, 2018, p. 40). Within this framework, these hybridized beliefs are conceptualized under terms such as 'Western esotericism' (Hanegraaff, 1996), 'contemporary alternative religions' (Hunt, 2003), and the 'spiritual marketplace' (Lyon) (Doğan, 2020, p. 29). These beliefs have recently experienced heightened demand, as they promise spiritual purification, happiness, abundance, prosperity, and healing to individuals seeking meaning amid the turmoil of modern life.

Since the 1970s, new religious formations, spreading as a global phenomenon, have paved the way for the emergence of mosaic societies through the development of pluralistic structures in the religious sphere. In this process, individuals' searches for meaning have given rise to hybrid socio-cultural structures formed by syncretic religious movements. Such hybrid structures are employed to characterize religious syncretism, multicultural amalgamations, or traditional symbolic meanings. Therefore, these hybrid structures refer to the concept of syncretism in the context of new religious beliefs (Kraidy, 2005, p. 1). In this context, syncretism is based on offering new approaches to the search for meaning through the blending of both different religious traditions and cultural influences. In line with individuals' search for meaning, syncretic (hybrid) structures and the merging of diverse religious traditions shape hybrid socio-cultural formations.

The age of effective communication is considered one of the most significant factors in the formation of hybrid structures. With the proliferation of communication technologies, the modern individual—through digital tools that serve as the window to the world—has become increasingly integrated into social life (Çoşkun, 2017, p. 23). In this context, the digitalization of hybrid beliefs emerges as an inevitable process. Digital platforms offer an alternative dimension for communication, representation, mass mobilization, and organization. Thus, technologies and digital tools—typically instruments of the secular world—are being appropriated for the practice of these belief systems (Dereli, 2019, p. 99). It is observed that the secular tools envisioned by modernity have become indispensable instruments for promoting, organizing, and coordinating membership in hybrid belief systems (Karaarslan, 2015, pp. 34–36). Communication technologies therefore play a critical role in the formation of such hybrid structures, as modern technologies facilitate the development and dissemination of hybrid beliefs.

There exist online spheres that enable individuals in search of meaning to engage in religious experiences through digital tools and applications. These digital spaces—such as Facebook, Instagram, and YouTube—facilitate such engagement through features like subscribing, following, sharing, commenting, and direct messaging or channel interaction. In the digital age, the transfer of oral, written, and visual cultures into accessible online platforms has greatly facilitated both the dissemination and reach of hybrid belief systems (Haberli, 2019, p. 30). Technology, perceived as an extension of the spiritual realm, facilitates spirituality in individuals' search for meaning through its certain applications (Campbell, 2005, p. 10). Thus, in the digital realm, hybrid beliefs display as modern forms of rituals that often reflect an individualistic orientation and bear little or no connection to traditional worship spaces such as mosques, churches, or temples. Hybrid belief platforms significantly contribute to fulfilling individuals' search for meaning by facilitating their engagement with such rituals through social media tools in digital realms.

11.4 The Journey of the Modern Individual: The Dark Retreat

In modern society, the processes of searching for, producing, and transmitting meaning are shaped by the invention of practices and teachings associated with new religious and hybrid beliefs. These teachings are offered to individuals through mass communication tools and the means of the digital world; they possess a syncretic character that brings together elements from different cultures and eras. In particular, meditation techniques imported from the East and modern psychotherapy practices (Berger & Luckmann, 2015, pp. 74–75) are considered to be new spaces that fill the search for meaning. Within this context, contemporary interpretations and forms of retreat are regarded as worldly moments of ecstasy in individuals' pursuit of peak experiences. These practices and teachings, which support individuals' spiritual satisfaction and search for meaning, enable them to establish a deep connection with themselves (Bauman, 2014, p. 268).

Retreat is a concept that signifies the individual's return to the self and an inner journey. This process allows the individual to engage in self-observation, as it involves bracketing the external world. Retreat is understood as a practice aimed at an individual attaining selfhood and self-knowledge, as well as experiencing both the soul and the body. This practice is associated with different concepts and definitions, such as a journey from the rhythm of the external world to the rhythm of the inner world, gazing, watching, contemplation, theoria, contemplation, and anschaunng (Taşdelen, 2021, p. 10). Today, retreat is practiced by combining it with meditation teachings in a mystical and spiritual context. This practice is carried out with the aim of detachment from worldly distractions, grounded in Christian and Buddhist mysticism and ascetic thought (zuhd) (Korkut, 2023, p. 374). Therefore, retreat, which constitutes the essence of religious, mystical, or Sufi experience and is based on the teaching of self-knowledge, has assumed a new form in the modern age.

In various religious traditions such as Islam, Christianity, Sufism, and monastic practices, retreat is considered a spiritual discipline aimed at purification and inner maturation. It serves as a means of deepening one's connection with the divine and cultivating spiritual awareness (Taşdelen, 2021, p. 16). In Islamic and Sufi teachings, retreat—referred to as khalwat—is described as a state of solitude, withdrawal into seclusion, detachment from the external world, minimal sleep in darkness, intense contemplation, prayer, and worship, and a complete cessation of contact with others (Aksöz, 2016, p. 109). This process is also considered a stage for maintaining psychological balance and rehabilitation (Aksöz, 2016, p. 115). In Eastern mysticism and Buddhism, retreat is understood as a form of asceticism involving mortification of the self (ego) and the renunciation of worldly pleasures, typically carried out in monastic settings (Polat, 2004, p. 7). In Christianity, similar to Sufi practices, a period of asceticism and a forty-day abstinence are observed, and caves and rock-hewn monasteries serve as places of worship. Today, the life of monks on the Athos (Aynaros) Peninsula is presented as a living example of the retreat tradition (Zafer,

2007, p. 45). In Far Eastern beliefs, retreat is associated with suffering and abstinence as a means of spiritual maturity and, ultimately, reaching nirvana. For example, Hindus who have retreated in places like the Himalayas and Devendranath Tagore have, over time, constructed multi-story temples within caves, transforming them into dedicated spaces of retreat (Sarıkçıoğlu, 2002, p. 19; 68).

Although a direct comparison of retreat practices across religions may not be entirely feasible, it can be said that they differ in accordance with their ultimate goals. In Far Eastern beliefs, the idea of attaining pure goodness forms the core teaching of retreat, whereas in Abrahamic religions, the aim is to attain the pleasure of God (Zafer, 2007, p. 55). In the modern era, hybrid beliefs inspired by traditions such as Sufism, Christianity, and Buddhism present practices and rituals—such as retreat or dark retreat—in contemporary forms. Individuals seeking escape from social labels, public perception, and societal pressures are increasingly turning to these modern adaptations of spiritual practices and teachings.

The practice of dark retreat presented in modern form differs from traditional understandings of retreat and is regarded as one of the core teachings of hybrid beliefs. It is described as a journey guided by the light of the heart—or as "Kaya Yalpa," a process believed to render the body immortal. It is said to derive its name from the belief that darkness has the power to slow down or halt the aging process in the individual. Dark retreat is practiced in two distinct forms. The first involves completely covering the eyes to prevent any exposure to light, enabling the individual to experience life entirely in darkness. The second entails withdrawing into a dark room and engaging in an uninterrupted meditation practice. Both methods, inspired by the transformative effect of darkness, aim to provide a process of physical and mental renewal to the individual. This practice, presented as a meditation technique in the modern world, plays a therapeutic and healing role in individuals' search for meaning and spiritual transformation.

The dark retreat is a meditative practice in which individuals embark on a journey of self-discovery through their intuition, accompanied by professional guides. This process typically concludes with the individual being released into the forest at the end of a three-day retreat to experience retracing their path back using only their intuition. The "dark room retreat" takes place entirely in a pitch-black environment within a 1.5-square-meter room. This type of retreat is a process spent in meditation after the individual has completed physical, mental, and breath preparation. It typically lasts for 6, 12, or 24 h—or alternatively for 3, 5, or 11 days—with participants beginning a fast after 5 p.m. on the evening prior to commencing the retreat. For retreats lasting up to three days, the fast is intended to promote internal purification; for those extending beyond three days, the practice is modified to include a 500 cal meal and soda water each evening.

Dark room retreats are a widely observed practice across different countries. In Tibetan Buddhism and the Bön belief, this form of retreat—carried out in complete darkness and conceived as a spiritual seclusion—is regarded as a practice that supports inner journeying and spiritual enlightenment. The practice of retreating in complete darkness is said to be a common practice found in many spiritual traditions throughout history. From Tibetan monks and lamas to the Kogi Mamos of

Colombia, the ancient Egyptians, and the mystics of fifteenth-century France, this practice is believed to have provided revelation and enlightenment to countless practitioners seeking inner illumination. Contemporary global examples include the Tara and Buddha Caves, located at the Hermitage of Lake Atitlan, Guatemala. Additionally, the Gut Saunstorf Monastery in Germany offers this retreat under the guidance of consultants. It is practiced in isolated 10-square-meter rooms, with dark room consultants and daily 30- to 60-min meditation sessions accompanied by knocking on the door.

The practice of dark retreat, which has recently gained popularity and become a widespread ritual in Türkiye, is offered by Çetin Çetintaş, who is known for his passion for biology and desire to acquire scientific knowledge about creation. Çetintaş spent many years studying yoga and meditation in various countries and monasteries across the Far East, eventually embracing the brahmacharya lifestyle as a yogi. He is also the founder of YogaKioo Schools, YogaKioo Publications, YogaKioo Magazine, and the Kioo Retreat Center in Kırklareli, through which he claims to have established a solid foundation for yoga's presence in Türkiye. His published works include Hanuman'ı Bulmak—Finding Hanuman (2016); Yoga Sutralar 1: Bir Yoginin El Kitabı—Yoga Sutras 1: A Handbook for Yogis—translated from Sanskrit (2018); the bestseller What Is Life Telling You? (2019); Sarı Çiçeği Koklayan Kedi—The Cat Who Smelled the Yellow Flower (2020); Temel Yoga Eğitmenlik Kitabı—Fundamentals of Yoga Teacher Training (2021); and Duyguların Efendisi—Master of Emotions (2023). For over fifteen years, Çetintaş has been delivering training not only in Türkiye but also around the world, introducing individuals to ancient yogic wisdom. Moreover, YogaKioo Institute—considered the largest yoga school in the world—has 23 branches, including seven in Istanbul, two in Ankara, and others in cities such as Antalya, Izmir, Adana, Bursa, Gaziantep, and Mersin. Çetin Çetintaş shares informative content with his followers through various platforms, including his website, Instagram, and YouTube, regularly posting video lessons and insights related to yoga practice.

11.5 Methodology

This study interprets hybrid religious expressions in the digital age as indicators of ongoing secularization, analyzing how social media platforms facilitate individualized and fragmented belief systems. It centers on videos from Çetin Çetintaş's YouTube channel, specifically analyzing the documentary "Kaya Yalpa," released in June 2024, which had 34,000 views, 1,800 likes, and 230 comments at the time of review. The documentary features the experiences of participants from various scientific disciplines before and after a dark retreat, offering valuable qualitative insights. It was selected for its depth on retreat and inclusion of participant observation. Çetintaş's channel, which is free to access and subscribe to, boasts 420,000 subscribers, 519 videos, and over 46 million views, featuring content that covers yoga postures, breathwork, energy practices, meditation, and a retreat-themed series.

This qualitative research analyzes the viewpoints of participants in the documentary The Dark Retreat by Kaya Yalpa, which was available on Çetin Çetintaş's YouTube channel. For data collection and analysis, the transcription and coding of the YouTube video content were conducted using MAXQDA Analytics Pro (version 24.3.0). The video transcription and coding were subjected to descriptive and content analysis methods.

11.6 Findings and Analysis

11.6.1 Video Content of the Dark Retreat "Kaya Kalpa" Documentary

The focus of the research is the "Kaya Yalpa" documentary, a Dark Retreat, released on Çetin Çetintaş's YouTube channel in June 2024, which has garnered 34,000 views, 1,800 likes, and 230 comments. It features the dark retreat experiences—before and after—of ten participants from various scientific disciplines. These participants include healthcare professionals such as psychiatrists, physicians, and doctors. The video under review has a total duration of 36 min. During the research process, attention was given to identifying contributors and the views and reflections they expressed. The video addresses themes such as dark retreat experiences, participants' perspectives on yoga and meditation, the modern human's search for meaning, meditative aspects, existential questioning, and worldly needs—fundamental factors that influence individuals' inclination toward.

11.6.1.1 Participants' Reflections Prior to the Dark Retreat

The dark retreat, designed as a practice to facilitate a profound meditation experience, provides a significant space for modern individuals to cultivate inner peace. Within this framework, the documentary features participants with meditation experience sharing their perspectives on yoga, meditation, and their professional insights prior to entering the dark room, addressing the contributions of yoga to life and the modern individual's turn toward yoga practice. In this sense, it seeks to explain the dark retreat, an object of curiosity and debate, not as a religious belief but as a scientific and health-related practice. Furthermore, the documentary presents hybrid beliefs, typically in the forms transmitted from the West, as a therapeutic method for individuals who have become individualized, isolated, and are engaged in a search for meaning within their inner worlds. By providing both informative and thought-provoking content, it raises awareness about such practices and rituals in modern society.

The documentary begins with a speech by the meditation leader, Çetintaş. He explains the concept of the dark room as "what we call the dark room is actually entering the womb of the universe, just like being in the mother's womb, like the sages who once withdrew into caves; by bringing the practice from caves into rooms, we embark on a journey into the womb of the universe." Presenting the dark room retreat as a modern form, Çetintaş notes that "the journey of meditation today, descending deep into our essence in dark rooms, continues to be practiced in many places such as America, Europe, the Czech Republic, and Asia." The retreat practice, once carried out in caves as a means of attaining self-essence and uniting with the divine in ancient traditions, is now often conducted in rooms in the contemporary context.

A participant (K1, a doctor/male) with 50 years of professional experience in psychotherapy states, "Yoga and meditation are practices that can relieve the diseases caused by the unfulfilled spiritual instinct in the secular world and provide preventive support against them," and describes yoga as a psychotherapy technique. Recently, yoga has become increasingly widespread in Türkiye, often regarded as both a psychotherapeutic technique and a physical activity. In this regard, yoga has gained popularity, particularly among modern individuals who, in the face of crises caused by individualization and isolation, have adopted it as a strategy to cope with the psychological burdens of modern life.

A participant (K2, medical doctor/female) with experience in meditation and yoga practice states, "I am an Ayurvedic therapist and a yoga and meditation instructor. Imagine being invited to someone's home as a guest. If no one offers you a chair, you will constantly be in a state of anxiety; a part of you remains preoccupied with that, observing the comings and goings, conversations, and dialogues, and your mind searches for a place to sit. Meditation, in a sense, pulls out that chair for you and says, 'Sit, and look from here.' This is perhaps what modern life imposes on us… so many responsibilities, so much to consider and manage in our lives. That is why the mind is constantly tired, always rushing—we call it the butterfly mind, flitting from one place to another…" In this reflection, the doctor highlights how, amid the chaos of modern life, individuals—disconnected from reality and exhausted by perpetual demands (Berger, 2015, p. 53)—find fulfillment in their spiritual practices and rituals through yoga. This tradition has been transmitted from the East.

A participant (K3, psychiatrist/female) stated, "I am a psychiatrist and also a yoga instructor. Most of the time, we are not aware of these thoughts, or we engage in various distractions to avoid becoming aware of them—especially with mobile phones and televisions. We occupy ourselves with cleaning or doing this and that, constantly evading ourselves. Indeed, studies have shown that even if a person stays at home all day and claims not to have thought about anything or experienced any negative thoughts, their depression scores increase in tests conducted before and after, indicating they feel more depressed by the end of the day." Through this observation, the psychiatrist draws attention to how modernization further isolates the individual by failing to cultivate awareness of one's own experiences and choices (Ünal, 2011, p. 183, religious individualism). In today's world, emerging spiritual practices such as yoga and meditation contribute to the development of such awareness, as individuals increasingly construct their meaning-making frameworks through these belief systems.

A participant (K4, cardiologist/male) who focuses on the therapeutic aspects of yoga, meditation, and dark room practices stated, "I have been a physician for approximately 23 years. The most significant effect of meditation and yoga is their ability to regulate the autonomic nervous system. In my view, the autonomic nervous system comprises two main branches: the parasympathetic and the sympathetic systems. When the sympathetic system becomes excessively active, our brain remains in a constant state of alertness, which in turn triggers anxiety and especially anger—emotions we find difficult to control." He thus highlights the capacity of yoga and meditation to manage anxiety and stress. Similarly, another participant (K5, neurologist/male) mentioned that, "Soon we need to get the child ready for school, prepare breakfast, and rush to work; the principal said something yesterday, a colleague said something else, and there is traffic—will we make it on time? This fear of not completing things builds up within us and activates stress hormones through the sympathetic system," noting that fear increases stress hormones, while yoga induces relaxation. Both participants, framing their views on yoga and meditation through the functioning of the autonomic and sympathetic nervous systems, argue that these practices are effective in treating panic and stress disorders. Indeed, numerous studies affirm the therapeutic potential of meditation for mental health (Hendriks et al., 2021, p. 10); however, many underscore that definitive conclusions remain premature.

Participants evaluate the meditation process in terms of making sense of the events they experience in the modern world and discovering their inner world. A participant (K6, psychologist/female) stated, "Through meditation, psychotherapy also invites us into a calm space—that is, to make sense of what we have experienced and to become aware of our thoughts and emotions. One common aspect of both is that they teach us to respond more consciously to negative experiences rather than reacting emotionally," referring to the common aspect of psychotherapy and meditation practices. Similarly, a participant (K7, psychological counselor/male) remarked, "Many methods have been developed to understand our inner world and uncover our shadows—these are referred to as shadow work. The meditation process is, in fact, a self-observation and understanding of one's inner world. Especially in conditions with minimal stimuli, such as darkness or fasting, one of the responses individuals exhibit is turning inward to discover themselves," interpreting the retreat and fasting process experienced in the dark room as a process of self-observation and self-discovery.

A participant (K4, cardiologist/male), who views yoga and meditation as tools for managing anxiety and stress, stated, "Through yoga and meditation, we activate what is known as the vagal system—commonly referred to as the vagus nerve—which corresponds to the parasympathetic nervous system. When the vagus is activated, it creates balance within the sympathetic system, allowing for regulation of heart rate, blood pressure, and breathing, thereby reducing anxiety and stress." For another participant (K7, psychological counselor/male), yoga and meditation consist of intentional acts carried out through individual will. He explained, "If there is an observing self capable of viewing the self from an external perspective, it can bypass the ego and observe it—including its defenses—as well as reveal the unconscious material that the ego avoids, that is, the shadow. The presence of such a structure provides an ideal space for synthesizing and integrating the conscious and unconscious realms."

The modern individual—whom we may refer to as the contemporary human being—is in search of a roadmap to a lost world of meaning. In this quest, there is a growing need for sources—be they individuals or groups—that offer temporary, ready-made packages pointing toward a meaningful existence, capable of filling the internal void and guiding one through life's challenges. Among the practices that contribute to this existential search, yoga and meditation hold a distinctive place (Doğan, 2020, p. 147). It is understood that these approaches, rooted in the view that the modern self is composed of a mind–body–soul triad and that past emotional wounds are repressed within the subconscious (Merter, 2012, p. 392), suggest that an inner transformation becomes possible through the purification of subconscious emotions, with yoga and meditation practices functioning as the spiritual sacred spaces mediating this transformation (Table 11.1).

Based on their professional and personal understandings, participants described the dark retreat as the ancient dungeon therapy, a path to enlightenment and spiritual maturity, deprivation of stimuli; and; a ritual of purification and rebirth that renders human existence more meaningful and empowered (K1, doctor/male); the pre-modern darkness and rest (K4, cardiologist/male); a space where hope and hidden treasures are stored (K7, psychological counselor/male); a place that accelerates tissue repair and slows cellular aging (K8, dietitian/female); a site that enhances universal love and compassion (K9, psychologist/female); a phenomenon has capacity to induce awareness (K10, doctor/male). These definitions suggest that the modern form of yoga and meditation, as practiced in such settings, is primarily approached from a therapeutic and health-oriented perspective (Table 11.2).

Additionally, participants expressed their emotions before the retreat and shared their concluding reflections prior to the event's commencement.

Çetin Çetintaş describes the dark room as a space, devoid of any light, stating, "There is absolutely nothing in the dark room. We are talking about an empty room, with no light entering whatsoever. The room is small, designed to prevent us from lying down and to encourage us to maintain an upright posture, which is essential for sustaining meditation. Contemporary science also demonstrates that the meditative state induces a deeper level of rest than sleep. Since the meditative state induces a resting condition in the body similar to deep sleep, during profound meditation, both our body and mind undergo renewal. After prolonged meditation, our skin begins to glow, we express ourselves more comfortably, our self-confidence increases, and our state of being is positively transformed." (Video, 12:33.6 min). With these words, he emphasizes that the dark room offers a profound state of rest akin to deep sleep, ultimately enhancing one's overall well-being.

Formulated with inspiration from ancient Indian religions, Far Eastern spiritual traditions, and mystical philosophies, the practice of dark retreat is presented as a remedy for individuals who have become distanced from or remain disconnected from spirituality. That is, it is offered as a response to the ailments of modern life—such as the search for meaning, psychological exhaustion, and existential distress—providing a path toward healing and well-being. Unlike traditional notions

Table 11.1 Participants' reflections prior to the dark retreat experience

Reflections (pre-dark retreat)	Coding
"Due to the overwhelming bombardment of stimuli, we find ourselves in distress. That is why, since ancient times, adults have undergone a kind of dungeon therapy. Individuals are placed in a chamber of affliction and deprived of all forms of stimulation—light, sound, everything. Through this deprivation, they are allowed to encounter the light within themselves—leading to experiences such as enlightenment or the attainment of spiritual maturity." (P1, doctor/male)	Dungeon therapy, enlightenment
"Before the modern age, we used to experience darkness directly, and I believe there must be certain reasons for the existence of darkness. Foremost among them, I think, is rest… As human beings, we need to rest and prepare our bodies for use again. In this sense, darkness—namely, the night—is extremely important." (P4, cardiologist/male)	Rest
"When I received this invitation, I was pleased. These kinds of practices fall within my area of interest—some even from abroad… The exit footage at the end of the process was quite striking. The cave you fear to enter might be holding the treasure you seek." (P7, psychological counselor/male)	Concealment of hope and treasure
"One of the positive effects of the dark retreat is not only accelerating tissue repair but also slowing down cellular aging. For people who remain in darkness for extended periods, the telomeres—the ends of chromosomes that shorten with aging—shorten less. What does this mean? We can say that those who enter the dark retreat are, in a sense, stopping time." (P8, dietitian/female)	Suspension of time
"In the publications I've read, there is evidence suggesting that the dark room experience significantly enhances the experience of universal love and compassion, which truly excites me." (P9, psychologist/female)	Love, compassion
"I believe it will hold a significant place within my personal meditation practice. I also think it will contribute meaningfully to my journey toward greater awareness." (P10, doctor/male)	Awareness
"Isn't the dark room a kind of purification and rebirth ritual—an experience designed to make a person's existence in ordinary life more meaningful and more resilient? I mean, when we look inward, we do so to relate to others more effectively and to be more productive in our interactions with them—otherwise, why would we engage in such self-reflection?" (P1, doctor/male)	Purification and rebirth ritual

of seclusion, this modern adaptation supports the contemporary individual's quest for meaning by enabling the discovery of new experiences and responses rooted in curiosity, self-exploration, integration, and the pursuit of quick yet profound solutions in a fast-paced world.

Table 11.2 Participants' emotions and practices prior to the dark retreat

Emotional states (pre-dark retreat)	Coding
"I anticipate that my hormonal balance will stabilize. To be honest, there's a bit of excitement and a bit of curiosity." (P4, cardiologist/male) "I felt an intense excitement; I believe this will be one of the most unique experiences I'll ever have in my life." (P9, psychologist/female)	Excitement, curiosity Excitement
"This will be my first 24-h experience. As one develops a degree of awareness and willpower in this process, you begin to realize that knowing oneself and becoming whole is what matters most." (P7, psychological counselor/male)	Self-discovery, integration
"A sweet kind of excitement, a new experience, anticipation, a sense of seeking…" (P2, medical doctor/female)	New experience, search

11.6.2 Participants' Reflections in the Aftermath of the Dark Retreat

Ten participants, who each spent 24 h fasting in the dark retreat rooms, began at 5:00 p.m. and shared their experiences of inhabiting a 1.5-square-meter space. They described the dark retreat as a journey toward understanding and realizing the depth and dimensions of life, the dialectic of imagination and reality, sleep and wakefulness, insight and existential questioning, dreams, the womb of the mother, an inner journey, and integration with the realm of meaning.

Regarding the environment and experience of a dark retreat, Çetintaş said, "You are in a dark room; you can neither stand up, lie down, nor do anything else; you can only sit. However, when you sit there, it is as if the entire universe becomes a part of your body. You sit there in such a way that it feels like you are expanding into the depths of space. From where you sit, you seem to be experiencing the whole universe; you do not feel as if you are confined to one place. Once you enter it, you feel as if you have opened yourself up to the depths of the universe. Sometimes, when you open your eyes in meditation, you find yourself in a completely dark space, but you do not feel like it is a small area; you feel as if you are inside something infinite. Because the mind moves into such a layer that our minds begin to experience all of life in its dimensions, and at that point, we realize that we actually experience life very limitedly; we do not fully perceive its depth, dimensions, or texture. Moreover, when the practice reaches a certain stage within that experience, we come to understand what it truly means to live." Expressing the dark retreat as a means of experiencing the universe and becoming aware of life's depth and dimensions, Çetintaş presents this form of seclusion, which also exists in traditional religions, through the distinctive lens of yoga and meditation.

The dark retreat experience revealed diverse perspectives among participants. Some participants reflected on the experience through the lens of blurred boundaries between imagination and reality. One participant (P5, neurologist/male) remarked, "You can no longer distinguish between imagination and reality… it felt like I travelled to many places," while another (P7, psychological counselor/male) stated, "I began to question whether I exist or not—am I imaginary or real, or does the external world even exist?" Through such reflections, participants expressed that the dark retreat had created a profound merging of imagination and reality, affecting them.

The dark retreat was interpreted as a state of consciousness situated between sleep and wakefulness, as well as in relation to the perception of time. A participant (P4, cardiologist/male) shared, "Honestly, I was surprised when the door was knocked. They said the time was up, and I was shocked. At certain moments, it felt as though you were suspended between sleep and wakefulness—sometimes you felt as if you were dreaming, sometimes you were truly seeing the dream—and I recalled it all with remarkable clarity and intensity. You are mostly oscillating between sleep and wakefulness…" Another participant (P3, psychiatrist/female) stated, "It was pitch dark all around, there was no clock, and you had no awareness of time. No light enters the room. Although it was a meditation practice, my mind kept generating new thoughts that seemed to wage a battle against me…" Similarly, (P5, neurologist/male) noted, "There is no difference between the moment you open your eyes and the moment you close them. Time does not exist there. I believe time belongs to life—it starts moving again once we leave that space. I mean, if you ask why this world was created, perhaps it was created just for that." These reflections reveal that the absence of light and external stimuli in the retreat caused participants to experience a dissolution of temporal boundaries, integrating meditation with altered states of consciousness.

Participants interpreted the dark retreat in terms of insight and existential inquiry. One participant (P4, cardiologist/male) reflected, "It is definitely something one should experience. Honestly, it is a good opportunity to focus on your own behaviors and actions and develop personal insight. Trying to understand why you react in certain ways—this is what the process of gaining insight means. In this regard, I think the dark retreat can be very beneficial. Personally, that is what I focused on during the retreat…" Another participant (P7, psychological counselor/male) stated, "I engaged in deep questioning—I questioned existence, life, and death. As Erich Fromm says, human beings are the only creatures burdened with the task of making sense of their existence and cannot escape it. My experience was largely about exploring such questions. My awareness certainly developed—definitely." These reflections suggest that the retreat is perceived as a temporary separation from the external world—a return, a re-encounter with the self; it facilitated existential questioning and supported the individual's search for meaning, as well as its function in fostering self-reflection and psychological depth. Within yogic traditions, which represent new religious movements, the retreat experience is considered a method for spiritual renewal and mental transformation (Taşdelen, 2021, p. 12).

A participant (P9, psychologist/female) associated her psychological journey in the dark room with a dream, stating, "At one point, I realized I had fallen asleep, and during that time, I had a dream—a reconciliation with a friend I had not seen or spoken to in nearly a year due to a falling out—and to be honest, I really liked it." Another participant (P2, medical doctor/female) likened the dark retreat to the experience of being in the womb, saying, "When I came out, they told me it had been minus ten degrees outside—one of the coldest days here—and yet I had retreated into that space. I completely likened it to the womb. In medicine, we often refer to the womb as a closed, dark box—just like a child in fetal form inside the mother's womb. It felt peaceful, safe, and calm in there, like a still sea." She related the sensations of safety and serenity experienced during the retreat to those of a fetus, which, though in darkness, perceives external stimuli. In this way, he connected the retreat experience to the womb and psychotherapy, noting that just as a baby in the womb perceives external stimuli, she experienced similar feelings during the retreat. Just as psychotherapy offers structured responses within a safe framework, the dark retreat appears to provide a therapeutic space for those seeking to feel valued and understood.

One participant (P7, psychological counselor/male) described the dark retreat as an inner journey and a process of integration with the realm of meaning, stating, "The hero sets out on a journey after receiving a call, and with that departure, enters a realm beyond the familiar horizon. In this second space, the hero confronts himself—his shadow. It is, in fact, a personal sanctuary, a journey into the inner world. Moreover, it is a challenging one—you confront emotions, fears, and repressed elements. If you engage in the right kind of questioning, you experience a form of enlightenment, a moment of integration. The goal here is to distance oneself from the worldly and unite with the realm of meaning. Symbolically, you die and are reborn. The first stage is departure, the second is initiation, and the third is return… I have just returned." Through this narrative, the participant portrays the human condition as one of constant motion and existential search within a world of becoming and dissolution. Such meaning-making pursuits are often explored through new religious movements, which attract individuals through philosophical teachings that emphasize self-knowledge, the search for essence, and the discovery of truth (Table 11.3).

Çetintaş stated that the practices of yoga, meditation, and the dark retreat are well established in other countries but relatively new in Türkiye. The dark retreat attracts individual interest because it differs from the retreats experienced in traditional religions. Addressing the perception that yoga and meditation constitute a religion, Çetintaş remarked, "A few years ago, a Thai football team and their coach became trapped in a cave during an excursion. During the ten days they were stranded, their coach, who had prior experience with meditation, taught them how to meditate. Through this practice, he helped the boys navigate the psychological and physical challenges of being trapped in the cave. In this context, yoga is neither a belief system nor merely a means of progressing through faith. It is a method that has been practiced for thousands of years, composed of techniques that help us understand ourselves, make sense of life, discover the connection between self and existence, and live as our best selves in harmony with life." Through this explanation, Çetintaş emphasizes yoga as a fundamentally scientific practice rather than a faith-based system. Thus, yoga practice may mirror an individual's external religious expression, yet it remains independent of any particular belief. As an application that includes mystical and spiritual phenomena, yoga is no longer merely defined in modernity as a bodily exercise; instead, it is viewed as part of new spiritual currents that transcend traditional religious boundaries.

Table 11.3 Participants' reflections and practices in the aftermath of the dark retreat

Emotional states (post-dark retreat)	Coding
"From being able to sit to even being able to swallow—everything felt so precious. A single drop of water, a single drop of sweat, was immensely valuable. The ability to speak felt like such a tremendous blessing." (P5, neurologist/male)	Blessing
"It was incredibly restorative and refreshing—I can truly say I feel as though I have been reborn." (P2, medical doctor/female)	Rebirth
"I feel more self-confident and more at peace with myself." (P3, psychiatrist/female)	Self-confidence, inner peace
"It was like sensing the very presence of life itself. Spending nearly 24 h in darkness was a powerful experience." (P7, psychological counselor/male)	Existence
"I feel profoundly rested—as if I have been completely rebooted, like a computer that has been reformatted. I am feeling an incredible sense of relief right now." (P4, cardiologist/male)	Rest
"I did not thank the person I was—I thanked the person I had become. I felt a deep sense of gratitude toward myself." (P2, medical doctor/female)	Transformation

During the three-day dark retreat, participants are deprived of food, water, and light. It is noted that the specially prepared single-occupancy rooms are designed in such a way that lying down or waking up in the conventional sense is not possible. Participants are informed that, should any issue arise, they may use a walkie-talkie provided in the room to communicate. This practice or ritual, which gained popularity in Türkiye in January 2024, represents a visible expression of the practices associated with new religious movements that respond to modern individuals' search for meaning. The creation of online ritual spaces in the digital world, in particular, has significantly increased individuals' participation in such experiences. The reflections of those who have experienced this practice have gained popularity in the form of modern godless religions, often shared through social media posts. It is stated that the retreat, achieved through yoga and meditation practice, strengthens the individual spiritually and mentally, and that this retreat is not tied to any particular belief or religion (Yitik, 2007, p. 346).

The dark retreat, as a modern form of traditional religious practices such as seclusion and fasting, reflects the eclectic and hybrid structure of new religious movements. A participant (P8, dietitian/female) interpreted the retreat through the lens of health, linking the fasting component of the experience to contemporary wellness discourses. She remarked, "After having the opportunity to witness the dark retreat, I became increasingly interested in practices in this field. There are several nutritional models here, one of which is a three-day fast. I learned that the participants selected for the dark retreat were all healthy individuals, which is essential because fasting should only be practiced by those with stable health indicators. One of the most important aspects is the activation of autophagy after the 24-h mark of fasting, especially by the third day. Simply put, autophagy is the process through which the cell breaks down and consumes molecules it identifies as harmful or foreign to create energy. Another significant effect of the dark retreat is its stimulation of melatonin production. Melatonin is secreted in darkness, precisely when cells require repair. Why do we age? Because the pace of cellular repair slows. Thus, one of the positive effects of the dark retreat is that it accelerates tissue regeneration and slows cellular aging. Research indicates that the telomeres—protective ends of chromosomes that shorten with age—shorten more slowly in those who spend extended time in darkness. In this sense, we might say that participants in the dark retreat are, metaphorically, pausing time." This health-centered interpretation positions darkness not only as a spiritual but also as a biological space of renewal. The growing popularity of practices like the dark retreat, yoga, and meditation supports Giddens's thesis that tradition has lost its authority in modernity and that global, secular forces now shape everyday life. The current trend toward yoga offers a framework, particularly for individuals who are searching and questioning, to complete their search for meaning.

11.7 Conclusion

The withdrawal of religion into the private sphere and the decline of its influence have given rise to extensive debates on secularization. In the modern era, elements such as the search for meaning, uncertainty, existential crisis, loneliness, and individualization have initiated a process in which secularization and religion increasingly intertwine, leading to the re-emergence of the sacred. Individuals' search for the sacred and their integration with it have laid the groundwork for new religious practices and formations beyond secularization. These new manifestations of religion in modern society are often viewed as compensatory mechanisms that address issues such as the search for meaning and spiritual voids. In this context, practices such as yoga and meditation—as well as increasingly widespread mystical and hybrid belief systems, ancient pagan teachings, and spiritual phenomena—are being presented in new forms that respond to the needs of modern societies.

These new religious formations, which gained popularity in the 1960s and 1970s and were shaped within the dialectic of modern society, are esoteric in nature and function as a form of emotional and existential first aid, offering temporary remedies to individuals' spiritual and existential crises. They represent practices and methods that respond to the search for self-realization, happiness, and a healthy, long life. In every era, such movements have emerged as responses to individuals' feelings of loneliness and spiritual deficiency, offering psychological and spiritual coping mechanisms for the stressful and demanding conditions of modern life. With advancements in technology and the rise of digital platforms, the social visibility of these rituals and practices has significantly increased. Modern technologies have made access to such practices more convenient by providing individuals with options to watch, follow, like, comment on, or subscribe to them at any time and from anywhere, thus enhancing their appeal and integration into contemporary lifestyles.

As part of the research, the YouTube channel of Çetin Çetintaş was examined, and the content related to yoga and meditation practices was analyzed. A search conducted on the channel using the keyword "dark retreat" focused on the documentary The Dark Retreat "by Kaya Yalpa." Uploaded in June 2024, the documentary had received 34,000 views, 1.8 thousand likes, and 230 comments at the time of analysis. Through descriptive and content analysis, the documentary was examined in terms of participants' reflections on yoga and meditation, as well as their emotional states and experiences before and after the dark retreat. Participants' emotional states were coded in the video transcription. It was identified that the contemporary appeal of yoga and meditation arises from a lack of spiritual fulfillment in a secular world, mental fatigue, the pressures imposed by modern life, a lack of self-awareness, and increasing experiences of anxiety, stress disorders, and anger. These findings suggest that the turn toward meditation reflects an effort to address the psychological and emotional imbalances of modern existence.

Participants' pre-retreat descriptions of the dark room prominently featured a range of expressions, including dungeon therapy, enlightenment, rest, the concealment of hope and treasure, the suspension of time, awareness, purification, and a ritual of rebirth. These descriptions and participants' views on meditation indicate the reasons why individuals burdened by the search for meaning and existential questioning in the overwhelming and exhausting conditions of modern life turn toward hybrid beliefs and practices. The emergence of new religious formations and the widespread adoption of yoga and meditation practices—particularly as they have been transmitted to Western societies—are understood as a result of the modern individual's search for meaning. Furthermore, prior to the dark retreat experience, participants expressed feelings of excitement and curiosity, aspirations for self-discovery and integration, openness to new experiences, and a sense of searching. These emotional codes suggest that the modern individual, distanced from the sacred due to secularization, attempts to complete his search for meaning through syncretic and eclectic religious formations. These new religious formations, blending teachings from the Far East, Indian traditions, or Tibetan Buddhism, not only offer individuals esoteric and rational knowledge but also promise a healthy lifestyle, existential meaning, and the hope of renewal.

Participants who shared their post-dark retreat experiences expressed their reflections in terms of gaining a deeper understanding of life's depth and dimensions, as well as recognizing what real life is. They described the dark retreat in terms such as the dialectic of dream and reality, the womb, inner journey, integration with the metaphysical realm, and the search and questioning of meaning. Emotional codes derived from participants' narratives included notions of blessing, rebirth, self-confidence, peace, rest, and transformation. These findings suggest that yoga and meditation practices and rituals, regarded within the framework of new religious formations, reflect the ongoing nature of the modern individual's search for the sacred. This search continues through teachings of alternative and hybrid beliefs, which present spiritual tools in modernized forms. The research also reveals that individuals' inclination toward such rituals, regardless of adherence to a specific belief system, stems from a desire to escape the negativities of modern life and spiritual emptiness. It highlights their preference for meditative and therapeutic techniques that offer inner relief and balance. Additionally, participants' professions and professional orientations significantly influenced their experience of the retreat. This also indicates that not everyone may be mentally, spiritually, or physically prepared for such an intense retreat. The selection of participants with medical credentials appears to be a deliberate strategy to lend credibility and minimize criticism toward this increasingly popular ritual. While the dark retreat is already a widely practiced phenomenon in the United States, Europe, and Asia, it has only recently been introduced in Türkiye. Çetin Çetintaş, the yoga and meditation instructor who founded the Kioo Retreat Center and facilitated this experience, emphasized his intention to make yoga and ancient knowledge accessible to all. Although new to Türkiye, this practice gained significant public attention after being undertaken by a well-known figure and widely shared on social media platforms. As a pioneering contribution to a largely unexplored subject in the existing literature, this study provides critical insights into why and how individuals adopt hybrid forms of belief.

References

Aksöz, T. (2016). *Modern psikolojik yaklaşımlar açısından nefs arınması* [Doctoral Dissertation]. Sakarya Üniversitesi Sosyal Bilimler Enstitüsü.

Altıntaş, R. (2005). *Din ve sekülerleşme.* Pınar Yayınları.

Arslan, M. (2006). Değişim sürecinde yeni dindarlık formları: "Yeni çağ" inanışları örneği. *Değerler Eğitimi Dergisi, 4*(11), 9–25.

Arslan, M. (2015). Postmodern yeni dinsel kimlik ve paranormal inançlar. *Milel ve Nihal, 12*(2), 55–72. https://doi.org/10.17131/milelnihal.88195

Arslan, M. (2016). Kitle iletişim araçları, medya ve din ilişkisi üzerine. *Birey ve Toplum Sosyal Bilimler Dergisi, 6*(1), 5–26.

Aupers, S., & Houtman, D. (2006). Beyond the spiritual supermarket: The social and public significance of new age spirituality. *Journal of Contemporary Religion, 21*(2), 201–222. https://doi.org/10.1080/13537900600655894

Aydınalp, H. (2023). Sekülerleşme, Türkiye ve din. *Nihayet Dergisi, 102*, 32–43.

Aydın, C. (2015). *İnsanın anlam arayışı ile yeni çağ inanışları arasındaki ilişki* [Doctoral Dissertation]. Samsun Ondokuz Mayıs Üniversitesi Sosyal Bilimler Enstitüsü.

Bahadur, M., & Çapcıoğlu, İ. (2021). Yeni dini hareketlerde çevrimiçi ve çevrimdışı yönelimler: Sahaja Yoga örneği. *İslami Araştırmalar, 32*(2), 372–386.

Bauman, Z. (2014). *Postmodernizmin hoşnutsuzlukları* (İ. Türkmen, Trans). Ayrıntı Yayınları.

Bayer, A. (2022). *Sekülerleşme ve din.* İKSAD Yayınevi.

Berger, P. L., & Huntington, S. P. (2002). *Many globalizations: Cultural diversity in the contemporary world.* Oxford University Press.

Berger, P. L., & Luckmann, T. (2022). *Modernite, çoğulculuk ve anlam krizi modern insanın yönelimi* (M. D. Dereli, Trans.). Albaraka Yayınları.

Berger, P. L., & Luckmann, T. (2015). *Gerçekliğin toplumsal inşası: Bilgi sosyolojisine bir katkı* (H. Aydın, Trans.). Heretik Yayıncılık.

Berk, S., & Nadir Çetin, B. (2023). Dijital çağda dini ritüel algısının dönüşümü. *Sosyolojik Bağlam Dergisi, 4*(3), 248–272. https://doi.org/10.52108/2757-5942.4.3.3

Biçer, R. (2006). Heretik bir new age tarikati: Dünya kardeşlik birliği Mevlana Yüce vakfı. *EKEV Akademi Dergisi, X*(29), 27–50.

Bruce, S. (2011). *Secularization: In defence of an unfashionable theory.* Oxford University Press.

Campbell, H. (2005). Spiritualising the internet. Uncovering discourses and narratives of religious internet usage. *Online Heidelberg Journal of Religions on the Internet, 1*(1), 1–25. https://doi.org/10.11588/rel.2005.1.381
Çapcıoğlu, İ., & Yürük, T. (2010). Modern dünyada insanın anlam arayışına teolojik katkı: Hz. İbrahim Kıssası örneği. *BİDDER Sosyal Bilimler Dergisi, 1*(2), 21–31.
Clarke, P. (2006). *New religions in global perspective: Religious change in the modern world*. Routledge.
Coşkun, H. (2017). Küreselleşme sürecinde din. *Gaziosmanpaşa Üniversitesi İlahiyat Fakültesi Dergisi, 5*(2), 115–134.
Dereli, M. D. (2019). Dinî kimliklerin siber uzamda akışkanlaşması. *İnsan ve Toplum, 9*(1), 85–116. https://doi.org/10.12658/M0301
Dereli, M. D. (2022). Kurgu ile ütopya arasında: Habermas'in dine yaklaşımında değişim ve post-seküler toplum projesi. *Bilimname, 47*, 303–342. https://doi.org/10.28949/bilimname.1079329
Doğan, E. (2020). *Türkiye'de new age hareketi: Şifacı grupların sosyo-ekonomik ve kültürel tabanı üzerine sosyolojik bir inceleme* [Master's Thesis]. Uludağ Üniversitesi Sosyal Bilimler Enstitüsü.
Francis, D. W., Cuff, E. C., & Sharrock, W. W. (2015). *Sosyolojide perspektifler* (Ü. Tatlıcan, Trans.). Say Yayınları.
Furseth, I., & Repstad, P. (2011). *Din sosyolojisine giriş klasik ve çağdaş kuramlar* (İ. Çapcıoğlu & H. Aydınalp, Trans.). Birleşik Dağıtım Kitabevi.
Giddens, A. (2021). *Modernliğin sonuçları* (E. Kuşdil, Trans.). Ayrıntı Yayınları.
Güneş, A. (2023). Toplumsal bir protesto: Yeni dini hareketler. *Fırat Üniversitesi Sosyal Bilimler Dergisi, 33*(1), 401–412. https://doi.org/10.18069/firatsbed.1189286
Haberli, M. (2013). Dinlerin internet ortamındakı temsili ve dağılımı. *The Journal of Academic Social Science Studies, VI*(1), 859–873.
Haberli, M. (2019). Dijital çağda din ve dindarlığınn dönüşümü. *Medya ve Din Araştırmaları Dergisi, 2*(2), 307–315.
Haberli, M. (2022). Gutenberg'den Zuckerberg'e medya ve din: Panaromik bakış. *Medya ve Din Araştırmaları Dergisi, 5*(2), 387–407. https://doi.org/10.47951/mediad.1197443
Habermas, J. (2005). *Religion in the public sphere*. Holberg Prize Lecture, Bergen, Norway.
Hanegraaff, W. J. (1999). New age spiritualities as secular religion: A historian's perspective. *Social Compass, 46*(2), 145–160. https://doi.org/10.1177/003776899046002004
Hendriks, T., Pritikin, J., Choudhary, D. R., & Danyluck, C. (2021). Exploring the relationship between character strengths and meditation: A cross-sectional study among long-term practitioners of Sahaja Yoga meditation. *International Journal of Applied Positive Psychology, 7*(2), 31–45. https://doi.org/10.1007/s41042-021-00052-0
Hondeet, M., & van der Beck, S. (Eds.). (2019). *Introduction. Ritual in a digital society* (pp. 1–27). Netherlands Studies in Ritual and Liturgy 21, Netherlands.
Karaarslan, F. (2015). Post seküler din halleri ve dinin dijitalleşmesi. In M. Çamdereli, B. O. Doğan, & N. K. Şener (Eds.), *Dijitalleşen Din: Medya ve Din 2* (pp. 13–45). Köprü Kitapları.
Kaygusuz, İ., Özkul, M., & Kaya, Y. (2020). Modernleşme sürecinde din ve dinde yeni eğilimler. *Tarih Okulu Dergisi, 13*(XLIX), 4467–4500. https://doi.org/10.29228/joh.47310
Kirman, M. A. (1999). Batı'da ortaya çıkan yeni dini hareketlerin bazı özellikleri ve toplumsal tabanları. *Dini Araştırmalar, 1*(4), 223–233.
Kirman, M. A. (2008). Küreselleşme sürecinde sekülerleşme ve dinin geleceği. *38. ICANAS Uluslararası Asya ve Kuzey Afrika Çalışmaları Kongresi* (pp. 279–295).
Kirman, M. A. (2013). *Yeni dinî hareketler sosyolojisi*. Nobel Akademik Yayıncılık.
Korkut, T. (2023). Turabdin bölgesi inziva sütunları (Estuno) (Mor Yakup Manastırı inziva sütunu örneği). *Ortaçağ Araştırmaları Dergisi, 6*(1), 371–398. https://doi.org/10.48120/oad.1091816
Köse, A. (Ed.). (2002). *Sekülerizm sorgulanıyor 21. yüzyılda dinin geleceği*. Ufuk Kitapları.
Köse, A. (2013). *Sekülerleşme teorileri bağlamında Türkiye'de din ve modernleşme*. Retrieved from May 5, 2025, from https://www.hazardernegi.org/wp-content/uploads/2013/01/sekulerles
Kraidy, M. M. (2005). *Hybridity, or the cultural logic of globalization*. Temple University Press. Retrieved from May 10, 2025, from https://www.jstor.org/stable/j.ctt1bw1k8m

Luckmann, T. (2016). *Görünmeyen din* (A. Coşkun & F. Aydın, Trans.). Rağbet Yayınları.
Main, R. (2002). Religion, science, and the new age. In J. Pearson (Ed.), *Religion Today: Tradition, Modernity & Change Belief Beyond Boundaries: Wicca, Celtic Spirituality, and the New Age* (pp. 173–225). Ashgate Publishing.
Merter, M. (2012). *Dokuz yüz katlı insan.* Kaknüs Yayınları.
Mirza, G. A. (2018). *Yeni dinselleşme eğilimleri ve maneviyat arayışları.* İstanbul Boğaziçi Üniversitesi Yayınları.
Öztan, A. (2019). *İnsanın anlam ve mutluluk arayışında inancın rolü* [Master's Thesis]. Uludağ Üniversitesi Sosyal Bilimler Enstitüsü.
Özkan, A. R. (2008). Seküler dindarlık biçimleri: Yeni dini hareketler. *Dinler Tarihi Araştırmaları Sempozyumu* (pp. 307–322).
Polat, S. (2004). *Hıristiyanlık'ta manastır hayatı* [Master's Thesis]. Ankara Üniversitesi Sosyal Bilimler Enstitüsü.
Sarıkçıoğlu, E. (2002). *Din fenomenolojisi.* Süleyman Demirel Üniversitesi Yayınları.
Şentürk, R. (2004). *Yeni din sosyolojileri.* Gelenek Yayıncılık.
Şenyayla, G. (2021). Post-seküler unsurların sosyolojik açıdan değerlendirilmesi: Bir Başkadır dizisi örneği. *Tezkire Dergisi, 77*, 196–219.
Slattery, M. (2007). *Sosyolojide temel fikirler* (Ü. Tatlıcan, Ed.). Sentez Yayınları.
Taşdelen, V. (2021). İnziva: İnsanın kendine yolculuğu. *Van İnsani ve Sosyal Bilimler Dergisi, 1*(1), 8–20.
Taylor, C. (2007). *A secular age.* Harvard University Press.
Turner, B. S. (2010). Religion in a post-secular society. In B. S. Turner (Ed.), *The New Blackwell Companion to the Sociology of Religion* (pp. 649–667). Wiley. https://doi.org/10.1002/9781444320787.ch29
Uysal, E. (2015). *20. yüzyıl new age akımı üzerine karşılaştırmalı bir analiz* [Master's Thesis]. Çukurova Üniversitesi Sosyal Bilimler Enstitüsü.
Wenzel, N. G. (2012). Postmodernizm ve din (A. Ayten, Trans.). In P. B. Clarke (İ. Çapcıoğlu, Trans. Ed.), *Din Sosyolojisi Kuram ve Yöntem* (pp. 281–312). İmge Kitabevi.
Wuthnow, R. (2002). Din sosyolojisi (A. Çiftçi, Trans.). In *Din ve Modernlik* (A. Çiftçi, Ed.). Ankara Okulu. Yayınları.
Yıldız, M., & Meçin, M. M. (2013). Dinlerde iç yolculuklar: Riyazetin kökenine dair. *Tarih Okulu Dergisi, 7*(XVII), 221–251. https://doi.org/10.14225/Joh470
Yitik, A. İ. (2007). Hint kaynaklı dinlerin ülkemizdeki faaliyetleri. *İslami Araştırmalar Dergisi, 20*(3), 340–347.
Zafer, H. (2007). *Dinî yaşantıda inzivâ* [Master's Thesis]. Sakarya Üniversitesi Sosyal Bilimler Enstitüsü.

Chapter 12
"Loose" Muslim "Strict" Opponent: Religion as an Object of Humor in Social Media Stand-Ups

Hüseyin Çil

12.1 Introduction

In recent years, humor has emerged as a visibly expanding cultural form in Türkiye. The increase in both the number and viewership of comedy films, the proliferation of humor-based social media channels, and the widening of their audiences collectively indicate the growing popularization and mass appeal of comedy. This expansion has occurred in parallel with the rapid dissemination of new media technologies. Social media, in particular, has facilitated both the production and the widespread circulation of comedic content, offering an accessible and low-cost platform for performers to reach large audiences. A notable example is Cem Gelinoğlu, who first gained visibility in the mid-2010s through short amateur videos on the Vine platform. Initially producing informal sketches recorded on smartphones in domestic and public settings, Gelinoğlu has since risen to national prominence, having produced two widely released comedy films. This trajectory exemplifies how social media ruptured conventional hierarchies in the field of humor, weakening the symbolic authority of established figures and contributing to a more democratized comedic landscape. Today, humor is increasingly generated by ordinary individuals and circulates broadly within digital publics.

This chapter focuses explicitly on how religion and religiosity are represented in stand-up performances disseminated through social media platforms. In recent years, religion has become one of the most prominent and controversial topics in the expanding field of digital humor in Türkiye. Almost every stand-up performance features religious references, and these references often ignite public debate and controversy. For example, in 2020, comedian Emre Günsal was arrested for insulting two historically and symbolically significant figures. During a performance, he described Mustafa Kemal Atatürk—the founding leader of the Republic

H. Çil (✉)
Department of Sociology, Selçuk University, Konya, Türkiye
e-mail: huseyin.cil@selcuk.edu.tr

M. D. Dereli and M. Eken (eds.), *Turkish Perspectives on Secularization and Media*,
https://doi.org/10.1007/978-3-032-16436-0_12

of Türkiye—as "the country's most successful alcoholic." He made a joke associating homosexuality with Mevlana, a central figure in the Islamic intellectual and spiritual tradition (Gök, 2021). As both figures symbolize the respective foundations of secular and Islamic identities, this incident sparked severe legal and social consequences for the comedian. It should also be noted that this is not unique to Türkiye; the cartoons of the Prophet Muhammad published in Denmark and France, along with the subsequent events, remain vivid in public memory (Lindekilde et al., 2009).

The appearance of religion in stand-up comedy is not exclusive to Türkiye. Christianity, for example, has long been a target of offensive humor in countries such as the United Kingdom and the United States (Gürler, 2020). However, several contextual factors render the Turkish case distinct. While processes such as secularization and individualization are commonly recognized as contributing to the transformation of religion into a subject of humor, it is important not to overlook the culturally specific conditions in which these transformations occur. These contextual dynamics form the foundation of the two primary arguments of this chapter.

First, I argue that the prominence of Islam and Muslim identity in stand-up performances in Türkiye is closely linked to a broader global trend shaped by neoliberal political economy and postmodern cultural sensibilities. These global forces not only circulate religious knowledge as a commodified product but also open it to reinterpretation, critique, and humor through increasingly individualized perspectives. Religion, while strengthening its presence in the public sphere, has simultaneously become entangled in new discursive arenas, including those defined by satire and humor.

Second, I contend that the increasing visibility of religious themes in stand-up performances is shaped by enduring sociopolitical tensions within Türkiye. The long-standing contestation between secular and Islamic worldviews, and their associated modes of life, renders the satirization of religion and the public reactions it provokes more intelligible. A significant number of stand-up comedians identify as atheists or secularists, which paves the way for them to make jokes about everyday or historical issues related to Islam. This is possible because they can lean on the global trend mentioned in the first point. However, the exact identification also explains the religiously motivated backlash they face. Hence, the presence of religion in stand-up comedy in Türkiye should be understood not only as an aesthetic or narrative choice but also as a site of ongoing social contestation.

The remainder of the chapter proceeds in two stages. First, it explores the global and local dynamics that shape the development of religious humor in the Turkish digital media landscape. Second, it offers a critical analysis of how religion is thematically and discursively represented in 25 stand-up performances published on YouTube.

12.2 From Global to Local: The Relationship Between Social Media Humor and Religion

12.2.1 Global Dynamics: Neoliberal Society/Postmodern Religion

Following the decline of the core claim of secularization theory—that religion would lose its influence in modern societies and eventually disappear—a new thesis emerged, often referred to as "the revenge of God" (Kepel, 1994). This idea not only pointed to the "return" of religion but also to the specific form that this return would take. The increasing visibility of religion and its encroachment into the center of public life occurred in ways and through forms quite different from those of previous decades. Türkiye, with its own specific nuances, has also been shaped by this process. The "Islamic revival," which gained visibility globally from the late 1970s and became undeniable by the 1990s, also unfolded as a sociopolitical phenomenon in Türkiye. Notably, the representation of Islam in Türkiye during this period reflected two overarching global developments: the rise of neoliberalism and the influence of postmodernity.

One of the most defining features of neoliberalism is that its logic is not confined to the economic realm but penetrates all aspects of life (Brown, 2015; Harvey, 2005). From consumption to art, from education to child-rearing, and from sports to religion, this new "economic rationality" becomes operative in all domains of everyday life. In a hyper-competitive environment in which individuals are regarded as both agents and bearers of full responsibility for their actions, religious belief too becomes subject to individual accountability. The individual, now positioned as the entrepreneur of their own life, is also held responsible for managing their own religious beliefs and practices in a market-driven world. Religion is no longer a matter of institutional affiliation, but rather a resource for personal meaning-making and fulfillment. In this context, individualized religion, having grown distant from traditional authorities, gains a more flexible and fragmented structure. As Guest (2023, p. 43) notes: "Religion in late modernity has reached an unprecedented level of unpredictability and flexibility. It is less bound to traditional forms and meanings and has become more capable of forming new connections with non-religious social phenomena." The once-dominant religious communities of the past now compete with one another to attract individuals into their ranks. Through extensive media campaigns, religious movements have not only accepted the competitive logic of the religious sphere but have also learned to operate within it.

In the neoliberal age, religious life is shaped not only by systems of belief but also through cultural performances, consumption patterns, and individualized practices. Patrick Haenni's (2014) concept of "Market Islam" exemplifies this transformation. Within this framework, religiosity is no longer limited to worship and traditional morality; it is also redefined through visibility and public display in the media, in clothing styles, in behavior, and in everyday practices. This emphasis on visibility enables religion to be performed as spectacle and to be rendered suitable for comedic representation. The transformation of religiosity into a performative act under neoliberal logic introduces a range of ethical and symbolic contradictions.

Undoubtedly, the postmodern condition, which famously proclaims the end of metanarratives (Lyotard, 2010), shares significant parallels with the neoliberal paradigm. A symbiotic relationship between neoliberalism and postmodernism shapes the emergence of new forms of religiosity. The principles that define the neoliberal subject, as outlined above, also characterize the postmodern individual. This subject is designed to navigate the complexities of dissolved identities, fluid subjectivities, and normative ambiguities. The secure life trajectories and collective moral frameworks once promised by modernity have lost their relevance; instead, individuals are now expected to assume full responsibility for the direction of their own lives. This condition has led the postmodern individual to seek new forms of spiritual support (Bauman, 2008). However, unlike the rigid norms and prohibitive language of the past, this quest often privileges pluralistic and experiential forms of religiosity. Postmodernism challenges the binary oppositions between religion and secularism that modernity once upheld. It reconceptualizes religion not as a fixed system of belief, but as a site of ritual, embodied practice, and cultural experience. This reframing dissolves the monopoly on absolute truth claims held by religion and transforms it into a collection of pluralistic, localized, and individually experienced practices. The experiential and plural nature of religion in the postmodern era makes it more amenable to humorous representation. As institutional sanctity weakens, religion becomes increasingly open to public critique, parody, and reinterpretation (Anderson, 2012). This approach also permits individuals to configure religious elements in accordance with their personal intuition (Crocket, 2003), thereby making religion simultaneously more flexible and more susceptible to critique. Humor, in this regard, functions as a cultural space in which the contradictions embedded in this flexible religiosity are rendered visible.

12.2.2 Local Dynamics: Culture Wars, Polarization, and Social Media Humor

In an era where global dynamics rapidly penetrate both individual and public expressions of religion, local socio-political dynamics have also been reshaped under the influence of these global trends. In Türkiye, the most critical local factor that renders religion a subject of public controversy is the extent to which it is experienced as a public rather than purely private practice. Following the foundation of the Republic, a secular nationalist "culture wars" emerged, aiming to restrict the influence of religion in public life (Çolak, 2017). The outlawing of religious groups, which had previously functioned as powerful political actors during the Ottoman Empire, also contributed significantly to the development of a religious-secular cleavage in

Türkiye. These historical narratives continue to serve as powerful reference points in current debates. Consequently, the tension between secularism and religiosity emerges as a key dynamic in understanding the structure of Turkish society. Indeed, a large body of literature referred to as "Türkish studies" identifies this tension as a core analytical lens for understanding the country (Baran, 2008; Başkan, 2010; Kalaycıoğlu, 2012; Somer, 2007).

Since the 2000s, this religious-secular divide has increasingly been reflected in political party preferences. Research indicates that individuals maintain a growing social distance from voters of rival parties and often perceive themselves as morally superior. For instance, voters of the Republican People's Party (CHP),[1] typically clustered around ideals of Atatürkism and secularism, and those of the ruling Justice and Development Party (AKP), clustered around religiosity and conservatism, have come to occupy antagonistic positions in the public imagination (Erdoğan & Uyan-Semerci, 2018, 2022). This political polarization, situated along axes of culture and identity, has increasingly infiltrated everyday life through the discourse of "lifestyle differences" (KONDA, 2008).

The proliferation of mass communication technologies, particularly the internet, smartphones, and social media, has made these contrasting lifestyles more visible and accessible. The growing visibility of religious individuals and groups on social media has also opened the door to renewed debates around religion and religiously inspired ways of life (Dereli, 2019, 2022). In contemporary Türkiye, it would be difficult to claim that there are any remaining taboos or hidden subjects related to Islam; nearly all religious matters are now openly discussed on online platforms. While scholars debate ongoing secularization trends (Ertit, 2023), it is also evident that we are witnessing a form of religion that articulates positions on almost every topic, from women's roles in public life to the Central Bank's interest rate policies, from electoral behavior to family policy, and rapidly disseminates these views via digital media. These religious discourses, whether originating from individual believers or organized religious communities, often present themselves as rooted in Islam and are capable of generating widespread public debate.

The increasing publicization of the views and actions of religious figures or self-identified devout individuals has, in turn, rendered these actors and their statements frequent subjects of humor. The uninhibited mischievousness of humor, on the one hand, and the seriousness of religious issues, on the other, sowed new seeds of polarization rather than sparking a public debate. One illustrative case involves Cem Yılmaz, one of Türkiye's most prominent comedians. In short, Yılmaz said that God first created man, identified the problematic features of this version (referring to the male genitalia), and then created woman, free of these faults. This joke drew intense backlash from Halil Konakçı, a popular Islamic preacher in Türkiye, who declared that anyone making such a joke could not be considered Muslim and had effectively left the religion. Furthermore, he claimed that those who laughed or applauded the joke had also apostatized.

[1] CHP was founded by Atatürk and is widely regarded as the primary proponent of secular policies. The party has been identified as the strongest opposition to the current conservative government.

This incident generated considerable public debate. Media outlets aligned with secular worldviews strongly criticized Konakçı, while conservative media defended him. What makes such cases particularly notable in Türkiye is that society becomes sharply divided in its reception of them. One segment of the population interprets Konakçı's comments as a significant theological matter. At the same time, another sees Cem Yılmaz's performance as an exercise in freedom of expression and views Konakçı's rhetoric as fundamentalist. The latter group often mocks religious figures like Konakçı, turning them into caricatures and thereby signaling a refusal to engage with their positions seriously. This dynamic continues to reinforce Türkiye's polarized socio-political landscape.

12.3 Methodology

This study is based on stand-up performances sourced from YouTube, which currently serves as the most prominent platform for broadcasting stand-up comedy within social media. Accordingly, an initial sample of 36 stand-up shows—each ranging between 40 and 110 min in duration and with a minimum of 100,000 views—was selected and watched. Of these, 25 performances were identified as containing jokes related to religion to varying degrees. These 25 shows were rewatched and subjected to detailed analysis.

The profiles of the comedians included in this study exhibit three primary orientations regarding their relationship with religion. It is important to note that identifying their religious orientation is not particularly difficult, as most comedians explicitly express their religious identity or worldview during their performances and use it as the basis for their jokes. The analysis includes individuals who predominantly grew up in religious or conservative families or circles and received a religious education during their childhood. However, they later distanced themselves from religion. Another group, comprising four comedians, openly identifies as atheists. Three comedians identify as Alevi.[2] Among the comedians, three are women and twenty-two are men. One female comedian noted that she had previously worn a headscarf but later chose to remove it due to various social pressures.

The selected stand-up performances were transcribed and analyzed using a thematic analysis approach. This approach emphasizes the identification of recurring patterns of meaning across the dataset. These patterns are typically organized into what are called "themes." As Braun and Clark (2019, p. 878) explain, "a theme captures something important about the data in relation to the research question and

[2] As noted, these identity statements are based on the comedians' own declarations. The Alevi identity has historically been situated at the center of religious tensions in Türkiye and is generally regarded by the Sunni Muslim majority as a heterodox Islamic tradition. For example, Alevis are frequently associated with the CHP, known for its secular orientation and policies. Despite being a religious group, public discourse often emphasizes Alevis' secular inclinations, leading to widespread stereotyping. For this reason, comedians who identify as Alevi often do so to underline their alignment with secular worldviews.

Table 12.1 Stand-up shows cited in the text

	Comedian	Access the performance's URL
1	Özkan Çelik	https://www.youtube.com/watch?v=9tlW7eeBUq0&t=789s
2	Cüneyt Nergiz	https://www.youtube.com/watch?v=vNSJ5jGNDNo
3	Hidayet Tılı	https://www.youtube.com/watch?v=0NpHN75XoGo
4	Doğan Tunçel	https://www.youtube.com/watch?v=7_YaL271F0Y&t=692s
5	Ömer Harmankaya	https://www.youtube.com/watch?v=MaZmVeOTHL0
6	Özgür Turhan	https://www.youtube.com/watch?v=C0St09C4pjQ&t=1621s
7	Nebiye Arı	https://www.youtube.com/watch?v=VouN-HeFH4E&t=1861s
8	Tuna Kalınsaz	https://www.youtube.com/watch?v=uHV-M1Rysdo&t=2391s
9	Berkan Priştina	https://www.youtube.com/watch?v=xX8U1aOoFb8

represents some level of patterned response or meaning within the dataset." Based on this approach, two central themes were identified within the performances analyzed. The section titles that follow—"All That Is Solid Melts into Air": Religious Fragments in Stand-Up Performances and The Intersection of Religion and Humor in the Axis of Social Tensions—represent these themes and are discussed in further detail within their respective sections.

As noted, the study incorporates 25 stand-up performances. However, consistent with the logic of thematic analysis, the objective is not to present data from each show separately but to highlight illustrative quotations that best represent the overarching narrative. Therefore, the study does not attribute data to each of the 25 performances individually. Instead, selected excerpts that best convey the core themes have been included in the analysis. A list of the original video links for all performances cited directly in the analysis is provided below (Table 12.1).

12.4 "All That Is Solid Melts into Air": Religious Fragments in Stand-Up Performances

12.4.1 The Erosion of the Boundaries Between God and Human

One of the most striking features of stand-up comedy in Türkiye is the inclusion of nearly all aspects of religion, including the foundational principles of Islam, as material for humorous content. Within this expanded discursive space, where traditional boundaries of religion are significantly loosened, even the position of God, traditionally regarded as beyond question within the Islamic tradition, becomes subject to individual interpretation. The ontological hierarchy that traditionally places God as absolutely superior to humans (Davutoğlu, 1994) is increasingly reconfigured within the narrative domain of the individual subject. As divine authority relatively diminishes, human agency ascends in parallel (Tekin, 2023). In this rising wave of humor, "Allah" is no longer consistently depicted as the exalted creator standing above His servants, but rather as an anthropomorphic figure positioned almost on equal footing with them.

> You know that viral video of the cat supposedly saying "Allah," right? Well, I said, …. at that moment. Then I was like, "Guys, why didn't you warn me? We nearly ended up in hell!"
>
> However, then I thought… wouldn't it be hilarious if that is really why I burned?
>
> Like, Allah says: "You are going to hell."
>
> Moreover, I go: "But my Allah, there was no evidence!"
>
> Moreover, Allah replies: "What do you mean, no evidence? Didn't you see the cat?"
>
> So he basically presents a cat as proof. (Özkan Çelik)

Özkan, who identifies himself as an atheist, constructs a fictional scenario in which he imagines an afterlife encounter with God, satirizing certain viral videos circulating on Turkish social media. These videos often feature animals making sounds that are interpreted by some as the word "Allah," and are occasionally cited as miraculous evidence of divine existence and power. Özkan turns this phenomenon into comedic material by imagining a dialogue with God in which the supposed "proof" of divine reality is, ironically, the utterance of a cat. The imagined conversation takes place in an almost casual tone, as if between two acquaintances on the street, suggesting a striking reduction in the ontological hierarchy traditionally maintained between God and humans.

In addition, Özkan's joke also references belief in the afterlife, particularly the concepts of heaven and hell. By saying, "We nearly burned," he humorously highlights the dissonance between his atheist stance and the possibility of divine judgment. However, this recklessness should not be interpreted solely as a byproduct of his atheism. Özkan is not an "atheist exception." His approach echoes similar tones found in the work of other comedians. Cüneyt was raised in a conservative religious household and reportedly received substantial religious education in his youth. As explored in the following example, Cüneyt recounts how his mother, a devout believer, prayed fervently for him not to become a comedian, adding another layer to the complex interplay between religion, family, and humor.

> Apparently, my mom went straight to the highest authority to stop me from performing-she went directly to Allah. After that prayer, my following four sets went terribly, and I was genuinely upset.
>
> I started wondering: "Was her prayer actually accepted?"
>
> Because years ago, when regime forces in Syria killed numerous civilians, my mom had also prayed for them. Her prayer was not answered back then; people continued to die.
>
> So now I am like… if her prayer for something that important was not accepted,
>
> Why did Allah intervene just because I made a few penis jokes?
>
> Was that really more important?…. (Cüneyt Nergiz)

Cüneyt's joke simultaneously engages with a classic theological issue—the "problem of evil"—and subverts the traditional hierarchical relationship between

God and human beings. In his performance, Cüneyt contrasts a God who seemingly remained inactive in the face of mass civilian deaths during the Syrian conflict with a God who actively interferes in response to a comedian's use of vulgar language. This ironic juxtaposition serves as a critique of divine priorities, implicitly questioning the moral consistency of divine will. Moreover, by portraying God as someone who would intervene to sabotage a comedy show over a few inappropriate jokes, Cüneyt anthropomorphizes the divine, effectively recasting God in the role of a meddling employer. This narrative narrows the ontological gap between the sacred and the profane, challenging the theological hierarchy at the heart of Islamic cosmology.

Such depictions, which undermine God's transcendental authority, can be deeply provocative for devout Muslims in Türkiye. However, the nature of the humor found in the stand-up routines analyzed here significantly differs from the explicitly confrontational atheism of Western comedians such as Ricky Gervais or George Carlin. For these figures, religion and especially the concept of God is something to be ridiculed, debunked, and dismissed entirely. Their acts are often guided by a didactic impulse aimed at dismantling religion through satire.

In contrast, the stand-up comedians examined in this study adopt a more ambivalent stance. While a few explicitly identify as atheists, many describe themselves in terms that suggest a residual or evolving connection to religion. Cüneyt, for instance, explicitly rejects the atheist label, preferring instead to describe himself as a "loose Muslim." This ambiguous positioning is reflected in the comedic material itself: rather than launching direct or political attacks on God or religious institutions, the comedians tend to treat religion as a cultural texture—an object of light-hearted irreverence rather than ideological opposition.

This tendency is further exemplified in the case of Hidayet, a comedian raised in a conservative family who characterizes himself as someone currently grappling with religious questions. His jokes reflect a kind of generational shift in attitudes toward faith—less about abandonment, more about uncertainty and negotiation. This nuanced relationship with religion helps explain why, in Türkiye, humor about God often takes on an exploratory rather than hostile tone.

> I am going through a period where I feel somewhat distant from religion.
>
> I discuss these topics, but I do not intend to offend anyone.
>
> I am already an indecisive person. I am confused.
>
> However, people still really do need religion.
>
> Sometimes, I catch myself praying like this: "Dear Allah... first of all, I hope You exist.
>
> Moreover, if you do not, please do not exist. Come into being from non-being."
>
> I find myself saying prayers like this.
>
> I cannot say I am an atheist, by the way. I would not define myself that way.
>
> Like I said, I am indecisive... and confused. (Hidayet Tılı)

Hidayet's use of expressions such as "feeling somewhat distant from religion," "I am confused," and "I cannot define myself as an atheist" aptly illustrates the hybrid and ambivalent narrative commonly observed in stand-up performances. These statements reflect neither a complete rejection of religion nor a firm commitment to it.

Instead, they point to a "loose" and unsettled connection between the individual and God/religion, one marked by uncertainty, fluctuation, and introspective hesitation.

12.4.2 From Parable to Humor: Rambling on Sacred Things

Prophets, stories, narratives (qisas), and ritual practices mentioned in the Qur'an are frequently transformed into comedic material in stand-up performances. Once topics as central as God and faith become fair game for humor, it is unsurprising that other elements of Islam also become comedic subjects. However, while jokes about core theological issues, such as belief in God and faith, can provoke strong public reactions (Önder, 2022), humor based on what might be considered "secondary" religious matters tends to carry lower social costs in Türkiye.

One of the most significant episodes mentioned in the Qur'an is the story of the sacrifice. According to Islamic belief, the parable of Abraham (Ibrahim) and his son Ishmael (Ismail) stands as one of the most potent symbols of submission and faith in Islam. Abraham, who remained childless for many years, was eventually blessed with a son by God. Later, he saw in a dream that he was to sacrifice his son for God. As a prophet, he interpreted the dream as a divine command. When he told Ishmael, the boy submitted without hesitation. Just as Abraham was about to carry out the act, God intervened and sent a ram to be sacrificed in place of Ishmael. This episode symbolizes the unwavering devotion and obedience of both Abraham and Ishmael. Muslims commemorate this event during the Feast of Sacrifice (Eid al-Adha) by sacrificing animals.

Doğan, a comedian, turns this sacred narrative into comedic material by referencing it in the context of a conversation with his atheist friend. His humor hinges on the perceived irrationality of the event, particularly the notion of a ram descending from the heavens, an element he contrasts with modern scientific reasoning. By doing so, Doğan generates laughter not by mocking the faith itself, but by highlighting the cognitive dissonance between deeply held religious narratives and contemporary secular logic.

> As I said, those Islamic reflexes have never wholly left me.
>
> For instance, my former roommate Emre was an atheist… He tried really hard to steer me away from religion. At home, he kept making me watch *Cosmos*, then Celal Şengör[3] …
>
> At one point, he showed me a video where Şengör says:
>
> "They claim in the Qur'an that God created mountains to protect people from earthquakes.
>
> However, in reality, mountains are one of the leading causes of earthquakes."
>
> Şengör argues that the Qur'an got it wrong on this. And then Emre turns to me and says:
>
> "Well? Go ahead, explain this one!"

[3] Celal Şengör is a well-known geologist in Türkiye who has gained prominence not only for his academic work but also for his outspoken atheism and frequent critiques of religious beliefs in public discourse.

And I replied: "Dude, I already believe a ram once descended from the sky-
You think *this* is what is going to trip me up?" (Doğan Tunçel)

Doğan's joke encapsulates the multidimensional nature of contemporary stand-up culture in Türkiye. By invoking the words of a prominent atheist scientist, the comedian uses a scientific critique as a springboard for addressing a core religious narrative—the story of Abraham's intended sacrifice of his son. This juxtaposition highlights the ongoing tension between scientific rationalism and religious belief in the country's socio-cultural climate. Doğan references the miraculous descent of a ram, a central element in the Islamic tradition of the feast of sacrifice, and frames it as a point of irrationality from a secular perspective. While this framing generates laughter by drawing attention to the implausibility of the story in scientific terms, it simultaneously affirms Doğan's continued identification with Islam. In this way, the performance does not signify a rejection of religion, rather exemplifies the "hybrid" and ambivalent religious subjectivity described earlier, one that is neither devoutly traditional nor strictly secular.

What is equally striking is the comedians' willingness to target sacred figures in Islam, including prophets and angels. This signals a shift in religious discourse, where not only traditional narratives (such as scriptural stories) but also central religious agents become subjects of satire. In the example that follows, the joke centers on Azrael, the angel of death, and Israfil, the angel tasked with blowing the trumpet on Judgment Day. While Azrael is portrayed as an overworked employee, Israfil is humorously likened to an unnecessary hire with minimal responsibilities. This analogy not only humanizes these celestial figures but also strips them of their transcendental aura, reflecting a postmodern impulse to demystify the sacred and embed it within everyday bureaucratic logic.

So, Azrael probably comes home every night like this: "Phew, what a day..."

He loosens his tie, unbuttons the top of his shirt—you can tell he has been working.

But guys... You know Israfil's job description, right?

Blow the trumpet. That is it—one task.

Now let me ask you: wasn't Israfil hired way too early?

I mean, sure, we do not know when the Day of Judgment will happen- But Allah does!

He could have hired him a month before. I am being generous here, just so he would get used to the place, go through orientation, or something.

Even the day before would have been fine! Because the job interview would have gone like this:

"Do you have any previous experience with trumpet-blowing?"

"No."

"That is fine. You are hired." I mean... they really brought the guy on board too early. (Ömer Harmankaya)

Ömer, the comedian who delivers this joke, introduces himself as someone originally from Konya, a city in Türkiye widely associated with devout and conservative social groups—but also as a graduate of Middle East Technical University[4] (commonly known in Türkiye as ODTÜ), one of the country's most prominent secular academic institutions. Ömer's joke does not stem from a position entirely detached from religion; instead, he pushes the boundaries on a topic considered highly sensitive within Islamic doctrine. In Islam, belief in angels is one of the six pillars of faith, involving the affirmation of divine beings created from light who carry out God's commands. Israfil is believed to sound the trumpet that signals the end of the world and the resurrection, while Azrael is the angel of death tasked with taking souls. In this joke, however, Ömer likens Azrael and Israfil to ordinary workers, and God to an employer—an analogy that anthropomorphizes these figures and brings them closer to human characteristics. As with the jokes involving God and human relations, Ömer's portrayal here blurs the metaphysical boundary between the earthly and the otherworldly, offering a postmodern subversion of traditional ontological hierarchies.

Throughout the performances analyzed, many jokes reflect characteristics associated with postmodern religiosity—such as flexibility, individualization, and a relative detachment from the sacred. Often raised in devout social environments, the comedians juxtapose these backgrounds with a secular, intellectual identity, creating a nuanced stance that bridges belief and cultural critique. What emerges is not merely a humorous inversion but a paradigmatic example of how the sacred is secularized in postmodern religious discourse. These representations illustrate the shifting status of religion in a time when its fixed ontological claims are increasingly dissolved and recontextualized within everyday experience, positioning humor as a key site for this transformation.

12.5 The Intersection of Religion and Humor in the Axis of Social Tensions

The growing visibility of a postmodern perception of religion within humor reflects what may be described as an "elective affinity" between this cultural development and the political and social context of Türkiye. Max Weber's concept of "elective affinities" is a key term used to describe how various social, cultural, or moral elements do not converge randomly, but instead come together through a specific inner compatibility or tendency (Swedberg, 2005). In the context of this study, an elective affinity is evident between the increasing prevalence of postmodern religious orientations that open religious topics to humor and parody, and the broader social tensions in

[4] ODTÜ holds significance precisely because it is positioned in stark contrast to the identity typically attributed to Konya. In other words, by stating in his performance that he was raised in a devout environment but graduated from a university known for its secular institutional identity, Ömer draws attention to a widely recognized social tension in Türkiye.

Türkiye, particularly those revolving around the religious-secular divide. As religious visibility in the public sphere continues to increase, this rise becomes material for politically charged humor, often approached with a postmodern recklessness.

12.5.1 Humor on a Thorny Path: The Religious-Secular Tension

As previously noted, political and cultural polarization in Türkiye has intensified in recent years. This polarization has placed cultural issues—most notably religion—at the center of social and political debates. The encounter between religious and secular lifestyles, as well as the overt or implicit conflicts between them, is widely showcased in both traditional and new media platforms. Social media does not merely disseminate these disputes passively; rather, it actively serves as a source of such conflicts and continually reproduces them (Kaya-Erdem, 2020). Humor circulating on social media occupies a similar position. On one hand, it brings underlying tensions to the surface through comedic expression; on the other, it reproduces these tensions in line with the comedians' identities and lifestyles.

Comedian Tuna Kalınsaz directly addresses this societal tension in one of his performances. He refers to it as the "conservative-secular conflict" and uses it as a central theme in his material, particularly in relation to how religious topics become subjects of humor. Tuna's joke is built around two standard greetings that reflect the opposition between religious and secular life: "Selamünaleyküm" and "Merhaba." Although both words have Arabic origins, over time the former has come to represent a religious lifestyle, while the latter has acquired associations with a secular one. These associations have led to minor tensions in everyday encounters.

> You know, I have been following this conservative–secular struggle since I was a kid.
>
> In fact, we are all following it. It is part of all our lives.
>
> Moreover, when the conservative–secular tension manifests itself in language, I find it quite amusing.
>
> Because both sides try not to use the exact words, right?
>
> Like: "Hayırlı sabahlar" vs. "Günaydın"; "Inshallah" vs. "Hopefully."
>
> What else comes to your mind?
>
> (Audience member): "Merhaba" vs. "Selamünaleyküm."
>
> Oh, that one is excellent - "Merhaba" versus "Aleyküm selam," the battle of greetings.
>
> I have seen many "Selamünaleyküm"s deflected with a "Merhaba."
>
> Moreover, just as often, I have seen "Merhaba" countered with "Aleyküm selam."
>
> There is a subtle tension in those moments.
>
> For example, when someone greets you with "Selamünaleyküm," what are they really saying?
>
> Is it "Peace be upon you"? Alternatively, is it more like: "Shall we merge religion and state affairs?"

> The same goes for the "Merhaba" camp. Like: "Merhaba, my friend. Sorry, but the only true guide in life is science."[5] Yeah… not buying it. (Tuna Kalınsaz)

Tuna's joke presents the religion-based tension in Türkiye through two key words, framing the issue as a kind of "battle." These words, "Selamünaleyküm" and "Merhaba," have come to carry symbolic meanings. In everyday language, their usage is often assumed to indicate the speaker's cultural identity and associated lifestyle. According to Tuna, saying "Selamünaleyküm" is not merely offering a religious greeting; it also signals an ideological stance that challenges secular norms, potentially suggesting a will to dismantle secular lifestyles. In contrast, replying with "Merhaba" instead of the customary "Aleyküm selam" is, in the context of the joke, interpreted as a secular counter-response—one that symbolically invokes Mustafa Kemal Atatürk's well-known maxim, "The only true guide in life is science."

Tuna's joke is significant because it extends a seemingly mundane act of greeting into a reflection on major historical and political cleavages in Türkiye. By juxtaposing Atatürk's legacy with conservative religious groups, the joke capitalizes on one of the most persistent sociopolitical divides in the country. Over the last two decades, political developments have seen religious groups become more prominent and aligned with the ruling government, while oppositional segments of society have increasingly rallied around secular principles and the symbolic figure of Atatürk. This polarization has made Atatürk a frequent subject in stand-up comedy, especially in jokes that frame the tension between secularism and religiosity. In this sense, the political divide in Türkiye has given rise to a style of humor where the religious and the political are inextricably intertwined. The following joke by Özgür Turhan, which directly engages with the relationship between religion and Atatürk, illustrates this point well. Özgür recounts an anecdote involving his aunt, a staunch supporter of the secularist CHP, who lives in İzmir.[6]

> I was four years old at the time. We were in İzmir, walking through Konak Square with my aunt.
>
> Some women in full-body black veils (çarşaf) walked past us.
>
> I had never seen anything like that before.
>
> I was just a kid, so I was curious. I asked, "Auntie, why are those women wearing that?"
>
> She turned to me with a solemn expression and said, "Because they do not believe in Atatürk." (Özgür Turhan)

Özgür's joke is also built upon a typical religion-based tension in Türkiye. According to the anecdote, his secular-minded aunt identifies the women wearing full-body coverings not as Muslims, but as opponents of Atatürk. In Türkiye, women's clothing and lifestyle practices have long been among the most contested issues

---

[5] This sentence is attributed to Atatürk, the founding figure of the Republic, and it is widely recognized as a reference to science as the foundational principle for establishing a secular way of life.

[6] İzmir is considered a symbolic city for the secular lifestyle in Türkiye. A significant portion of its electorate is known to be staunch followers of Atatürk's political principles and predominantly votes for the Republican People's Party.

within the modernization process. Whether women should wear attire reflecting an Islamic way of life or adopt Western-style clothing symbolizing a modern/secular lifestyle has often been framed as a significant political choice. As such, women's dress has become a key point of polarization in debates surrounding religion. This ongoing tension is also reflected in humor, as in this example, where religious clothing is portrayed as incompatible with Atatürk's vision of a modern Türkiye. The opposition between a religious outfit and a political figure, such as Atatürk, frequently found in many jokes, illustrates how religion is filtered through a political lens in stand-up comedy, highlighting the politicized nature of religious representation in this genre.

12.5.2 The Islamic and Secular Character of Space: Humor About Cities

One of the most visible ways religion becomes a subject of humor in stand-up performances in Türkiye is through representations of cities, which are symbolically divided according to the secular-religious binary previously discussed. While religion and religiosity are associated with specific cities, a secular lifestyle and a distanced attitude toward religion are likewise associated with other particular cities or urban spaces. Cities located in Türkiye's central regions, such as Konya, Karaman, Yozgat, and Tokat, are commonly identified with religiosity, particularly because they tend to support the ruling party in elections. In contrast, İzmir and districts like Kadıköy and Ataköy in Istanbul are portrayed as bastions of secular life.

At this point, Nebiye Arı serves as a striking example: She is not only a female comedian, but also originally from Konya, a city widely associated with conservatism and religiosity. Having spent a significant part of her life wearing the headscarf, she later decided to remove it and pursue a career in stand-up comedy. Despite identifying as a "Muslim feminist/leftist" even during her veiled years—thereby challenging common stereotypes about covered women—her transition into a comedian who occasionally makes what might be seen as offensive jokes about religion sets her apart. The following joke by Nebiye exemplifies the symbolic division between cities in Türkiye based on their cultural attitudes toward religion. In her performance, she builds her joke around İzmir and Konya, two cities that represent opposite sides of the religious-secular spectrum.

> Some people from İzmir act as if Atatürk was actually born among them.
>
> However, really, the only thing İzmir has produced that resembles Atatürk… is a man who looks like him. Still, İzmir has welcomed him, taken him in as one of their own; he is now known as an İzmir native.
>
> There is this event in Konya: the Prophet's *sakal-ı şerif* (holy beard)-some hair … something like that. Wherever it is taken, women gather in that house.
>
> Likewise, in İzmir, wherever this man who resembles Atatürk is taken, women gather at that house as well. (Nebiye Arı)

In the joke, two contrasting symbols of sanctity are juxtaposed: on one hand, the beard of the Prophet Muhammad, to which devout Muslims attribute religious reverence; on the other, a man known for his resemblance to Atatürk, who is viewed with near-sacred admiration by some secular women in Türkiye. At its core, Nebiye's joke offers a critical stance on both forms of sanctification, using Konya and İzmir as symbolic opposites to frame this dichotomy. However, in doing so, she adopts a reckless tone toward the religious ritual by referring to the Prophet's beard with dismissive terms such as "hair" or "fuzz," a move likely to be perceived as offensive by devout audiences.

Given Nebiye's personal background, however, this tone becomes more intelligible. Having once worn the headscarf and later choosing to remove it, Nebiye positions this comedic critique as a reaction to what she perceives as "religious oppression." The ritual she references takes place in a city commonly symbolized as a stronghold of conservative religiosity—thus, her joke reflects a personal and political rejection of that symbolic order through satire.

This form of critique, frequently observed in stand-up performances, resonates within the broader context of Türkiye's polarized cultural climate, especially the tension between religious and secular lifestyles. In recent years, there has been a growing concern among secular segments of society that state policies are actively promoting the Islamization of the public sphere. The increasing visibility of religious groups and rituals is often cited as evidence of this perceived shift, interpreted by many as a form of ideological imposition. In such a political atmosphere, religion becomes filtered through a lens of contention, and satire emerges as a means of symbolic resistance. All of the stand-up comedians examined in this study self-identify as politically oppositional figures, and their performances frequently frame them—and their audiences—as part of a shared front against the conservative ruling establishment. This oppositional positioning directly informs how religion is represented and critiqued in their acts.

A typical example of how cities are interpreted through their relationship with religion can be seen in a joke by Berkan Priştina, in which he assesses İzmir and Kadıköy, a district in Istanbul known for its secular identity, through their perceived distance from religious practice.

> I gave up on Friday prayers; I stuck with the easier one -holiday prayers.
>
> You know, there are no holiday prayers in İzmir, right? I figured as much.
>
> I struggle telling this joke in İzmir and Kadıköy.
>
> Every time I say Eid prayer,' someone goes, 'You mean like October 29th,[7] bro?'
>
> However, off the record, yes -these are holiday prayers.
>
> They happen twice a year. Moreover, in İzmir, apparently, no one seems to have a clue. (Berkan Priştina)

[7] The Republic of Türkiye was officially established on October 29, 1923, and this event is celebrated annually with official ceremonies. The founding of the Republic is especially embraced by secular segments of society, who regard it as a major historical turning point.

Berkan's joke makes visible through humor the phenomenon of categorizing Turkish cities according to their perceived levels of secularism and religiosity. The joke relies on existing stereotypes about places such as Kadıköy and İzmir, which are often associated with secular identities and presumed to be distant from religious knowledge and practice. By suggesting that the audience might mistake the phrase "Eid prayer" for a reference to the Republic Day celebrations on October 29, the comedian humorously highlights the presumed unfamiliarity with religious rituals in these locales. In doing so, Berkan sketches a spatial map of the religion-politics tension in Türkiye, not through a direct critique of belief, but rather by presenting secular indifference to religion as a source of comedic potential.

Within this joke, one can also discern a postmodern stance toward religion that complements the political symbolism of the spatial-religious divide. By referencing his past religious practices while simultaneously turning religion into a comedic resource, Berkan positions himself in a space that is neither entirely secular nor wholly devout. This is where Weber's notion of "elective affinities," introduced earlier, becomes especially relevant. The postmodern religious subject selectively draws from past religious identity while reinterpreting religion through a lens shaped by contemporary political tensions. In this way, the political and social context of Türkiye, as well as the postmodern religiosity observable in stand-up performances, appear as mutually reinforcing and converging dynamics.

12.6 Conclusion

This study has examined the recent rise of stand-up comedy in Türkiye through the lens of its engagement with religion and religiosity, focusing on both the transformation of individual belief systems and the broader context of social polarization. Two key themes have emerged from the analysis. First, the postmodern cultural transformation has created a context in which religious symbols are individualized, reinterpreted, and consequently rendered suitable as material for humor. Second, the growing secular-religious divide in Türkiye's sociopolitical landscape has a significant influence on both the content and form of stand-up performances.

The comedians analyzed in this study generally approach religious figures, rituals, and belief systems not through outright attacks or systematic critiques, but rather through an ambiguous, hybrid, and distanced comedic discourse. This reflects the selective and flexible form of religiosity that characterizes the postmodern era. Most of the comedians examined do not present themselves as entirely disconnected from or absolutely committed to religion. As Grace Davie (1990) puts it, their stance could be described as "believing without belonging."

Furthermore, the humor in stand-up shows goes beyond personal narrative to encompass collective representations shaped by spatial and cultural codes. The frequent references to cities and districts, such as Konya, İzmir, and Kadıköy, used symbolically in relation to religious or secular identities, illustrate how cultural boundaries between religiosity and secularism are spatially mapped in contemporary Türkiye.

Islam retains its public character in Türkiye. As José Casanova (2014) notes, Islam has been a "unique example" among public religions since its inception. In practice, it appears increasingly unlikely for it to be confined to the private realm of individual conscience. While the benefits that devout individuals derive from the public power of religion could be the subject of a separate study, it is clear that religion continues to serve as a strong resource for public actors in Türkiye, informing their decisions in decision-making processes.

Building on this reality, Jürgen Habermas argues that the healthy functioning of the public sphere requires religious claims and perspectives not to be excluded from public discourse; on the contrary, their inclusion offers potential benefits for society as a whole (Habermas, 2016). His concept of the "post-secular society" is grounded in the idea that "religious communities are increasingly assuming the role of interpretive communities in the public arenas of secular societies" (Habermas, 2008, p. 20). With the advent of digital platforms, the visibility of religion has intensified (Karaarslan, 2015), not only enabling religious views and demands to enter public discourse more actively but also exposing them to critique— and at times, to humor.

In Türkiye's highly polarized political atmosphere, the views, demands, rituals, and practices of religious groups or individuals have become more visible than ever, primarily through social media. However, this same visibility has also invited a variety of responses, ranging from critical engagement to satirical representation. Humor is just one of these forms of response.

In conclusion, stand-up comedy in Türkiye is situated at the intersection of post-modern religiosity and political polarization. The transformation of religion into a subject of humor reflects not only the repositioning of the sacred in postmodern societies but also serves as a critical commentary on the politicized nature of religion in the Turkish context. As religion becomes increasingly visible through a political filter in the public sphere, the line between political satire and religious humor begins to blur. As a result, politically offensive humor can turn into religiously offensive comedy, generating narratives that challenge and often transgress traditional boundaries surrounding religion.

References

Anderson, P. S. (2012). Postmodernism and religion. In S. Sim (Ed.), *The Routledge Companion to Postmodernism* (3rd ed., pp. 73–85). Routledge. https://doi.org/10.4324/9780203813201-9

Baran, Z. (2008). Turkey divided. *Journal of Democracy*. Retrieved May 7, 2025, from https://www.journalofdemocracy.org/articles/turkey-divided/

Başkan, F. (2010). Religious versus secular groups in the age of globalization in Turkey. *Totalitarian Movements and Political Religions, 11*(2), 167–183. https://doi.org/10.1080/14690764.2010.511458

Bauman, Z. (2008). *Postmodern ethics*. Blackwell.

Braun, V., & Clark, V. (2019). Psikolojide tematik analizin kullanımı (N. Özer, & A. Atli, Trans.). *Eğitimde Nitel Araştırmalar Dergisi, 7*(2), 873–898. https://dergipark.org.tr/tr/pub/enad/issue/45025/561459
Brown, W. (2015). Undoing the demos: Neoliberalism's stealth revolution. *Zone Books*. https://doi.org/10.2307/j.ctt17kk9p8
Casanova, J. L. (2014). *Modern dünyada kamusal dinler* (M. M. Şahin, Trans.). Sakarya Üniversitesi Yayınları.
Çolak, Y. (2017). *Türkiye'de kültürel iktidarın kuruluşu 1923–1945*. Liberte Yayınları.
Crocket, C. (2003). Post-modernism and its secrets: Religion without religion. *Cross Currents, 52*(4), 499–515. https://www.jstor.org/stable/24460636
Davie, G. (1990). Believing without belonging: Is this the future of religion in Britain? *Social Compass, 37*(4), 455–469. https://doi.org/10.1177/003776890037004004
Davutoğlu, A. (1994). *Alternative paradigms: The impact of Islamic and Western Weltanschauungs on political theory*. University Press of America.
Dereli, M. D. (2019). Dinî kimliklerin siber uzamda akışkanlaşması. *İnsan ve Toplum, 9*(1), 85–116. https://doi.org/10.12658/M0301
Dereli, M. D. (2022). *Sanala veda: Sosyal medya ve dönüşen dindarlık*. Albaraka Yayınları.
Erdoğan, E., & Uyan-Semerci, P. (2018). *Fanusta diyaloglar: Türkiye'de kutuplaşmanın boyutları*. Istanbul Bilgi Üniversitesi Yayınları.
Erdoğan, E., & Uyan-Semerci, P. (2022). Kutuplaşmayı nasıl aşarız? *Turkuazlab*. Retrieved May 10, 2025, from https://www.turkuazlab.org/yayinlar/
Ertit, V. (2023). *Endişeli muhafazakarlar çağı: Dinden uzaklaşan Türkiye* (8th ed.). Orient Yayınları.
Gök, D. (2021). Stand-up'çı Emre Günsal'a hapis cezası: "20 dakika için 3 yıl 5 ay." *Onedio*. Retrieved April 3, 2025, from https://onedio.com/haber/stand-up-ci-emre-gunsal-a-hapis-cezasi-20-dakika-stand-up-icin-3-yil-5-ay-957343
Guest, M. (2023). *Neoliberal din: 21. yüzyılda inanç ve güç* (M. Pekdemir, Trans.). Fol Kitap.
Gürler, G. (2020). Ofansif mizah, toplumsal eşitsizlikler ve politik doğruculuk: Stand-Up komedileri üzerine eleştirel bir analiz. *İlef Dergisi, 7*(1), 137–166. https://doi.org/10.24955/ilef.736032
Habermas, J. (2008). Notes on post-secular society. *New Perspectives Quarterly, 25*(4), 17–29. https://doi.org/10.1111/j.1540-5842.2008.01017.x
Habermas, J. (2016). Kamusal alanda din (M. A. Kirman, Trans.). *Şırnak Üniversitesi İlahiyat Fakültesi Dergisi, 7*(14), 183–206. https://dergipark.org.tr/tr/pub/sirnakifd/issue/34156/384871
Haenni, P. (2014). *Piyasa İslamı: İslam surentinde neoliberalizm* (L. Ünsaldı, Trans.). Heretik Yayıncılık.
Harvey, D. (2005). *A brief history of neoliberalism*. Oxford University Press. https://doi.org/10.1093/oso/9780199283262.001.0001
Kalaycıoğlu, E. (2012). Kulturkampf in Turkey: The constitutional referendum of 12 September 2010. *South European Society and Politics, 17*(1), 1–22. https://doi.org/10.1080/13608746.2011.600555
Karaarslan, F. (2015). Postseküler din halleri ve dinin dijitalleşmesi. In M. Çamdereli, B. Önay-Doğan, & N. Kocabay-Şener (Eds.), *Dijitalleşen Din (Medya ve Din 2)* (pp. 13–44). Köprü Kitapları.
Kaya-Erdem, B. (2020). Yeni medyada homo ridensin saldirgan yükselişi: Ofansif mizah ve ötekileştirici temsiller. *Social Sciences Studies Journal, 6*(75), 5537–5549. https://doi.org/10.26449/sssj.2917
Kepel, G. (1994). *The revenge of God: The resurgence of Islam, Christianity, and Judaism in the modern world*. Polity.
KONDA. (2008). Biz kimiz: Hayat tarzları araştırması. *KONDA*. Retrieved April 3, 2025, from https://konda.com.tr/rapor/165/biz-kimiz-hayat-tarzlari-arastirmasi-2008
Lindekilde, L., Mouritsen, P., & Zapata-Barrero, R. (2009). The Muhammad cartoons controversy in comparative perspective. *Ethnicities, 9*(3), 291–313. https://doi.org/10.1177/1468796809337434

Lyotard, J.-F. (2010). *The postmodern condition: A report on knowledge.* University of Minnesota Press.

Önder, N. (2022). *Türkiye'nin mizah anlayışı değişti! Marketing Türkiye.* Retrieved March 12, 2025, from https://www.marketingturkiye.com.tr/haberler/turkiyenin-mizah-anlayisi-degisiyor/

Somer, M. (2007). Moderate Islam and secularist opposition in Turkey: Implications for the world, Muslims and secular democracy. *Third World Quarterly, 28*(7), 1271–1289. https://doi.org/10.1080/01436590701604888

Swedberg, R. (2005). *The Max Weber dictionary.* Stanford University Press.

Tekin, M. (2023). Postmodern dinsellikler. *UMDE Dini Tetkikler Dergisi, 6*(2), 241–260. https://doi.org/10.54122/umde.1379969

Chapter 13
Remembrance and Mourning Rituals in Digital Cemeteries

Gülsen Çankal

13.1 Introduction

The digital age has profoundly impacted all areas of life, significantly altering daily routines and causing numerous social consequences. While these effects are observed in a wide range of areas, from the economy to politics, education to communication, the world of meaning regarding death and its aftermath has also been impacted by these changes. As a matter of fact, after the death of individuals who exist on social media platforms with their digital identities, their presence in the digital space continues in some way. Especially on platforms such as Instagram and Facebook, the profiles that individuals create about their identities continue to exist after their deaths and somehow become the subject of digital rituals. Therefore, the online profiles of the deceased are digital entities that persist even after biological death. In this context, it will be inevitable that the online presence of the deceased will surpass that of the living of the time. Accordingly, the subject of this study is to examine the appearance of posthumous commemoration and mourning rituals in the digital world.

These profiles, conceptualized as digital cemeteries,[1] are created as a result of the social media platforms used by individuals during their lifetime being visited by other individuals after their death. In this respect, digital cemeteries are the digital

[1] While the notion of digital cemeteries emphasizes the transformation of traditional burial and mourning practices into digital environments, it partially overlaps with concepts such as digital memorials and virtual gravespaces. However, unlike digital memorials, which often focus on commemorative expressions and online tributes, digital cemeteries underline the spatial and communal aspects of mourning in cyberspace. Similarly, the term differs from virtual gravespaces by highlighting the continuity of social interactions with the deceased rather than static digital representation.

G. Çankal (✉)
Department of Sociology, Bartın University, Bartın, Türkiye
e-mail: gcankal@bartin.edu.tr

M. D. Dereli and M. Eken (eds.), *Turkish Perspectives on Secularization and Media*,
https://doi.org/10.1007/978-3-032-16436-0_13

equivalent of traditional cemeteries, which can be accessed over the internet and allow deceased individuals to be remembered. According to Dilmaç (2016), this remembrance is provided through simulations on online platforms. Instead of disappearing completely in the traditional sense with death, individuals are perceived as a constant presence in the online environment and become extremely visible. Due to this hyper-presence enabled by internet technology, death and mourning practices have also gone beyond physical boundaries. Interacting with the dead has created new ways of keeping their memory alive and transformed the processes of commemorating, remembering and honoring the dead through the possibilities offered by the internet.

Social media platforms support the digital culture of remembrance by enabling constant communication and interaction between the living and the dead, and enable the digitization of memorial practices. The profiles of the deceased, which first start to receive a large number of visitors after the announcement of the death, then host various commemorative events. Posting emotional messages about deceased users, sharing photos, and remembering them on the anniversaries of their deaths and births is an aspect of this commemoration activity that has been transferred to digital environments, and it is almost impossible to draw the boundaries of this practice within the possibilities of digital environments. In this framework, with the development of communication technologies, death and mourning practices have evolved and transformed. Within the possibilities provided by the Internet, it facilitates the perpetuation of the memories of the deceased and the transfer of their legacy to future generations. In this context, death is no longer just an end but has become part of an ongoing process of interaction and communication. In fact, the memories experienced during life are linked to the existence of the individual. Therefore, when life comes to an end, there will be no more new experiences, so memories will also come to an end (Foer, 2015, p. 26). However, the remnants of memories collected on digital memory are transformed back into a digital life reality even after the death of individuals. In this process where digital immortality gains meaning with the past, the fact that the past is hidden and that it accumulates and forms a pile of memories provides basic data for digital immortalization. After death, digital life shows continuity by holding on to these memories (Molo, 2021, p. 93). In this study, in order to explore the rituals of remembrance and mourning in digital cemeteries, the netnography method was used to analyze social media users who visit and comment on the social media profiles of deceased people on platforms such as Instagram and Facebook. Thus, examining the role of the secularization process in the digitalization of post-mortem rituals, together with the results obtained, offers an important perspective to the literature on the effects of digitalization on social and cultural practices. While prior studies have examined digital mourning practices, this study contributes to the literature by conceptualizing 'digital cemeteries' as a new form of posthumous commemoration and by providing a netnographic analysis of user interactions, highlighting how social, emotional, and ritual functions are performed in digital spaces.

13.2 Secularization and Death

The digital age has profoundly impacted all areas of life, significantly altering daily routines and causing numerous social consequences. While these effects are observed in a wide range of areas, from the economy to politics, education to communication, the world of meaning regarding death and its aftermath has also been impacted by these changes. As a matter of fact, after the death of individuals who exist on social media platforms with their digital identities, their presence in the digital space continues in some way. Especially on platforms such as Instagram and Facebook, the profiles that individuals create about their identities continue to exist after their deaths and somehow become the subject of digital rituals. Therefore, the online profiles of the deceased are digital entities that persist even after biological death. In this context, it will be inevitable that the online presence of the deceased will surpass that of the living of the time. Accordingly, the subject of this study is to examine the appearance of posthumous commemoration and mourning rituals in the digital world.

The process of secularization has also changed the perception of death and rituals related to death, and has distanced them from traditional religious understandings. Rational elements such as science and technology won great victories in the fight against deadly threats such as disease and epidemics, and in this case science replaced religion and acquired a mythic content (Allan, 2020, p. 50). Seventeenth century medical technology provided assessments on the timing of death and whether the treatment process would be successful or not, putting death, which had previously been determined by a divine power at a specific time and situation, under human control. In this period, death was mostly attributed to older age groups and accepted as a natural process (Illich, 2004, p. 107). Modernism found every death other than the one it accepted as natural death intriguing. Modernism wanted to understand the cause of death that did not occur within the boundaries it set and to follow the disease process leading to death. Therefore, in the eighteenth century, diseases became more important than patients. However, by the nineteenth century, the concept of a disease separate from the body disappeared from visibility. The modern medical perspective placed the disease in the patient's body. The medical authority, which had previously investigated the what, now centered on the how. According to this new clinical perspective, the disease continues to exist in the body by showing symptoms. The idea that the disease exists in the body has led to the study of the human body in parts, revealing the how and objectifying the body (Allan, 2020, pp. 228–229). This has resulted in the perception of a living being with a soul in the past being perceived as a machine in the modern western world.

This course of medical developments has encouraged people to fight against death. However, modern Western culture has made efforts to discredit death or remove it from thoughts, since it has not achieved a complete victory over death (Becker, 2015). One of the strategies developed by the modern period to defeat death was to act with a progressive understanding of history and to create a belief that even if death is not defeated today, it will be defeated tomorrow (Hökelekli, 2008, p. 44).

Another strategy developed by the modern period was shaped through discourses on death. The discourses on death have turned into a war of struggle in which all interventions are made but without success. Moreover, the acceptance of death and death processes as a displeasing phenomenon in the modern period is a result of this strategy (Baudrillard, 2002, pp. 330–331). At a certain point, the phenomenon of death, which Ariès (1991) domesticated in the pre-modern period, has been thrown out of the house in the modern period. Modernity was defeated in its struggle against death and found even the mention of death disturbing. It has also tried to achieve a mental success against death by characterizing death in the minds as something ugly, dirty, bad and shameful (Ariès, 1991; Bauman, 2000).

For modernity, which used to regard death as a purely physical phenomenon, death is now considered a biological or medical phenomenon. Therefore, by dividing death into small parts, modernity has made it difficult to determine which stage is a real death. In Illich's words, in medical death, which excludes beliefs and ignores spiritual and moral dimensions, a person no longer breathes his last breath or dies because his heart stops, but dies when the electroencephalogram draws a straight line (Illich, 2004, pp. 119–120). This situation has led to a change in the meaning attributed to space. In the process, instead of individuals going to the hospital for treatment, there has been a change where they have to go to the hospital to die (Ariès, 1991). Therefore, the perception of death as a biological and even technical reality in the modern period led to the transfer of places of death from homes to hospitals. A similar change is also related to the processes that take place upon the death of another. Encountering the death of another requires first of all a confrontation with medical authority and bureaucracy. In order for the process of death to gain validity, the necessary rationalist explanations must be provided; otherwise, in order to obtain these explanations, the body must be subjected to certain research processes in autopsy laboratories. Therefore, in the modern period, death and life have been taken away from the individual and controlled to the extent determined by social permissions and bureaucracy (Baudrillard, 2002, pp. 315–316). With the acceptance of the right to die as a right in the last twenty years, Western societies have reconsidered the issue of death and led to the discussion of the individual's right to die (Onur, 2004, p. 367). In this context, in places such as the Netherlands, Belgium, Luxembourg, Germany, Canada, Washington, Oregon and Montana, the right to die has been presented as a social service policy within the framework of certain rules and kept under the control of the bureaucracy.

13.3 Digital Graveyards of Social Media

The concept of social media refers to the social aspects of online applications (Constantinides & Fountain, 2008, p. 232). Social media are the activities, practices and behaviors among communities of people who come together online to share information, knowledge and ideas in mutual interaction (Safko & Brake, 2009, p. 6). A social person is one who adapts to the requirements of the environment in which he/she is open to communication with another. The most fundamental effect that gives dynamism to this concept is communication. In this respect, social media is a communication tool that allows people to share their lives, thoughts and experiences with other(s) regardless of time and place.

The society in the digitalized world is a society characterized by the widespread use of digital technologies such as social media. As Martin (2008) points out, the people who produce the knowledge and digital technologies that lead to digitalization form an important part of the digital society. Therefore, when defining the concept of digital society, it is important to focus on the social effects and interactions of social media. In this context, the concept of social media emerges as one of the main characteristics of a digitalized society. Social media platforms have radically changed the way individuals communicate, exchange information, interact and maintain social relations. As people interact both individually and socially through social media, these platforms significantly affect the dynamics of society. In this context, social media is considered as an important indicator and driver of social changes and transformations in the digitalized world.

Unlike traditional media tools, social media requires a receiver to organize and interpret the message. The individual is not a passive recipient of the message, but an active user who organizes, interprets and objects to it (Lester, 2012, p. 118). Indeed, being an active user in social media has certain requirements. According to Lietsala and Sirkkunen (2008), these requirements are content creation, sharing, interaction, and the existence of profile accounts that enable all these to be done. In their social media accounts, individuals can display identifying characteristics such as profile photo, date of birth, age, gender, country, etc. In addition, they are involved in the process of content production with thoughts, experiences and information on what they like or dislike and share them with other users. Sharing is the communication mechanism through which human-system-human interaction is established, which brings along the processes of liking, commenting or re-sharing the content produced for how they want to define themselves.

This active participation in social media also extends to how individuals encounter and engage with topics such as death, transforming the way death is experienced and represented compared to traditional media. In traditional media, death is presented not as a reality but as a spectacle, and the individual who is satisfied with the death images presented is left alone with death, which eventually loses its meaning (Baudrillard, 2002). In the process of transition from traditional media to new media, death, which is presented to individuals in a packaged form, has been replaced by an environment where individuals can choose and interact with the content related to death according to their own preferences. In other words, the individual can now control news, images and comments about death more effectively. The death of social media users has led to the existence of "dead profiles" in the digital world and has triggered a debate on whether social media accounts can be inherited. This situation has raised important questions about the future of individuals online assets by addressing the legal, ethical and social dimensions of digital inheritance (Yılmaz & Erken, 2020). Even after the death of individuals who were alive on social media platforms, these accounts continued to exist in the online world and provided a kind of continuity by allowing other individuals to access these accounts. This situation, which has evolved through human, process and technology adaptation, has not only profoundly changed human-system interaction, but has also affected interpersonal interaction, stretching the concepts of space and time and fundamentally changing human perception. The transformation of the material foundations of time and space has strengthened the emergence of a culture of virtuality (Castells, 2008, p. 501). Now, the social media accounts left behind by individuals have turned into a kind of digital cemetery where visitors are welcomed on birthdays, death days and important moments (Çankal, 2022).

Platforms such as Facebook, MySpace, Virtual Eternity, Instagram and MyDeathSpace are some of the websites that make it possible to interact with deceased individuals. These platforms revitalize the profiles of deceased users together with the interactions of other individuals, thus digitally engaging them in processes of remembrance and commemoration. In this context, digital platforms such as social networking sites are becoming important sites in the culture of digital remembrance, as they allow users to maintain their presence after death, making them part of the practices of remembrance and commemoration (Church, 2013, p. 184). According to the We Are Social Digital 2023 Report, by 2023 there are 4.76 billion social media users worldwide, which is approximately 60% of the global population. In addition, Facebook ranks the highest among social media platforms. In addition, Facebook remains the most widely used social media platform, followed by other major platforms such as YouTube, WhatsApp, Instagram, WeChat, TikTok, Telegram, Twitter, and Pinterest. These platforms differ in terms of user base and engagement, yet all contribute to the formation and maintenance of digital memorial spaces. The expression we conceptualize as digital cemeteries is that the digital assets left behind by individuals active on social media platforms after their deaths focus on the continued interaction of other people.

In the first research on death profiles, Scott Church (2013) in his article "Digital Gravescapes: Digital Memorializing on Facebook", Scott Church (2013) examines the processes of remembering, grieving, and memorializing a deceased Facebook user's account, the spread of the news of the death, and the subsequent remembering, grieving, and memorializing processes of friends, family members, and other users. The research begins with a case study analysis of the unexpected death of a user named Clarissa. It examines how the posts and interactions on Clarissa's Facebook account functioned as a digital cemetery. In the aftermath of the death, it analyzes in detail how users remember Clarissa, their emotional reactions and posts. This analysis reveals how digital identity is preserved and remembered even after death. Church's research thus makes an important contribution to understanding the impact of social media platforms on personal and collective memory and how posthumous digital memorialization rituals function. Çankal (2022), in his research on death profiles and digital commemoration rituals on Instagram, examined how users' digital legacies are shaped and how their digital assets are perceived after death. The research emphasized that accounts that do not have any restrictions on access to other users' profiles while they are alive, especially the causes of death reflected in the media, attract more visitors. Çankal's (2022) study examined the effects of the life constructed in the digital world and especially the association of women's beauty with death. The study concluded that the idealization of the life presented on social media platforms or the inability to associate women's beauty with death creates a perception that makes it difficult to accept death. The perception of individuals as if they are not dead has created the feeling of an ongoing existence in the digital world. In conclusion, Çankal's (2022) research on Instagram has made an important contribution to the blurring of the boundaries between life and death on digital platforms and how simulations affect the perception of reality. Indeed, the characteristic feature of the simulative order is that what is real is not the truth, but illusion and visual images. Such a situation reveals that the digital world has an effect that questions the perception of reality and metaphysical values (Dağ, 2020, p. 41).

As a matter of fact, every society transfers rituals about death to digital by relying on its own cultural accumulation and mobilizing its cultural elements. However, it is also important to consider the relationship between digital rituals and secularization. Traditionally performed in religious and cultural contexts, death rituals tend to secularize in the process of digitalization. That is, digital rituals can break away from traditional, religious or cultural contexts and take on a more general, universal structure. However, digital rituals also deepen the secularization process. Because death rituals performed on digital platforms move away from the influence of religious or traditional structures and turn into a more individual, subjective experience. This is an indication of the change in social and cultural norms on death, the impact of the secularization process and the social dynamics of digitalization. At this point, understanding how digital rituals relate to secularization offers an important perspective for understanding social transformation and cultural change.

13.4 Methodology

The subject of the research is the appearance of posthumous commemoration and mourning rituals in the digital world. The digitalization process transforms many aspects of life and causes changes. One of these changes is seen in death rituals. Traditionally performed in religious or cultural contexts, death rituals tend to secularize with the digitalization process. The aim of the research is to reveal how death rituals performed on digital platforms differ from traditional religious or cultural contexts and how they transform into individual experiences. Thus, the research will make an important contribution to the literature on the role of the secularization process in the digitalization of post-mortem rituals and the effects of digitalization on social and cultural practices. Netnography method was preferred in order to understand the appearance of these commemoration and mourning rituals in the digital world. Indeed, considering that channels such as Instagram and Facebook are important tools that individuals use to construct their digital identities, the digitalization of post-mortem rituals takes place prominently on these platforms. By 2100, it is estimated that the number of Facebook's dead users will exceed the number of living users (Öhman & Watson, 2019), and for Instgram, which hosts 2 billion users, the overwhelming majority of the number of living and deceased users will be for dead profiles, if not in 2100, then in the next century. However, the social media profiles of deceased individuals continue to exist even after their deaths and are the subject of some kind of digital rituals. In this context, the focus of the research is to examine the appearance of posthumous commemoration and mourning rituals in the digital world with the netnography method. Netnography offers the opportunity to observe and analyze real-time interactions on social media platforms (Kozinets, 1999). According to Kozinets (Kozinets, 2010), netnography treats online communication not only contextually, but also as social interaction, embedded expression of meaning, and cultural construction. Therefore, tracking the behavior of users who visit and interact with the social media profiles of deceased individuals on platforms such as Instagram and Facebook helps to develop a detailed understanding of the digitalization of post-mortem rituals. In this way, the research aims to understand the role of the secularization process in the digitalization of post-mortem rituals and to make a significant contribution to the literature on the effects of digitalization on social and cultural practices.

Considering that it may be ethically objectionable to examine such profiles without the permission of the families of the profile owners, the profiles of the dead to be analyzed were predetermined before starting the study. In determining the profiles, a distinction was made between accounts that could be accessed without being on the friends list and accounts that could not be accessed. No permission was requested from any family member on accounts that could be accessed without being included in the friends list, but permissions were requested from the relevant family members for accounts with restricted access. In the analyses, observations were made based on the available data and any textual findings related to the posthumous commemoration and mourning ritual were included in the research. In addition, as part of the research, a semi-structured interview form was applied with 10 people. The interviews were conducted in settings requested by the participants and each interview lasted 45–50 min on average. Participants were asked about their experiences of post-mortem memorialization and mourning rituals and their observations on digital platforms. These interviews, combined with netnographic analysis, aimed to gain an in-depth understanding of the digitalization of post-mortem rituals and the impact of social media use on these rituals (Table 13.1).

In the research process, firstly, it was determined whether individuals had social media accounts, and then the presence of profiles of a deceased person on these platforms was determined. As a result of the analyses, it was discovered that there were more women among those who interacted with the dead, and this increased the proportion of women among the participants. When the age distribution is analyzed, the ages of the participants vary between 19 and 67. While the youngest participant is 19 years old, the oldest participant is 67 years old. Education levels vary. The participants with postgraduate education level are P1, P2 and P5. The participants with undergraduate education are K6, K8 and K9; the only participant with associate's degree is K10 and the other participants have high school education. When the occupational distribution is analyzed, it is observed that the participants belong to various occupational groups. The participants who are students are P1 and P9.

Table 13.1 Socio-demographic features of the interviewees

Code	Gender	Age	Education	Occupation
K1	Female	30	Postgraduate	Student
K2	Male	35	Postgraduate	Private Sector
K3	Male	66	High School	Retired
K4	Female	67	High School	Retired
K5	Female	32	Bachelor's	Teacher
K6	Female	31	Bachelor's	Not Working
K7	Female	43	High School	Not Working
K8	Female	29	Bachelor's	Not Working
K9	Female	19	Bachelor's	Student
K10	Male	34	Associate's	Private Sector

Participants working in the private sector are P2 and P10. The participants who are retired are P3 and P4. The other participants are not working.

13.5 Findings

13.5.1 Social Aspects of Death Profiles

As a result of the research, some functions have emerged with the death of social media users and the leaving behind of their accounts. Participants generally stated that these accounts are useful for remembering the deceased. Fewer participants emphasized the necessity of visiting deceased profiles on social media in order to be accepted in digital culture. However, fewer participants emphasized that remembering the deceased has a role not only for the deceased but also for the relatives of the deceased, such as making them happy and solidarity. Other participants state that they receive the message "live life, be happy" through these profiles.

> I think it's nice to keep the past alive, so look at the old ones, who remembers the deceased or who shares something like talking to him. Then it is always forgotten. For example, there are gravestones in cemeteries where no one prays. The inscriptions are in the old language, so the name is not clear, the rest is not clear, but that is not here. (P10)

> It makes me happy to see that people do not forget. I read who remembers and how they remember. It is as if people are actually troubling, that is, it pleases me that they express with their messages that they do not forget and do not forget. In this way, it is not forgotten and always remembered. For example, sometimes they tag and share old pictures taken with her, so if there is a picture of her that I have not seen before, I see it. (P4)

> For example, there are very few pictures of people who died in the past, there are one or two pictures and they are constantly looked at. For example, great-grandfathers are known by name and surname, who they are, what they are, what kind of life they had is not known. They die themselves and the information about them is limited to their children who know

> them. But the information about someone who is active on social media is no longer limited to people who know him very closely. For example, even a hundred years after I die, my grandchildren who have never seen me will be able to access all the information about me as long as the internet exists. (P5)

> I think it is beneficial in terms of not being forgotten. I mean, it is not possible to forget. For example, people have difficulty in remembering the faces of the dead, but this way you do not forget their faces. It feels as if he has never died and will continue to share. (P8)

Participants think that dead profiles on social media serve the function of keeping memories of the past alive and remembering the forgotten ones. In particular, the participants state that the deceased, who are traditionally forgotten, can be remembered more by having a profile on social media. This prevents people from being forgotten and keeps their memories alive, and the profiles of the dead fulfill people's desire to remember and commemorate after death. In addition, the participants stated that the dead profiles on social media function like an abstract tombstone and give people the opportunity to communicate with them and share their memories as well as reminding them of the deceased.

> I often read what other people write after death, as if it was written for themselves and not for the deceased. Writing there does not help the deceased, but no one prays either. The meaning of expressions such as "God have mercy" does not seem real to me there. It feels as if they are saying, "I am writing my condolences too, look, don't forget. So it feels like a show against others. Therefore, it feels a bit like a show to me. (P2)

> I shared the news of his death both on my own wall with his picture and I tagged my friend. Because there was the thought that he was murdered and if this was true, I wanted to create interaction so that the perpetrator would be prosecuted. Not only me but many people did this. But now I do not make any posts. (P5)

Another function of death profiles is for the continuation of the culture created by the digital space. Based on the statements of the participants, it is seen that death profiles have become a ritual for people in the digital environment and commenting on the deceased is accepted as a necessity of the digital. According to the statements of P2, the comments and shares made to the deceased on social media actually aim to adapt to social norms in the digital environment. Similarly, as P5 stated, another function of the dead profiles is to adapt to people in the digital environment and to participate in digital interactions.

> It's always clear who he is here, what he likes and what he does. His face smiles, for example, in his pictures. There are no bad memories, you don't remember them badly, they are always happy, always smiling, always cheerful. That's why you always imagine them happy after they die, so I think it is a good situation for the rest. (P10)

> So a family member reads what I have written and says, you know, his friends haven't forgotten. They will be happy. At least someone from his family will be happy to see that I haven't forgotten. Even if I'm no use to her, I'll be useful to someone who is alive. I mean, I would be happy too, I would think that my daughter has not been forgotten, there are still people who love her and think about her. (P6)

Profiles of the deceased provide comfort to the survivors. Comments and posts on social media provide a form of consolation to the family or relatives of the deceased, as they show that the deceased is not forgotten and is still loved. Based on the participants statements, it generates a perception that the profiles of the deceased often reflect positive memories and happy moments, thus helping to ensure that the deceased is always remembered in a happy and joyful way.

For bereaved people, death profiles are important for empathy, solidarity, strength and inspiration. Bereaved individuals empathize by observing how others cope with similar losses through death profiles, enabling them to better cope with their own losses. For people who visit death profiles and see other people's life struggles, seeing the processes of coping with the difficulties exhibited by others in the digital space inspires them to overcome the grief process. Therefore, death profiles are actually a source for understanding the social and cultural dimensions of the process of loss and grief. The content in these profiles reflects society's norms, rituals and emotional reactions to death and grief.

> I lost my mother at a very young age, then I lost my brother from the same disease, and now I am struggling to save my brother and my wife from the grip of this disease. I am afraid of losing my relatives, but seeing other people who have lost their relatives gives me a little strength. I mean, I am curious about the lives of people who have lost their son, lost their daughter, lost their mother. I mean, I wonder how they recover, what they are doing, and seeing them somehow gives me strength. Because yes, there are people with loss, I like to see them recovering. I mean, seeing how they recovered, what they did, how they eat, drink and where they go makes me think that there is life after death. (P7)

The last function, which refers to the social aspect of death profiles, is to enable individuals to focus on life by thinking about death:

> I mean, it depends on how you follow it, actually. I mean, if you look and think about him, it's a good thing if you think about him, but if you don't learn from his death, it's a problem. So we will die, we will all die one day, and you see how empty this world is. No matter how long you live, you will die one day. You need to learn this lesson, you need to live life well. The internet actually shows this. So live, do what you want, but it gives the message that you will die one day. If you are going to die one day, it is not worth hurting. It gives the message that we should be happy and make people happy. (P7)

Profiles of the dead fulfil an important social function by reminding people of the transience of life and the inevitability of death. These profiles convey the message that people should evaluate their lives, be happy and make the people around them happy. In this respect, profiles of the dead serve as a warning to people that they should appreciate what is precious, live their lives to the fullest and have positive interactions.

13.5.2 Key Motivations Behind Visits to Profiles of the Dead

It is seen that curiosity is the main factor behind the motivation for individuals to visit death profiles. Seeing the lives of the deceased in relation to their relatives and how the living remember them are among the factors that fuel curiosity the most. This situation often arises primarily through the comment culture. In addition, the role of associations has as much importance as curiosity among the reasons for visiting the deceased profiles for the participants. For participants, events, people, or situations that remind them of the deceased person cause them to visit the deceased's profile. For fewer participants, remembering is not based on any associations or curiosity, but rather on the fact that notifications through platforms such as Facebook are a reminder tool. Again, fewer participants stated that they visit these profiles because of the news of death in traditional media. These statements reflect the diversity of motivations and reasons for visiting death profiles. In general, factors such as curiosity, associations, and notifications influence people's tendency to visit death profiles.

> I could not find anything for him. I went to his relatives and then to his father. His father put a picture up, and I looked at the date on the picture. I look to see if there are any recent posts, if people have shared anything, who still remembers, who is still sad, whose mourning process continues, or who has forgotten. I am just looking at that moment and reading the comments. I mean, I do not actually think of an act of prayer, I am just curious, I read the comments because I am curious. (P1)

> I just wonder if someone has written something. Sometimes I go down to old pictures. I like to read what is written. I like to read who wrote what and how they expressed their pain. (P5)

> I have not lost anyone close to me, but if I hear about it on the news, I wonder about the life of the deceased. If they are a martyr, for example, I wonder about their family, spouse, or lover, and I also wonder about their lives. I immediately look them up on Facebook or Instagram to learn about their lives. I look at them, but I think I am most interested in looking at their relatives and seeing their pain through their eyes. (P9)

Curiosity in participant responses is a key factor in determining people's motivation to visit the profiles of deceased individuals. In fact, curiosity carries the desire to know the unknown. For people who act to know the unknown and discover what is different, death continues to preserve all its mystery. In fact, although the existence of profiles left behind by the deceased on social media still allows for some form of interaction, the direction of this interaction is one-way. With the desire to understand the lives of the deceased in relation to their relatives and how the living remember them, the participants act with a need to read the comments and posts written on the deceased's profile. For visitors to the deceased's profile, the articles, photographs, and other content shared on the profile arouse curiosity because they are related to death.

> We have mutual friends on the internet. There was a girl he liked in primary school, and she was my friend. When I saw her on Instagram, I thought of my friend who died, and then I wanted to look at her profile. (P1)

For example, if our team wins, let us say we won, I even log in to say, "We won, brother" (P10).

> A friend of mine from university was murdered. Now, for example, when I see a very close friend of his on Instagram, I think of my friend who died, and that is why I especially look at his profile. Everyone got married, had a job, and had children, but he could not experience any of these processes. What would he have shared if he had lived? I enter his profile, and that is how I see that time has frozen for him. For example, his last picture is full of everyone's comments, but the dates are from ancient times. For me, as I said, when I see something that will remind me of her, I enter it especially, otherwise I do not think about her. (P5)

> For example, if someone died or I received such news, I think of my friends or acquaintances who died and I enter their accounts. (P6)

> As my husband's illness progresses, I do not know if I think about it or I think about it when I see pictures of people who have lost their lives. Sometimes I like to visit the accounts of deceased people, if they are added. However, if they are not added as friends, I also cannot access their content. In such cases, I look at the pictures and posts of their acquaintances. You know, to see if they have forgotten or what they are doing. (P7)

> As a matter of fact, I do not remember anything in particular, but whenever I have the opportunity, I go on Instagram, I browse on Discover, I watch a video there, and if there is somehow an association, I think of it. For example, my cousin was a member of walking clubs; she used to walk frequently, and if I see such a walking activity, I think of it. (P8)

The behavior of logging into profiles of the deceased is often triggered by associations that occur while browsing the internet or consuming certain types of content. Participants often experience moments when something specific reminds them of a deceased friend, such as while browsing online platforms, watching a video, or attending an event. In this respect, the Internet offers an environment where users can easily revive their past relationships, memories, and experiences. Associations occur when watching a video, attending an event, or seeing a post on a particular topic. This suggests that visiting the profiles of the deceased can be triggered by instant associations and that these visits are linked to memories. The act of visiting the profiles of the dead based on associations reflects the participants' desire to revive their past relationships and memories, to remember and commemorate the person they have lost.

> In the digital world, such deaths are a constant reminder of death. For example, I forget about him/her because they are not a relative of mine, but I receive a notification, and then I go and look at it, and I feel sad. I do not know what good it will do when I feel sad, but for example, there was a brother here and I get a notification for his/her birthday. (P1)

> Facebook gives notifications on birthdays, so when my friend's birthday comes, there is a notification like write something on your wall. In this way, I remember him, then I go to his profile on Facebook and see what people are writing rather than writing something. Some, for example, celebrate his birthday as if he never died. There are even people who write 'Happy Birthday, Happy Healthy Birthday.' I wonder if they do not know that my friend is dead. (P2)

> I have lost friends or relatives on Facebook, and I like to commemorate them on special days. For example, the mother of my daughter-in-law, whom I loved very much, was a retired teacher, and we lost her 4 years ago. I like to visit her profile on Teacher's Day and write something. I go to her profile on her birthday, teacher's day, or on the anniversary of her death and write a message. (P4)

The role of notifications in visiting dead profiles is vital. Participants visit their dead profiles through notifications from social media platforms. For example, platforms such as Facebook send notifications to remind users of their friends' birthdays or other special occasions. These notifications remind them of the special days of a deceased relative.

13.5.3 Emotional Experiences in Death Profiles

The mental and emotional processes of people who enter the profiles of the dead differ between individuals. When they are exposed to the content and interactions on dead profiles, they may feel that the deceased person is still alive and experience the strange and eerie aspects of interacting with a digital presence.

> I know that he knows that I do not forget, and I am sure that he would not be comfortable in his grave if I forget. So this feeling gives me strength. (P10)

> I am sure that he feels what is written there somewhere. Because I have not forgotten, and I do not express that I have not forgotten with simple messages. I open up. Moreover, I am sure he feels them, and at such times, if I am experiencing very intense emotions, I definitely see them in my dreams. I receive the message that I am fine, and as long as this continues, I believe what I am doing is the right thing. I do not know, at least it feels good for me. (P6)

The emotional bond experienced through the dead profiles offers a postmodern perspective that questions the perception of reality. In particular, the interaction with deceased profiles suggests that it can offer a different life experience by transcending the boundaries of reality, and that the distinction between reality and the virtual world is gradually blurring. This situation offers an in-depth reflection on how modern communication technology alters human experiences and shapes perceptions. This strangeness and the perception of the deceased as digitally present can be further understood through posthumanist and digital embodiment perspectives, which highlight how technology extends human experience beyond biological life and challenges traditional boundaries between the living, the dead, and digital existence (Ferrando, 2013; Hayles, 1999).

Post-mortem digital assets have a value that questions the limits of life and human existence. The fact that the age is fixed in the deceased profiles and the posthumous experiences are depicted through the pictures reminds us that the deceased person was once alive. However, the fact that the dead will no longer age and will not change like those who are alive stands out as one of the reasons why such celebrations feel strange. In addition, seeing the deceased person's past life experiences and shares, thinking that they still exist in some way, evokes strange feelings in people. The feeling that posthumous digital beings stand as if they are not dead and cannot update their profile causes people to experience strange and frightening feelings in relation to the concept of death.

> Some of them celebrate your birthday again and write that we have not forgotten you, for example, it seems strange to me. I say, why celebrate the birthday of a dead person? He does not get older anymore. He stopped, that is, his age was fixed at 28. It feels strange, I mean, I see his experiences through pictures. I feel a sense of strangeness when I see them, for example, that he once lived, traveled, laughed, had fun, or had a problem and shared it. It is like he does not know he is dead, like he is standing there somewhere. He cannot update his profile anymore, for example, he cannot share a new article or picture, but it feels like he is there. (P2)

> I think it should be closed. I think the things belonging to him should be destroyed after his death. What is the use of keeping them? If the important thing is photographs, you know, his son and daughter already have them. It should be appreciated while you are already "alive,

what is the point after death? Also, it is not pleasant, I mean, when the notification comes from Facebook, you know, when it is his birthday, then the person is startled and confused, wasn't this man dead? That is why I do not welcome this situation. It makes me uneasy. What will the dead man do, and what will he do there? You get a message as if he is not dead, and it startles you. (P3)

13.5.4 *Pagan Behavioral Patterns in the Virtual Guestbook*

The process of mourning in the digital space is realized through various practices. These practices include processes such as profile visits, comment culture, and sharing pictures or content. Each process is subject to its own order, but different dynamics are at play within the comment culture. According to Roberts, comment culture is rooted in Pagan beliefs. According to Roberts, who describes the comments made on online platforms as a virtual guestbook, this practice is similar to the pagan customs of the past and the notes left on tombstones. Those who are left behind often leave messages on virtual platforms to share their memories of the deceased and update others on their lives (Roberts, 2004).

> I like to commemorate them on special occasions, such as on their birthday, Teacher's Day, or death anniversary. I go to their profile and read what they have written, and then I write a message myself. I do not make labelling, I write what I feel. (P4)

> I like to commiserate. I mean, I enter, look at their profiles, get sad, and write what I want to write. About life, about time, I actually write down the things that pass through me there. For example, I see on Facebook or Instagram that people usually write articles on death days and birthdays; I do not like that. I do not like a simple message, "May your grave be light" or "May God have mercy". I think of these as things made for other people. I write things from myself. I mean, I feel as if they are there and reading it, and I know that they feel such sincere things. (P6)

The context of virtual guestbooks in pagan culture, used for commiseration, is linked to the need for communication and contact with the spirits of deceased loved ones. In this belief, it is important to maintain ties with the spirits. In this context, virtual guestbooks can be seen as a means of establishing an emotional bond and communicating with them.

13.5.5 *Postmortem Tasks*

Post-mortem practices, which vary across different geographies, have social value as they strengthen solidarity among people, while also being an important religious duty. Religious practices include prayers for the deceased with the intention of forgiving their sins, paying the debts left behind by their relatives, fulfilling their will, if any, performing the funeral prayer, and burial. In this way, it is hoped that the soul of the deceased will find peace. The social aspect of post-mortem practices is a social duty as it relieves the pain of the survivors. The participants who participated in the research and lost their relatives were asked whether they had any material or spiritual practices after death, and the following answers were received:

> If what you mean is visiting the cemetery, I do not even go to my relatives. It does not matter whether you have been there or not. I think the important thing is to remember. (P10)
>
> I was really sad when he died. (P2)
>
> No, I do not. (P5)
>
> I am commenting, so what else can I say? If you are asking about visiting the cemetery, I mean, what is the point? I cannot see it there, at least I can see it here. (P6)
>
> No, I do not do it, I mean, I guess those who do it do it. (P7)
>
> I mean, I do not know what can be done, I do not do it. (P9)

For some participants, the primary reason for visiting the cemetery is to remember, and therefore, they believe it is not necessary to visit in person. Indeed, the importance of visiting the grave stems from the act of remembering, but here lies the problem of what to remember. Is it the dead or the deceased that is to be remembered? The purpose of writing "Every soul will taste death" in the 57th verse of Surah Ankebüt at the entrances of the graveyards is to remind us of the necessity of remembering death. The post-mortem commemoration and mourning practices exhibited in the digital world differ in this respect. In fact, based on Nietzsche's philosophy, it would not be incorrect to say that the digital field reconstructs Stoic philosophy. The philosophy of Amor Fati and commemoration practices in the digital space encourage living with pleasure by fostering a similar perspective on accepting life and understanding the value of the moment.

13.6 Conclusion

The fact that the profiles left behind by the death of social media users are somehow subject to visits shows that religious practices occupy less space in social life and that the digital environment has replaced religious rituals. The digital practices exhibited in the profiles of the dead are closely related to the posthumous digital commemoration and mourning process. The intensity of interactions is generally higher immediately after the news of death. In the mourning process that follows the initial news of death, entering the digital profiles of the deceased and posting comments expressing shock, denial, anger, amazement, and using sad or crying emojis are all part of the digital mourning process. However, over time, as the effect of the pain decreases and the routine of daily life returns, the number and intensity of these interactions decrease. Afterward, these profiles are now more subject to the culture of remembrance and commemoration. This situation, when examined sociologically, reveals the dynamics of the digital mourning process, which is a component of the posthumous mourning process. While intense emotional reactions and commemoration activities are evident in the early stages, the gradual decrease in these activities over time is a natural part of the mourning process.

In addition to the purpose of keeping the memory of the deceased alive and commemorating their legacy, the fact that digital tagging and sharing are seen as necessary is evidence that new norms in digital culture are replacing traditional religious ones. Moreover, the fact that death profiles function to provide comfort and strength to the deceased's loved ones again indicates that the role of religion in providing comfort and spiritual support has been transferred to secular norms. This suggests that the use of death profiles to fulfill emotional and psychological needs in society indicates a decline in the need for support and solace provided by religious institutions. For individuals, profiles of the dead encourage a focus on life by reminding them of the transience of life and the inevitability of death. This situation suggests that secular norms emphasizing the value of life have been established. Indeed, for believers, it is the afterlife that matters, and death symbolizes the beginning of the end, rather than the end itself. For this reason, while death, not the deceased, should be commemorated in cemeteries, the value of life is emphasized through the deceased in death profiles. In this respect, death profiles point to death as a point that disrupts the rhythm of life, where beautiful moments and happiness come to an end.

Traditionally, death and memorialization rituals have been closely tied to religious beliefs and ceremonies. However, the motivations for visiting death profiles on digital platforms point to a more secular nature. Through factors such as curiosity, associations, and notifications when visiting death profiles, the culture of death and remembrance is increasingly diversifying, and the internet allows these processes to be reshaped. In this respect, it can be said that the motivations for visiting death profiles provide an alternative space to traditional commemoration rituals. Visiting dead profiles and the emotional experiences created by this act reflect the impact of digital transformation and modern communication technology on human perceptions. Dead profiles first emerged as a modern application that could replace traditional grave visits or commemoration ceremonies, and then took this one step further, causing the perception of reality to be questioned with features such as the digital presence of the deceased person still appearing active and past life experiences being visible. This has led people to examine the concepts of death and existence from a more complex and nuanced perspective.

The popularity of virtual guestbooks constructed through comments is similar to the pagan customs of the past and the notes left on tombstones. It addresses the need to communicate and relate to the spirits of deceased loved ones in a non-religious context. While the resurgence of pagan commentary culture on digital platforms shows that people are integrating traditional rituals related to death with modern communication technology, the influence of a non-religious perspective is clearly visible behind this situation. Increasingly, people tend to manage the process of death and mourning through non-religious rituals or rituals with fewer religious elements. Finally, profiles of the dead reinforce the tendency for societies to move away from religious norms by constructing for believers the value of an earth-oriented way of life rather than an afterlife.

References

Allan, K. (2020). *Çağdaş sosyal ve sosyolojik teori* (A. Bora et al., Trans.) İstanbul Bilgi Üniversitesi Yayınları.

Ariès, P. (1991). *Batılının ölüm karşısında tavırları* (M. A. Kılıçbay, Trans.). Gece Yayınları.

Baudrillard, J. (2002). Simgesel değiş tokuş ve ölüm (O. Adanır, Trans.). Boğaziçi Üniversitesi Yayınevi.

Bauman, Z. (2000). *Ölümlülük, ölümsüzlük ve diğer hayat stratejileri* (N. Demirdöven, Trans.). Ayrıntı Yayınları.

Becker, E. (2015). *Ölümü inkar* (A. Özdoğan, Trans.). İz Yayıncılık.

Çankal, G. (2022). Bedensel ritüellerden dijital ritüellere: Ölmüş kişilerin Instagram profilleri üzerine netnografik bir araştırma. In A. T. Türkmenoğlu (Ed.), *Medya Tartışmaları* (pp. 89–111). NEÜ Press.

Castells, M. (2008). *Enformasyon toplumu: Ekonomi, toplum ve kültür: Ağ toplumunun yükselişi.* (E. Kılıç, Trans.). İstanbul: Bilgi Üniversitesi Yayınları.

Church, S. H. (2013). Digital gravescapes: Digital memorializing on Facebook. *The Information Society, 29*(3), 184–189.

Constantinides, E., & Fountain, S. J. (2008). Web 2.0: Conceptual foundations and marketing issues. *Journal of Direct, Data and Digital Marketing Practice, 9*(3), 231–244. https://doi.org/10.1057/PALGRAVE.DDDMP.4350098

Dağ, A. (2020). İnsanın dönüşümü. In R. Umut (Ed.), *Dijital Çağda İnsan Kalmak* (pp. 41–43). Kadem Yayınları.

Dilmaç, J. A. (2016). The new forms of mourning: Loss and exhibition of the death on the internet. *Journal of Death and Dying, 77*(3), 280–295. https://doi.org/10.1177/0030222816633240

Ferrando, F. (2013). Posthumanism, transhumanism, antihumanism, metahumanism, and new materialisms: Differences and relations. *Existenz, 8*(2), 26–32.

Foer, J. (2015). *Einstein ile Ay yürüyüşü / her şeyi hatırlama sanatı.* Altın Kitaplar Yayınevi.

Hayles, N. K. (1999). *How we became posthuman: Virtual bodies in cybernetics, literature, and informatics.* University of Chicago Press.

Hökelekli, H. (2008). *Ölüm, ölüm ötesi psikolojisi ve din.* Dem Yayınları.

Illich, I. (2004). Ölüme karşı ölüm. *Cogito, 40*, 107–121.

Kozinets, R. V. (1999). E-tribalized marketing? The strategic implications of virtual communities of consumption. *European Management Journal, 17*(3), 252–264. https://doi.org/10.1016/S0263-2373(99)00004-3

Kozinets, R. V. (2010). *Netnography: Redefined.* Sage Publications Inc.

Lester, D. H. (2012). Social media: Changing advertising education. *Online Journal of Communication and Media Technologies, 2*(1), 116–125. https://doi.org/10.29333/OJCMT/2373

Lietsala, K., & Sirkkunen, E. (2008). *Social media. Introduction to the tools and processes of participatory economy.* Tampere University Press.

Martin, A. (2008). Digital literacy and the "digital society". In C. Lankshear & M. Knobel (Eds.), *Digital Literacies: Concepts, Policies and Practices* (pp. 151–176). Peter Lang Publishing

Molo, Ü. (2021). Artırılmış sonsuzluk: Dijital kalıntılar ile ölümsüzleşme arayışları. *Kesit Akademi Dergisi, 7*(27), 82–98. https://doi.org/10.29228/kesit.51387

Öhman, C. J., & Watson, D. (2019). Are the dead taking over Facebook? A big data approach to the future of death online. *Big Data and Society, 6*(1), 1–13. https://doi.org/10.1177/2053951719842540

Onur, B. (2004). *Gelişim psikolojisi.* İmge Kitabevi.

Roberts, P. (2004). Here today and cyberspace tomorrow: Memorials and bereavement support on the web. *Generations, 28*(2), 41–46.

Safko, L., & Brake, D. (2009). *The social media bible: Tactics, tools and strategies for business success.* Wiley.

Yılmaz, S., & Erken, V. U. (2020). Sosyal medya hesaplarının miras yoluyla intikal edip edemeyeceği sorusunun kişisel verileri koruma hukuku kapsamında incelenmesi. *İnönü Üniversitesi Hukuk Fakültesi Dergisi, 11*(2), 567–586. https://doi.org/10.21492/inuhfd.789817

Chapter 14
Social Reflections of Smart City Applications in Türkiye: Konya Metropolitan Municipality Practices (Youth Culture Card)

İbrahim Nacak

14.1 Introduction

The historical emergence of cities and the transformations they have undergone to the present day have been widely discussed by various scientific disciplines. A fundamental divergence has emerged in the approaches to the phenomenon of cities within the European and American social science traditions. The European tradition has highlighted the historical dynamics that gave rise to cities. For example, thinkers such as Max Weber (2012), Henri Pirenne (2019), and Lewis Mumford (2019) have presented narratives that focus specifically on European and, more broadly, world history. In Ancient Greece, cities also formed city-states (polis). The fundamental characteristics of cities, highlighted in the works of Weber and Pirenne, draw attention to their economic, administrative, political, legal, and military attributes. The existence of an army, a castle, a marketplace, and autonomous law and administration are cited as fundamental parameters (Kömürcüoğlu, 2019, pp. 24–28). These characteristics demonstrate that cities also possessed state-like features.

When we turn to ancient human knowledge, the first cities emerged in the Mesopotamian region. The city of Susa, which still bears the same name in the Khuzestan region of Iran, the city of Uruk, the ancient capital of the Achaemenids north of the Persian Gulf, and Çatalhöyük (Konya) in Anatolia are among the earliest known examples (Hout et al., 2000, p. 43; Tekin, 2017, p. 19). Their standard features include the settlement spreading over a specific geographical area and the presence of structures corresponding to cultural functions, such as shelters and temples. Ongoing archaeological studies continue to reveal new findings.

İ. Nacak (✉)
Department of Sociology, Selçuk University, Konya, Türkiye
e-mail: ibrahimnacak557@gmail.com

M. D. Dereli and M. Eken (eds.), *Turkish Perspectives on Secularization and Media*,
https://doi.org/10.1007/978-3-032-16436-0_14

The historical transformation that enables us to understand the urbanisation experience of the modern world emerged alongside industrialization. While industrialisation fundamentally created differences in production methods (economic), it also brought about profound transformations in areas such as population, political structure, religious life, health, education, and consumption. When we talk about the modern city phenomenon today, we refer to the opportunities brought about by the industrial age: the use of steam power and machinery at the end of the eighteenth century, the use of electricity and assembly systems at the beginning of the twentieth century, the development of electronics, automation, and information systems in the late twentieth century, and finally, the widespread adoption of cyber-physical systems (autonomous robots, augmented reality, the Internet of Things, etc.) in various production areas today. The current stage reached by the industrial age is referred to in the literature as "Industry 4.0." Industry 4.0 emphasises the level reached by intelligent automation systems that can control themselves, based on information and communication technologies and cyber-physical systems, with potential in advanced robotics, big data, cloud computing, and artificial intelligence (Erdal, 2023, p. 36). These developments initially indicate technological advances in the economic sphere. However, as every new technological tool created by the digital world becomes available for people's daily use through computers and smartphones, every practice (action or behaviour) occurring in social life leaves a trace in the digital or cyber world (Dereli, 2019, 2022). Consequently, information generated in all areas of social life, such as production, services, finance, communication, transportation, health, energy, climate, environmental issues, city management, and public services, is transformed into a data extension in the cyber world. In summary, individuals and society, as actors in the real, cultural, and public world, create their digital twins in the cyber universe.

The integration of technological applications in the fields of information and cyberspace since 2000 has been expressed through the concept of "Society 5.0" in society.[1] It was first officially proposed in 2016 by the Japanese Cabinet, in line with the Fifth Science and Technology Basic Plan. Society 5.0, in its broadest sense, presents a vision of creating a sustainable society that enhances people's productivity and quality of life. Technological solutions produced through human-machine collaboration are expected to create opportunities that facilitate and improve individual and social life (Duman, 2022, p. 313). Therefore, intelligent systems are being designed to make human relationships—both with nature and with other humans—healthy, comfortable, and sustainable.

The noteworthy aspect of smart technological systems from a social sciences perspective is that they give rise to applications that directly impact mass living. One area where this can be observed through concrete examples is the smart city vision and the strategies developed by local governments. This is because cosmopolitan cities, where the population is increasingly dense, demographic diversity is rising, and people live under different economic conditions, make it challenging to provide

[1] For a study examining Society 5.0 discussions in the context of data and capitalism, see Karaarslan and Erdal Avcı (2025).

urban services quickly, directly, transparently, successfully, and fairly. Therefore, local governments need to utilise smart systems to produce functional solutions to complex urban problems. The smart city vision represents the process of effectively utilising software applications that respond to urban needs, developing the skills of city residents, involving all stakeholders in city management, and producing effective planning and solutions. Two key variables determine the effectiveness of smart city applications. The first is the innovative steps taken by the institutional authority that develops and manages the application, and the second is the urban areas and residents affected by the application (Komninos et al., 2015, pp. 31–35). Therefore, smart city applications enable user-centred autonomous systems while also contributing to the development of a participatory governance approach between administrators and city residents.

The most significant impact of technology in today's world is that it enables global trends to spread more rapidly and policies to be implemented swiftly. This is because the anticipated or foreseen problems regarding the future of the world and humanity are based on the idea that they can be prevented with the help of digital technologies. The vision developed by international organisations and the concrete applications of countries at the forefront of technology—such as the 500 smart city pilot projects in China and the 100 smart city projects in the USA—reveal the components on which smart city design is based (Babaoğlu, 2024, p. 35) (Table 14.1).

These components essentially emphasise the fundamental principles that will enable healthy, safe, and comfortable living in large cities with high demographic density. They encompass a multidimensional process, ranging from planning economic needs, production, distribution, and consumption processes to transport systems that facilitate fast and comfortable human mobility; from applications that enhance the living standards of city residents to the participation of public, private, and civil initiatives in local government. Based on this, many sub-components, actions, and applications are being developed.

Gökalp and Şenol (2020) examined smart city applications through global examples in their study, evaluating the practices of 170 countries and determining their maturity levels. Accordingly, Barcelona, Amsterdam, London, Los Angeles, and Tokyo were categorised as leading cities; Milan, Rome, Dubai, Moscow, and Istanbul as transition-level cities; and Houston, Detroit, Santiago, Kiev, and Konya as starting-level cities. For example, Barcelona (Spain) is one of the first European cities to use data-driven smart city technologies. It has developed solutions in transportation, environment, and sustainable energy, smart mobile sensor networks, and open data. Amsterdam (Netherlands) began its smart city movement in 1993. The Amsterdam Smart City (ASC) initiative is involved in developing smart city applications and creating network structures, as well as open and big data systems (Gökalp & Şenol, 2020, pp. 6–8). Although Gökalp and Şenol mention Istanbul and Konya as examples from Türkiye, as of 2020, neither city had established a long-term strategic plan. In 2021, the Istanbul Metropolitan Municipality and in 2022, the Konya Metropolitan Municipality transformed the information technology-based smart city applications they had developed into comprehensive smart city strategies and roadmaps.

Table 14.1 Characteristics and factors of a smart city (Giffinger & Gudrun, 2010; Vienna Univ., etc., 2007)

Smart economy (Competitiveness)	**Smart people (Social and Human Capital)**
❑ Innovative spirit ❑ Entrepreneurship ❑ Economic image & trademarks ❑ Productivity ❑ Flexibility of the labour market ❑ International embeddedness ❑ Ability to transform	❑ Level of qualification ❑ Affinity to lifelong learning ❑ Social and ethnic plurality ❑ Flexibility ❑ Creativity ❑ Cosmopolitanism/Open-mindedness ❑ Participation in public life
Smart governance (Participation)	**Smart mobility (Transport and ICT)**
❑ Participation in decision-making ❑ Public and social services ❑ Transparent governance ❑ Political strategies & perspectives	❑ Local accessibility ❑ (Inter-)national accessibility ❑ Availability of ICT infrastructure ❑ Sustainable, innovative, and safe transport systems
Smart environment (Natural resources)	**Smart living (Quality of life)**
❑ Attractivity of natural conditions ❑ Pollution ❑ Environmental protection ❑ Sustainable resource management	❑ Cultural facilities ❑ Health conditions ❑ Individual safety ❑ Housing quality ❑ Education facilities ❑ Touristic attractivity ❑ Social cohesion

After providing general information about smart city strategies and applications, sociological assessments are needed to critically evaluate the social transformation that smart urbanisation aims to achieve. In doing so, the focus will be on the functional dimensions of the smart city phenomenon, emphasising its transformative impact on social life rather than its technological aspects.

14.2 The Phenomenon of Smart Cities with Sociological Reflections

The fundamental criterion required to define a city as smart is the ability to manage the resources and tools necessary to achieve strategic goals in an effective, efficient, and systematic manner. Achieving this is possible through the consistent and integrated actions of urban actors, institutions, organisations, and infrastructure elements. This is because it is this coordination that influences the decisions of city administrators and regulates the daily lives of city residents. Data tracking systems that record the dynamics of city life fulfil the basic function of a smart city system by making this data easily, quickly, and in real-time available to users (individuals and institutions)

(Smart Cities, 2014). If these real-time data are available to city residents and generate instant feedback, this structure is referred to as an autonomous intelligent system. However, if the data are recorded in the IT infrastructure, processed and analysed by experts, and then corporate intervention occurs, these applications are considered non-autonomous intelligent systems. For example, a passenger who knows through smart applications that a public transport vehicle is approaching the station will prefer to wait at the stop. If the passenger knows that the bus will not arrive soon, they will consider alternative transportation options. Similarly, suppose a bus driver knows that no passengers are waiting at the station. In that case, they can save time and energy by choosing a shorter route as an example of autonomous systems, smart junction systems (with integrated cameras) that can detect the number of vehicles waiting at an intersection grant the right of way to the direction with higher traffic density, thereby increasing driver comfort (human-friendly) on the one hand and reducing ecological damage (environmentally friendly) on the other.

Although smart city strategies have many dimensions, when evaluated in terms of academic disciplines, it can be said that they have two fundamental backgrounds: technical and social. The use of a range of knowledge-based digital and electronic technologies, and their integration into urban infrastructure, constitutes the technical dimension. In contrast, the aspects of learning, innovation development, and communication with people for the purpose of transforming urban life (Pourahmad et al., 2018, p. 15) constitute the social dimension. In other words, information obtained from human behaviour in urban life and new applications (policies or solutions) developed based on this information fall within the scope of disciplines such as public administration, urban planning, and sociology. Therefore, making technology- or information-based applications available to public institutions and urban users can be considered the first step towards the vision of regulating urban life. However, the perspective of the social sciences focuses on what kind of functional transformation it creates in the lives of city dwellers.

The active use of smart systems in city management and citizens acting in accordance with the requirements of these systems are not sufficient for the functionality of the "smart city" concept. Smart systems can fulfil their social function only if they are designed according to citizens' needs, adapt to changes in city life, and generate solutions to potential problems through feedback. Therefore, the use or increase in the number of smart technological systems will remain ineffective unless feedback is obtained from city residents. In other words, unless smart technologies analyse the data they collect from urban users and develop applications that meet the expectations, comfort, and well-being of city dwellers, they will not generate collective benefits. For this reason, demonstrating the transformative impact of smart technologies on social life is a sociological necessity.

For smart city systems to tangibly demonstrate their social function, the developed applications must be comprehensible and understandable to everyone, provide measurable indicators, be accessible to all segments of society, realistically present resources and opportunities, and ensure uninterrupted operation and continuity (Velibeyoğlu, 2016). In other words, it is a prerequisite that urban actors consciously use the digital tools developed and continuously feed data into smart systems. Furthermore, it is necessary to answer the following questions: Which authorised institutions evaluate the data generated through the applications and transform it into practical policies? Or what kinds of problems are identified, and what solutions are produced thanks to digital data? Another point where we can observe a social function is in the areas where digital applications affect urban dwellers. How do these tools transform the daily lives of urban residents? What behavioural changes do smart applications create in their lives? In summary, the transformative effect of smart applications on social life must be identified based on the observations and experiences of both city administrators and city residents. This should be the goal of social scientists, particularly sociologists.

14.3 Smart City Applications in Türkiye and Konya

Examining the progress made in Türkiye's urbanisation journey in recent years, it is evident that the country has closely followed global developments. Since the 2000s, technological and IT-based applications have been widely used in many cities. These applications were initially developed to improve the efficient use of energy resources. Automatic irrigation systems in landscaped areas, smart metres (for water, electricity, and natural gas) in homes and workplaces, and smart lighting systems in places such as streets, avenues, and squares are smart public measures focussed on energy efficiency. Digital infrastructure services have been widely utilised in recent years in major cities such as Istanbul, Ankara, İzmir, Bursa, and Konya. Smart traffic systems, smart parking systems, smart transportation systems, smart waste collection systems, and smart buildings are some examples (Örselli & Akbay, 2019). However, it was not until 2019 that the national smart city vision was presented, and local governments announced their strategies and roadmaps.

Public institutions and private organisations in Türkiye have conducted various studies to establish national standards for smart city visions and strategies. The initial studies took the form of preliminary meetings to develop the strategies. Numerous workshops, fairs, and meetings were organised by various institutions and organisations, such as the Urban Transformation and Smart Cities Congress (2016), organised by the Ministry of Environment and Urbanisation, and the Smart Municipalities Summit (2016), organised by the Marmara Municipalities Union. Additionally, public platforms such as the Smart Cities Portal, Smart City Ecosystem, and Smart City Index have been established to track current developments in municipalities implementing smart city strategies and applications. These platforms facilitate cooperation between central government agencies, local governments, and civil society organisations. Thus, a nationwide organisational network has been established to determine successful smart city strategies, initiate implementation processes, plan and develop projects, monitor project effectiveness, and conduct evaluations (Uçar et al., 2017). This will enable the preparation of model examples for small-scale cities that will later join smart urbanisation programmes.

As highlighted in the 2020–2023 National Smart Cities Strategy and Action Plan (2020), prepared by the Ministry of Environment, Urbanisation and Climate Change, it has been determined that 80.2% of local administrations in Türkiye do not have smart city strategies. The strategy and action plan, prepared to address this need, serves as a roadmap for local governments. Therefore, each city must focus on different priorities according to its own characteristics and adopt a practical, sustainable, phased, and incremental approach in line with its objectives. The smart city management mechanism of metropolitan cities and other provinces is implemented with the participation and coordination of all stakeholders. This aims to prevent inter-institutional incompatibility and duplicate investments.

The 2020–2023 National Smart Cities Strategy and Action Plan (2020) identifies smart city components under sixteen headings. These components are designed to encompass all aspects of urban life, including health, environment, economy, infrastructure, security, energy, transportation, disasters, and governance. They also include components based on technological hardware and software, encompassing information and communication systems, institutional structures, and spatial management. These components correspond to the diverse areas of activity of local governments, ensuring that urban services are integrated into smart systems through the development of projects. This aims to establish coherence between the smart city vision, urban life, and digital data systems. Ultimately, digital data systems can enable the rapid identification of problem areas in urban life and the swift development of solutions (autonomous or non-autonomous) (Fig. 14.1).

Smart city components constitute the areas that regulate today's urban life on the broadest scale. As local authorities develop targets and applications in line with these parameters, systematic and comprehensive steps will be taken that are compatible with smart urban strategies and integrated into national policies. The Smart City Ecosystem and Smart City Index, prepared in coordination with the Ministry, categorises cities based on the projects they have developed and designed. Accordingly, Konya, Istanbul, Bursa, Kütahya, Kayseri, Sakarya, and Kocaeli are among the leading cities in Turkey. Konya Metropolitan Municipality is one of the local administrations that has set the most successful examples in this regard. With 296 completed and designed applications, it ranks first in Türkiye. Between 2020 and 2023, the local administration has used smart city technologies most effectively for four consecutive years (Figs. 14.2 and 14.3).[2]

Konya Metropolitan Municipality and ASELSAN have collaborated to prepare a guide and roadmap for planning smart city solutions specific to Konya, in line with the national action plan, and for determining the vision, objectives, and implementation of the proposed actions. The Konya Smart City Strategy and Roadmap (2022–2030) includes long-term, inclusive, and sustainable actions. Its fundamental vision is to improve the quality of life for the people of Konya by using high-tech, integrated

---

[2] For the source of the news, see: https://www.konya.bel.tr/haber/konya-ulusal-akilli-sehir-endeksinde-4-yildir-zirvede.

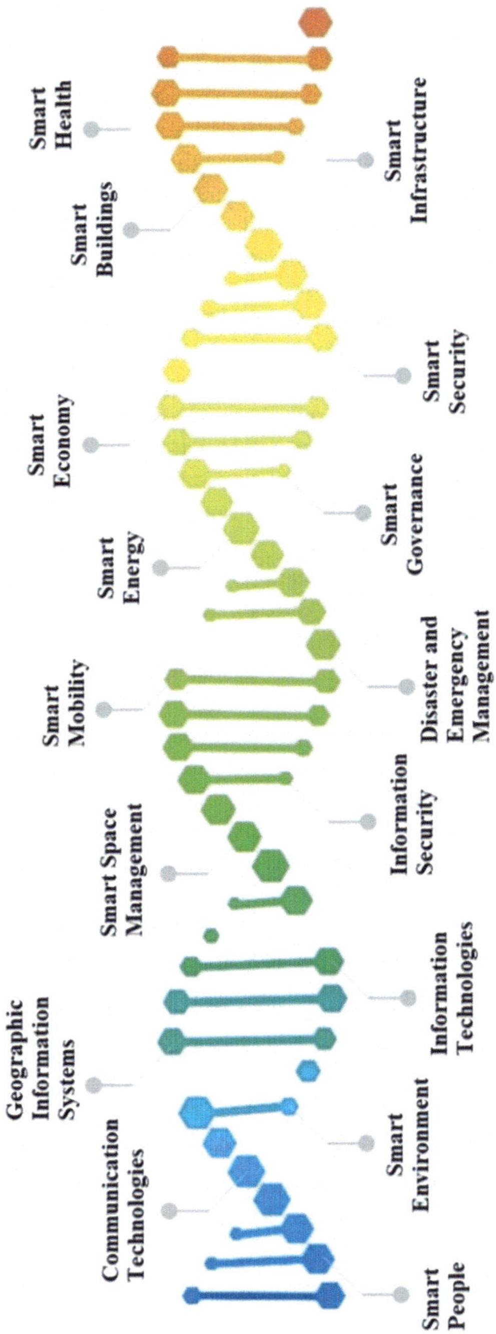

Fig. 14.1 2020–2023 National Smart Cities Strategy and Action Plan Smart City Components (www.akillisehirler.gov.tr)

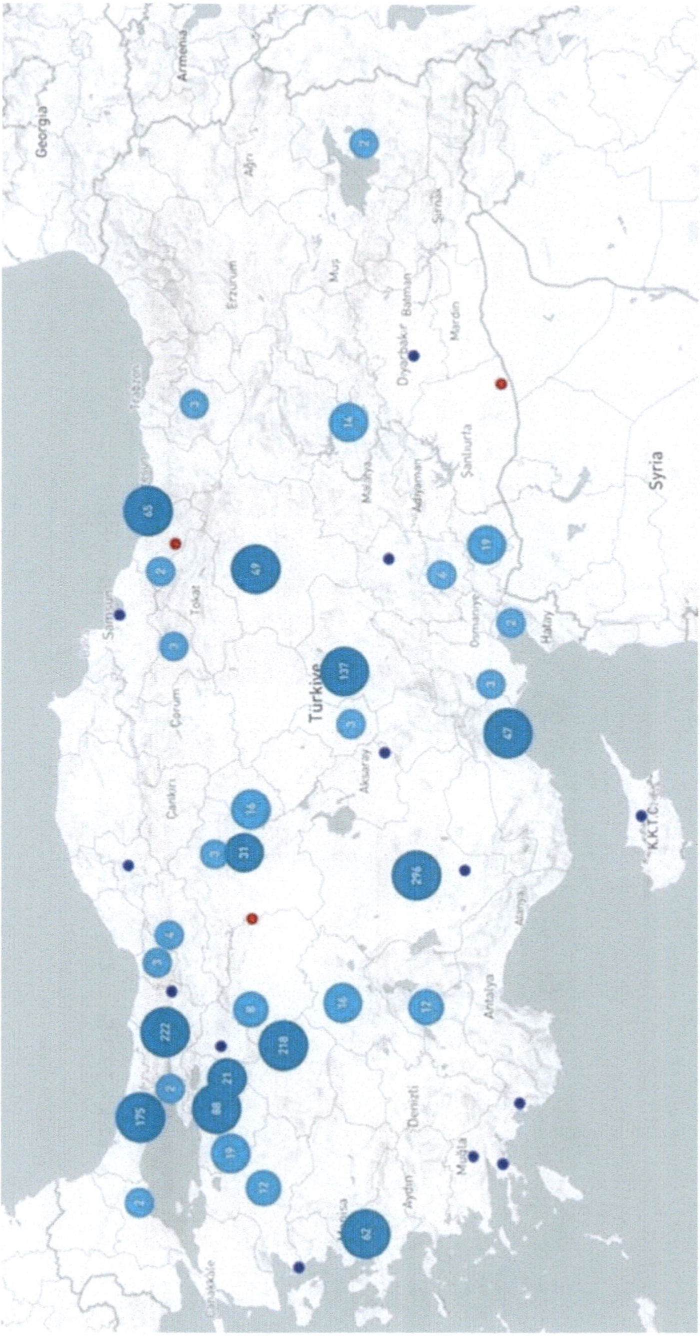

Fig. 14.2 Konya ranks first in Türkiye with 296 applications in terms of the number of completed and planned projects in the Smart City Ecosystem (https://akillisehirekosistem.csb.gov.tr/ProjectMap)

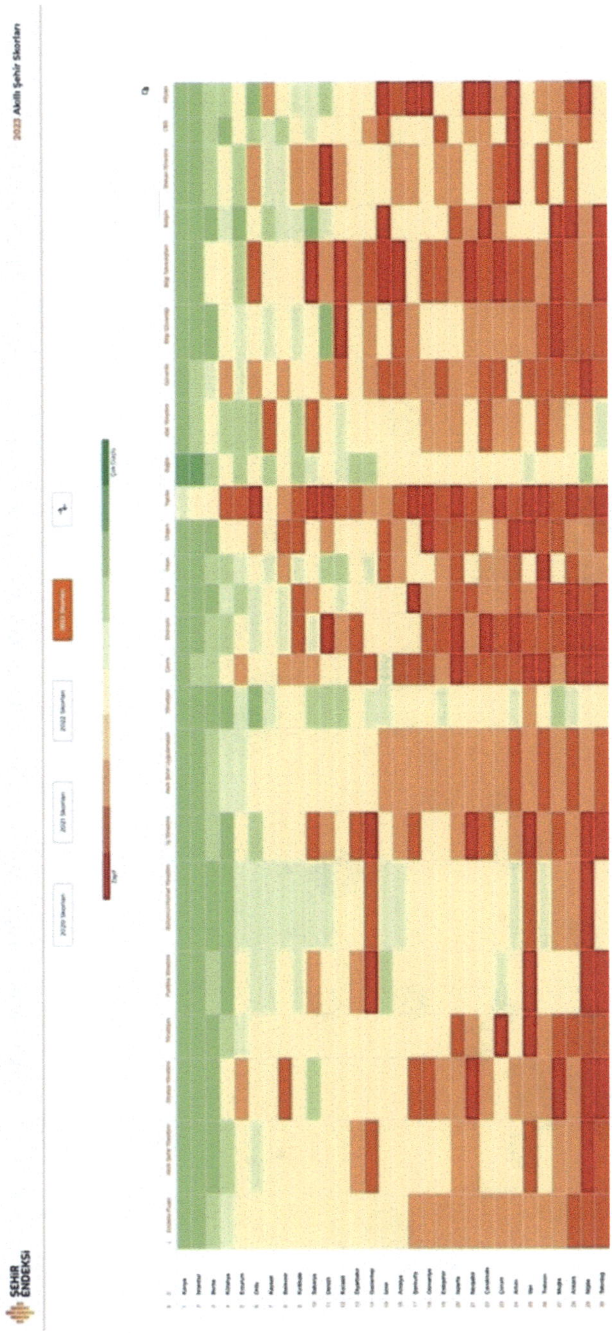

Fig. 14.3 National City Index—2023 Smart City Scores (https://sehirendeksi.gov.tr/endekspublic)

smart systems.[3] Additionally, the smart city roadmap of Konya Metropolitan Municipality has introduced several innovations within its institutional framework. One of these is the website www.akillisehir.konya.bel.tr, established as an open-access platform. This website contains information about the purpose, capabilities, stakeholders, and target audience of all smart city applications developed by the municipality. Furthermore, the Smart City Management Department has been established under the umbrella of the Information Processing Directorate. The duties, powers, and responsibilities of the Smart City Management Department are as follows:

(a) To support the Council in its strategy formulation and action planning efforts related to the concept of Smart City Development.
(b) To coordinate the activities and systems carried out by departments within the framework of Smart City Development.
(c) To conduct studies and research on new Smart City applications, identify those suitable for Konya, and provide advice and consultancy support to departments on these matters.[4]

It is possible to examine Konya Metropolitan Municipality's smart city applications in several dimensions. One of these is to identify the strategies, plans, and applications developed by the local administration through open sources and make a superficial assessment. Another is the compilation and evaluation of digital data obtained from active smart city applications by responsible and authorised institutions. A further method is to conduct an analysis based on the knowledge, experience, perceptions, and attitudes of city residents, who are the stakeholders and users of smart city applications. Essentially, this method will be a sociological initiative that demonstrates both the functionality and efficiency of smart city applications, as well as their social implications.

Konya Metropolitan Municipality has developed 142 applications utilising eighteen smart components in line with the national action plan outlined in its Smart City Strategy and Roadmap (2022–2030). Although the Ministry of Environment, Urbanisation and Climate Change's national action plan includes sixteen components (as mentioned above), Konya Metropolitan Municipality has added smart agriculture and smart tourism components, taking into account its own regional dynamics. The areas with the highest number of applications developed per component are smart environment (17), smart energy (12), smart people (22), smart transport (23), smart governance (20), and information technologies (13) (KBB, 2022, p. 98). When examining the website www.akillisehir.konya.bel.tr, prepared by the metropolitan municipality, some of the prominent applications are as follows:

- Konya Zero Waste Information System—2023 (Smart Environment)
- Smart Lighting—2023 (Smart Energy)
- Accessible Konya—2024 (Smart People)

---

[3] For the source of the information, see: https://www.konya.bel.tr/proje/konya-akilli-sehir-stratejisi-ve-yol-haritasi.

[4] For the source of the information, see: https://www.konya.bel.tr/birim/akilli-sehir-yonetimi-sube-mudurlugu.

- Youth Culture Card—2023 (Smart People)
- ATUS Smart Public Transport System—2023 (Smart Transport)
- MUBİS Village Administration Information System—2023 (Smart Governance)
- City Information System—2007 (Information Technologies)

The preparation of the smart city strategy and roadmap, as well as the development of applications, involved examining scientific studies conducted both worldwide and in Türkiye, international standards and indices, and successful pilot projects, resulting in comprehensive preparatory work of a guiding nature. Furthermore, all stakeholders and contributing components identified in the Konya smart city ecosystem were evaluated, and meetings were held at various times, with a total of 681 internal and external stakeholders participating. This led to the preparation of 985 project proposals and the creation of a project pool. The expectations and opinions of members of parliament, local administrators, university rectors, and other institutional administrators were taken into account. Finally, a field survey was conducted with a sample size of 2,400 participants to identify the views, requests, and expectations of city residents.

The fact that smart city projects are most intensively implemented in the city of Konya within the Turkish context has attracted the attention of academic studies. These studies primarily ensure that smart projects are evaluated from a scientific perspective and discussed at an exploratory and descriptive level. However, there are relatively few studies analysing the functionality, efficiency, and social benefits generated by smart city applications. One study specifically focussing on the Konya example was published in 2018. It found that, at a time when the municipality did not yet have a smart city roadmap, many smart projects had already been implemented (such as Smart Public Transport, Smart Bicycles, and Smart Waste Management). However, a comprehensive strategic approach had not yet been established (Bilici & Babahanoğlu, 2018, p. 137). Another study, published in 2021, found that Konya's smart city projects focused on transportation, environment, and governance parameters; however, these applications primarily facilitated the monitoring and coordination of tasks and processes carried out by municipal departments. Instead, it was emphasised that the concept of governance should be implemented in the city management process through mutual interaction, such as sharing municipal activities with citizens and obtaining their opinions prior to implementation (Karasoy & Kıraç, 2021, p. 62). Therefore, increasing the number and variety of smart applications will not, by itself, contribute to long-term social goals. For this reason, each application should directly contribute to the environment, society, and, specifically, the human factor. Due to the integrated execution of smart applications with the digital data management process, they should not lead to the neglect of the human factor and the social, cultural, historical, psychological, and spiritual aspects of human beings.

The most fundamental criticism of smart city projects is that the investments made and the digital applications developed are neither widely known nor actively used by citizens in their everyday urban life. The most important step in enhancing functionality is ensuring that city residents are aware of smart applications and use them to meet their various needs. In this regard, the Konya Mobile Application holds a significant advantage with over 500,000 users (Erdal, 2023, p. 103). The Konya Mobile Application, compatible with all smart devices, offers comprehensive and up-to-date information about the city of Konya. It includes data on health institutions, pharmacies, hospitals, district governor's offices, educational institutions, libraries, mosques, municipal service points, public health centres, neighbourhood offices, bus terminals, industrial areas, banks, shopping centres, taxi ranks, bicycle stations, cemeteries, fountains, marketplaces, gathering places, free Wi-Fi hotspots, notaries, Bilgehane, the High School Civilisation Academy, and Fenni Fırınlar. Users can also access municipal online services and public transport systems through this application.

In addressing contemporary urban challenges and ensuring social welfare and harmony, it is essential to critically evaluate both the positive and negative approaches associated with the smart city ideal. This is because smart city policies focus on solutions grounded in scientific principles and centred on technological infrastructure. Consequently, smart cities are conceptualised as technologically advanced urban environments that utilise digital automation. However, the interdisciplinary dimension of this phenomenon should not be neglected (Şenyüz, 2024, p. 123). Due to their structure comprising numerous components, smart city applications must be examined by the relevant disciplines while adhering to their own conceptual and methodological principles. The fundamental parameters on which the social science perspective will focus centre around human and social life.

It is an undeniable fact that smart city policies have been institutionalised and visionary steps have been taken, particularly within the Konya Metropolitan Municipality. Through the development of various smart projects, Konya has gained visibility at both national and international levels, implementing practices that could serve as models for other cities across the country. However, determining how these smart applications influence urban life, how they reflect on the social life of city residents, whether they meet the needs and expectations of urban dwellers, and ultimately identifying their shortcomings and areas for improvement, is only possible through in-depth investigation. This research aims to examine a concrete example of smart applications implemented by the Konya Metropolitan Municipality, thereby assessing the functionality and efficiency of these applications using sociological indicators.

14.4 Method and Results

Smart City 6.0, considered the most recent iteration of the smart city concept, emphasises citizen participation and data-driven decision-making, extending beyond approaches primarily focused on technology and infrastructure.[5] This approach also encourages institutions and organisations developing smart city programmes to place the human factor at the centre of their initiatives. This article focuses on a group of city residents to analyse the effectiveness of smart city projects implemented by the Konya Metropolitan Municipality. Considering the scope and limitations of the study, the aim is to assess a specific smart city application and its usage patterns among city residents. To this end, open-access sources were utilised to examine Konya Metropolitan Municipality's smart city projects. The Smart City Strategy and Roadmap (2022) document and the https://akillisehir.konya.bel.tr/ website served as the two primary data sources. As of August 2025, Konya's smart city statistics indicate the existence of 121 active applications, 142 ongoing projects, seven awards, 256 stakeholders, 50 services provided, and seven smart city markets. Within these, the research specifically focused on the smart people component and its related activity areas. This focus was chosen because other components predominantly emphasise technological, IT, and digital infrastructure systems, some of which function as automated systems. The smart people parameter, in contrast, directly targets areas that enhance the social lives of city residents—such as education, culture, arts, health, tourism, sports, and social assistance.

The smart city application specifically identified in this research is the Youth Culture Card initiative. This application is specifically designed to serve young people and students aged 18–26 residing in Konya. The Youth Culture Card was developed to promote the socio-cultural development of young people and to enable them to socialise through various activities. Its target audience consists of university students enrolled in formal education in Konya. The project supports young students' participation in cultural, artistic, educational, and sporting activities, while also encouraging their involvement in social responsibility projects.

Within the scope of this research, semi-structured interviews were conducted with 28 students.[6] Diversity was ensured in the selection of participants, taking into account their hometowns, departments, and class levels. However, due to its status as the university with the highest student population in Konya, Selçuk University was predominantly represented. A small number of students reported not

---

[5] The core elements of the Smart City 6.0 concept are listed as follows: (1) Citizen-centricity, (2) Data-driven decision-making, (3) Sustainability, (4) Innovation and entrepreneurship, (5) Collaboration, (6) Resilience. (Source: https://www.thesmartcityjournal.com/en/cities/the-key-characteristics-of-the-smart-city-6-0-concept).

[6] During the spring term of the 2024–2025 academic year, a group of students from the Department of Sociology at Selçuk University who were enrolled in the *Urban Sociology* course voluntarily contributed to the data collection process for this research. I would like to express my sincere gratitude to the following students for their valuable contributions to the data collection phase of our smart city research: A. Basılgan, B. Circir, F. Tufan, H. M. Gür, H. Öztürk, H. N. Akay, H. Yaşkır, M. R. Kaya, and Y. Kaya.

using mobile applications. They were nevertheless included in the study, as it was believed that their participation would provide alternative and valuable insights for the research. Accordingly, the demographic profile of the students included in the study is presented in the Table 14.2.

The data collection process and procedures applied in data analysis can be summarised as follows. A semi-structured interview form was prepared prior to conducting the field research. This interview form included demographic questions, young people's general thoughts about Konya and municipal services, their practices in using the Youth Culture Card, the services they benefited from through the smart application, and finally, suggestions that would contribute to the functionality of the Youth Culture Card application. These themes formed the most general question groups. New codes were created based on the students' answers to the questions. For example, based on the answers given regarding Konya and municipal services, satisfaction and expectations were expressed in the areas of infrastructure and transportation, social and cultural activities, education, and job opportunities. In the context of Young Culture Card usage areas and functionality, codes such as participation in festivals, trips, and camp programs, socialisation, adaptation to the city, and cultural accumulation were identified. Regarding smart practices, young users' overseas activities, young people presenting their own projects, and career and job-focused programmes were identified as sub-codes. The main headings in the findings section represent the general themes, while the participant statements classified under the content section display the sub-codes.

14.4.1 General Opinions About Konya and the Municipality

Firstly, to understand the satisfaction and dissatisfaction experienced by young people and university students living in Konya, questions were asked regarding how they spend their daily lives, their level of satisfaction with the city, and their expectations of the city's administrators. Students from different cities compared their experiences, highlighting both the advantages and disadvantages. One of the main advantages noted was that the city offers affordable, convenient, and comfortable transportation options for students. Infrastructure and municipal services were also generally well regarded.

> Compared to other cities, we can clearly understand Konya's advantages and disadvantages because we come from a different city. One of its advantages is that it is truly a student city. It is inexpensive, like a student city, especially in terms of transportation; I can say it is cheaper than most cities, huge cities. As for disadvantages, I think Konya's geographical location could be a disadvantage. It is a large city so that transportation can be challenging in that sense. However, the city council makes it easy for students. (YP17, Female, ND, Afyonkarahisar)

> As I said, transport is very advantageous. Additionally, as a region, it is advantageous that the university area is located far from the city centre. However, why do we refer to it as a student city? A separate area has been allocated, and all students are on that side; everything

Table 14.2 Youth participants included in this study

Participant	Gender	Age	Hometown	Period	Place	University	Department	Class	Youth Culture Card
1	M	20	Van	1	Halls	Selcuk Univ	International Relations	1	Yes
2	F	20	Karaman	1	Halls	Selcuk Univ	Psychology	1	No
3	M	20	Karaman	1	Halls	Selcuk Univ	Psychology	1	No
4	M	20	Konya	7	Family H	N. Erbakan Univ	Theology	1	Yes
5	M	24	Ankara	4	Halls	Selcuk Univ	German Language	3	No
6	F	20	Eskişehir	1,5	Halls	Karatay Univ	Midwifery	3	Yes
7	F	23	Konya	23	Family H	Selcuk Univ	International Relations	3	Yes
8	F	22	Konya	22	Halls	Selcuk Univ	Turkish Language	3	Yes
9	M	23	Adıyaman	2	Halls	Selcuk Univ	Law	2	Yes
10	M	21	Aksaray	2	Halls	Selcuk Univ	Law	2	Yes
11	M	21	Aksaray	2	Halls	Selcuk Univ	Law	2	Yes
12	F	22	Konya	22	Family H	N. Erbakan Univ	Nursing	2	Yes
13	M	23	Konya	23	Family H	Selcuk Univ	Industrial Design	3	Yes
14	M	25	Konya	25	Family H	Selcuk Univ	Guidance, Counseling	4	Yes
15	M	20	İzmir	3	Halls	Selcuk Univ	Computer Eng	3	Yes
16	F	21	Trabzon	2	Halls	Selcuk Univ	Psychology	2	Yes
17	F	19	Afyon	4	Halls	Selcuk Univ	Nutrition and Dietetics	2	Yes
18	M	21	Afyon	2	Halls	Selcuk univ	History	2	Yes

(continued)

Table 14.2 (continued)

Participant	Gender	Age	Hometown	Period	Place	University	Department	Class	Youth Culture Card
19	F	23	Uşak	4	Student H	Selcuk Univ	Midwifery	4	Yes
20	F	23	Konya	23	Family H	Selcuk Univ	Painting	3	Yes
21	F	22	Konya	22	Family H	Karatay Univ	Nutrition and Dietetics	4	Yes
22	F	20	Konya	20	Family H	Selcuk Univ	Sociology	2	No
23	F	22	Konya	22	Family H	Selcuk Univ	Sociology	2	Yes
24	F	24	Adıyaman	5	Halls	Selcuk Univ	Theology	4	Yes
25	F	22	Burdur	2	Halls	Selcuk Univ	Pharmacy	2	No
26	F	20	Antalya	1	Halls	K. Teknik Univ	Chemical engineering	1	No
27	M	21	Adana	3	Halls	Selcuk Univ	Mechanical engineering	3	Yes
28	M	20	Kayseri	2	Halls	Selcuk Univ	Pharmacy	2	Yes

is available in terms of transportation, and they can access everything they need. I think this is the situation where being a student city is at the forefront. (YP20, Female, P, Konya)

The advantage is that Konya is relatively cheap to live in, and transport is generally easy. We had much trouble with this in Antalya, so we felt very comfortable when we arrived here. My friend is studying here anyway, and I came on his recommendation. I have not seen any major disadvantages yet. (YP26, Female, CE, Antalya)

I like the municipality; the infrastructure and transport are good. The municipality's cafés are affordable, and we go there with friends. (YP10, Male, L, Aksaray)

One of the areas where young people have the highest expectations of a city is socio-cultural activities. One participant, who stated that the city was generally peaceful and safe, emphasised that social activities were limited compared to larger cities. (YP12)

In addition, when participants were asked about the socio-cultural opportunities in their city, they responded positively but also indicated that these opportunities needed further development. Travel, sporting activities, the city's historical and cultural aspects, cafés, conference and sports centres, and park areas were mentioned as advantages in terms of spatial diversity. However, the view that events such as theatre, concerts, and cinema are both expensive and need to be increased was prominent.

You can take advantage of everything—from sightseeing to sporting activities to exploring the city. It is a beautiful city for me from a cultural and historical perspective, which is enough for me. (YP18, Male, H, Afyonkarahisar)

I think the advantage is the variety of venues. Cafés, conference centres, sports centres, large areas, large parks—you can find all kinds of venues. Because it is good in this respect, Konya is preferred for some events. Again, because there are many conference centres, it is a large area. (YP19, Female, M, Uşak)

Let me put it this way, I cannot attend much. I actually love theatre, concerts, cinema, and other fun activities, but with the current economic situation, I cannot attend them as often as I would like. I think theatre, concerts, and cinema are costly in terms of fees and costs. (YP20, Female, P, Konya)

I find it sufficient, thank you. Additionally, what types of services and opportunities should they provide? There could be more concert-style events. Now that summer is here, they have actually organised some spring festivals, summer festivals, and events that are similar to festivals. They are doing it, but it could be even more and in a nicer way. (YP3, Male, P, Karaman)

I would like them to increase the number of concerts and make ticket prices more affordable, including theatre. As a student, I am struggling financially. There are not enough libraries; they could build one near the bus station, and public libraries could be established in areas with dormitories. In general, I find it difficult to find space in libraries. (YP9, Male, L, Adıyaman)

Considering that young people's expectations of the city primarily relate to socio-cultural life, the inadequacy of such opportunities or their inaccessibility due to economic reasons also shapes their expectations of city administrators. The Youth Culture Card initiative demonstrates that the municipality fulfils an important function by offering students the opportunity to participate in such activities. At this point, it is also necessary to highlight the areas where students' expectations differ. In addition to these, alternative academic education opportunities and employment prospects are important issues for students in terms of their future careers. When all these factors are evaluated together, the basic requirements for Konya to become a youth-friendly city emerge.

The academy is, of course, critical, and increasing job opportunities is also important. The fact is, there are a large number of students in Konya. That is, there are many university students, and if job opportunities are increased, I think the vast majority of these students would want to continue their vocational education in Konya. That is why such job opportunities are significant. (YP2, Female, P, Karaman)

Actually, I think Konya is youth-friendly to some extent. However, academic and educational opportunities need to be developed. That is, it could lead to young people preferring this place more. As people coming from outside—especially for those coming from outside the city, not those like us who are in the city—these academic opportunities could attract young people here more. (YP4, Male, T, Konya)

Developing academic and educational opportunities could be one way. For example, if there were places that could offer internships, that would be great. (YP6, Female, M, Eskişehir)

There are very few opportunities. There are few job opportunities, and it is difficult for us to establish contact with companies. My job requires me to meet with industry representatives, but my family does not approve due to the distance. I have communication difficulties because the industries are located outside the city. (YP7, Female, IR, Konya)

This section did not include questions specifically about the Youth Culture Card application. Instead, questions arose in the context of expectations from the city of

Konya and its municipal services. The fact that students emphasised their expectations regarding academic and job opportunities demonstrates their awareness that they are at a crucial stage in their careers. It also emerged that they wish to prepare for professional achievements during their student years and are concerned about their lives after graduation. Accordingly, the findings highlight their need for greater institutional and public support in areas such as technology, entrepreneurship, innovation, and internships.

> The municipality's youth-oriented applications are generally good, but more support and opportunities could be provided, especially in the field of technology. For example, events such as software development camps and entrepreneurship competitions could be organised. (YP15, Male, CE, Izmir)

> For Konya to become a youth-friendly city, job opportunities need to be increased, social and cultural areas need to be enriched, and academic and educational opportunities need to be developed. Projects targeting young people, especially in the fields of technology and innovation, are significant. (YP15, Male, CE, Izmir)

To summarise what young people generally expect from a city and its administrators, it can be said that they want easy and affordable access to activities that enrich their social and cultural lives. Although Konya is a large city in terms of area, it has been positively evaluated by students in terms of transportation options. The promotion of travel, cultural-artistic, and sporting events has been highlighted as a fundamental expectation. Furthermore, as all participants were university students, they expressed a desire for specific initiatives in the areas of academic and employment opportunities, as well as early access to experiences relevant to their professional development.

14.4.2 Youth Culture Card Application: Areas of Use and Functionality

The previous section assessed young people's expectations of city life, specifically in Konya. In this section, students' views were gathered on the Youth Culture Card application, which is designed to address these expectations. This smart application, developed as part of Konya Metropolitan Municipality's smart city vision, is examined through the approaches and usage practices of students. The Youth Culture Card application appears to offer a significant advantage when compared to those in other cities. The fact that students from different cities make such comparisons highlights the functional aspects of the application. The opportunity to participate in social, cultural, and artistic events in Konya at no cost is viewed as both positive and beneficial for students. Furthermore, the application is emphasised as functional in enabling students to get to know the city, socialise, adapt to urban life, and develop a sense of belonging. Based on the perspectives and experiences of students who benefit from the application, it can be argued that the Youth Culture Card serves as a practical component of Konya's smart city strategies.

> I think it has a positive effect. I have not heard of such things happening in other cities. Even if they do, I do not think they are as active and lively. I think it is very nice. It attracts students here. (YP6, Female, M, Eskişehir)

> First of all, all the activities are free, which is economically advantageous and appealing to students who have recently arrived in the city. It is a great opportunity to say that Konya is beautiful and active in the future. Apart from that, it is useful for socialising, but I am not sure if people attend events to adapt to the city. Konya has a very different charm. (YP1, Male, IR, Van)

> Yes, especially for students like me who come from a different city, the Youth Culture Card is a great opportunity to get to know the city and meet new people. (YP15, Male, CE, İzmir)

> It is particularly advantageous for new students who have recently arrived in the city to adapt to it. Providing students with free concert tickets, book raffles, and coffee raffles is very nice. (YP17, Female, ND, Afyonkarahisar)

> The biggest advantage is that it facilitates access to cultural events and reduces the financial burden. This allows students to increase their artistic and cultural knowledge. At the same time, it is a great tool for discovering the city and the social opportunities it offers. (YP27, Male, ME, Adana)

> Absolutely yes. When I came from Adana, it took me some time to get used to Konya. Thanks to the Youth Culture Card, I discovered different places, participated in cultural events, and met new people. This accelerated my adaptation process and made me feel at home more quickly. (YP27, Male, ME, Adana)

As Konya is a large city, not all activities taking place on an urban scale fall under the direct responsibility of local authorities. Various sources contribute to the city's socio-economic capital. Universities, industrial and commercial organisations, civil society organisations, and public institutions organise numerous activities at both national (local) and international levels. However, Konya Metropolitan Municipality plans large-scale programmes by integrating its own organisational capacity with the city's collective resources. Particularly in recent years, in line with the principle of social municipalism, fairs, festivals, and public celebrations have been organised that invite participation from all segments of the city's population. Students reported their participation in these programmes and expressed their satisfaction as follows:

> The last one was Biz Bize Fest. My friend and I went to it. It was quite enjoyable. Kıvanç and Burak were there. Workshops were organised. We had much fun. It was nice. I liked it. (YP6, Female, M, Eskişehir)

> I only participated in the marathon event organised by Spor Konya once. The people there were friendly; it had a family atmosphere. (YP11, Male, L, Aksaray)

> About two years ago, there was a Coffee and Chocolate Festival. There were various concerts on the same day, and I attended them. Additionally, this year, there was the Biz Bize Fest, which was recently held. Comedians and people we see on television were invited. We listened to them, and we attended workshops. We received free coffee, which was a nice perk. Concerts, I think, give off excellent energy. It is really nice to shout out the name of someone you love and always listen to. It also helps us relieve stress. These are the things that make me happy. (YP19, Female, M, Uşak)

Looking at the activities highlighted by the students, it appears that they are primarily focused on sports, entertainment, culture, and the arts. Students reported feeling happy, having fun, and enjoying participating in these activities. Furthermore, young people who took advantage of cinema discounts (YP13, YP15) and attended theatre (YP14, YP27) and concert events (YP15, YP10) through the Youth Culture Card expressed their satisfaction with meeting new people and expanding their social circles as a result of their participation. In addition, the camp activities organised by the municipality provided students with the opportunity to get to know Konya and its districts more closely.

> I have participated in events. I went to the districts of Konya. I went to Çatalhöyük, the Beyşehir camp, and the Taşkent women's camp, and I had much fun. It was an event for female students. (YP8, Female, TL, Konya)

> Yes, I participated in an event. They organised a Beyşehir camp, and I joined it. At our event, we had friends from many different departments and cities. We built friendships there. I participated in social, cultural, and sporting activities — it was an excellent experience. We travelled to different districts and saw places we had never visited before. We strengthened our friendships. We stayed there for a few days, benefited from various sporting activities, and competed, performing quite effectively. We organised Survivor-style games, held an archery competition, played paintball, and held other contests. The games were a great experience for me. I enjoyed paintball the most; it was an amazing event. (YP18, Male, H, Afyonkarahisar)

> I think it contributes to students because many of those from outside Konya participate in activities with the Youth Culture Card. I also think these events are a great opportunity to get to know Konya. As I mentioned, the gathering of people from different cities in large groups and the blending of cultures is a unique and meaningful phenomenon. (YP20, Female, P, Konya)

> I think the Youth Culture Card increases young people's participation in socio-cultural activities in the city. Thanks to this card, I discovered events I had never even heard of before. I can say that this enriched me both socially and culturally. When I feel motivated, I can sense this positive energy reflected in my academic life. (YP24, Female, T, Adıyaman)

In summary, the Youth Culture Card application functions effectively in line with the objectives of local administrations due to its diverse range of applications and the various events in which young people participate. However, collecting various forms of feedback is essential to identify potential problem areas and ensure continuous improvement.

14.4.3 Feedback on Smart Applications

One of the most important missions of contemporary urban policies is the implementation of smart city projects. In addition to advancing their technological dimensions, understanding how these projects influence urban life has become a crucial concern. Accordingly, it is necessary to provide concrete answers to the question of how smart applications regulate the daily lives of city dwellers. This constitutes one of the primary issues addressed in this study. Specifically, the following questions are central: How do smart applications positively or negatively affect the lives of city residents? What kinds of suggestions have residents made regarding aspects that are not yet included in smart applications but should be developed? This section seeks to answer these questions. Feedback from young people provides valuable insights for improving the functionality and efficiency of the Youth Culture Card application, which serves as a concrete example of smart city initiatives.

The opportunities that students most frequently benefit from within the Youth Culture Card programme are social and cultural activities. They stated that they mainly participate in events such as educational, entertainment, sporting, concert, cinema, and theatre activities. Nevertheless, participants made suggestions to increase, expand, and diversify these opportunities (YP4, YP11, YP14). In addition, it was suggested that benefits related to food, shopping, and stationery—such as raffles, discounts, and promotional campaigns—should also be enhanced (YP9, YP12, YP17, YP19).

Another area where young people wish to see further development in the Youth Culture Card programme concerns voluntary activities, particularly social responsibility projects. Participants emphasised the need for projects that would facilitate communication between young people and civil society organisations, raise environmental awareness, and promote social consciousness. Collaborations with organisations such as Yeşilay (Green Crescent), Kızılay (Turkish Red Crescent), and LÖSEV (Foundation for Children with Leukemia) (YP1), as well as environmental and zero-waste projects to be carried out in cooperation with institutions such as TÜBİTAK (The Scientific and Technological Research Council of Türkiye) (YP17, YP22), were suggested as ways to enhance young people's social engagement and sense of responsibility towards the city they live in.

Another key demand expressed by young people towards local authorities concerns social and cultural excursion programs, which they are often unable to afford due to economic reasons. In fact, the Konya Metropolitan Municipality organises regional and national cultural excursion programs for city residents from different age groups, occupational categories, and social backgrounds—including students, women, and children—on various occasions. However, the programme most frequently emphasised by students is that of overseas excursion opportunities.

> As someone from Konya, I know that Konya has a vibrant history. Therefore, it could include visits to Mevlâna or showcase the numerous historical artefacts left behind by the Seljuk Empire. Plans and tours could be organised for this purpose. (YP20, Female, P, Konya)

> Overseas trips would be excellent. Those who cannot participate in the Erasmus programme could take advantage of this opportunity. This could attract a large audience. (YP7, Female, IR, Konya)

> If events such as trips abroad are organised, the popularity of the Youth Culture Card among young people will definitely increase. Such events allow young people to socialise and learn about different cultures. (YP15, Male, CE, İzmir)

> If events such as trips abroad are organised, the appeal of the Youth Culture Card will increase significantly. It offers the opportunity to learn about different cultures and meet new people. This is also a great investment in personal development. Thus, students can broaden their horizons. (YP27, Male, ME, Adana)

The widespread use of social media has played a significant role in shaping overseas trips as a key aspiration among young people. They express a strong desire to go abroad, both to take advantage of educational opportunities and to promote personal development. Furthermore, alongside the other opportunities offered within the Youth Culture Card programme, the inclusion of an international excursion initiative, despite its high economic cost, would likely ensure the programme's broader recognition and adoption among young people. From these findings, it can be understood that while the Youth Culture Card currently meets the minimum expectations of young people regarding urban life, there remains a strong desire for more unique and innovative programmes—particularly those that provide experiences perceived as otherwise unattainable for students.

The fact that the majority of the young participants in this research are university students necessitates the preparation of more dynamic and flexible programmes within the scope of innovative applications. Considering the diversity of the student population –including those from disciplines such as health, engineering, agriculture, science, law, the arts, and the social sciences—offering pre-designed, standardised activities does not produce sufficiently satisfying results. In other words, travel, entertainment, cultural, artistic, sporting, and educational activities often appear monotonous, routine, and repetitive to students. At this point, it becomes essential to develop strategies that allow young people to generate innovative ideas and content, and to realise them through smart applications.

> There should be areas where everyone can present their ideas. (YP21, Female, ND, Konya)
>
> It would be better if the projects designed by young people within their own plans were implemented — if they could make their own plans and put them into practice. Young people's ideas should be valued more; they should be able to present their ideas, take part in projects, and see their own initiatives realised in daily life. (YP18, Male, H, Afyonkarahisar)
>
> Yes, a forum or platform where young people can organise and publicise their own activities could be added to the programme. This would allow them to organise events based on their interests and meet new people. (YP15, Male, CE, İzmir)
>
> I would like to see more interactive activities in the application. For example, workshops, filmmaking, and digital art — activities that encourage creativity. Because just being a spectator is no longer enough; young people want to be creators. Activities connected with nature are also particularly beneficial for young people's mental health. (YP24, Female, T, Adıyaman)

When evaluating smart city strategies developed by local authorities, it is important to note that smart applications should not merely serve as instrumental platforms for delivering services to users. Rather, they should also provide opportunities for users to share ideas and initiatives that contribute to urban life, thereby fulfilling the principle of participatory governance. A platform enabling young people to present innovative ideas for both their personal development and the improvement of the cities they inhabit would enhance the functionality and effectiveness of smart applications. The findings of this research indicate that young people are actively seeking a platform where they can bring their ideas to life, based on their own aspirations and needs.

In addition to the findings discussed above, one of the most prominent needs expressed by young people concerns career planning and employment programmes. University-aged individuals, being at the final stage of their education, seek to complete their preparations for entering professional life. Accordingly, they aim to take proactive steps to explore job opportunities, gain professional experience, and strengthen their employability throughout their education.

> As young people, we face the greatest difficulties in terms of education and job opportunities. For example, finding internships and jobs can be quite challenging. We expect more support in this regard. Additionally, social spaces are inadequate; there should be more cafés and youth centres. I want the city's administrators to listen more to young people's ideas and organise events and projects for us. That way, we will feel more valued and want to stay in the city. Some young people may want to leave because of economic concerns. They want experience because of job opportunities. That's why we want internships. We need references. (YP25, Female, PH, Burdur)

> The scope of the programme could be expanded by creating more career-focused events, mentoring programmes, and job networks for young professionals. This would contribute not only to the cultural but also to the professional development of young people. It would also increase the city's attractiveness to young talent. (YP27, Male, ME, Adana)

> The current services are not sufficient. More employment and career-oriented projects should be offered to young people. In addition, platforms should be created to increase young people's participation in social issues. (YP13, Male, ID, Konya)

> I do not find it sufficient. There should be more support for young people's careers. For example, they should help with internship opportunities or job placements. (YP12, Female, N, Konya)

It can be said that Konya Metropolitan Municipality offers a wide range of services for young people. Various initiatives have been organised specifically for young people to participate in and benefit from. For example, the Konya Metropolitan Municipality Career Support Education Centre (KADEME), Youth Assembly, Vocational Training Courses (KOMEK), KOMEK Distance Education Centre, Capsule Technology Platform, and Bilgehane are alternative organisations that young people can benefit from. In addition, local administrations make significant contributions to career fairs organised at national and regional levels, alongside public institutions, universities, and the business world. The Konya Metropolitan Municipality Career Support Education Centre has been a key partner in the Central Anatolia Career Fair (İKAF-2025), held in Konya. Through such initiatives, career counselling and meetings with employers are facilitated to prepare young people effectively for the business world.

Although the young people who participated in our research requested the expansion of career-focused programmes, they were not sufficiently aware of the activities organised by the municipality. In particular, when we asked questions about the Career Centre and Career Mentoring, they stated that they did not have enough information about these programmes or that they did not benefit from them. Therefore, university students should be provided with more information about organisations in the field of career education and counselling. The fact that a participant who emphasised the need to develop career support programs was unaware of the municipality's career mentoring program (YP12) indicates that the services offered do not reach a broad audience.

> I am following it. I see that a sufficient explanation is not provided. The event has a very nice brochure, but the explanation is brief, and there is little information. I have heard of Career

Mentoring, but I have no idea what it entails. I think there is not enough advertising on this subject. Very little information is provided. (YP7, Female, IR, Konya).

I have heard of Career Mentoring, but have not had the opportunity to attend. I heard about it from a friend. More emphasis should be placed on this topic. It should be advertised. It has not been advertised as much as Teteri. This is a shortcoming. (YP8, Female, TL, Konya).

I have heard of Career Mentoring, but I did not know about it. I am thinking of researching it. It would be beneficial for guiding our lives after graduation." (YP10, Male, L, Aksaray).

"I do not know about the Career Mentoring programme, but I would consider using it for my career—of course, for career development. (YP17, Female, ND, Afyonkarahisar).

Yes, I definitely plan to take advantage of it to guide my career after graduation and take the right steps in the sector. Getting mentoring from an experienced engineer in my field would be particularly valuable. (YP27, Male, ME, Adana)

In this chapter, where we evaluate the usage practices and functionality of smart applications, we sought to gather feedback on the policies and services developed by Konya Metropolitan Municipality for young people. We had the opportunity to thoroughly examine the thoughts, attitudes, and experiences of young people (university students) living in Konya regarding the Youth Culture Card application, developed as a smart city practice. Our aim here is to explore the social implications of smart city applications through their usage practices. The findings we have attempted to classify using the participant views above highlight the points where the Youth Culture Card application is helpful for young people. In addition, the issues that young people consider to be lacking or insufficient constitute points that need to be developed from the perspective of local administrations.

14.5 Conclusion

The areas of application for smart city policies around the world and in Türkiye are diversifying on a daily basis. In Türkiye specifically, some cities have developed pioneering applications. One such city, Konya Metropolitan Municipality, ranks among the leaders in the development and implementation of smart city projects. The fact that local administrations have prepared long-term strategies and roadmaps demonstrates that smart city objectives play a crucial role in urban planning and urban policy. In today's metropolitan cities, where the population is increasing daily, the demographic structure is diversifying, the spatial structure is expanding, and the organisational structure is changing, problem areas are also increasing at a similar rate. The widespread and effective use of digital technologies is the most functional tool for reducing and resolving these problems. The projects, programmes, and applications developed within the scope of the smart city vision are aimed at directly ensuring urban welfare, comfort, and order. The digital data obtained is also expected to support urban management policies indirectly.

In this study, the Youth Culture Card Application (mobile), one of the smart city applications of Konya Metropolitan Municipality, was selected as an example. The primary target audience for this application is young people studying at university.

Within the scope of our research, the functionality and efficiency of the Youth Culture Card smart city application were evaluated through interviews conducted with young university students. In other words, questions were asked about the extent to which young users benefited from the smart application, in which areas it met their needs and expectations, and what areas were lacking or needed improvement. Based on the answers obtained from the interviews, the impact of the smart city application on the daily and social lives of young people was evaluated.

According to the results obtained, young people utilise the Youth Culture Card application to take advantage of the services provided by Konya Metropolitan Municipality. The application provides valuable opportunities to participate in and benefit from social, cultural, artistic, educational, and sporting events held in Konya. It enables students, especially those from different cities, to become more familiar with the city of Konya and develop a sense of belonging to the city where they live. It also provides students with the opportunity to participate in cultural and artistic events that they would otherwise find difficult to access due to financial constraints. The opportunity to benefit from discounts in areas such as food, textiles, stationery, cafes, and restaurants has been welcomed by young people. The fundamental mission of the Youth Culture Card, as stated in its founding purpose, is to ensure that young people are actively engaged in social, cultural, and educational activities. Based on the research findings, it is assessed that this mission is being fulfilled.

According to the research results, the issues that participants consider lacking and in need of improvement are organisations that will strengthen their gains in their professional lives. They want programmes to be prepared that are career and employment-focused and that will evaluate job opportunities. They also demand that platforms be established where young people and students can bring their own ideas to life. Furthermore, requests were made for the opportunities offered by the Youth Culture Card application to be shared/announced in a timely, fast, detailed, and transparent manner (YP14, YP27), for quotas to be increased (YP1, YP24), and for it to be made more widespread for those studying in high schools and districts (YP18, YP24).

Finally, a significant portion of the expectations and demands expressed by students regarding the use of the Youth Culture Card are being met by Konya Metropolitan Municipality. In particular, a centre has been established and is providing services for career planning and accessing job opportunities. The fact that local administrations have not made sufficient announcements and promotions may be a factor in students' lack of awareness in this regard. In new academic studies to be conducted in the long term, "how digital data obtained from smart applications is transformed into a decision-making mechanism in the municipality's authorised bodies" could be a subject of research. This is because smart cities will enable more effective city management by facilitating the flow of data between citizens and administrators through digital tools.

References

Babaoğlu, P. (2024). *İnsan odaklı akıllı kentleşme: Türkiye için bir çerçeve önerisi* [Doctoral Dissertation]. Isparta Süleyman Demirel Üniversitesi Sosyal Bilimler Enstitüsü.

Bilici, Z., & Babahanoğlu, V. (2018). Smart city implementations and the case of Konya. *Journal of Academic Approaches, 9*(2), 124–139.

Dereli, M. D. (2019). Dinî kimliklerin siber uzamda akışkanlaşması. *İnsan ve Toplum Dergisi, 9*(1), 85–116. https://doi.org/10.12658/M0301

Dereli, M. D. (2022). *Sanala veda: Sosyal medya ve dönüşen dindarlık.* Albaraka Yayınları.

Duman, M. Ç. (2022). Society 5.0: Human-focused digital transformation. *Journal of Social Policy Conferences, 82*, 309–336.

Erdal, E. (2023). *Toplum 5.0 üzerine yeni tartışmalar: Konya akıllı şehir uygulamaları* [Master's Thesis]. Necmettin Erbakan Üniversitesi Sosyal Bilimler Enstitüsü.

Giffinger, R., & Gudrun, H. (2010). Smart cities ranking: An effective instrument for positioning. *Architecture, City and Environment, 12*, 7–25. https://doi.org/10.5821/ace.v4i12.2483

Gökalp, D., & Şenol, P. (2020). Akıllı kentlerin gelişimi ve kent planlama ilişkisi üzerine bir değerlendirme. *SKETCH Journal of City and Regional Planning, 2*(2), 1–20. https://doi.org/10.5505/sjcrp.2021.43531

Hout, J. L., Thalmann, J. P., & Valbelle, D. (2000). *Kentlerin doğuşu* (A. B. Girgin, Trans.). İmge Kitabevi Yayınları.

Karaarslan, F., & Erdal Avcı, E. (2025). Industry-based society definitions: Society 5.0. *Journal of Civilization and Society, 9*(1), 1–17. https://doi.org/10.51117/metder.2025.86

Karasoy, H. A., & Kıraç, Z. K. (2021). Smart city applications in Türkiye: Case of Konya province. *International Journal of Tourism, Economic and Business Sciences, 5*(1), 55–64.

KBB. (2022). *Konya Büyükşehir Belediyesi akıllı şehir stratejisi ve yol haritası.* ASELSAN & Sabancı Üniversitesi.

Komninos, N., Bratsas, C., Kakderi, C., et al. (2015). Smart city ontologies: Improving the effectiveness of smart city applications. *Journal of Smart Cities, 1*(1), 31–46. https://doi.org/10.18063/JSC.2015.01.001

Kömürcüoğlu, M. (2019). *Türkiye'de şehir ve toplum: Tarih, teori ve temel meseleler.* Ketebe Yayınları.

Mumford, L. (2019). *Tarih boyunca kent: Kökenleri, geçirdiği dönüşümler ve geleceği* (G. Koca & T. Tosun, Trans.). Ayrıntı Yayınları.

Örselli, E., & Akbay, C. (2019). Technology and transformation in urban life: Smart cities. *International Journal of Management Academy, 2*(1), 228–241. https://doi.org/10.33712/mana.544549

Pirenne, H. (2019). *Ortaçağ kentleri: Kökenleri ve ticaretin canlanması* (Ş. Karadeniz, Trans.), İletişim Yayınları.

Pourahmad, A., Keramattolah, Z., Hataminejad, H., & Parsa, S. (2018). Explanation of concept and features of a smart city. *Bagh-e Nazar, 15*(58), 5–26.

Smart Cities. (2014). *Priminary report: Information thecnology.* ISO/IEC JTC 1, Switzerland. Retrieved September 3, 2025, from https://www.iso.org/files/live/sites/isoorg/files/developing_standards/docs/en/smart_cities_report-jtc1.pdf

Şenyüz, F. Y. (2024). *Türkiye'de skıllı kent deneyiminin temelleri ve uygulamaları üzerine eleştirel bir değerlendirme* [Master's Thesis]. Giresun Üniversitesi Sosyal Bilimler Enstitüsü.

Tekin, M. (2017). Dünya tarihinde ilk şehir ve şehir devleti'nin ortaya çıkışı ve gelişimi. *Gaziosmanpaşa Üniversitesi Sosyal Bilimler Araştırmaları Dergisi, 12*(2), 17–30. https://doi.org/10.19129/sbad.327

Uçar, A., Şemşit, S., & Negiz, N. (2017). Smart city implementations in the EU and reflections in Türkiye. *Süleyman Demirel Üniversitesi İktisadi ve İdari Bilimler Fakültesi Dergisi, 22*(15), 1785–1798.

Velibeyoğlu, K. (2016). *Akıllı kentler: Vaatler ve ötesi. Yenilikçi sürdürülebilir gelişme stratejileri bağlamında Türkiye ekonomisinin geleceğine yönelik çözüm arayışları* (S. Şanlısoy, Ed.). İlkim Ofset.
Vieanna Univ. & Ljubljana Univ. & Delft Univ. (2007). *Smart cities ranking of European medium-sized cities*. Retrieved September 1, 2025, from www.smart-cities.eu
Weber, M. (2012). *Şehir: Modern kentin oluşumu* (M. Ceylan, Trans.). Yarın Yayınları.
https://www.thesmartcityjournal.com/en/cities/the-key-characteristics-of-the-smart-city-6-0-concept. Access Date: May 25, 2025.
https://www.akillisehirler.gov.tr/. Access Date: May 23, 2025.
https://akillisehirekosistem.csb.gov.tr/. Access Date: May 13, 2025.
https://akillisehir.konya.bel.tr/. Access Date: May 12, 2025.

Index

M. D. Dereli and M. Eken (eds.), *Turkish Perspectives on Secularization and Media*,
https://doi.org/10.1007/978-3-032-16436-0

The manufacturer's authorised representative in the EU is Springer Nature Customer Service Centre GmbH, Europaplatz 3, 69115 Heidelberg, Germany. If you have any concerns regarding our products, please contact ProductSafety@springernature.com

Printed and bound by CPI Group (UK) Ltd, Croydon, CR0 4YY
21/09/2026
02220012-0009